Effective Python

Third Edition

Effective Python

125 SPECIFIC WAYS TO WRITE BETTER PYTHON

Third Edition

Brett Slatkin

✦▾Addison-Wesley

Visit us on the Web: informit.com/aw

Library of Congress Control Number: 2024945552

Copyright © 2025 Pearson Education, Inc.

Hoboken, NJ

Cover image: Victoria Moloman/Shutterstock

ISBN-13: 978-0-13-817218-3

ISBN-10: 0-13-817218-8

1 2024

To our family

Contents at a Glance

Contents

Chapter 8 Metaclasses and Attributes   265

Chapter 9 Concurrency and Parallelism   319

Preface

The Python programming language has unique strengths and charms that can be hard to grasp. Many programmers familiar with other languages approach Python from a limited mindset instead of embracing its full capabilities. Some programmers go too far in the other direction, overusing Python features that can cause big problems later.

This book provides insight into the *Pythonic* way of writing programs: the best way to use Python. It builds on a fundamental understanding of the language that I assume you already have. Novice programmers will learn the best practices of Python's critical features. Experienced programmers will learn how to embrace a new tool with confidence.

With this book I hope to help you use Python to accomplish your goals, whatever they may be, or at least to help you have more fun on your journey with programming.

What This Book Covers

Each chapter in this book contains a broad but related set of items. Feel free to jump between items and follow your interest. Each item contains concise and specific guidance explaining how you can write Python programs more effectively. Items include advice on what to do, what to avoid, how to strike the right balance, and why this is the best choice. Items reference each other to make it easier to fill in the gaps as you read.

This third edition covers the language up through Python version 3.13 (see Item 1: "Know Which Version of Python You're Using"). This book includes 35 completely new items compared to the second edition. Most of the items from the second edition have been revised and included, but many have undergone substantial updates. For some items, my advice has completely changed due to best practices evolving as Python has matured over the past five years.

Python takes a "batteries included" approach to its standard library. Many of these built-in packages are so closely intertwined with idiomatic Python that they may as well be part of the language specification. The full set of standard modules is too large to cover in this book, but I've included the ones that I feel are critical to be aware of and use.

Python also has a vibrant ecosystem of community-built modules that extend the language in valuable ways. Although I mention important packages to know about in various items, this book is not intended to be a thorough reference. Similarly, despite the importance of Python package management, I avoid going into the details about it because it's rapidly changing and evolving.

Chapter 1: Pythonic Thinking

The Python community has come to use the adjective *Pythonic* to describe code that follows a particular style. The idioms of Python have emerged over time through experience using the language and collaborating with other programmers. This chapter covers the best ways to do the most common things in Python.

Chapter 2: Strings and Slicing

Python has built-in syntax, methods, and modules for string and sequence processing. These capabilities are so essential that you'll see them in nearly every program. They make Python an excellent language for parsing text, inspecting data formats, and interfacing with the low-level binary representations used by computers.

Chapter 3: Loops and Iterators

Processing through sequential data is a critical need in programs. Loops in Python feel natural and capable for the most common tasks involving built-in data types, container types, and user-defined classes. Python also supports iterators, which enable a more functional-style approach to processing arbitrary streams of data with significant benefits.

Chapter 4: Dictionaries

Python's built-in dictionary type is a versatile data structure for bookkeeping in programs. Compared to simple lists, dictionaries provide much better performance for adding and removing items. Python also has special syntax and related built-in modules that enhance dictionaries beyond what you might expect from hash tables in other languages.

Chapter 5: Functions

Functions in Python have a variety of extra features that can make a programmer's life easier. Some are similar to capabilities in other programming languages, but many are unique to Python. This chapter covers how to use functions to clarify intention, promote reuse, and reduce bugs.

Chapter 6: Comprehensions and Generators

Python has special syntax for quickly iterating through lists, dictionaries, and sets to generate derivative data structures. It also allows for a stream of iterable values to be incrementally returned by a function. This chapter covers how these features can provide better performance, reduced memory usage, and improved readability.

Chapter 7: Classes and Interfaces

Python is an object-oriented language. Getting things done in Python often requires writing new classes and defining how they interact through their interfaces and hierarchies. This chapter covers how to use classes to express intended behaviors with objects.

Chapter 8: Metaclasses and Attributes

Metaclasses and dynamic attributes are powerful Python features. However, they also enable you to implement extremely bizarre and unexpected behaviors. This chapter covers the common idioms for using these mechanisms to ensure that you follow the *rule of least surprise*.

Chapter 9: Concurrency and Parallelism

With features such as threads and asynchronous coroutines, Python makes it easy to write concurrent programs that do many different things seemingly at the same time. Python can also be used to do parallel work through system calls, subprocesses, and special modules. This chapter covers how to best utilize Python in these subtly different situations.

Chapter 10: Robustness

Making programs dependable when they encounter unexpected circumstances is just as important as making programs with correct functionality. Python has built-in features and modules that aid in hardening your programs so they are robust in a wide variety of situations.

Chapter 11: Performance

Python includes a variety of capabilities that enable programs to achieve surprisingly impressive performance with relatively low amounts of effort. Using these features, it's possible to extract maximum performance from a host system while retaining the productivity gains afforded by Python's high-level nature.

Chapter 12: Data Structures and Algorithms

Python includes optimized implementations of many standard data structures and algorithms that can help you achieve high performance with minimal effort. The language also provides battle-tested data types and helper functions for common tasks (e.g., working with currency and time) that allow you focus on your program's core requirements.

Chapter 13: Testing and Debugging

You should always test your code, regardless of what language it's written in, but with Python, testing is especially important. Python's dynamic features can increase the risk of runtime errors in unique ways. Luckily, they also make it easier to write tests and diagnose malfunctioning programs. This chapter covers Python's built-in tools for testing and debugging.

Chapter 14: Collaboration

Collaborating on Python programs requires you to be deliberate about how you write your code. Even if you're working alone, you'll want to understand how to use modules written by others. This chapter covers the standard tools and best practices that enable people to work together on Python programs.

Conventions Used in This Book

Python code snippets in this book are in monospace font and have syntax highlighting. When lines are long, I use ➥ characters to show when they wrap. I truncate some snippets with ellipses (...) to indicate regions where code exists that isn't essential for expressing the point. You'll need to download the full example code (see below on where to get it) in order to get these truncated snippets to run correctly on your computer.

I take some artistic license with the Python style guide in order to make the code examples better fit the format of a book or to highlight the most important parts. I've also left out embedded documentation to reduce the size of code examples. I strongly suggest that you don't emulate this in your projects; instead, you should follow the style guide (see Item 2: "Follow the PEP 8 Style Guide") and write documentation (see Item 118: "Write Docstrings for Every Function, Class, and Module").

Most code snippets in this book are accompanied by the corresponding output from running the code. When I say "output," I mean console or terminal output: what you see when running the Python program in an interactive interpreter. Output sections are in monospace font, and each is preceded by a >>> line (the Python interactive prompt). The idea is that you could type the code snippets into a Python shell and reproduce the expected output.

Finally, there are some other sections in monospace font that are not preceded by a >>> line. These represent the output of running programs besides the Python interpreter. These examples often begin with $ characters to indicate that I'm running programs from a command-line shell like Bash. If you're running these commands on Windows or another type of system, you may need to adjust the program names and arguments accordingly.

Where to Get the Code and Errata

It's useful to view many of the examples from this book as whole programs without interleaved prose. This also gives you a chance to tinker with the code yourself and understand why the program works as described. You can find the source code for all code snippets in this book on the book's website, https://effectivepython.com. The website also provides instructions on how to report errors. Thank you in advance for contacting me about any errors you find.

Register your copy of *Effective Python: 125 Specific Ways to Write Better Python, 3rd Edition* on the InformIT site for convenient access to updates and/or corrections as they become available. To start the registration process, go to informit.com/register and log in or create an account. Enter the product ISBN (**9780138172183**) and click Submit. If you would like to be notified of exclusive offers on new editions and updates, please check the box to receive email from us.

Acknowledgments

Thank you for reading this book. I must emphasize that this book would not have been possible without guidance, support, and encouragement from many people.

Thanks to Scott Meyers for the Effective Software Development series of books. I discovered the joy of computer programming at a young age, but when I read his book *Effective C++* when I was 15 years old, something clicked. There's no doubt that Scott's books led to my college education and first job. I'm thrilled to have had the opportunity to write all three editions of *Effective Python*. I've learned so much in the process, and I'm deeply grateful for the experience.

Thanks to the team who made this third edition a reality. Thanks to my executive editor, Debra Williams, for being so supportive throughout the process. Thanks to development editor Chris Zahn, production editor Mary Roth, copy editor Kitty Wilson, cover designer Chuti Prasertsith, and marketing manager Chike Lawrence-Mitchell. Thanks to my technical reviewers—Karry Lu, David N. Cohron, and Andy Chu—for the depth and thoroughness of their feedback.

Thanks to everyone who supported me in creating the first and second editions of this book: Debra Williams, Trina MacDonald, Olivia Basegio, Mike Bayer, Titus Brown, Brett Cannon, Andy Chu, Tom Cirtin, Nick Cohron, Leah Culver, Andrew Dolan, Pamela Fox, Stephanie Geels, Adrian Holovaty, Toshiaki Kurokawa, Michael Levine, Lori Lyons, Asher Mancinelli, Wes McKinney, Julie Nahil, Stephane Nakib, Stephane Nakib, Marzia Niccolai, Ade Oshineye, Chuti Prasertsith, Brandon Rhodes, Tavis Rudd, Katrina Sostek, Mike Taylor, Simon Willison, Kitty Wilson, and Chris Zahn.

Thanks to all of the readers who reported errors and room for improvement in the book. Please keep the feedback coming! Thanks to all of the translators who made the book available around the world; nothing brings a smile to my face quite like seeing my book in other languages.

xxiv   Acknowledgments

Thanks to the wonderful Python programmers I've known and worked with: Anthony Baxter, Brett Cannon, Wesley Chun, Jeremy Hylton, Alex Martelli, Neal Norwitz, Guido van Rossum, Andy Smith, Greg Stein, Ka-Ping Yee, and Gregory Smith. I appreciate your tutelage and leadership. Python has an excellent community, and I feel lucky to be a part of it.

Thanks to my teammates over the years for letting me be the worst player in the band. Thanks to Kevin Gibbs for helping me take risks. Thanks to Ken Ashcraft, Ryan Barrett, and Jon McAlister for showing me how it's done. Thanks to Brad Fitzpatrick for taking it to the next level. Thanks to Paul McDonald for being an amazing co-founder. Thanks to Jeremy Ginsberg, Jack Hebert, John Skidgel, Evan Martin, Tony Chang, Troy Trimble, Tessa Pupius, Erick Armbrust, and Dylan Lorimer for helping me learn. Thanks to Sagnik Nandy, Waleed Ojeil, and Will Grannis for your mentorship.

Thanks to the inspiring programming and engineering teachers that I've had: Ben Chelf, Glenn Cowan, Vince Hugo, Russ Lewin, Jon Stemmle, Derek Thomson, Daniel Wang, Dean Nevins, Stephen Strenn, and Alex Guy. Without your instruction, I would never have pursued our craft or gained the perspective required to teach others.

Thanks to my mother for giving me a sense of purpose and encouraging me to become a programmer. Thanks to my family and friends for their support. Thanks to my wife for her love and friendship.

About the Author

Brett Slatkin has been programming with Python professionally for the past 19 years. He currently works as a principal software engineer in the Office of the CTO at Google, developing technology strategies and rapid prototypes.

His prior experience includes founding Google Surveys, an internal startup for collecting machine learning and market research data sets; launching Google App Engine, the company's first cloud computing product; scaling Google's A/B experimentation products to billions of users; co-creating PubSubHubbub, the W3C standard for real-time RSS feeds; and making various contributions to open source projects.

Brett earned a bachelor's degree in computer engineering from Columbia University in the City of New York. Outside of his day job, he enjoys playing piano, surfing, and spending time with his family. He lives in California. You can find him online at https://onebigfluke.com.

Pythonic Thinking

The idioms of a programming language are defined by its users. Over the years, the Python community has come to use the adjective *Pythonic* to describe code that follows a particular style. The Pythonic style isn't regimented or enforced by the compiler. It has emerged over time through experience using the language and working with others. Python programmers prefer to be explicit, to choose simple over complex, and to maximize readability. (Type `import this` into your interpreter to read *The Zen of Python*.)

Programmers familiar with other languages may try to write Python as if it's C++, Java, or whatever they know best. New programmers may still be getting comfortable with the vast range of concepts that can be expressed in Python. It's important for you to know the best—the *Pythonic*—way to do the most common things in Python. These patterns will affect every program you write.

Item 1: Know Which Version of Python You're Using

Throughout this book, the majority of example code is for Python 3.13 (released in October 2024). This book does not cover Python 2, although it sometimes mentions older versions of Python 3 to provide background information about how the language has evolved over time.

Many computer operating systems ship with multiple versions of the standard CPython interpreter preinstalled. However, the default meaning of python on the command line may not be clear. python is usually an alias for python2.7, but it can sometimes be an alias for even older versions, like python2.6 or python2.5. To find out exactly which version of Python you're using, you can use the --version flag:

```
$ python --version
Python 2.7.10
```

On many systems, Python 2 is no longer installed, and the python command causes an error:

```
$ python --version
-bash: python: command not found
```

Python 3 is usually available under the name python3:

```
$ python3 --version
Python 3.12.3
```

To use alternative Python runtimes, such as PyPy (https://www.pypy.org), to run Python programs, you need to use their specific commands:

```
$ pypy3 --version
Python 3.10.14 (75b3de9d9035, May 28 2024, 18:06:40)
[PyPy 7.3.16 with GCC Apple LLVM 15.0.0 (clang-1500.3.9.4)]
```

You can also figure out the version of Python you're using at runtime by inspecting values in the sys built-in module:

```
import sys

print(sys.platform)
print(sys.implementation.name)
print(sys.version_info)
print(sys.version)

>>>
darwin
cpython
sys.version_info(major=3, minor=12, micro=3,
➥releaselevel='final', serial=0)
3.12.3 (main, Apr  9 2024, 08:09:14)
➥[Clang 15.0.0 (clang-1500.3.9.4)]
```

For a long time, the Python core developers and community were actively maintaining support for both Python 2 and Python 3. The versions are different in significant ways and have incompatibilities that made porting difficult. The migration from version 2 to version 3 was an extremely long and painful period that finally came to an end on April 20, 2020, when Python version 2.7.18 was published. This was the final official release of Python 2. For anyone who still needs security patches and bug fixes for Python 2, the only remaining options are to pay a commercial software vendor for support or do it yourself.

Since then, the Python core developers and community have been focused on Python version 3. The functionality of the core language, the standard library, and the ecosystem of packages and tools are constantly being improved. Keeping up with all the changes and innovations that are happening can be overwhelming. One good way to find out about what's new is to read the release notes (https:// docs.python.org/3/whatsnew/index.html), which highlight additions and changes for each version. There are other websites out there that will also notify you when the community packages you rely on are updated (see Item 116: "Know Where to Find Community-Built Modules").

Things to Remember

✦ Python 3 is the most up-to-date and well-supported version of Python, and you should use it for your projects.

✦ Be sure that the command-line executable for running Python on your system is the version you expect it to be.

✦ Python 2 is no longer officially maintained by the core developers.

Item 2: Follow the PEP 8 Style Guide

Python Enhancement Proposal #8, otherwise known as PEP 8, is the style guide for how to format Python code. You are welcome to write Python code any way you want, as long as it has valid syntax. However, using a consistent style makes your code more approachable and easier to read. Sharing a common style with other Python programmers in the larger community facilitates collaboration on projects. But even if you are the only one who will ever read your code, following the style guide will make it easier for you to change things later and can help you avoid many common errors.

PEP 8 provides a wealth of details about how to write clear Python code. It continues to be updated as the Python language evolves. It's worth reading the whole guide online (https://www.python.org/dev/peps/pep-0008/). Here are a few rules you should be sure to follow.

Whitespace

In Python, whitespace is syntactically significant. Python programmers are especially sensitive to the effects of whitespace on code clarity. Follow these guidelines related to whitespace:

- Use spaces instead of tabs for indentation.
- Use four spaces for each level of syntactically significant indenting.
- Lines should be 79 characters in length or less.

- Continuations of long expressions onto additional lines should be indented by four extra spaces from their normal indentation level.

- In a file, functions and classes should be separated by two blank lines.

- In a class, methods should be separated by one blank line.

- In a dictionary, put no whitespace between each key and colon; put a single space before the corresponding value if it fits on the same line.

- Put one—and only one—space before and after the = operator in a variable assignment.

- For type annotations, ensure that there is no separation between the variable name and the colon, and use a space before the type information.

Naming

PEP 8 suggests unique styles of naming for different parts in the language. These conventions make it easy to distinguish which type corresponds to each name when reading code. Follow these guidelines related to naming:

- Functions, variables, and attributes should be in `lowercase_underscore` format.

- Protected instance attributes should be in `_leading_underscore` format.

- Private instance attributes should be in `__double_leading_underscore` format.

- Classes (including exceptions) should be in `CapitalizedWord` format.

- Module-level constants should be in `ALL_CAPS` format.

- Instance methods in classes should use `self`, which refers to the object, as the name of the first parameter.

- Class methods should use `cls`, which refers to the class, as the name of the first parameter.

Expressions and Statements

The Zen of Python states: "There should be one—and preferably only one—obvious way to do it." PEP 8 attempts to codify this style in its guidance for expressions and statements:

- Use inline negation (`if a is not b`) instead of negation of positive expressions (`if not a is b`).

- Don't check for empty containers or sequences (like [] or "") by comparing the length to zero (if `len(somelist) == 0`). Use `if not somelist` and assume that empty values will implicitly evaluate to `False`.

- The same thing goes for non-empty containers or sequences (like `[1]` or `"hi"`). The statement `if somelist` is implicitly `True` for non-empty values.

- Avoid single-line `if` statements, `for` and `while` loops, and `except` compound statements. Spread these over multiple lines for clarity.

- If you can't fit an expression on one line, surround it with parentheses and add line breaks and indentation to make it easier to read.

- Prefer surrounding multiline expressions with parentheses over using the \ line continuation character.

Imports

PEP 8 suggests some guidelines for how to import modules and use them in your code:

- Always put `import` statements (including `from x import y`) at the top of a file.

- Always use absolute names for modules when importing them, not names relative to the current module's own path. For example, to import the `foo` module from within the `bar` package, you should use `from bar import foo`, not just `import foo`.

- If you must do relative imports, use the explicit syntax `from . import foo`.

- Imports should be in sections in the following order: standard library modules, third-party modules, your own modules. Each subsection should have imports in alphabetical order.

Automation

If what you've read so far seems like a lot to remember, I have good news: The Python community is coalescing around a common tool for automatic PEP 8 formatting: It's called black (https://github.com/psf/black), and it's an official Python Software Foundation project. black provides very few configuration options, which makes it easy for developers working on the same codebase to agree on the style of code. Installing and using black is straightforward:

```
$ pip install black
$ python -m black example.py
reformatted example.py
```

```
All done! ✦ 🍰 ✦
1 file reformatted.
```

Besides black, there are many other community tools to help you improve your source code automatically. Many IDEs and editors include style-checking tools, auto-formatters, and similar plug-ins. One popular code analyzer is `pylint` (https://github.com/pylint-dev/pylint); it helps enforce the PEP 8 style guide and detects many other types of common errors in Python programs (see Item 3: "Never Expect Python to Detect Errors at Compile Time" for more examples).

Things to Remember

✦ Always follow the Python Enhancement Proposal #8 (PEP 8) style guide when writing Python code.

✦ Sharing a common style with the larger Python community facilitates collaboration with others.

✦ Using a consistent style makes it easier to modify your own code later.

✦ Community tools like `black` and `pylint` can automate compliance with PEP 8, making it easy to keep your source code in good style.

Item 3: Never Expect Python to Detect Errors at Compile Time

When loading a Python program and preparing for execution, the source code is parsed into abstract syntax trees and checked for obvious structural errors. For example, a poorly constructed `if` statement will raise a `SyntaxError` exception indicating what's wrong with the code:

```
if True  # Bad syntax
  print('hello')

>>>
Traceback ...
SyntaxError: expected ':'
```

Errors in value literals will also be detected early and raise exceptions:

```
1.3j5  # Bad number

>>>
Traceback ...
SyntaxError: invalid imaginary literal
```

Unfortunately, that's about all the protection you can expect from Python before execution. Anything beyond basic tokenization errors and parse errors will not be flagged as a problem.

Even simple functions that seem to have obvious errors will not be reported as having problems before program execution due to the highly dynamic nature of Python. For example, here I define a function where the my_var variable is clearly not assigned before it's passed to print:

```
def bad_reference():
    print(my_var)
    my_var = 123
```

But this won't raise an exception until the function is executed:

```
bad_reference()

>>>
Traceback ...
UnboundLocalError: cannot access local variable 'my_var'
➥where it is not associated with a value
```

The reason this isn't considered a *static* error is because it's valid for Python programs to dynamically assign local and global variables. For example, here I define a function that is valid or not depending on the input argument:

```
def sometimes_ok(x):
    if x:
        my_var = 123
    print(my_var)
```

This call runs fine:

```
sometimes_ok(True)

>>>
123
```

This one causes a runtime exception:

```
sometimes_ok(False)

>>>
Traceback ...
UnboundLocalError: cannot access local variable 'my_var'
➥where it is not associated with a value
```

Python also won't catch math errors upfront. It would seem that this is clearly an error before the program executes:

```
def bad_math():
    return 1 / 0
```

But it's possible for the meaning of the division operator to vary based on the values involved, so checking for errors like this is similarly deferred until runtime:

```
bad_math()

>>>
Traceback ...
ZeroDivisionError: division by zero
```

Python also won't statically detect problems with undefined methods, too many or too few supplied arguments, mismatched return types, and many more seemingly obvious issues. There are community tools that can help you detect some of these errors before execution, such as the flake8 linter (https://github.com/PyCQA/flake8) and type checkers that work with the typing built-in module (see Item 124: "Consider Static Analysis via typing to Obviate Bugs").

Ultimately, when writing idiomatic Python, you're going to encounter most errors at runtime. The Python language prioritizes runtime flexibility over compile-time error detection. For this reason, it's important to check that your assumptions are correct at runtime (see Item 81: "assert Internal Assumptions and raise Missed Expectations") and verify the correctness of your code with automated tests (see Item 109: "Prefer Integration Tests over Unit Tests").

Things to Remember

✦ Python defers nearly all error checking until runtime, including detection of problems that seem like they should be obvious during program startup.

✦ Community projects like linters and static analysis tools can help catch some of the most common sources of errors before program execution.

Item 4: Write Helper Functions Instead of Complex Expressions

Python's pithy syntax makes it easy to write single-line expressions that implement a lot of logic. For example, say that I want to decode the query string from a website URL. Here each query string parameter represents an integer value:

```
from urllib.parse import parse_qs

my_values = parse_qs("red=5&blue=0&green=",
                     keep_blank_values=True)
print(repr(my_values))

>>>
{'red': ['5'], 'blue': ['0'], 'green': ['']}
```

Some query string parameters may have multiple values, some may have single values, some may be present but have blank values, and some may be missing entirely. Using the get method on the result dictionary will return different values in each circumstance:

```
print("Red:     ", my_values.get("red"))
print("Green:   ", my_values.get("green"))
print("Opacity:", my_values.get("opacity"))

>>>
Red:      ['5']
Green:    ['']
Opacity: None
```

It'd be nice if a default value of 0 were assigned when a parameter isn't supplied or is blank. I might initially choose to do this with Boolean expressions because it feels like this logic doesn't merit a whole if statement or helper function quite yet.

Python's syntax makes this choice all too easy. The trick here is that the empty string, the empty list, and zero all evaluate to False implicitly. Thus, the expressions below will evaluate to the subexpression after the or operator when the first subexpression is False:

```
# For query string 'red=5&blue=0&green='
red = my_values.get("red", [""])[0] or 0
green = my_values.get("green", [""])[0] or 0
opacity = my_values.get("opacity", [""])[0] or 0
print(f"Red:     {red!r}")
print(f"Green:   {green!r}")
print(f"Opacity: {opacity!r}")

>>>
Red:      '5'
Green:    0
Opacity: 0
```

The red case works because the key "red" is present in the my_values dictionary. The value retrieved by the get method is a list with one member: the string "5". This item is retrieved by accessing index 0 in the list. Then the or expression determines that the string is not empty and thus is the resulting value of that operation. Finally, the variable red is assigned to the value "5".

The green case works because the value in the my_values dictionary is a list with one member: an empty string. The item at index 0 in the list is retrieved. The or expression determines that the string is empty, and thus its return value should be the right-side argument to the operation, which is 0. Finally, the variable green is assigned to the value 0.

The opacity case works because the value in the my_values dictionary is missing altogether. The behavior of the get method is to return its second argument if the key doesn't exist in the dictionary (see Item 26: "Prefer get over in and KeyError to Handle Missing Dictionary Keys"). The default value in this case is a list with one member: an empty string. Thus, when opacity isn't found in the dictionary, this code does exactly the same thing as the green case.

The complex expression with get, [""], [0], and or is difficult to read, and yet it still doesn't do everything I need. I also want to ensure that all the parameter values are converted to integers so I can immediately use them in mathematical expressions. To do that, I wrap each expression with the int built-in function to parse the string as an integer:

```
red = int(my_values.get("red", [""])[0] or 0)
```

This logic is now extremely hard to read. There's so much visual noise. The code isn't approachable. A new reader of the code would have to spend too much time picking apart the expression to figure out what it actually does. Even though it's nice to keep things short, it's not worth trying to fit this all on one line.

Although Python does support conditional expressions for inline if/else behavior, using them in this situation results in code that's not much clearer than the Boolean operator example above (see Item 7: "Consider Conditional Expressions for Simple Inline Logic"):

```
red_str = my_values.get("red", [""])
red = int(red_str[0]) if red_str[0] else 0
```

Alternatively, I can use a full `if` statement over multiple lines to implement the same logic. Seeing all of the steps spread out like this makes the dense version seem even more complex:

```
green_str = my_values.get("green", [""])
if green_str[0]:
    green = int(green_str[0])
else:
    green = 0
```

Now that this logic is spread across multiple lines, it's a bit harder to copy and paste for assigning other variables (e.g., red). If I want to reuse this functionality repeatedly—even just two or three times, as in this example—then writing a helper function is the way to go:

```
def get_first_int(values, key, default=0):
    found = values.get(key, [""])
    if found[0]:
        return int(found[0])
    return default
```

The calling code is much clearer than the complex expression using or and the two-line version using the conditional expression:

```
green = get_first_int(my_values, "green")
```

As soon as your expressions get complicated, it's time to consider splitting them into smaller pieces—such as intermediate variables—and moving logic into helper functions. What you gain in readability always outweighs what brevity may have afforded you. Avoid letting Python's pithy syntax for complex expressions get you into a mess like this. Follow the *DRY principle*: Don't repeat yourself.

Things to Remember

✦ Python's syntax makes it all too easy to write single-line expressions that are overly complicated and difficult to read.

✦ Move complex expressions into helper functions, especially if you need to use the same logic repeatedly.

Item 5: Prefer Multiple-Assignment Unpacking over Indexing

Python has a built-in tuple type that can be used to create immutable, ordered sequences of values (see Item 56: "Prefer dataclasses for

Creating Immutable Objects" for similar data structures). A tuple can be empty, or it can contain a single item:

```
no_snack = ()
snack = ("chips",)
```

A tuple can also include multiple items, as in these key/value pairs from a dictionary:

```
snack_calories = {
    "chips": 140,
    "popcorn": 80,
    "nuts": 190,
}
items = list(snack_calories.items())
print(items)
```

```
>>>
[('chips', 140), ('popcorn', 80), ('nuts', 190)]
```

The members in tuples can be accessed through numerical indexes and slices, just like in a list:

```
item = ("Peanut butter", "Jelly")
first_item = item[0]    # Index
first_half = item[:1]   # Slice
print(first_item)
print(first_half)
```

```
>>>
Peanut butter
('Peanut butter',)
```

Once a tuple is created, you can't modify it by assigning a new value to an index:

```
pair = ("Chocolate", "Peanut butter")
pair[0] = "Honey"
```

```
>>>
Traceback ...
TypeError: 'tuple' object does not support item assignment
```

Python also has syntax for *unpacking*, which allows for assigning multiple values in a single statement. The patterns that you specify in unpacking assignments look a lot like trying to mutate tuples—which isn't allowed—but they actually work quite differently. For example, if you know that a tuple is a pair, instead of using indexes to access its values, you can assign it to a tuple of two variable names:

```
item = ("Peanut butter", "Jelly")
first, second = item  # Unpacking
print(first, "and", second)
```

```
>>>
Peanut butter and Jelly
```

Unpacking has less visual noise than accessing the tuple's indexes, and it often requires fewer lines of code. The same pattern-matching syntax of unpacking works when assigning to lists, sequences, and multiple levels of arbitrary iterables within iterables. I don't recommend doing the following in your code, but it's important to know that it's possible and how it works:

```
favorite_snacks = {
    "salty": ("pretzels", 100),
    "sweet": ("cookies", 180),
    "veggie": ("carrots", 20),
}
((type1, (name1, cals1)),
 (type2, (name2, cals2)),
 (type3, (name3, cals3))) = favorite_snacks.items()

print(f"Favorite {type1} is {name1} with {cals1} calories")
print(f"Favorite {type2} is {name2} with {cals2} calories")
print(f"Favorite {type3} is {name3} with {cals3} calories")
```

```
>>>
Favorite salty is pretzels with 100 calories
Favorite sweet is cookies with 180 calories
Favorite veggie is carrots with 20 calories
```

Newcomers to Python may be surprised to learn that unpacking can even be used to swap values in place without the need to create temporary variables. Here I use typical syntax with indexes to swap the values between two positions in a list as part of an ascending-order sorting algorithm:

```
def bubble_sort(a):
    for _ in range(len(a)):
        for i in range(1, len(a)):
            if a[i] < a[i - 1]:
                temp = a[i]
                a[i] = a[i - 1]
                a[i - 1] = temp
```

```
names = ["pretzels", "carrots", "arugula", "bacon"]
bubble_sort(names)
print(names)

>>>
['arugula', 'bacon', 'carrots', 'pretzels']
```

However, with unpacking syntax, it's possible to swap indexes in a single line:

```
def bubble_sort(a):
    for _ in range(len(a)):
        for i in range(1, len(a)):
            if a[i] < a[i - 1]:
                a[i - 1], a[i] = a[i], a[i - 1]   # Swap

names = ["pretzels", "carrots", "arugula", "bacon"]
bubble_sort(names)
print(names)

>>>
['arugula', 'bacon', 'carrots', 'pretzels']
```

The way this swap works is that the right side of the assignment (a[i], a[i-1]) is evaluated first, and its values are put into a new temporary, unnamed tuple (such as ("carrots", "pretzels") on the first iteration of the loops). Then the unpacking pattern from the left side of the assignment (a[i-1], a[i]) is used to receive that tuple value and assign it to the variable names a[i-1] and a[i], respectively. This replaces "pretzels" with "carrots" at index 0 and "carrots" with "pretzels" at index 1. Finally, the temporary unnamed tuple silently goes away.

Another valuable application of unpacking is in the target lists of for loops and similar constructs, such as comprehensions and generator expressions (see Item 40: "Use Comprehensions Instead of map and filter" and Item 44: "Consider Generator Expressions for Large List Comprehensions"). For example, here I iterate over a list of snacks without using unpacking:

```
snacks = [("bacon", 350), ("donut", 240), ("muffin", 190)]
for i in range(len(snacks)):
    item = snacks[i]
    name = item[0]
    calories = item[1]
    print(f"#{i+1}: {name} has {calories} calories")
```

```
>>>
#1: bacon has 350 calories
#2: donut has 240 calories
#3: muffin has 190 calories
```

This works, but it's noisy. There are a lot of extra characters required in order to index into the various levels of the snacks structure. Now I achieve the same output by using unpacking along with the `enumerate` built-in function (see Item 17: "Prefer `enumerate` over `range`"):

```
for rank, (name, calories) in enumerate(snacks, 1):
    print(f"#{rank}: {name} has {calories} calories")
```

```
>>>
#1: bacon has 350 calories
#2: donut has 240 calories
#3: muffin has 190 calories
```

This is the Pythonic way to write this type of loop; it's short and easy to understand. There's usually no need to access anything by using indexes.

Python provides additional unpacking functionality for `list` construction (see Item 16: "Prefer Catch-All Unpacking over Slicing"), function arguments (see Item 34: "Reduce Visual Noise with Variable Positional Arguments"), keyword arguments (see Item 35: "Provide Optional Behavior with Keyword Arguments"), multiple return values (see Item 31: "Return Dedicated Result Objects Instead of Requiring Function Callers to Unpack More Than Three Variables"), structural pattern matching (see Item 9: "Consider `match` for Destructuring in Flow Control; Avoid When `if` Statements Are Sufficient"), and more.

Using unpacking wisely will enable you to avoid indexing when possible, resulting in clearer and more Pythonic code. However, these features are not without pitfalls to consider (see Item 6: "Always Surround Single-Element Tuples with Parentheses"). Unpacking also doesn't work in assignment expressions (see Item 8: "Prevent Repetition with Assignment Expressions").

Things to Remember

✦ Python has special syntax called unpacking for assigning multiple values in a single statement.

✦ Unpacking is generalized in Python and can be applied to any iterable, including many levels of iterables within iterables.

✦ You can reduce visual noise and increase code clarity by using unpacking to avoid explicitly indexing into sequences.

Item 6: Always Surround Single-Element Tuples with Parentheses

In Python there are four kinds of tuple literal values. The first kind is a comma-separated list of items inside open and close parentheses:

```
first = (1, 2, 3)
```

The second kind is just like the first but with an optional trailing comma included, which allows for consistency when going across multiple lines and eases editing:

```
second = (1, 2, 3,)
second_wrapped = (
    1,
    2,
    3,  # Optional comma
)
```

The third kind is a comma-separated list of items without any surrounding parentheses:

```
third = 1, 2, 3
```

And finally, the fourth kind is just like the third but with an optional trailing comma:

```
fourth = 1, 2, 3,
```

Python treats all of these constructions as the same value:

```
assert first == second == third == fourth
```

However, there are also three special cases in creating tuples that need to be considered. The first case is the empty tuple, which is merely open and close parentheses:

```
empty = ()
```

The second special case is the form of single-element tuples: You must include a trailing comma. If you leave out the trailing comma, then what you have is a parenthesized expression instead of a tuple:

```
single_with = (1,)
single_without = (1)
assert single_with != single_without
assert single_with[0] == single_without
```

And the third special case is similar to the second one except without the parentheses:

```
single_parens = (1,)
single_no_parens = 1,
assert single_parens == single_no_parens
```

This third special case—a trailing comma with no parentheses—can cause unexpected problems that are hard to diagnose. Consider the following function call from an e-commerce website that has a difficult-to-spot bug:

```
to_refund = calculate_refund(
    get_order_value(user, order.id),
    get_tax(user.address, order.dest),
    adjust_discount(user) + 0.1),
```

You might expect that the return type is an integer, a float, or a decimal number containing the amount of money to be refunded to a customer. But, in fact, it's a tuple!

```
print(type(to_refund))
```

```
>>>
<class 'tuple'>
```

The problem is the extraneous comma at the end of the final line. Removing the comma fixes the code:

```
to_refund2 = calculate_refund(
    get_order_value(user, order.id),
    get_tax(user.address, order.dest),
    adjust_discount(user) + 0.1)  # No trailing comma
```

```
print(type(to_refund2))
```

```
>>>
<class 'int'>
```

A comma character like this could be inserted into your code by accident, causing a change in behavior that's hard to track down even upon close inspection. The errant separator could also be left over from editing the items in a tuple, list, set, or function call and forgetting to remove a leftover comma. This happens more often than you might expect!

Another problem with single-element tuples without surrounding parentheses is that they can't be easily moved from assignments into expressions. For example, if I want to copy the single-element tuple 1, into a list, I have to surround it with parentheses. If I forget to do that,

I end up passing more items or arguments to the surrounding form instead of a tuple:

```
value_a = 1,     # No parentheses, right
list_b = [1,]    # No parentheses, wrong
list_c = [(1,)]  # Parentheses, right
print('A:', value_a)
print('B:', list_b)
print('C:', list_c)

>>>
A: (1,)
B: [1]
C: [(1,)]
```

A single-element tuple may also be on the left side of an assignment as part of the unpacking syntax (see Item 5: "Prefer Multiple-Assignment Unpacking over Indexing," Item 31: "Return Dedicated Result Objects Instead of Requiring Function Callers to Unpack More Than Three Variables," and Item 16: "Prefer Catch-All Unpacking over Slicing"). Surprisingly, all of these assignments are allowed, depending on the value returned, but they produce three different results:

```
def get_coupon_codes(user):
    ...
    return [['DEAL20']]
    ...

(a1,), = get_coupon_codes(user)
(a2,) = get_coupon_codes(user)
(a3), = get_coupon_codes(user)
(a4) = get_coupon_codes(user)
a5, = get_coupon_codes(user)
a6 = get_coupon_codes(user)

assert a1 not in (a2, a3, a4, a5, a6)
assert a2 == a3 == a5
assert a4 == a6
```

Sometimes automatic source code formatting tools (see Item 2: "Follow the PEP 8 Style Guide") and static analysis tools (see Item 3: "Never Expect Python to Detect Errors at Compile Time") can make the trailing comma problem more visible. But often it goes unnoticed until a program or test suite starts acting strange. The best way to avoid this situation is to always write single-element tuples with surrounding parentheses, whether they're on the left or the right of an assignment.

Things to Remember

✦ Tuple literal values in Python may have optional surrounding parentheses and optional trailing commas, except in a few special cases.

✦ A single-element tuple requires a trailing comma after the one item it contains and may have optional surrounding parentheses.

✦ It's all too easy to have an extraneous trailing comma at the end of an expression, which changes the meaning of the expression into a single-element tuple that breaks a program.

Item 7: Consider Conditional Expressions for Simple Inline Logic

Python `if` statements are not expressions. The `if` block, `elif` blocks, and `else` block each can contain a number of additional statements. The whole group of blocks doesn't evaluate to a single value that can be stored in a variable or passed as a function argument.

Python also supports *conditional expressions* that let you insert `if`/`elif`/`else` behavior nearly anywhere an expression is allowed. For example, here I use a conditional expression to assign a variable's value depending on a Boolean test:

```
i = 3
x = "even" if i % 2 == 0 else "odd"
print(x)

>>>
odd
```

This expression structure seems convenient, especially for one-of-a-kind uses, and is reminiscent of the *ternary operator* you might know from C and other languages (e.g., `condition ? true_value : false_value`). For simple assignments like this, or even in function call argument lists (e.g., `my_func(1 if x else 2)`), conditional expressions can be a good choice for balancing brevity with flexibility in code.

It's important to note one key detail about how conditional expressions in Python are different from ternary operators in other languages: In C, the test expression comes first; in Python, the expression to evaluate when the test expression is truthy comes first. For example, you might expect that the following code calls the `fail` function and raises an exception; instead, the `fail` function is never executed because the test condition is `False`:

```
def fail():
    raise Exception("Oops")
```

```
x = fail() if False else 20
print(x)
```

```
>>>
20
```

if clauses in Python comprehensions have similar syntax and behavior for filtering (see Item 40: "Use Comprehensions Instead of map and filter" and Item 44: "Consider Generator Expressions for Large List Comprehensions"). For example, here I use the if clause in a list comprehension to only include even values of x when computing the resulting list:

```
result = [x / 4 for x in range(10) if x % 2 == 0]
print(result)
```

```
>>>
[0.0, 0.5, 1.0, 1.5, 2.0]
```

The expression to evaluate (x / 4) comes before the if test expression (x % 2 == 0), just like in a conditional expression.

Before conditional expressions were available in Python, people would sometimes use Boolean logic to implement similar behavior (see Item 4: "Write Helper Functions Instead of Complex Expressions" for details). For example, the following expression is equivalent to the conditional expression above:

```
x = (i % 2 == 0 and "even") or "odd"
```

This form of logic is quite confusing because you need to know that and returns the first falsey value or the last truthy value, while or returns the first truthy value or the last falsey value (see Item 23: "Pass Iterators to any and all for Efficient Short-Circuiting Logic" for details).

Also, the approach of using Boolean operators doesn't work if you want to return a falsey value as a result of a truthy condition (e.g., x = (i % 2 == 0 and []) or [1] always evaluates to [1]). It's all non-obvious and error prone, which is part of why conditional expressions were added to the language in the first place.

Now consider the same logic as a four-line if statement instead of the earlier single-line example:

```
if i % 2 == 0:
    x = "even"
else:
    x = "odd"
```

Although this is longer, it can be better for a few reasons. First, if I later want to do more inside each of the condition branches, like printing debugging information, I can without structurally changing the code:

```
if i % 2 == 0:
    x = "even"
    print("It was even!")   # Added
else:
    x = "odd"
```

I can also insert additional branches with `elif` blocks in the same statement:

```
if i % 2 == 0:
    x = "even"
elif i % 3 == 0:   # Added
    x = "divisible by three"
else:
    x = "odd"
```

If I really need to achieve brevity and put this logic in a single expression, I can do that by moving it all into a helper function that I call inline:

```
def number_group(i):
    if i % 2 == 0:
        return "even"
    else:
        return "odd"

x = number_group(i)   # Short call
```

As an added benefit, the helper function can be reused in multiple places instead of being a one-off, as a conditional expression would be.

Whether you should use conditional expressions, full `if` statements, or `if` statements wrapped in helper functions is going to depend on the specific situation.

You should avoid conditional expressions when they must be split over multiple lines. For example, here the function calls I make are so long that the conditional expression must be line-wrapped with surrounding parentheses:

```
x = (my_long_function_call(1, 2, 3) if i % 2 == 0
        else my_other_long_function_call(4, 5, 6))
```

This is quite difficult to read. And if you apply an auto-formatter (see Item 2: "Follow the PEP 8 Style Guide") to this code, the conditional expression will likely be rewritten to use more lines of code than a standard if/else statement anyway:

```
x = (
    my_long_function_call(1, 2, 3)
    if i % 2 == 0
    else my_other_long_function_call(4, 5, 6)
)
```

Another Python language feature to compare with conditional expressions is assignment expressions (see Item 8: "Prevent Repetition with Assignment Expressions"), which also allow statement-like behavior in expressions. The critical difference is that assignment expressions must be surrounded by parentheses when they're used in an ambiguous context; conditional expressions do not require surrounding parentheses, and lacking parentheses can hurt readability.

For example, this if statement with an assignment expression in parentheses is permitted:

```
x = 2
y = 1

if x and (z := x > y):
    ...
```

But this if statement without wrapping parentheses is a syntax error:

```
if x and z := x > y:
    ...
```

```
>>>
Traceback ...
SyntaxError: cannot use assignment expressions with expression
```

With conditional expressions, parentheses aren't required. It's difficult to decipher what the original intent of the programmer was since both of these forms are allowed:

```
if x > y if z else w:    # Ambiguous
    ...

if x > (y if z else w):  # Clear
    ...
```

Assignment expressions also need surrounding parentheses when used inside a function call argument list:

```
z = dict(
    your_value=(y := 1),
)
```

Leaving out the parentheses is a syntax error:

```
w = dict(
    other_value=y := 1,
)
```

```
>>>
Traceback ...
SyntaxError: invalid syntax
```

Conditional expressions, in contrast, don't require surrounding parentheses in this context, and the lack of parentheses can make code noisier and hard to read:

```
v = dict(
    my_value=1 if x else 3,
)
```

The bottom line: Use your judgment. In many situations, conditional expressions can be valuable and improve clarity. Sometimes they're better with surrounding parentheses and sometimes not. Conditional expressions can all too easily be overused to write obfuscated code that's difficult for new readers to understand. When in doubt, choose a normal if statement.

Things to Remember

✦ Conditional expressions in Python allow you to put an if statement nearly anywhere an expression would normally go.

✦ The order of the test expression, true result expression, and false result expression in a conditional expression is different than the order with ternary operators in other languages.

✦ Don't use conditional expressions in places where they increase ambiguity or harm readability for new readers of the code.

✦ Prefer standard if statements and helper functions when it's unclear whether conditional expressions provide a compelling benefit.

Item 8: Prevent Repetition with Assignment Expressions

An assignment expression—also known as the *walrus operator*—is a new syntax feature introduced in Python 3.8 to solve a long-standing problem with the language that can cause code duplication. Whereas normal assignment statements are written a = b and pronounced "a equals b," these assignments are written a := b and pronounced "a *walrus* b" (because := looks like a pair of eyeballs and tusks).

Assignment expressions are useful because they enable you to assign variables in places where assignment statements are disallowed, such as in the test expression of an if statement. An assignment expression's value evaluates to whatever was assigned to the identifier on the left side of the walrus operator.

For example, say that I have a basket of fresh fruit that I'm trying to manage for a juice bar. Here I define the contents of the basket:

```
fresh_fruit = {
    "apple": 10,
    "banana": 8,
    "lemon": 5,
}
```

When a customer comes to the counter to order some lemonade, I need to make sure there is at least one lemon in the basket to squeeze. Here I do this by retrieving the count of lemons and then using an if statement to check for a nonzero value:

```
def make_lemonade(count):
    ...

def out_of_stock():
    ...

count = fresh_fruit.get("lemon", 0)
if count:
    make_lemonade(count)
else:
    out_of_stock()

>>>
Making 5 lemons into lemonade
```

The problem with this seemingly simple code is that it's noisier than it needs to be. The count variable is used only within the first block of the if statement. Defining count above the if statement causes it to appear to be more important than it really is—as if all code that follows, including the else block, will need to access the count variable, when that is not the case.

This pattern of fetching a value, checking to see if it's truthy, and then using it is extremely common in Python. Many programmers try to work around the multiple references to count with a variety of tricks that hurt readability (see Item 4: "Write Helper Functions Instead of Complex Expressions" and Item 7: "Consider Conditional Expressions for Simple Inline Logic"). Luckily, assignment expressions were added to the language to streamline this type of code. Here I rewrite the example above using the walrus operator:

```
if count := fresh_fruit.get("lemon", 0):
    make_lemonade(count)
else:
    out_of_stock()
```

Although this is only one line shorter, it's a lot more readable because it's now clear that count is only relevant to the first block of the if statement. The assignment expression first assigns a value to the count variable and then evaluates that value in the context of the if statement to determine how to proceed with flow control. This two-step behavior—assign and then evaluate—is the fundamental nature of the walrus operator.

Lemons are quite potent, so only one is needed for my lemonade recipe, which means a nonzero, truthy check is good enough. If a customer orders a cider, though, I need to make sure that I have at least four apples. Here I do this by fetching the count value from the fresh_fruit dictionary and then using a comparison in the if statement test expression:

```
def make_cider(count):
    ...

count = fresh_fruit.get("apple", 0)
if count >= 4:
    make_cider(count)
else:
    out_of_stock()

>>>
Making cider with 10 apples
```

This has the same problem as the lemonade example, where the assignment of count puts distracting emphasis on that variable. Here I improve the clarity of this code by also using the walrus operator:

```
if (count := fresh_fruit.get("apple", 0)) >= 4:
    make_cider(count)
else:
    out_of_stock()
```

This works as expected and makes the code one line shorter. It's important to note how I needed to surround the assignment expression with parentheses to compare it with 4 in the if statement. In the lemonade example, no surrounding parentheses were required because the assignment expression stood on its own as a nonzero, truthy check; it wasn't a subexpression of a larger expression. As with other expressions, you should avoid surrounding assignment expressions with parentheses when possible to reduce visual noise.

Another common variation of this repetitive pattern occurs when I need to assign a variable in the enclosing scope depending on some condition and then reference that variable shortly afterward in a function call. For example, say that a customer orders some banana smoothies. In order to make them, I need to have at least two bananas' worth of slices, or else an OutOfBananas exception is raised. Here I implement this logic in a typical way:

```
def slice_bananas(count):
    ...

class OutOfBananas(Exception):
    pass

def make_smoothies(count):
    ...

pieces = 0
count = fresh_fruit.get("banana", 0)
if count >= 2:
    pieces = slice_bananas(count)

try:
    smoothies = make_smoothies(pieces)
except OutOfBananas:
    out_of_stock()

>>>
Slicing 8 bananas
Making smoothies with 32 banana slices
```

The other common way to do this is to put the `pieces = 0` assignment in the `else` block:

```
count = fresh_fruit.get("banana", 0)
if count >= 2:
    pieces = slice_bananas(count)
else:
    pieces = 0  # Moved

try:
    smoothies = make_smoothies(pieces)
except OutOfBananas:
    out_of_stock()
```

This second approach can feel odd because it means that the `pieces` variable has two different locations—in each block of the `if` statement— where it can be initially defined. This split definition technically works because of Python's scoping rules (see Item 33: "Know How Closures Interact with Variable Scope and `nonlocal`"), but it isn't easy to read or discover, which is why many people prefer the construct above, where the `pieces = 0` assignment is first.

The walrus operator can be used to shorten this example by one line of code. This small change removes any emphasis on the `count` variable. Now it's clearer that `pieces` will be important beyond the `if` statement:

```
pieces = 0
if (count := fresh_fruit.get("banana", 0)) >= 2:  # Changed
    pieces = slice_bananas(count)

try:
    smoothies = make_smoothies(pieces)
except OutOfBananas:
    out_of_stock()
```

Using the walrus operator also improves the readability of splitting the definition of `pieces` across both parts of the `if` statement. It's eas- ier to trace the `pieces` variable when the `count` definition no longer precedes the `if` statement:

```
if (count := fresh_fruit.get("banana", 0)) >= 2:
    pieces = slice_bananas(count)
else:
    pieces = 0  # Moved
```

```
try:
    smoothies = make_smoothies(pieces)
except OutOfBananas:
    out_of_stock()
```

One frustration that programmers who are new to Python often have is the lack of a flexible switch/case statement. The general style for approximating this type of functionality is to have a deep nesting of multiple if, elif, and else blocks.

For example, imagine that I want to implement a system of precedence so that each customer automatically gets the best juice available and doesn't have to order. Here I define logic to make it so banana smoothies are served first, followed by apple cider, and then finally lemonade:

```
count = fresh_fruit.get("banana", 0)
if count >= 2:
    pieces = slice_bananas(count)
    to_enjoy = make_smoothies(pieces)
else:
    count = fresh_fruit.get("apple", 0)
    if count >= 4:
        to_enjoy = make_cider(count)
    else:
        count = fresh_fruit.get("lemon", 0)
        if count:
            to_enjoy = make_lemonade(count)
        else:
            to_enjoy = "Nothing"
```

Ugly constructs like this are surprisingly common in Python code. Luckily, the walrus operator provides an elegant solution that can feel nearly as versatile as dedicated syntax for switch/case statements:

```
if (count := fresh_fruit.get("banana", 0)) >= 2:
    pieces = slice_bananas(count)
    to_enjoy = make_smoothies(pieces)
elif (count := fresh_fruit.get("apple", 0)) >= 4:
    to_enjoy = make_cider(count)
elif count := fresh_fruit.get("lemon", 0):
    to_enjoy = make_lemonade(count)
else:
    to_enjoy = "Nothing"
```

The version that uses assignment expressions is only five lines shorter than the original, but the improvement in readability is vast due to the reduction in nesting and indentation. If you ever see the previous ugly constructs emerge in your code, I suggest that you move them over to using the walrus operator if possible (see Item 9: "Consider match for Destructuring in Flow Control; Avoid When if Statements Are Sufficient" for another approach).

Another common frustration of new Python programmers is the lack of a do/while loop construct. For example, say that I want to bottle juice as new fruit is delivered until there's no fruit remaining. Here I implement this logic with a while loop:

```
def pick_fruit():
    ...

def make_juice(fruit, count):
    ...

bottles = []
fresh_fruit = pick_fruit()
while fresh_fruit:
    for fruit, count in fresh_fruit.items():
        batch = make_juice(fruit, count)
        bottles.extend(batch)
    fresh_fruit = pick_fruit()
```

This is repetitive because it requires two separate fresh_fruit = pick_fruit() calls: one before the loop to set initial conditions and another at the end of the loop to replenish the list of delivered fruit.

A strategy for improving code reuse in this situation is to use the *loop-and-a-half* idiom. This eliminates the redundant lines, but it also undermines the while loop's contribution by making it a dumb infinite loop. Now all of the flow control of the loop depends on the conditional break statement:

```
bottles = []
while True:                      # Loop
    fresh_fruit = pick_fruit()
    if not fresh_fruit:          # And a half
        break
    for fruit, count in fresh_fruit.items():
        batch = make_juice(fruit, count)
        bottles.extend(batch)
```

The walrus operator obviates the need for the loop-and-a-half idiom by allowing the fresh_fruit variable to be reassigned and then conditionally evaluated each time through the while loop. This solution is short and easy to read, and it should be the preferred approach in your code:

```
bottles = []
while fresh_fruit := pick_fruit():  # Changed
    for fruit, count in fresh_fruit.items():
        batch = make_juice(fruit, count)
        bottles.extend(batch)
```

There are many other situations where assignment expressions can be used to eliminate redundancy (see Item 42: "Reduce Repetition in Comprehensions with Assignment Expressions" for an example). In general, when you find yourself repeating the same expression or assignment multiple times within a grouping of lines, it's time to consider using assignment expressions in order to improve readability.

Things to Remember

✦ Assignment expressions use the walrus operator (:=) to both assign and evaluate variable names in a single expression, thus reducing repetition.

✦ When an assignment expression is a subexpression of a larger expression, it must be surrounded with parentheses.

✦ Although switch/case statements and do/while loops are not available in Python, their functionality can be emulated much more clearly by using assignment expressions.

Item 9: Consider match for Destructuring in Flow Control; Avoid When if Statements Are Sufficient

The match statement is a relatively new Python feature, introduced in version 3.10. With so many distinct capabilities, the learning curve for match is steep: It feels like another mini-language embedded within Python, similar to the unique ergonomics of comprehensions (see Item 40: "Use Comprehensions Instead of map and filter" and Item 44: "Consider Generator Expressions for Large List Comprehensions"). At first glance, match statements appear to provide Python with long-sought-after behavior that's similar to switch statements from other programming languages (see Item 8: "Prevent Repetition with Assignment Expressions" for another approach).

For example, say that I'm writing a vehicle assistant program that reacts to a traffic light's color. Here I use a simple Python if statement for this purpose:

```python
def take_action(light):
    if light == "red":
        print("Stop")
    elif light == "yellow":
        print("Slow down")
    elif light == "green":
        print("Go!")
    else:
        raise RuntimeError
```

I can confirm that this function works as expected:

```python
take_action("red")
take_action("yellow")
take_action("green")

>>>
Stop
Slow down
Go!
```

To use the match statement, I can create case clauses corresponding to each of the if, elif, and else conditions:

```python
def take_match_action(light):
    match light:
        case "red":
            print("Stop")
        case "yellow":
            print("Slow down")
        case "green":
            print("Go!")
        case _:
            raise RuntimeError
```

Using a match statement seems better than using an if statement because I can remove repeated references to the light variable, and I can leave out the == operator for each conditional branch. However, this code still isn't ideal because of how it uses string literals for everything. To fix this, what I'd normally do is create a constant at the module level for each light color and modify the code to use them, like this:

```
# Added these constants
RED = "red"
YELLOW = "yellow"
GREEN = "green"

def take_constant_action(light):
    match light:
        case RED:                # Changed
            print("Stop")
        case YELLOW:             # Changed
            print("Slow down")
        case GREEN:              # Changed
            print("Go!")
        case _:
            raise RuntimeError

>>>
Traceback ...
SyntaxError: name capture 'RED' makes remaining patterns
➥unreachable
```

Unfortunately, this code has an error—and a cryptic one at that. The issue is that the match statement assumes that simple variable names that come after the case keyword are *capture patterns*. To demonstrate what this means, here I shorten the match statement to have only a single branch that should match RED:

```
def take_truncated_action(light):
    match light:
        case RED:
            print("Stop")
```

Now I call the function by passing GREEN. I expect the match light clause to be evaluated first and the light variable lookup in the current scope to resolve to "green". Next, I expect the case RED clause to be evaluated and the RED variable lookup to resolve to "red". These two values don't match (i.e., "green" vs. "red"), and so I expect no output:

```
take_truncated_action(GREEN)

>>>
Stop
```

Surprisingly, the match statement executed the RED branch. Here I use print to figure out what's happening:

```
def take_debug_action(light):
    match light:
        case RED:
            print(f"{RED=}, {light=}")


take_debug_action(GREEN)

>>>
RED='green', light='green'
```

The case clause didn't look up the value of RED. Instead, it assigned RED to the value of the light variable! What the match statement is doing is similar to the behavior of unpacking (see Item 5: "Prefer Multiple-Assignment Unpacking over Indexing"). Instead of case RED translating to light == RED, Python determines if the multiple assignment (RED,) = (light,) would execute without an error, similar to this:

```
def take_unpacking_action(light):
    try:
        (RED,) = (light,)
    except TypeError:
        # Did not match
        ...
    else:
        # Matched
        print(f"{RED=}, {light=}")
```

The original syntax error above occurred because Python determines at compile time that the assignment (RED,) = (light,) will work for any value of light, and thus the subsequent clauses with case YELLOW and case GREEN are unreachable.

One work-around for this problem is to ensure that a . character is in the case clause's variable reference. The presence of a dot operator causes Python to look up the attribute and do an equality test instead of treating the variable name as a capture pattern. For example, here I achieve the original intended behavior by using the enum built-in module and the dot operator to access each constant name:

```
import enum                       # Added

class ColorEnum(enum.Enum):       # Added
    RED = "red"
    YELLOW = "yellow"
    GREEN = "green"
```

```
def take_enum_action(light):
    match light:
        case ColorEnum.RED:      # Changed
            print("Stop")
        case ColorEnum.YELLOW:   # Changed
            print("Slow down")
        case ColorEnum.GREEN:    # Changed
            print("Go!")
        case _:
            raise RuntimeError
```

Although this code now works as expected, it's hard to see the benefits of the match version over the simpler if version in the take_action function above. The if version is 9 lines versus 10 lines with match. The if version repeats the light == prefix for each branch, but the match version repeats the ColorEnum. prefix for the constants. Superficially, it seems like a wash. Why did Python add match statements to the language if they're not a compelling feature?

match **Is for Destructuring**

Destructuring is a programming language technique for extracting components from a complex nested data structure with minimal syntax. Python programmers use destructuring all the time without even thinking about it. For example, the multiple assignment of index, value to the return value of enumerate in this for loop is a form of destructuring (see Item 17: "Prefer enumerate over range"):

```
for index, value in enumerate("abc"):
    print(f"index {index} is {value}")

>>>
index 0 is a
index 1 is b
index 2 is c
```

Python has supported destructuring assignments for deeply nested tuples and lists for a long time (see Item 16: "Prefer Catch-All Unpacking over Slicing"). The match statement extends the language to also support this unpacking-like behavior for dictionaries, sets, and user-defined classes solely for the purpose of control flow. The *structural pattern matching* technique that match enables is especially valuable when your code needs to deal with heterogeneous object graphs and semi-structured data. (Similar idioms in functional-style programming are *algebraic data types*, *sum types*, and *tagged unions*.)

For example, say that I want to search a binary tree and determine if it contains a given value. I can represent the binary tree as a three-item tuple, where the first index is the value, the second index is the left (lower-value) child, and the third index is the right (higher-value) child. None in the second position or third position indicates the absence of a child node. In the case of a leaf node, I can just put the value inline instead of using another nested tuple. Here I define a nested tree containing five values (7, 9, 10, 11, 13):

```
my_tree = (10, (7, None, 9), (13, 11, None))
```

I can implement a recursive function to test whether a tree contains a value by using simple if statements. The tree argument might be None (for an absent child node) or a non-tuple (for a leaf node), so this code needs to ensure that those conditions are handled before unpacking the three-tuple node representation:

```
def contains(tree, value):
    if not isinstance(tree, tuple):
        return tree == value

    pivot, left, right = tree

    if value < pivot:
        return contains(left, value)
    elif value > pivot:
        return contains(right, value)
    else:
        return value == pivot
```

This function works as expected when the node values are comparable:

```
assert contains(my_tree, 9)
assert not contains(my_tree, 14)
```

Now I can rewrite this function using the match statement:

```
def contains_match(tree, value):
    match tree:
        case pivot, left, _ if value < pivot:
            return contains_match(left, value)
        case pivot, _, right if value > pivot:
            return contains_match(right, value)
        case (pivot, _, _) | pivot:
            return pivot == value
```

Using match, the call to isinstance is eliminated, the unpacking assignment can be avoided, the structure of the code (using case clauses) is more regular, the logic is simpler and easier to follow, and the function is only seven lines of code instead of the nine lines required for the if version. This makes the match statement appear quite compelling (see Item 76: "Know How to Port Threaded I/O to asyncio" for another example).

In this function, the way that match works is each of the case clauses tries to extract the contents of the tree argument by using the given destructuring pattern. After Python determines that the structure matches, it evaluates any subsequent if clauses, which work similarly to if clauses in comprehensions. When the if clause, sometimes called a *guard expression*, evaluates to True, the indented statements for that case block are executed, and the rest are skipped. If no case clauses match the input value, then the match statement does nothing and falls through.

This code also uses the | pipe operator to add an *or pattern* to the final case branch. This allows the case clause to match either of the given patterns: (pivot, _, _) or pivot. As you might recall from the traffic light example above that tried to reference the RED constant, the second pattern (pivot) is a capture pattern that will match any value. Thus, when tree is not a tuple with the right structure, the code assumes that it's a leaf value that should be tested for equality.

Now imagine that my requirements change yet again, and I want to use a class instead of a tuple to represent the nodes in my binary tree (see Item 29: "Compose Classes Instead of Deeply Nesting Dictionaries, Lists, and Tuples" for how to make that choice). Here I define a new class for nodes:

```python
class Node:
    def __init__(self, value, left=None, right=None):
        self.value = value
        self.left = left
        self.right = right
```

I can create another instance of the tree by using this class. Again, I specify leaf nodes simply by providing their value instead of wrapping them in an additional Node object:

```python
obj_tree = Node(
    value=10,
    left=Node(value=7, right=9),
    right=Node(value=13, left=11),
)
```

Modifying the if statement version of the contains function to handle the Node class is straightforward:

```
def contains_class(tree, value):
    if not isinstance(tree, Node):
        return tree == value
    elif value < tree.value:
        return contains_class(tree.left, value)
    elif value > tree.value:
        return contains_class(tree.right, value)
    else:
        return tree.value == value
```

The resulting code is similarly complex to the earlier version that used three-tuples. In some ways the class makes the function better (e.g., accessing object attributes instead of unpacking), and in other ways it makes the function worse (e.g., repetitive tree. prefixes).

I can also adapt the match version of the contains function to use the Node class:

```
def contains_match_class(tree, value):
    match tree:
        case Node(value=pivot, left=left) if value < pivot:
            return contains_match_class(left, value)
        case Node(value=pivot, right=right) if value > pivot:
            return contains_match_class(right, value)
        case Node(value=pivot) | pivot:
            return pivot == value
```

The way this works is each case clause implicitly does an isinstance check to test whether the value of tree is a Node object. Then it extracts the object's attributes using the capture patterns (pivot, left, right), similar to how tuple destructuring works. The capture variables can be used in guard expressions and case blocks to avoid more verbose attribute accesses (e.g., tree.left). The power and clarity provided by match works just as well with objects as it does with nested built-in data structures.

Semi-structured Data vs. Encapsulated Data

match also excels when the structure of data and its interpretation are decoupled. For example, a deserialized JSON object is merely a nesting of dictionaries, lists, strings, and numbers (see Item 54: "Consider Composing Functionality with Mix-in Classes" for an example). It lacks the clear encapsulation of responsibilities provided by an explicit class hierarchy (see Item 53: "Initialize Parent Classes with super"). But the way in which these basic JSON types are nested—the keys, values, and elements that are present at each level—gives the data semantic meaning that programs can interpret.

For example, imagine that I'm building billing software, and I need to deserialize customer records that are stored as JSON. Some of the records are for customers who are individuals, and other records are for customers that are businesses:

```
record1 = """{"customer": {"last": "Ross", "first": "Bob"}}"""
record2 = """{"customer": {"entity": "Steve's Painting Co."}}"""
```

I'd like to take these records and turn them into well-defined Python objects that I can use with my program's data processing features, UI widgets, and so on (see Item 51: "Prefer dataclasses for Defining Lightweight Classes" for background):

```
from dataclasses import dataclass

@dataclass
class PersonCustomer:
    first_name: str
    last_name: str

@dataclass
class BusinessCustomer:
    company_name: str
```

I can use the match statement to interpret the structure and values within the JSON data and map it to the concrete PersonCustomer and BusinessCustomer classes. This uses the match statement's unique syntax for destructuring dictionary literals with capture patterns:

```
import json

def deserialize(data):
    record = json.loads(data)
    match record:
        case {"customer": {"last": last_name,
                            "first": first_name}}:
            return PersonCustomer(first_name, last_name)
        case {"customer": {"entity": company_name}}:
            return BusinessCustomer(company_name)
        case _:
            raise ValueError("Unknown record type")
```

This function works as expected on the records defined above and produces the objects I need:

```
print("Record1:", deserialize(record1))
print("Record2:", deserialize(record2))

>>>
Record1: PersonCustomer(first_name='Bob', last_name='Ross')
Record2: BusinessCustomer(company_name="Steve's Painting Co.")
```

These examples give you merely a small taste of what's possible with match statements. There's also support for set patterns, as patterns, positional constructor patterns (with __match_args__ customization), exhaustiveness checking with type annotations (see Item 124: "Consider Static Analysis via typing to Obviate Bugs"), and more. Given the intricacies, it's best to refer to the official tutorial (https://peps.python.org/pep-0636/) to determine how to leverage match for your specific use case.

Things to Remember

✦ Although you can use match statements to replace simple if statements, doing so is error prone. The structural nature of capture patterns in case clauses is unintuitive for Python programmers who aren't already familiar with the gotchas of match.

✦ match statements provide a concise syntax for combining isinstance checks and destructuring behaviors with flow control. They're especially useful when processing heterogeneous object graphs and interpreting the semantic meaning of semi-structured data.

✦ case patterns can be used effectively with built-in data structures (e.g., lists, tuples, dictionaries) and user-defined classes, but each type has unique semantics that aren't immediately obvious.

2

Strings and Slicing

Python initially grew in popularity as a scripting language for orchestrating command-line utilities and processing input and output data. With built-in syntax, methods, and modules for string and sequence processing, Python was an attractive alternative to traditional shells and other common scripting languages (e.g., Perl). Since then, Python has continued to grow into adjacent domains, becoming an ideal programming language for parsing text, generating structured data, inspecting file formats, analyzing logs, and so on.

By using bytes and str types, Python programs can interface with human language text, manipulate low-level binary data formats, and perform input/output (I/O) and communicate with the outside world. Python abstracts over these character types, lists, and other types to provide a common interface for indexing, subsequencing, and more. These capabilities are so essential that you'll see them in nearly every program.

Item 10: Know the Differences Between bytes and str

In Python, there are two types that represent sequences of character data: bytes and str. Instances of bytes contain raw, unsigned 8-bit values (often displayed in ASCII encoding):

```
a = b"h\x65llo"
print(type(a))
print(list(a))
print(a)

>>>
<class 'bytes'>
[104, 101, 108, 108, 111]
b'hello'
```

Instances of `str` contain Unicode *code points* that represent textual characters from human languages:

```
a = "a\u0300 propos"
print(type(a))
print(list(a))
print(a)

>>>
<class 'str'>
['a', '`', ' ', 'p', 'r', 'o', 'p', 'o', 's']
à propos
```

Importantly, a `str` instance does not have an associated binary encoding, and a `bytes` instance does not have an associated text encoding. To convert Unicode data to binary data, you must call the encode method of `str`. To convert binary data to Unicode data, you must call the decode method of `bytes`. You can explicitly specify the encoding you want to use for these methods, or you can accept the system default, which is commonly *UTF-8* (but not always, as you'll see shortly).

When you're writing Python programs, it's important to do encoding and decoding of Unicode data at the furthest boundary of your interfaces; this approach is often called the *Unicode sandwich*. The core of your program should use the `str` type, which contains Unicode data, and should not assume anything about character encodings. This setup allows you to be very accepting of alternative text encodings (such as *Latin-1*, *Shift JIS*, and *Big5*) while being strict about your output text encoding (ideally, UTF-8).

The split between character data types leads to two common situations in Python code:

◆ You want to operate on raw 8-bit sequences that contain UTF-8-encoded strings (or some other encoding).

◆ You want to operate on Unicode strings that have no specific encoding.

You'll often need two helper functions to convert between these cases and to ensure that the type of input values matches your code's expectations.

The first function takes a `bytes` or `str` instance and always returns a `str`:

```
def to_str(bytes_or_str):
    if isinstance(bytes_or_str, bytes):
```

```
        value = bytes_or_str.decode("utf-8")
    else:
        value = bytes_or_str
    return value  # Instance of str

print(repr(to_str(b"foo")))
print(repr(to_str("bar")))

>>>
'foo'
'bar'
```

The second function takes a bytes or str instance and always returns a bytes:

```
def to_bytes(bytes_or_str):
    if isinstance(bytes_or_str, str):
        value = bytes_or_str.encode("utf-8")
    else:
        value = bytes_or_str
    return value  # Instance of bytes

print(repr(to_bytes(b"foo")))
print(repr(to_bytes("bar")))
```

There are two big gotchas when dealing with raw 8-bit values and Unicode strings in Python.

The first issue is that bytes and str seem to work the same way, but their instances are not compatible with each other, so you must be deliberate about the types of character sequences that you're passing around.

By using the + operator, you can add bytes to bytes and str to str, respectively:

```
print(b"one" + b"two")
print("one" + "two")

>>>
b'onetwo'
onetwo
```

But you can't add str instances to bytes instances:

```
b"one" + "two"

>>>
Traceback ...
TypeError: can't concat str to bytes
```

You also can't add bytes instances to str instances:

```
"one" + b"two"
```

```
>>>
Traceback ...
TypeError: can only concatenate str (not "bytes") to str
```

By using binary operators, you can compare bytes to bytes and str to str, respectively:

```
assert b"red" > b"blue"
assert "red" > "blue"
```

But you can't compare a str instance to a bytes instance:

```
assert "red" > b"blue"
```

```
>>>
Traceback ...
TypeError: '>' not supported between instances of 'str' and
➥'bytes'
```

And you also can't compare a bytes instance to a str instance:

```
assert b"blue" < "red"
```

```
>>>
Traceback ...
TypeError: '<' not supported between instances of 'bytes' and
➥'str'
```

Comparing bytes and str instances for equality will always evaluate to False, even when they contain exactly the same characters (in this case, ASCII-encoded "foo"):

```
print(b"foo" == "foo")
```

```
>>>
False
```

The % operator works with format strings for each type (see Item 11: "Prefer Interpolated F-Strings over C-Style Format Strings and str.format" for background):

```
blue_bytes = b"blue"
blue_str = "blue"
print(b"red %s" % blue_bytes)
print("red %s" % blue_str)
```

```
>>>
b'red blue'
red blue
```

But you can't pass a str instance to a bytes format string because Python doesn't know what binary text encoding to use:

```
print(b"red %s" % blue_str)
```

```
>>>
Traceback ...
TypeError: %b requires a bytes-like object, or an object that
➥implements __bytes__, not 'str'
```

However, you *can* pass a bytes instance to a str format string by using the % operator, or you can use a bytes instance in an interpolated format string, but it doesn't do what you'd expect:

```
print("red %s" % blue_bytes)
print(f"red {blue_bytes}")
```

```
>>>
red b'blue'
red b'blue'
```

In these cases, the code actually invokes the __repr__ special method (see Item 12: "Understand the Difference Between repr and str when Printing Objects") on the bytes instance and substitutes that in place of %s or {blue_bytes}, which is why the b"blue" literal appears in the output.

The second gotcha is that operations involving file handles (returned by the open built-in function) default to requiring Unicode strings instead of raw bytes. This can cause surprising failures, especially for programmers accustomed to Python 2. For example, say that I want to write some binary data to a file. This seemingly simple code breaks:

```
with open("data.bin", "w") as f:
    f.write(b"\xf1\xf2\xf3\xf4\xf5")
```

```
>>>
Traceback ...
TypeError: write() argument must be str, not bytes
```

The cause of the exception is that the file was opened in write text mode ("w") instead of write binary mode ("wb"). When a file is in text mode, write operations expect str instances containing Unicode data instead of bytes instances containing binary data. Here, I fix this by changing the open mode to "wb":

```
with open("data.bin", "wb") as f:
    f.write(b"\xf1\xf2\xf3\xf4\xf5")
```

A similar problem exists for reading data from files. For example, here I try to read the binary file that was written above:

```
with open("data.bin", "r") as f:
    data = f.read()
```

```
>>>
Traceback ...
UnicodeDecodeError: 'utf-8' codec can't decode byte 0xf1 in
➥position 0: invalid continuation byte
```

This fails because the file was opened in read text mode ("r") instead of read binary mode ("rb"). When a handle is in text mode, it uses the system's default text encoding to interpret binary data using the bytes.decode (for reading) and str.encode (for writing) methods. On most systems, the default encoding is UTF-8, which can't accept the binary data b"\xf1\xf2\xf3\xf4\xf5", thus causing the error above. Here, I solve this problem by changing the open mode to "rb":

```
with open("data.bin", "rb") as f:
    data = f.read()
assert data == b"\xf1\xf2\xf3\xf4\xf5"
```

Alternatively, I can explicitly specify the encoding parameter to the open function to make sure I'm not surprised by any platform-specific behavior. For example, here I assume that the binary data in the file was actually meant to be a string encoded as "cp1252" (a legacy Windows encoding):

```
with open("data.bin", "r", encoding="cp1252") as f:
    data = f.read()
assert data == "ñòóôõ"
```

The exception is gone, and the string interpretation of the file's contents is very different from what was returned when reading raw bytes. The lesson here is that you should check the default encoding on your system (using python3 -c 'import locale; print(locale.getpreferred-encoding())') to understand how it differs from your expectations. When in doubt, you should explicitly pass the encoding parameter to open.

Things to Remember

✦ bytes contains sequences of 8-bit values, and str contains sequences of Unicode code points.

✦ Use helper functions to ensure that the inputs you operate on are the type of character sequence you expect (8-bit values, UTF-8-encoded strings, Unicode code points, etc).

✦ bytes and str instances can't be used together with operators (like
>, ==, +, and %).

✦ If you want to read or write binary data to/from a file, always open
the file using a binary mode (like "rb" or "wb").

✦ If you want to read or write Unicode data to/from a file, be careful about your system's default text encoding. Explicitly pass the
encoding parameter to open to avoid surprises.

Item 11: Prefer Interpolated F-Strings over C-Style Format Strings and str.format

Strings are present throughout Python codebases. They're used for
rendering messages in user interfaces and command-line utilities.
They're used for writing data to files and sockets. They're used for
specifying what's gone wrong in Exception details (see Item 88: "Consider Explicitly Chaining Exceptions to Clarify Tracebacks"). They're
used in logging and debugging (see Item 12: "Understand the Difference Between repr and str When Printing Objects").

Formatting is the process of combining predefined text with data values into a single human-readable message that's stored as a string.
Python has four different ways of formatting strings that are built
into the language and standard library. All but one of them, which is
covered last in this item, have serious shortcomings that you should
understand and avoid.

C-Style Formatting

The most common way to format a string in Python is by using the %
formatting operator. A predefined text template is provided on the left
side of the operator in a *format string*. A value to insert into the template is provided as a single value or as a tuple of multiple values on
the right side of the format operator. For example, here I use the %
operator to convert difficult-to-read binary and hexadecimal values to
integer strings:

```
a = 0b10111011
b = 0xC5F
print("Binary is %d, hex is %d" % (a, b))

>>>
Binary is 187, hex is 3167
```

The format string uses format specifiers (like %d) as placeholders
that will be replaced by values from the right side of the formatting

expression. The syntax for format specifiers comes from C's `printf` function, which has been inherited by Python (as well as by other programming languages). Python supports all of the usual options you'd expect from `printf`, such as %s, %x, and %f format specifiers, as well as control over decimal places, padding, fill, and alignment. Many programmers who are new to Python start with C-style format strings because they're familiar and simple to use.

There are four problems with C-style format strings in Python.

The first problem is that if you change the type or order of data values in the `tuple` on the right side of a formatting expression, you can get errors due to type conversion incompatibility. For example, this simple formatting expression works:

```
key = "my_var"
value = 1.234
formatted = "%-10s = %.2f" % (key, value)
print(formatted)

>>>
my_var     = 1.23
```

But if you swap key and value, you get an exception at runtime:

```
reordered_tuple = "%-10s = %.2f" % (value, key)

>>>
Traceback ...
TypeError: must be real number, not str
```

Leaving the right side parameters in the original order but changing the format string results in the same error:

```
reordered_string = "%.2f = %-10s" % (key, value)

>>>
Traceback ...
TypeError: must be real number, not str
```

To avoid this gotcha, you need to constantly check that the two sides of the % operator are in sync; this process is error prone because it must be done manually for every change.

The second problem with C-style formatting expressions is that they become difficult to read when you need to make small modifications to values before formatting them into a string—and this is an extremely common need. Here, I list the contents of my kitchen pantry, without any inline changes to the values:

```
pantry = [
    ("avocados", 1.25),
    ("bananas", 2.5),
    ("cherries", 15),
]
for i, (item, count) in enumerate(pantry):
    print("#%d: %-10s = %.2f" % (i, item, count))

>>>
#0: avocados   = 1.25
#1: bananas    = 2.50
#2: cherries   = 15.00
```

Now, I make a few modifications to the values that I'm formatting to make the printed message more useful. This causes the `tuple` in the formatting expression to become so long that it needs to be split across multiple lines, which hurts readability:

```
for i, (item, count) in enumerate(pantry):
    print(
        "#%d: %-10s = %d"
        % (
            i + 1,
            item.title(),
            round(count),
        )
    )

>>>
#1: Avocados   = 1
#2: Bananas    = 2
#3: Cherries   = 15
```

The third problem with formatting expressions is that if you want to use the same value in a format string multiple times, you have to repeat it in the right-side `tuple`:

```
template = "%s loves food. See %s cook."
name = "Max"
formatted = template % (name, name)
print(formatted)

>>>
Max loves food. See Max cook.
```

This is especially annoying and error prone if you have to repeat small modifications to the values being formatted. For example, here I call the title() method on one reference to name but not the other, which causes mismatched output:

```
name = "brad"
formatted = template % (name.title(), name)
print(formatted)

>>>
Brad loves food. See brad cook.
```

The % operator in Python helps solve some of these problems because it has the ability to also do formatting with a dictionary instead of a tuple. The keys from the dictionary are matched with format specifiers that have the same name, such as %(key)s. Here, I use this functionality to change the order of values on the right side of the formatting expression with no effect on the output, thus solving problem #1 from above:

```
key = "my_var"
value = 1.234

old_way = "%-10s = %.2f" % (key, value)

new_way = "%(key)-10s = %(value).2f" % {
    "key": key,   # Key first
    "value": value,
}

reordered = "%(key)-10s = %(value).2f" % {
    "value": value,
    "key": key,   # Key second
}

assert old_way == new_way == reordered
```

Using dictionaries in formatting expressions also solves problem #3 from above by allowing multiple format specifiers to reference the same value, thus making it unnecessary to supply that value more than once:

```
name = "Max"

template = "%s loves food. See %s cook."
before = template % (name, name)    # Tuple
```

```
template = "%(name)s loves food. See %(name)s cook."
after = template % {"name": name}   # Dictionary
```

```
assert before == after
```

However, dictionary format strings introduce and exacerbate other issues. For problem #2 above, regarding making small modifications to values before formatting them, formatting expressions become longer and more visually noisy because of the presence of the dictionary key and colon operator on the right side. Here, I render the same string with and without dictionaries to show this problem:

```
for i, (item, count) in enumerate(pantry):
    before = "#%d: %-10s = %d" % (
        i + 1,
        item.title(),
        round(count),
    )

    after = "#%(loop)d: %(item)-10s = %(count)d" % {
        "loop": i + 1,
        "item": item.title(),
        "count": round(count),
    }

    assert before == after
```

Using dictionaries in formatting expressions also increases verbosity, which is problem #4 with C-style formatting expressions in Python. Each key must be specified at least twice—once in the format specifier, once in the dictionary as a key, and potentially once more for the variable name that contains the dictionary value:

```
soup = "lentil"
formatted = "Today's soup is %(soup)s." % {"soup": soup}
print(formatted)
```

```
>>>
Today's soup is lentil.
```

Besides involving duplicative characters, this redundancy causes formatting expressions that use dictionaries to be long. These expressions often must span multiple lines, with format strings concatenated across multiple lines and dictionary assignments with one line per value to use in formatting:

```
menu = {
    "soup": "lentil",
    "oyster": "kumamoto",
    "special": "schnitzel",
}
template = (
    "Today's soup is %(soup)s, "
    "buy one get two %(oyster)s oysters, "
    "and our special entrée is %(special)s."
)
formatted = template % menu
print(formatted)

>>>
Today's soup is lentil, buy one get two kumamoto oysters, and
➥our special entrée is schnitzel.
```

To understand what this formatting expression is going to produce, your eyes have to keep going back and forth between the lines of the format string and the lines of the dictionary. This disconnect makes it hard to spot bugs, and readability gets even worse if you need to make small modifications to any of the values before formatting.

There must be a better way.

The format Built-in Function and str.format

Python 3 added support for *advanced string formatting* that is more expressive than the old C-style format strings that use the % operator. For individual Python values, this new functionality can be accessed through the format built-in function. For example, here I use some of the new options (, for thousands separators and ∧ for centering) to format values:

```
a = 1234.5678
formatted = format(a, ",.2f")
print(formatted)

b = "my string"
formatted = format(b, "^20s")
print("*", formatted, "*")

>>>
1,234.57
*       my string        *
```

You can use this functionality to format multiple values together by calling the new `format` method of the `str` type. Instead of using C-style format specifiers like %d, you can specify placeholders with {}. By default the placeholders in the format string are replaced by the corresponding positional arguments passed to the `format` method in the order in which they appear:

```
key = "my_var"
value = 1.234

formatted = "{} = {}".format(key, value)
print(formatted)

>>>
my_var = 1.234
```

Within each placeholder you can optionally provide a colon character followed by format specifiers to customize how values will be converted into strings (see https://docs.python.org/3/library/string.html#format-specification-mini-language for the full range of options):

```
formatted = "{:<10} = {:.2f}".format(key, value)
print(formatted)

>>>
my_var     = 1.23
```

The way to think about how this works is that the format specifiers will be passed to the `format` built-in function along with the value (format(value, ".2f") in the example above). The result of that function call is what replaces the placeholder in the overall formatted string. You can customize the formatting behavior per class by using the `__format__` special method.

Another detail to be careful about with `str.format` is escaping braces ({}). You need to double them ({{) so they're not accidentally interpreted as placeholders (much as you need to double the % character to escape it properly with C-style format strings):

```
print("%.2f%%" % 12.5)
print("{} replaces {{}}".format(1.23))

>>>
12.50%
1.23 replaces {}
```

Within the braces you may also specify the positional index of an argument passed to the `format` method to use for replacing the placeholder. This allows the format string to be updated to reorder the output without requiring you to also change the right side of the formatting expression, thus addressing problem #1 from above:

```
formatted = "{1} = {0}".format(key, value)
print(formatted)
```

```
>>>
1.234 = my_var
```

The same positional index may also be referenced multiple times in the format string without the need to pass the value to the format method more than once, which solves problem #3 from above:

```
formatted = "{0} loves food. See {0} cook.".format(name)
print(formatted)
```

```
>>>
Max loves food. See Max cook.
```

Unfortunately, the new format method does nothing to address problem #2 from above, leaving your code difficult to read when you need to make small modifications to values before formatting them. There's little difference in readability between the old and new options, which are similarly noisy:

```
for i, (item, count) in enumerate(pantry):
    old_style = "#%d: %-10s = %d" % (
        i + 1,
        item.title(),
        round(count),
    )

    new_style = "#{}: {:<10s} = {}".format(
        i + 1,
        item.title(),
        round(count),
    )

    assert old_style == new_style
```

There are even more advanced specifier options for the str.format method, such as using combinations of dictionary keys and list indexes in placeholders and coercing values to Unicode and repr strings:

```
formatted = "First letter is
➥{menu[oyster][0]!r}".format(menu=menu)
print(formatted)
```

```
>>>
First letter is 'k'
```

But these features don't help reduce the redundancy of repeated keys from problem #4 above. For example, here I compare the verbosity of using dictionaries in C-style formatting expressions to the new style of passing keyword arguments to the format method:

```
old_template = (
    "Today's soup is %(soup)s, "
    "buy one get two %(oyster)s oysters, "
    "and our special entrée is %(special)s."
)
old_formatted = old_template % {
    "soup": "lentil",
    "oyster": "kumamoto",
    "special": "schnitzel",
}

new_template = (
    "Today's soup is {soup}, "
    "buy one get two {oyster} oysters, "
    "and our special entrée is {special}."
)
new_formatted = new_template.format(
    soup="lentil",
    oyster="kumamoto",
    special="schnitzel",
)

assert old_formatted == new_formatted
```

This style is slightly less noisy because it eliminates some quotes in the dictionary and a few characters in the format specifiers, but it's hardly compelling. Further, the advanced features of using dictionary keys and indexes within placeholders are only a tiny subset of Python's expression functionality. This lack of expressiveness is so limiting that it undermines the value of the str.format method overall.

Given these shortcomings and the problems from C-style formatting expressions that remain (problems #2 and #4 from above), I suggest that you avoid using the str.format method in general. It's important to know about the new mini-language used in format specifiers (everything after the colon) and how to use the format built-in function. But the rest of the str.format method should be treated as a historical artifact to help you understand how Python's new *f-strings* work and why they're so great.

Interpolated Format Strings

Python 3.6 added interpolated format strings—*f-strings* for short—to solve these issues once and for all. This new language syntax requires you to prefix a format string with an f character, which is similar to how a byte string is prefixed with a b character and a raw (unescaped) string is prefixed with an r character.

F-strings take the expressiveness of format strings to the extreme, solving problem #4 from above by completely eliminating the redundancy of providing keys and values to be formatted. They achieve this pithiness by allowing you to reference all names in the current Python scope as part of a formatting expression:

```
key = "my_var"
value = 1.234

formatted = f"{key} = {value}"
print(formatted)

>>>
my_var = 1.234
```

All of the same options from the new format built-in mini-language are available after the colon in the placeholders within an f-string, as is the ability to coerce values to Unicode and repr strings, similar to the str.format method (i.e., with !r and !s):

```
formatted = f"{key!r:<10} = {value:.2f}"
print(formatted)

>>>
'my_var'    = 1.23
```

Formatting with f-strings is shorter than using C-style format strings with the % operator and the str.format method in all cases. Here, I show every option together, in order from shortest to longest, and line up the left sides of the assignments so you can easily compare them:

```
f_string = f"{key:<10} = {value:.2f}"

c_tuple  = "%-10s = %.2f" % (key, value)

str_args = "{:<10} = {:.2f}".format(key, value)

str_kw   = "{key:<10} = {value:.2f}".format(key=key,
➥value=value)
```

```
c_dict    = "%(key)-10s = %(value).2f" % {"key": key, "value":
➥value}

assert c_tuple == c_dict == f_string
assert str_args == str_kw == f_string
```

F-strings also enable you to put a full Python expression within the placeholder braces, solving problem #2 from above by allowing small modifications to the values being formatted with concise syntax. What took multiple lines with C-style formatting and the str.format method now easily fits on a single line:

```
for i, (item, count) in enumerate(pantry):
    old_style = "#%d: %-10s = %d" % (
        i + 1,
        item.title(),
        round(count),
    )

    new_style = "#{}: {:<10s} = {}".format(
        i + 1,
        item.title(),
        round(count),
    )

    f_string = f"#{i+1}: {item.title():<10s} = {round(count)}"

    assert old_style == new_style == f_string
```

Or, if it's clearer, you can split an f-string over multiple lines by relying on adjacent-string concatenation (see Item 13: "Prefer Explicit String Concatenation over Implicit, Especially in Lists"). Even though this is longer than the single-line version, it's still much clearer than any of the other multiline approaches:

```
for i, (item, count) in enumerate(pantry):
    print(f"#{i+1}: "
          f"{item.title():<10s} = "
          f"{round(count)}")

>>>
#1: Avocados   = 1
#2: Bananas    = 2
#3: Cherries   = 15
```

Python expressions may also appear within the format specifier options. For example, here I parameterize the number of digits to print by using a variable instead of hard-coding it in the format string:

```
places = 3
number = 1.23456
print(f"My number is {number:.{places}f}")

>>>
My number is 1.235
```

The combination of expressiveness, terseness, and clarity provided by f-strings makes them the best built-in option for Python programmers. Any time you find yourself needing to format values into strings, choose f-strings over the alternatives.

Things to Remember

✦ C-style format strings that use the % operator suffer from a variety of gotchas and verbosity problems.

✦ The str.format method introduces some useful concepts in its formatting specifiers mini-language, but it otherwise repeats the mistakes of C-style format strings and should be avoided.

✦ F-strings are a new syntax for formatting values into strings that solves the biggest problems with C-style format strings.

✦ F-strings are succinct yet powerful because they allow for arbitrary Python expressions to be directly embedded within format specifiers.

Item 12: Understand the Difference Between repr and str when Printing Objects

As you debug a Python program, using the print function and format strings (see Item 11: "Prefer Interpolated F-Strings over C-Style Format Strings and str.format") or outputting via the logging built-in module will get you surprisingly far. Python object internals are often easy to access via plain attributes (see Item 55: "Prefer Public Attributes over Private Ones"). All you need to do is call print to see how the state of your program changes while it runs and deduce where it goes wrong (see Item 114: "Consider Interactive Debugging with pdb" for a more advanced approach).

The print function outputs a human-readable string version of whatever you supply it. For example, I can use print with a basic string to see the contents of the string without the surrounding quote characters:

```
print("foo bar")
```

```
>>>
foo bar
```

This is equivalent to all of these alternatives:

- Calling the str function before passing the value to print
- Using the "%s" format string with the % operator
- Using the default formatting of the value with an f-string
- Calling the format built-in function
- Explicitly calling the __format__ special method
- Explicitly calling the __str__ special method

Here, I show that they all produce the same output:

```
my_value = "foo bar"
print(str(my_value))
print("%s" % my_value)
print(f"{my_value}")
print(format(my_value))
print(my_value.__format__("s"))
print(my_value.__str__())
```

```
>>>
foo bar
foo bar
foo bar
foo bar
foo bar
foo bar
```

The problem is that the human-readable string for a value doesn't make it clear what the actual type and the specific composition of the value are. For example, notice how in the default output of print you can't distinguish between the types of the number 5 and the string "5":

```
int_value = 5
str_value = "5"
print(int_value)
print(str_value)
print(f"Is {int_value} == {str_value}?")
```

```
>>>
5
5
Is 5 == 5?
```

If you're debugging a program with `print`, these type differences matter. What you almost always want while debugging is to see the `repr` version of an `object`. The `repr` built-in function returns the *printable representation* of an object, which should be its most clearly understandable string serialization. For many built-in types, the string returned by `repr` is a valid Python expression:

```
a = "\x07"
print(repr(a))
```

```
>>>
'\x07'
```

Passing the value returned by `repr` to the `eval` built-in function often results in the same Python object that you started with:

```
b = eval(repr(a))
assert a == b
```

Of course, in practice you should only use `eval` with extreme caution (see Item 91: "Avoid `exec` and `eval` Unless You're Building a Developer Tool").

When you're debugging with `print`, you should call `repr` on a value before printing to ensure that any difference in types is clear:

```
print(repr(int_value))
print(repr(str_value))
```

```
>>>
5
'5'
```

This is equivalent to using the `"%r"` format string with the % operator or an f-string with the `!r` type conversion:

```
print("Is %r == %r?" % (int_value, str_value))
print(f"Is {int_value!r} == {str_value!r}?")
```

```
>>>
Is 5 == '5'?
Is 5 == '5'?
```

When the `str` built-in function is given an instance of a user-defined class, it first tries to call the `__str__` special method. If that's not defined, it falls back to call the `__repr__` special method instead.

If __repr__ also wasn't implemented by the class, then the call goes through method resolution (see Item 53: "Initialize Parent Classes with super"), eventually calling the default implementation from the object parent class. Unfortunately, the default implementation of repr for object subclasses isn't especially helpful. For example, here I define a simple class and then print one of its instances, which ultimately leads to a call to object.__repr__:

```
class OpaqueClass:
    def __init__(self, x, y):
        self.x = x
        self.y = y

obj = OpaqueClass(1, "foo")
print(obj)

>>>
<__main__.OpaqueClass object at 0x1009be510>
```

This output can't be passed to the eval function, and it says nothing about the instance fields of the object. To improve this, here I define my own __repr__ special method that returns a string containing the Python expression that re-creates the object (see Item 51: "Prefer dataclasses for Defining Lightweight Classes" for another approach to defining __repr__):

```
class BetterClass:
    def __init__(self, x, y):
        self.x = x
        self.y = y

    def __repr__(self):
        return f"BetterClass({self.x!r}, {self.y!r})"
```

Now the repr value is much more useful:

```
obj = BetterClass(2, "bar")
print(obj)

>>>
BetterClass(2, 'bar')
```

Calling str on an instance of this class produces the same result because the __str__ special method isn't defined, causing Python to fall back to __repr__:

```
print(str(obj))

>>>
BetterClass(2, 'bar')
```

To have `str` print out a different human-readable format of the string—for example, to display in a UI element—I can define the corresponding `__str__` special method:

```
class StringifiableBetterClass(BetterClass):
    def __str__(self):
        return f"({self.x}, {self.y})"
```

Now `repr` and `str` return different human-readable strings for each of the different purposes:

```
obj2 = StringifiableBetterClass(2, "bar")
print("Human readable:", obj2)
print("Printable:     ", repr(obj2))

>>>
Human readable: (2, bar)
Printable:      BetterClass(2, 'bar')
```

Things to Remember

✦ Calling `print` on built-in Python types produces the human-readable string version of a value, which hides type information.

✦ Calling `repr` on built-in Python types produces a string that contains the printable representation of a value. `repr` strings can often be passed to the `eval` built-in function to get back the original value.

✦ `%s` in format strings produces human-readable strings like `str`. `%r` produces printable strings like `repr`. F-strings produce human-readable strings for replacement text expressions unless you specify the `!r` conversion suffix.

✦ You can define the `__repr__` and `__str__` special methods on your classes to customize the printable and human-readable representations of instances, which can help with debugging and can simplify integrating objects into human interfaces.

Item 13: Prefer Explicit String Concatenation over Implicit, Especially in Lists

Earlier in its history, Python inherited many attributes directly from C, including notation for numeric literals and `printf`-like format strings. The language has evolved considerably since then; for example, octal numbers now require a `0o` prefix instead of only `0`, and the new string interpolation syntax is far superior (see Item 11: "Prefer Interpolated F-Strings over C-Style Format Strings and str.format"). However, one C-like feature that remains in Python is implicit string concatenation. This causes string literals that are adjacent expressions to be concatenated without the need for an infix + operator. Therefore, these two assignments actually do the same thing:

```
my_test1 = "hello" "world"
my_test2 = "hello" + "world"
assert my_test1 == my_test2
```

This implicit concatenation behavior can be useful when you need to combine different types of string literals with varying escaping requirements, which is a common need in programs that do text templating or code generation. For example, here I implicitly merge a raw string, an f-string, and a single-quoted string:

```
x = 1
my_test1 = (
    r"first \ part is here with escapes\n, "
    f"string interpolation {x} in here, "
    'this has "double quotes" inside'
)
print(my_test1)
```

```
>>>
first \ part is here with escapes\n, string interpolation 1 in
➥here, this has "double quotes" inside
```

Having each type of string literal on its own line makes this code easier to read, and the absence of operators reduces visual noise. In contrast, when implicit concatenation happens on a single line, it can be difficult to anticipate what the code is going to do without having to pay extra attention:

```
y = 2
my_test2 = r"fir\st" f"{y}" '"third"'
print(my_test2)
```

```
>>>
fir\st2"third"
```

Implicit concatenation like this is also error prone. If you accidentally slip in a comma character between adjacent strings, the meaning of the code will be completely different (see a similar issue in Item 6: "Always Surround Single-Element Tuples with Parentheses"):

```
my_test3 = r"fir\st", f"{y}" '"third"'
print(my_test3)
```

```
>>>
('fir\\st', '2"third"')
```

Another problem can occur if you do the opposite and accidentally delete a comma instead of adding one. For example, imagine that I want to create a list of strings to output, with one element for each line:

```
my_test4 = [
    "first line\n",
    "second line\n",
    "third line\n",
]
print(my_test4)
```

```
>>>
['first line\n', 'second line\n', 'third line\n']
```

If I delete the middle comma, the resulting data will have similar structure, but the last two lines will be merged together silently.

```
my_test5 = [
    "first line\n",
    "second line\n"  # Comma removed
    "third line\n",
]
print(my_test5)
```

```
>>>
['first line\n', 'second line\nthird line\n']
```

As a new reader of this code, you might not even see the missing comma at first glance. If you use an auto-formatter (see Item 2: "Follow the PEP 8 Style Guide"), it might rewrap the two lines to make this implicit behavior more discoverable, like this:

```
my_test5 = [
    "first line\n",
    "second line\n" "third line\n",
]
```

But even if you do notice that implicit concatenation is happening, it's unclear whether it's deliberate or accidental. Thus, my advice is to always use an explicit + operator to combine strings inside a list or tuple literal to eliminate any ambiguity caused by implicit concatenation:

```
my_test6 = [
    "first line\n",
    "second line\n" +  # Explicit
    "third line\n",
]
assert my_test5 == my_test6
```

When the + operator is present, an auto-formatter might still change the line wrapping, but in this state, it's at least clear what the author of the code originally intended:

```
my_test6 = [
    "first line\n",
    "second line\n" + "third line\n",
]
```

Another place that implicit string concatenation might cause issues is in function call argument lists. Sometimes using implicit concatenation within a call looks fine, such as with the print function:

```
print("this is my long message "
      "that should be printed out")
```

```
>>>
this is my long message that should be printed out
```

Implicit concatenation can even be readable when you provide additional keyword arguments after a single positional argument:

```
import sys

print("this is my long message "
      "that should be printed out",
      end="",
      file=sys.stderr)
```

However, when a call takes multiple positional arguments, implicit string concatenation can be confusing and error prone, just as it is with list and tuple literals. For example, here I create an instance of a class with implicit concatenation in the middle of the initialization argument list—how quickly can you spot it?

```
import sys

first_value = ...
second_value = ...
```

```
class MyData:
    ...

value = MyData(123,
               first_value,
               f"my format string {x}"
               f"another value {y}",
               "and here is more text",
               second_value,
               stream=sys.stderr)
```

Changing the string concatenation to be explicit makes this code much easier to scan:

```
value2 = MyData(123,
               first_value,
               f"my format string {x}" +  # Explicit
               f"another value {y}",
               "and here is more text",
               second_value,
               stream=sys.stderr)
```

My advice is to always use explicit string concatenation when a function call takes multiple positional arguments in order to avoid any confusion (see Item 37: "Enforce Clarity with Keyword-Only and Positional-Only Arguments" for a similar example). If there's only a single positional argument, as with the print example above, then using implicit string concatenation is fine. Keyword arguments can be passed using either explicit or implicit concatenation—whichever maximizes clarity—because sibling string literals can't be misinterpreted as positional arguments after the = character.

Things to Remember

✦ When two string literals are next to each other in Python code, they will be merged as if the + operator were present between them, in a similar fashion to the implicit string concatenation feature of the C programming language.

✦ Avoid implicit string concatenation of items in list and tuple literals because it creates ambiguity about the original author's intent. Instead, you should use explicit concatenation with the + operator.

✦ In function calls, it is fine to use implicit string concatenation with one positional argument and any number of keyword arguments, but you should use explicit concatenation when there are multiple positional arguments.

Item 14: Know How to Slice Sequences

Python includes syntax for *slicing* sequences into pieces. Slicing allows you to access a subset of a sequence's items with minimal effort. The simplest uses for slicing are the built-in types list, tuple, str, and bytes. Slicing can be extended to any Python class that implements the __getitem__ and __setitem__ special methods (see Item 57: "Inherit from collections.abc Classes for Custom Container Types").

The basic form of the slicing syntax is somelist[start:end], where start is inclusive and end is exclusive:

```
a = ["a", "b", "c", "d", "e", "f", "g", "h"]
print("Middle two:  ", a[3:5])
print("All but ends:", a[1:7])

>>>
Middle two:   ['d', 'e']
All but ends: ['b', 'c', 'd', 'e', 'f', 'g']
```

When slicing from the start of a sequence, you should leave out the zero index to reduce visual noise:

```
assert a[:5] == a[0:5]
```

When slicing to the end of a sequence, you should leave out the final index because it's redundant:

```
assert a[5:] == a[5:len(a)]
```

Using negative numbers for slicing is helpful for doing offsets relative to the end of a sequence. All of these forms of slicing would be clear to a new reader of your code:

```
a[:]       # ["a", "b", "c", "d", "e", "f", "g", "h"]
a[:5]      # ["a", "b", "c", "d", "e"]
a[:-1]     # ["a", "b", "c", "d", "e", "f", "g"]
a[4:]      #                 ["e", "f", "g", "h"]
a[-3:]     #                      ["f", "g", "h"]
a[2:5]     #           ["c", "d", "e"]
a[2:-1]    #           ["c", "d", "e", "f", "g"]
a[-3:-1]   #                      ["f", "g"]
```

There are no surprises here, and I encourage you to use these variations.

Slicing deals properly with start and end indexes that are beyond the boundaries of a list by silently omitting missing items. This behavior makes it easy for your code to establish a maximum length to consider for an input sequence:

```
first_twenty_items = a[:20]
last_twenty_items = a[-20:]
```

In contrast, directly accessing the same missing index causes an exception:

```
a[20]
```

```
>>>
Traceback ...
IndexError: list index out of range
```

Note

Beware that indexing a list by a negated variable is one of the few situations in which you can get surprising results from slicing. For example, the expression somelist[-n:] will work fine when n is greater than zero (e.g., somelist[-3:] when n is 3). However, when n is zero, the expression somelist[-0:] is equivalent to somelist[:], which results in a copy of the original list.

The result of slicing a list is a whole new list. Each of the items in the new list will refer to the corresponding objects from the original list. Modifying the list created by slicing won't affect the contents of the original list:

```
b = a[3:]
print("Before:    ", b)
b[1] = 99
print("After:     ", b)
print("No change:", a)
```

```
>>>
Before:     ['d', 'e', 'f', 'g', 'h']
After:      ['d', 99, 'f', 'g', 'h']
No change: ['a', 'b', 'c', 'd', 'e', 'f', 'g', 'h']
```

When used in assignments, slices replace the specified range in the original list. Unlike unpacking assignments (e.g., a, b = c[:2]; see Item 5: "Prefer Multiple-Assignment Unpacking over Indexing" and Item 16: "Prefer Catch-All Unpacking Over Slicing"), the lengths of slice assignments don't need to be the same. All of the values before and after the assigned slice will be preserved, with the new values stitched in between. Here, the list shrinks because the replacement list is shorter than the specified slice:

```
print("Before ", a)
a[2:7] = [99, 22, 14]
print("After   ", a)

>>>
Before  ['a', 'b', 'c', 'd', 'e', 'f', 'g', 'h']
After   ['a', 'b', 99, 22, 14, 'h']
```

And here the list grows because the assigned list is longer than the specified slice:

```
print("Before ", a)
a[2:3] = [47, 11]
print("After   ", a)

>>>
Before  ['a', 'b', 99, 22, 14, 'h']
After   ['a', 'b', 47, 11, 22, 14, 'h']
```

If you leave out both the start and the end indexes when slicing, you end up with a copy of the whole original list:

```
b = a[:]
assert b == a and b is not a
```

If you assign to a slice with no start or end indexes, you replace the entire contents of the list with references to the items from the sequence on the right side (instead of allocating a new list):

```
b = a
print("Before a", a)
print("Before b", b)
a[:] = [101, 102, 103]
assert a is b                # Still the same list object
print("After a ", a)         # Now has different contents
print("After b ", b)         # Same list, so same contents as a

>>>
Before a ['a', 'b', 47, 11, 22, 14, 'h']
Before b ['a', 'b', 47, 11, 22, 14, 'h']
After a  [101, 102, 103]
After b  [101, 102, 103]
```

Things to Remember

✦ Avoid being verbose when slicing: Don't supply 0 for the start index
  or the length of the sequence for the end index.

✦ Slicing is forgiving of start or end indexes that are out of bounds,
  which means it's easy to express slices on the front or back boundaries of a sequence (e.g., a[:20] or a[-20:]).

✦ Assigning to a list slice replaces that range in the original sequence
  with what's referenced even when the lengths are different.

Item 15: Avoid Striding and Slicing in a Single
Expression

In addition to basic slicing (see Item 14: "Know How to Slice
Sequences"), Python has special syntax for the *stride* of a slice in the
form somelist[start:end:stride]. This lets you take every *n*th item
when slicing a sequence. For example, the stride makes it easy to
group by even and odd ordinal positions in a list:

```
x = ["red", "orange", "yellow", "green", "blue", "purple"]
odds = x[::2]    # First, third, fifth
evens = x[1::2]  # Second, fourth, sixth
print(odds)
print(evens)

>>>
['red', 'yellow', 'blue']
['orange', 'green', 'purple']
```

The problem is that the stride syntax often causes unexpected behavior that can introduce bugs. For example, a common Python trick for
reversing a byte string is to slice the string with a stride of -1:

```
x = b"mongoose"
y = x[::-1]
print(y)

>>>
b'esoognom'
```

This also works correctly for Unicode strings (see Item 10: "Know the
Differences Between bytes and str"):

```
x = "寿司"
y = x[::-1]
print(y)

>>>
司寿
```

But it will break when Unicode data is encoded as a UTF-8 byte string:

```
w = "寿司"
x = w.encode("utf-8")
y = x[::-1]
z = y.decode("utf-8")
```

```
>>>
Traceback ...
UnicodeDecodeError: 'utf-8' codec can't decode byte 0xb8 in
➥position 0: invalid start byte
```

Are negative strides besides -1 useful? Consider the following examples:

```
x = ["a", "b", "c", "d", "e", "f", "g", "h"]
x[::2]    # ["a", "c", "e", "g"]
x[::-2]   # ["h", "f", "d", "b"]
```

Here, ::2 means "Select every second item starting at the beginning." Trickier, ::-2 means "Select every second item starting at the end and moving backward."

What do you think 2::2 means? What about -2::-2 vs. -2:2:-2 vs. 2:2:-2?

```
x[2::2]     # ["c", "e", "g"]
x[-2::-2]   # ["g", "e", "c", "a"]
x[-2:2:-2]  # ["g", "e"]
x[2:2:-2]   # []
```

```
>>>
['c', 'e', 'g']
['g', 'e', 'c', 'a']
['g', 'e']
[]
```

The point is that the stride part of the slicing syntax can be extremely confusing. Having three numbers within the brackets is hard enough to read because of its density. Then, it's not obvious when the start and end indexes come into effect relative to the stride value, especially when the stride is negative.

To prevent problems, I suggest that you avoid using a stride along with start and end indexes. If you must use a stride, prefer making it a positive value and omit start and end indexes. If you must use a stride with start or end indexes, consider using one assignment for striding and another for slicing:

```
y = x[::2]    # ["a", "c", "e", "g"]
z = y[1:-1]   # ["c", "e"]
```

Striding and then slicing creates an extra shallow copy of the data. The first operation should try to reduce the size of the resulting slice by as much as possible. If your program can't afford the time or memory required for two steps, consider using the itertools built-in module's islice method (see Item 24: "Consider itertools for Working with Iterators and Generators"), which is clearer to read and doesn't permit negative values for the start, end, or stride.

Things to Remember

✦ Specifying start, end, and stride together in a single slice can be extremely confusing.

✦ If striding is necessary, try to use only positive stride values without start or end indexes; avoid negative stride values.

✦ If you need start, end, and stride in a single slice, consider doing two assignments (one to stride and another to slice) or using islice from the itertools built-in module.

Item 16: Prefer Catch-All Unpacking over Slicing

One limitation of basic unpacking (see Item 5: "Prefer Multiple-Assignment Unpacking over Indexing") is that you must know the length of the sequences you're unpacking in advance. For example, here I have a list of the ages of cars that are being traded in at a car dealership. When I try to take the first two items of the list with basic unpacking, an exception is raised at runtime:

```
car_ages = [0, 9, 4, 8, 7, 20, 19, 1, 6, 15]
car_ages_descending = sorted(car_ages, reverse=True)
oldest, second_oldest = car_ages_descending
```

```
>>>
Traceback ...
ValueError: too many values to unpack (expected 2)
```

Newcomers to Python often rely on indexing and slicing (see Item 14: "Know How to Slice Sequences") for this type of situation. For example, here I extract the oldest, second oldest, and other car ages from a list of at least two items:

```
oldest = car_ages_descending[0]
second_oldest = car_ages_descending[1]
others = car_ages_descending[2:]
print(oldest, second_oldest, others)
```

```
>>>
20 19 [15, 9, 8, 7, 6, 4, 1, 0]
```

This works, but all of the indexing and slicing is visually noisy. In practice, it's also error prone to divide the members of a sequence into various subsets this way because you're much more likely to make off-by-one errors; for example, you might change boundaries on one line and forget to update the others.

To better handle this situation, Python also supports catch-all unpacking through a *starred expression*. This syntax allows one part of the unpacking assignment to receive all values that didn't match any other part of the unpacking pattern. Here, I use a starred expression to achieve the same result as above without any indexing or slicing:

```
oldest, second_oldest, *others = car_ages_descending
print(oldest, second_oldest, others)
```

```
>>>
20 19 [15, 9, 8, 7, 6, 4, 1, 0]
```

This code is shorter, easier to read, and no longer has the error-prone brittleness of boundary indexes that must be kept in sync between lines.

A starred expression may appear in any position—start, middle, or end—so you can get the benefits of catch-all unpacking any time you need to extract one optional slice (see Item 9: "Consider match for Destructuring in Flow Control, Avoid When if Statements Are Sufficient" for another situation where this is useful):

```
oldest, *others, youngest = car_ages_descending
print(oldest, youngest, others)

*others, second_youngest, youngest = car_ages_descending
print(youngest, second_youngest, others)
```

```
>>>
20 0 [19, 15, 9, 8, 7, 6, 4, 1]
0 1 [20, 19, 15, 9, 8, 7, 6, 4]
```

However, when you use a starred expression in an unpacking assignment, you must have at least one required part, or else you'll get a syntax error. You can't use a catch-all expression on its own:

```
*others = car_ages_descending
```

```
>>>
Traceback ...
SyntaxError: starred assignment target must be in a list or
➥tuple
```

You also can't use multiple catch-all expressions in a single unpacking pattern:

```
first, *middle, *second_middle, last = [1, 2, 3, 4]
```

```
>>>
Traceback ...
SyntaxError: multiple starred expressions in assignment
```

But it is possible to use multiple starred expressions in an unpacking assignment statement, as long as they're catch-alls for different levels of the nested structure being unpacked. I don't recommend doing the following (see Item 31: "Return Dedicated Result Objects Instead of Requiring Function Callers to Unpack More Than Three Variables" for related guidance), but understanding it should help you develop an intuition for how starred expressions can be used in unpacking assignments:

```
car_inventory = {
    "Downtown": ("Silver Shadow", "Pinto", "DMC"),
    "Airport": ("Skyline", "Viper", "Gremlin", "Nova"),
}
((loc1, (best1, *rest1)),
 (loc2, (best2, *rest2))) = car_inventory.items()
print(f"Best at {loc1} is {best1}, {len(rest1)} others")
print(f"Best at {loc2} is {best2}, {len(rest2)} others")
```

```
>>>
Best at Downtown is Silver Shadow, 2 others
Best at Airport is Skyline, 3 others
```

Starred expressions become list instances in all cases. If there are no leftover items from the sequence being unpacked, the catch-all part will be an empty list. This is especially useful when you're processing a sequence that you know in advance has at least *N* elements:

```
short_list = [1, 2]
first, second, *rest = short_list
print(first, second, rest)
```

```
>>>
1 2 []
```

You can also unpack arbitrary iterators with the unpacking syntax. This isn't worth much with a basic multiple-assignment statement. For example, here I unpack the values from iterating over a range of length 2. This doesn't seem useful because it would be easier to just assign to a static list that matches the unpacking pattern (e.g., [1, 2]):

```
it = iter(range(1, 3))
first, second = it
print(f"{first} and {second}")
```

```
>>>
1 and 2
```

But with the addition of starred expressions, the value of unpacking iterators becomes clear. For example, here I have a generator that yields the rows of a CSV (comma-separated values) file containing all car orders from the dealership this week:

```
def generate_csv():
    yield ("Date", "Make", "Model", "Year", "Price")
    ...
```

Processing the results of this generator using indexes and slices is fine, but it requires multiple lines and is visually noisy:

```
all_csv_rows = list(generate_csv())
header = all_csv_rows[0]
rows = all_csv_rows[1:]
print("CSV Header:", header)
print("Row count: ", len(rows))
```

```
>>>
CSV Header: ('Date', 'Make', 'Model', 'Year', 'Price')
Row count:  200
```

Unpacking with a starred expression makes it easy to process the first row—the header—separately from the rest of the iterator's contents. This is much clearer:

```
it = generate_csv()
header, *rows = it
print("CSV Header:", header)
print("Row count: ", len(rows))
```

```
>>>
CSV Header: ('Date', 'Make', 'Model', 'Year', 'Price')
Row count:  200
```

Keep in mind, however, that because a starred expression is always turned into a list, unpacking an iterator also risks using up all the memory on your computer and causing your program to crash (see Item 115: "Use tracemalloc to Understand Memory Usage and Leaks" for how to debug this). So you should only use catch-all unpacking on iterators when you have good reason to believe that the result data will all fit in memory (see Item 21: "Be Defensive when Iterating over Arguments" for another approach).

Things to Remember

✦ Unpacking assignments may include a starred expression to store all values that weren't assigned to the other parts of the unpacking pattern in a list.

✦ Starred expressions may appear in any position of the unpacking pattern. They will always become a list instance containing zero or more values.

✦ When dividing a list into non-overlapping pieces, catch-all unpacking is much less error prone than using separate statements that do slicing and indexing.

3

Loops and Iterators

Programs often need to process through sequential data—of fixed or dynamic length. As a primarily imperative programming language, Python makes it easy to implement sequential processing using loops. This is the general pattern: On each pass through a loop, read data—stored in variables, lists, dictionaries, and so on—and carry out corresponding state modifications or I/O operations. Loops in Python feel natural and capable for the most common tasks involving built-in data types, container types, and user-defined classes.

Python also supports iterators, which enable a more functional-style approach to processing arbitrary streams of data. Instead of directly interacting with how the sequential data is stored, you can use iterators, which provide a common abstraction that hides the details. Iterators can make programs more efficient, easier to refactor, and capable of handling arbitrarily sized data. Python also includes functionality to compose iterators together and fully customize their behavior by using generators (see more in Chapter 6, "Comprehensions and Generators").

Item 17: Prefer enumerate over range

The `range` built-in function is useful for loops that iterate over sequences of integers. For example, here I generate a 32-bit random number by flipping a coin for each bit position:

```python
from random import randint

random_bits = 0
for i in range(32):
    if randint(0, 1):
        random_bits |= 1 << i
```

```
print(bin(random_bits))

>>>
0b1110100010010000011100001000001
```

When you have a data structure to iterate over, such as a list of strings, you can loop directly over the sequence:

```
flavor_list = ["vanilla", "chocolate", "pecan", "strawberry"]
for flavor in flavor_list:
    print(f"{flavor} is delicious")

>>>
vanilla is delicious
chocolate is delicious
pecan is delicious
strawberry is delicious
```

Often, you'll want to iterate over a list and also know the index of the current item in the list. For example, say that I want to print the ranking of my favorite ice cream flavors. One way to do this is by using range to generate an offset for each position in the list:

```
for i in range(len(flavor_list)):
    flavor = flavor_list[i]
    print(f"{i + 1}: {flavor}")

>>>
1: vanilla
2: chocolate
3: pecan
4: strawberry
```

This looks clumsy compared with the other examples of a for statement over flavor_list or range. I have to get the length of the list. I have to index into the array. The multiple steps make it harder to read.

Python provides the enumerate built-in function to simplify this situation. enumerate wraps any iterator with a lazy generator (see Item 43: "Consider Generators Instead of Returning Lists"). enumerate yields pairs of the loop index and the next value from the given iterator. Here, I manually advance the returned iterator with the next built-in function to demonstrate what it does:

```
it = enumerate(flavor_list)
print(next(it))
print(next(it))

>>>
(0, 'vanilla')
(1, 'chocolate')
```

Each pair yielded by enumerate can be succinctly unpacked in a for statement (see Item 5: "Prefer Multiple-Assignment Unpacking over Indexing" for how that works). The resulting code is much clearer:

```
for i, flavor in enumerate(flavor_list):
    print(f"{i + 1}: {flavor}")
```

```
>>>
1: vanilla
2: chocolate
3: pecan
4: strawberry
```

I can make this even shorter by specifying the number for enumerate to use to begin counting (1 in this case) as the second parameter:

```
for i, flavor in enumerate(flavor_list, 1):
    print(f"{i}: {flavor}")
```

Things to Remember

✦ enumerate provides concise syntax for looping over an iterator and getting the index of each item from the iterator as you go.

✦ Prefer enumerate instead of looping over a range and indexing into a sequence.

✦ You can supply a second, optional parameter to enumerate that specifies the beginning number for counting (zero is the default).

Item 18: Use `zip` to Process Iterators in Parallel

Often in Python you find yourself with many lists of related objects. List comprehensions make it easy to take a source list and produce another derived list by applying an expression to each item (see Item 40: "Use Comprehensions Instead of map and filter"). For example, here I take a list of names and create a corresponding list of how many characters are in each name:

```
names = ["Cecilia", "Lise", "Marie"]
counts = [len(n) for n in names]
print(counts)
```

```
>>>
[7, 4, 5]
```

The items in the derived list (counts) are related to the items in the source list (names) by their corresponding positions in the sequences. To access items from both lists in a single loop, I can iterate over the length of the source list (names) and use the offsets generated by range to index into either list. For example, here I use parallel indexing to determine which name is the longest:

```
longest_name = None
max_count = 0

for i in range(len(names)):
    count = counts[i]
    if count > max_count:
        longest_name = names[i]
        max_count = count

print(longest_name)

>>>
Cecilia
```

The problem is that this whole for statement is visually noisy. The indexing operations—names[i] and counts[i]—make the code hard to read. Indexing into two arrays by the same loop index i seems redundant. I can use the enumerate built-in function (see Item 17: "Prefer enumerate over range") to improve this slightly, but it's still not ideal because of the counts[i] indexing operation:

```
longest_name = None
max_count = 0

for i, name in enumerate(names):  # Changed
    count = counts[i]
    if count > max_count:
        longest_name = name         # Changed
        max_count = count
```

To make this code clearer, Python provides the zip built-in function. zip wraps two or more iterators with a lazy generator. The zip generator yields tuples containing the next value from each iterator. These tuples can be unpacked directly within a for statement (see Item 5: "Prefer Multiple-Assignment Unpacking over Indexing" for background). By eliminating indexing operations, the resulting code is much cleaner than the code above that separately accesses two lists:

```
longest_name = None
max_count = 0

for name, count in zip(names, counts):  # Changed
    if count > max_count:
        longest_name = name
        max_count = count
```

zip consumes the iterators it wraps one item at a time, which means it can be used with infinitely long inputs without risk of your program using too much memory and crashing (see Item 43: "Consider Generators Instead of Returning Lists" and Item 44: "Consider Generator Expressions for Large List Comprehensions" for how to create such inputs).

However, it's important to beware of zip's behavior when the input iterators have different lengths. For example, say that I add another item to the names list, but I forget to update the counts list. Running zip on the two input lists has an unexpected result:

```
names.append("Rosalind")
for name, count in zip(names, counts):
    print(name)

>>>
Cecilia
Lise
Marie
```

The new item for "Rosalind" isn't in the output. Why not? This is just how zip works. It keeps yielding tuples until any one of the wrapped iterators is exhausted. Its output is only as long as its shortest input. If premature truncation could be a problem for your program, you can pass the strict keyword argument to zip—a new option since Python 3.10—which will cause the returned generator to raise an exception if any of the inputs is exhausted before the others:

```
for name, count in zip(names, counts, strict=True):  # Changed
    print(name)

>>>
Cecilia
Lise
Marie
Traceback ...
ValueError: zip() argument 2 is shorter than argument 1
```

Alternatively, you can solve this truncation problem by using the zip_longest function from the itertools built-in module to fill in a missing item with a default value (see Item 24: "Consider itertools for Working with Iterators and Generators").

Things to Remember

✦ The zip built-in function can be used to iterate over multiple iterators in parallel.

✦ zip creates a lazy generator that produces tuples; it can be used on infinitely long inputs.

+ `zip` truncates its output silently to the shortest iterator if you supply it with iterators of different lengths.

+ Pass the `strict` keyword argument to `zip` if you want to ensure that silent truncation is not possible and mismatched iterator lengths should result in a runtime error.

Item 19: Avoid `else` Blocks After `for` and `while` Loops

Python loops have an extra feature that is not available in most other programming languages: You can put an `else` block immediately after a loop's repeated interior block:

```
for i in range(3):
    print("Loop", i)
else:
    print("Else block!")
```

```
>>>
Loop 0
Loop 1
Loop 2
Else block!
```

Surprisingly, the `else` block runs immediately after the loop finishes. Why is the clause called `else`? Why not `and`? In an `if`/`else` statement, `else` means "Do this if the block before this doesn't happen" (see "Item 7: Consider Conditional Expressions for Simple Inline Logic". In a `try`/`except` statement, `except` has the same definition: "Do this if trying the block before this failed."

Similarly, `else` from `try`/`except`/`else` follows this pattern (see Item 80: "Take Advantage of Each Block in `try`/`except`/`else`/`finally`") because it means "Do this if there was no exception to handle." `try`/`finally` is also intuitive because it means "Always do this after trying the block before."

Given all of the uses of `else`, `except`, and `finally` in Python, a new programmer might assume that the `else` part of `for`/`else` means "Do this if the loop wasn't completed." In reality, it does exactly the opposite. Using a break statement in a loop actually skips the `else` block:

```
for i in range(3):
    print("Loop", i)
    if i == 1:
        break
else:
    print("Else block!")
```

```
>>>
Loop 0
Loop 1
```

Another surprise is that the else block runs immediately if you loop over an empty sequence:

```
for x in []:
    print("Never runs")
else:
    print("For else block!")
```

```
>>>
For else block!
```

The else block also runs when while loops are initially False:

```
while False:
    print("Never runs")
else:
    print("While else block!")
```

```
>>>
While else block!
```

The rationale for these behaviors is that else blocks after loops are useful when you're searching for something. For example, say that I want to determine whether two numbers are coprime (that is, their only common divisor is 1). Here, I iterate through every possible common divisor and test the numbers. After every option has been tried, the loop ends. The else block runs when the numbers are coprime because the loop doesn't encounter a break:

```
a = 4
b = 9
for i in range(2, min(a, b) + 1):
    print("Testing", i)
    if a % i == 0 and b % i == 0:
        print("Not coprime")
        break
else:
    print("Coprime")
```

```
>>>
Testing 2
Testing 3
Testing 4
Coprime
```

In practice, I wouldn't write the code this way. Instead, I'd write a helper function to do the calculation. Such a function can be written using either of two common styles.

The first approach is to return early when I match the condition I'm looking for. I only return the default outcome if I fall through the loop:

```
def coprime(a, b):
    for i in range(2, min(a, b) + 1):
        if a % i == 0 and b % i == 0:
            return False
    return True

assert coprime(4, 9)
assert not coprime(3, 6)
```

The second way is to have a result variable that indicates whether I've found what I'm looking for in the loop. Here, I break out of the loop as soon as I find something and then return that indicator variable:

```
def coprime_alternate(a, b):
    is_coprime = True
    for i in range(2, min(a, b) + 1):
        if a % i == 0 and b % i == 0:
            is_coprime = False
            break
    return is_coprime

assert coprime_alternate(4, 9)
assert not coprime_alternate(3, 6)
```

Both of these approaches are much clearer to readers of unfamiliar code. Depending on the situation, either may be a good choice. However, the expressivity you gain from the else block doesn't outweigh the burden you put on people (including yourself) who want to understand your code in the future. Simple constructs like loops should be self-evident in Python. You should avoid using else blocks after loops entirely.

Things to Remember

✦ Python has special syntax that allows else blocks to immediately follow for and while loop interior blocks.

✦ The else block after a loop runs only if the loop body did not encounter a break statement.

✦ Avoid using else blocks after loops because their behavior isn't intuitive and can be confusing.

Item 20: Never Use for Loop Variables After the Loop Ends

When you are writing a for loop in Python, you might notice that the variable you create for iteration continues to persist after the loop has finished:

```
for i in range(3):
    print(f"Inside {i=}")
print(f"After  {i=}")

>>>
Inside i=0
Inside i=1
Inside i=2
After  i=2
```

It's possible to use this loop variable assignment behavior to your advantage. For example, here I implement an algorithm for grouping together periodic elements by searching for their indexes in a list:

```
categories = ["Hydrogen", "Uranium", "Iron", "Other"]
for i, name in enumerate(categories):
    if name == "Iron":
        break
print(i)

>>>
2
```

In the case that a given element isn't found in the list, the last index will be used after iteration is exhausted to group the item into the "Other" catch-all category (index 3 in this case):

```
for i, name in enumerate(categories):
    if name == "Lithium":
        break
print(i)

>>>
3
```

The assumption in this algorithm is that either the loop will find a matching item and end early due to a break statement, or the loop will iterate through all the options and fall through. Unfortunately, there's a third possibility, where the loop never begins because the iterator is initially empty—which can result in a runtime exception:

```
categories = []
for i, name in enumerate(categories):
    if name == "Lithium":
        break
print(i)
```

```
>>>
Traceback ...
NameError: name 'i' is not defined
```

There are alternative approaches for dealing with a loop that never processes anything (see Item 19: "Avoid else Blocks After for and while Loops"). But the point is the same: You can't always be sure that a loop variable will exist when you try to access it after the loop, so it's best to never do this in practice.

Fortunately—or perhaps unfortunately—other Python features do not have this problem. The loop variable leakage behavior is not exhibited by list comprehensions or generator expressions (see Item 40: "Use Comprehensions Instead of map and filter" and Item 44: "Consider Generator Expressions for Large List Comprehensions"). If you try to access a comprehension's inner variables after execution, you'll find that they're never present, and thus you can't inadvertently encounter this pitfall:

```
my_numbers = [37, 13, 128, 21]
found = [i for i in my_numbers if i % 2 == 0]
print(i)  # Always raises
```

```
>>>
Traceback ...
NameError: name 'i' is not defined
```

However, it's possible for assignment expressions in comprehensions to change this behavior (see Item 42: "Reduce Repetition in Comprehensions with Assignment Expressions"). Exception variables also don't have this problem of leakage, although they are quirky in their own way (see Item 84: "Beware of Exception Variables Disappearing").

Things to Remember

✦ The loop variable from for loops can be accessed in the current scope even after the loop terminates.

✦ for loop variables will not be assigned in the current scope if the loop never did a single iteration.

◆ Generator expressions and list comprehensions do not leak loop variables by default.

◆ Exception handlers do not leak exception instance variables.

Item 21: Be Defensive when Iterating over Arguments

When a function takes a list of objects as a parameter, it's often important to iterate over that list multiple times. For example, say that I want to analyze tourism numbers for the U.S. state of Texas. Imagine that the data set is the number of visitors to each city (in millions per year). I'd like to figure out what percentage of overall tourism each city receives.

To do this, I need a normalization function that sums the inputs to determine the total number of tourists per year and then divides each city's individual visitor count by the total to find that city's contribution to the whole:

```
def normalize(numbers):
    total = sum(numbers)
    result = []
    for value in numbers:
        percent = 100 * value / total
        result.append(percent)
    return result
```

This function works as expected when given a list of visits:

```
visits = [15, 35, 80]
percentages = normalize(visits)
print(percentages)
assert sum(percentages) == 100.0
```

```
>>>
[11.538461538461538, 26.923076923076923, 61.53846153846154]
```

To scale this up, I need to read the data from a file that contains every city in all of Texas. I define a generator to do this because then I can reuse the same function later, when I want to compute tourism numbers for the whole world—a much larger data set with higher memory requirements (see Item 43: "Consider Generators Instead of Returning Lists" for background):

```
def read_visits(data_path):
    with open(data_path) as f:
        for line in f:
            yield int(line)
```

Surprisingly, calling `normalize` on the `read_visits` generator's return value produces no results:

```
it = read_visits("my_numbers.txt")
percentages = normalize(it)
print(percentages)
```

```
>>>
[]
```

This behavior occurs because an iterator produces its results only a single time. If you iterate over an iterator or a generator that has already raised a StopIteration exception, you won't get any results the second time around:

```
it = read_visits("my_numbers.txt")
print(list(it))
print(list(it))  # Already exhausted
```

```
>>>
[15, 35, 80]
[]
```

Confusingly, an exception won't be raised when you iterate over an already exhausted iterator. for loops, the list constructor, and many other functions throughout the Python standard library expect the StopIteration exception to be raised during normal operation. These functions can't tell the difference between an iterator that has no output and an iterator that had output and is now exhausted.

To solve this problem, you can explicitly exhaust an input iterator and keep a copy of its entire contents in a list. You can then iterate over the list version of the data as many times as you need to. Here's the same function as before, but now it defensively copies the input iterator:

```
def normalize_copy(numbers):
    numbers_copy = list(numbers)  # Copy the iterator
    total = sum(numbers_copy)
    result = []
    for value in numbers_copy:
        percent = 100 * value / total
        result.append(percent)
    return result
```

Now the function works correctly on the `read_visits` generator's return value:

```
it = read_visits("my_numbers.txt")
```

```
percentages = normalize_copy(it)
print(percentages)
assert sum(percentages) == 100.0

>>>
[11.538461538461538, 26.923076923076923, 61.53846153846154]
```

The problem with this approach is that the copy of the input iterator's contents could be extremely large. Copying the iterator could cause the program to run out of memory and crash (see Item 115: "Use tracemalloc to Understand Memory Usage and Leaks" on how to debug this). This potential for scalability issues undermines the reason that I wrote read_visits as a generator in the first place. One way around this is to accept a function that returns a new iterator each time it's called:

```
def normalize_func(get_iter):
    total = sum(get_iter())    # New iterator
    result = []
    for value in get_iter():   # New iterator
        percent = 100 * value / total
        result.append(percent)
    return result
```

To use normalize_func, I can pass in a lambda expression that produces a new generator iterator each time it's called:

```
path = "my_numbers.txt"
percentages = normalize_func(lambda: read_visits(path))
print(percentages)
assert sum(percentages) == 100.0

>>>
[11.538461538461538, 26.923076923076923, 61.53846153846154]
```

Although this works, having to pass a lambda function like this is clumsy. A better way to achieve the same result is to define a new container class that implements the *iterator protocol*.

The iterator protocol is what Python for loops and related expressions use to traverse the contents of a container type. When Python sees a statement like for x in foo, it actually calls iter(foo) to discover the iterator to loop through. The iter built-in function calls the foo.__iter__ special method in turn. The __iter__ method must return an iterator object (which itself implements the __next__ special method). Then, the for loop repeatedly calls the next built-in function on the iterator object until it's exhausted (as indicated by a StopIteration exception being raised).

It sounds complicated, but practically speaking, you can enable all of this behavior for your own classes by implementing the __iter__ method as a generator. Here, I define an iterable container class that reads the file containing tourism data and uses yield to produce one line of data at a time:

```
class ReadVisits:
    def __init__(self, data_path):
        self.data_path = data_path

    def __iter__(self):
        with open(self.data_path) as f:
            for line in f:
                yield int(line)
```

This new container type can be passed to the original function without any modifications:

```
visits = ReadVisits(path)
percentages = normalize(visits)   # Changed
print(percentages)
assert sum(percentages) == 100.0
```

```
>>>
[11.538461538461538, 26.923076923076923, 61.53846153846154]
```

This works because the sum method in normalize calls ReadVisits.__iter__ to allocate a new iterator object. The for loop to normalize the numbers also calls __iter__ to allocate a second iterator object. Each of those iterators will be advanced and exhausted independently, ensuring that each unique iteration sees all of the input data values. The only downside of this approach is that it reads the input data multiple times.

Now that you know how containers like ReadVisits work, you can write your functions and methods to ensure that parameters aren't just iterators. The protocol states that when an iterator is passed to the iter built-in function, iter returns the iterator itself. In contrast, when a container type is passed to iter, a new iterator object is returned each time. Thus, you can test an input value for this behavior and raise a TypeError to reject arguments that can't be repeatedly iterated over:

```
def normalize_defensive(numbers):
    if iter(numbers) is numbers:  # An iterator -- bad!
        raise TypeError("Must supply a container")
    total = sum(numbers)
    result = []
```

```
    for value in numbers:
        percent = 100 * value / total
        result.append(percent)
    return result
```

Alternatively, the collections.abc built-in module defines an Iterator class that can be used in an isinstance test to recognize the potential problem (see Item 57: "Inherit from collections.abc Classes for Custom Container Types"):

```
from collections.abc import Iterator


def normalize_defensive(numbers):
    if isinstance(numbers, Iterator):  # Another way to check
        raise TypeError("Must supply a container")
    total = sum(numbers)
    result = []
    for value in numbers:
        percent = 100 * value / total
        result.append(percent)
    return result
```

The approach of expecting a container is ideal if you don't want to copy the full input iterator—as in the normalize_copy function above—but you also need to iterate over the input data multiple times. Here, I show how the normalize_defensive function can accept a list, a ReadVisits object, or theoretically any container that follows the iterator protocol:

```
visits_list = [15, 35, 80]
list_percentages = normalize_defensive(visits_list)

visits_obj = ReadVisits(path)
obj_percentages = normalize_defensive(visits_obj)

assert list_percentages == obj_percentages
assert sum(percentages) == 100.0
```

The normalize_defensive function raises an exception if the input is an iterator rather than a container:

```
visits = [15, 35, 80]
it = iter(visits)
normalize_defensive(it)

>>>
Traceback ...
TypeError: Must supply a container
```

The same approach of checking for compliance with the iterator proto-col can also be used with asynchronous iterators (see Item 76: "Know How to Port Threaded I/O to asyncio" for an example).

Things to Remember

✦ Beware of functions and methods that iterate over input arguments multiple times. If these arguments are iterators, you might see strange behavior and missing values.

✦ Python's iterator protocol defines how containers and iterators inter-act with the iter and next built-in functions, for loops, and related expressions.

✦ You can easily define your own iterable container type by imple-menting the __iter__ method as a generator.

✦ You can detect that a value is an iterator (instead of a container) if calling iter on it produces the same value that you passed in. Alter-natively, you can use the isinstance built-in function along with the collections.abc.Iterator class.

Item 22: Never Modify Containers While Iterating over Them; Use Copies or Caches Instead

There are many gotchas in Python caused by surprising iteration behaviors (see Item 21: "Be Defensive when Iterating over Arguments" for another common situation). For example, if you add a new item to a dictionary while iterating over it, Python will raise a runtime exception:

```
search_key = "red"
my_dict = {"red": 1, "blue": 2, "green": 3}

for key in my_dict:
    if key == "blue":
        my_dict["yellow"] = 4  # Causes error
```

```
>>>
Traceback ...
RuntimeError: dictionary changed size during iteration
```

A similar error occurs if you delete an item from a dictionary while iterating over it:

```
for key in my_dict:
    if key == "blue":
        del my_dict["green"]  # Causes error
```

```
>>>
Traceback ...
RuntimeError: dictionary changed size during iteration
```

An error won't occur if, instead of adding or deleting keys from a dictionary, you only change their associated values—which is surprisingly inconsistent with the behaviors above:

```
for key in my_dict:
    if key == "blue":
        my_dict["green"] = 4  # Okay
print(my_dict)
```

```
>>>
{'red': 1, 'blue': 2, 'green': 4}
```

Sets work similarly to dictionaries, and if you change their size by adding or removing items during iteration, you will encounter an exception at runtime:

```
my_set = {"red", "blue", "green"}


for color in my_set:
    if color == "blue":
        my_set.add("yellow")  # Causes error
```

```
>>>
Traceback ...
RuntimeError: Set changed size during iteration
```

However, the behavior of set also seems inconsistent because trying to add an item that already exists in a set won't cause any problems while you're iterating over it. Re-adding is allowed because the set's size didn't change:

```
for color in my_set:
    if color == "blue":
        my_set.add("green")  # Okay

print(my_set)
```

```
>>>
{'green', 'blue', 'red'}
```

Much as with dictionaries, and also surprisingly inconsistently, lists can have any existing index overwritten during iteration with no problems:

```
my_list = [1, 2, 3]

for number in my_list:
    print(number)
    if number == 2:
        my_list[0] = -1  # Okay

print(my_list)
```

```
>>>
1
2
3
[-1, 2, 3]
```

But if you try to insert an element into a list before the current iterator position, your code will get stuck in an infinite loop:

```
my_list = [1, 2, 3]
for number in my_list:
    print(number)
    if number == 2:
        my_list.insert(0, 4)  # Causes error
```

```
>>>
1
2
2
2
2
2
...
```

However, appending to a list after the current iterator position is not a problem—the index-based iterator hasn't gotten that far yet—which is, again, surprisingly inconsistent behavior:

```
my_list = [1, 2, 3]

for number in my_list:
    print(number)
    if number == 2:
        my_list.append(4)  # Okay this time

print(my_list)
```

```
>>>
1
2
3
4
[1, 2, 3, 4]
```

Looking at each of the examples above, it can be hard to guess whether the code will work in all cases. Modifying containers during iteration can be especially error prone in situations where the modification point changes based on input to the algorithm. In some cases it'll work, and in others there will be an error. Thus, my advice is to never modify containers while you iterate over them.

If you still need to make modifications during iteration due to the nature of your algorithm, you should simply make a copy of the container you want to iterate and apply modifications to the original (see Item 30: "Know That Function Arguments Can Be Mutated"). For example, with dictionaries I can copy the keys:

```
my_dict = {"red": 1, "blue": 2, "green": 3}


keys_copy = list(my_dict.keys())    # Copy
for key in keys_copy:               # Iterate over copy
    if key == "blue":
        my_dict["green"] = 4        # Modify original dict

print(my_dict)
```

```
>>>
{'red': 1, 'blue': 2, 'green': 4}
```

For lists I can copy the whole container:

```
my_list = [1, 2, 3]


list_copy = list(my_list)       # Copy
for number in list_copy:        # Iterate over copy
    print(number)
    if number == 2:
        my_list.insert(0, 4)    # Inserts in original list

print(my_list)
```

```
>>>
1
2
3
[4, 1, 2, 3]
```

And the same approach works for sets:

```
my_set = {"red", "blue", "green"}


set_copy = set(my_set)          # Copy
for color in set_copy:          # Iterate over copy
    if color == "blue":
        my_set.add("yellow")    # Add to original set


print(my_set)
```
```
>>>
{'yellow', 'green', 'blue', 'red'}
```

For some extremely large containers, copying might be too slow (see Item 92: "Profile Before Optimizing" to verify your assumptions). One way to deal with poor performance is to stage modifications in a separate container and then merge the changes into the main data structure after iteration. For example, here I modify a separate dictionary and then use the update method to bring the changes into the original dictionary:

```
my_dict = {"red": 1, "blue": 2, "green": 3}
modifications = {}


for key in my_dict:
    if key == "blue":
        modifications["green"] = 4  # Add to staging


my_dict.update(modifications)          # Merge modifications
print(my_dict)
```
```
>>>
{'red': 1, 'blue': 2, 'green': 4}
```

The problem with staging modifications is that they won't be immediately visible in the original container during iteration. If the logic in the loop relies on modifications being immediately visible, the code won't work as expected. For example, here the programmer's intent might have been to cause "yellow" to be in the resulting dictionary, but it won't be there because the modifications aren't visible during iteration:

```
my_dict = {"red": 1, "blue": 2, "green": 3}
modifications = {}
```

```
for key in my_dict:
    if key == "blue":
        modifications["green"] = 4
    value = my_dict[key]
    if value == 4:                      # This condition is never true
        modifications["yellow"] = 5

my_dict.update(modifications)     # Merge modifications
print(my_dict)

>>>
{'red': 1, 'blue': 2, 'green': 4}
```

This code can be fixed by looking in both the original container (my_dict) and the modifications container (modifications) for the latest value during iteration, essentially treating the staging dictionary as an intermediate cache:

```
my_dict = {"red": 1, "blue": 2, "green": 3}
modifications = {}

for key in my_dict:
    if key == "blue":
        modifications["green"] = 4
    value = my_dict[key]
    other_value = modifications.get(key)   # Check cache
    if value == 4 or other_value == 4:
        modifications["yellow"] = 5

my_dict.update(modifications)                 # Merge modifications
print(my_dict)

>>>
{'red': 1, 'blue': 2, 'green': 4, 'yellow': 5}
```

This type of reconciliation works, but it's hard to generalize to all situations. When developing an algorithm like this, you'll need to take your specific constraints into account. This can be quite difficult to get right, especially with all of the edge cases, so I recommend writing automated tests to verify correctness (see Item 109: "Prefer Integration Tests over Unit Tests"). Similarly, you can use microbenchmarks to measure the performance of various approaches and pick the best one (see Item 93: "Optimize Performance-Critical Code Using timeit Microbenchmarks").

Things to Remember

✦ Adding or removing elements from lists, dictionaries, and sets while you're iterating over them can cause runtime errors that are often hard to predict.

✦ You can iterate over a copy of a container to avoid runtime errors that might be caused by mutation during iteration.

✦ If you need to avoid copying for better performance, you can stage modifications in a second container cache that you later merge into the original.

Item 23: Pass Iterators to `any` and `all` for Efficient Short-Circuiting Logic

Python is a great language for building programs that do logical reasoning. For example, imagine that I'm trying to analyze the nature of flipping a coin. I can define a function that will return a random coin flip outcome—True for heads or False for tails—each time it's called:

```
import random

def flip_coin():
    if random.randint(0, 1) == 0:
        return "Heads"
    else:
        return "Tails"

def flip_is_heads():
    return flip_coin() == "Heads"
```

If I want to flip a coin 20 times and see if every result is consecutively heads, I can use a simple list comprehension (see Item 40: "Use Comprehensions Instead of `map` and `filter`") and membership test with the in operator (see Item 57: "Inherit from `collections.abc` Classes for Custom Container Types"):

```
flips = [flip_is_heads() for _ in range(20)]
all_heads = False not in flips
```

However, the chance of this sequence of 20 coin flips producing nothing but heads is roughly one in a million—extremely rare. If coin flips were somehow expensive to do, I'd almost always waste a lot of resources on unnecessary work in the list comprehension because it keeps flipping coins even after seeing a tails result. I can improve this situation by using a loop that terminates the sequence of coin flips as soon as a non-heads outcome is seen:

```
all_heads = True
for _ in range(100):
    if not flip_is_heads():
        all_heads = False
        break
```

Although this code is more efficient, it's much longer than the list comprehension from before. To keep the code short while also ending execution early, I can use the all built-in function. all steps through an iterator, checks whether each item is truthy (see Item 7: Consider Conditional Expressions for Simple Inline Logic" for background), and immediately stops processing if not. all always returns a Boolean value of True or False, which is different from how the and logical operator returns the last value that's tested:

```
print("All truthy:")
print(all([1, 2, 3]))
print(1 and 2 and 3)

print("One falsey:")
print(all([1, 0, 3]))
print(1 and 0 and 3)
```

```
>>>
All truthy:
True
3
One falsey:
False
0
```

Using the all built-in function, I can rewrite the coin-flipping loop using a generator expression (see Item 44: "Consider Generator Expressions for Large List Comprehensions"). It will stop doing more coin flips as soon as the flip_is_heads function returns False:

```
all_heads = all(flip_is_heads() for _ in range(20))
```

Critically, if I pass a list comprehension instead of a generator expression—note the presence of the surrounding [and] square brackets—the code will create a list of 20 coin-flip outcomes before passing them to the all function. The computed result will be the same, but the code's performance will be far worse:

```
all_heads = all([flip_is_heads() for _ in range(20)])  # Wrong
```

Alternatively, I can use a yielding generator function (see Item 43: "Consider Generators Instead of Returning Lists") or any other type of iterator to achieve similar efficiency:

```
def repeated_is_heads(count):
    for _ in range(count):
        yield flip_is_heads()  # Generator


all_heads = all(repeated_is_heads(20))
```

Once `repeated_is_heads` yields a `False` value, the `all` built-in function will stop moving the generator iterator forward and return `False`. The reference to the generator's iterator that was passed to `all` will be thrown away and garbage collected, ensuring that the loop never completes (see Item 89: "Always Pass Resources into Generators and Have Callers Clean Them Up Outside" for details).

Sometimes, you'll have a function that behaves in the opposite way of `flip_is_heads`, returning `False` most of the time and `True` only when a certain condition is met. Here, I define a function that behaves this way:

```
def flip_is_tails():
    return flip_coin() == "Tails"
```

In order to use this function to detect consecutive heads, `all` won't work. Instead, I can use the any built-in function. any similarly steps through an iterator, but it terminates upon seeing the first truthy value. any always returns a Boolean value, unlike the or logical operator that it mirrors:

```
print("All falsey:")
print(any([0, False, None]))
print(0 or False or None)

print("One truthy:")
print(any([None, 3, 0]))
print(None or 3 or 0)

>>>
All falsey:
False
None
One truthy:
True
3
```

With any, I can use `flip_is_tails` in a generator expression to compute the same results as before:

```
all_heads = not any(flip_is_tails() for _ in range(20))
```

Or I can create a similar generator function:

```
def repeated_is_tails(count):
    for _ in range(count):
        yield flip_is_tails()


all_heads = not any(repeated_is_tails(20))
```

When should you choose any vs. all? It depends on what you're doing and the difficulty of testing the conditions that you care about. If you want to end early with a True value, then use any. If you want to end early with a False value, then use all. Ultimately, these built-in functions are equivalent, as demonstrated by *De Morgan's laws* for Boolean logic:

```
for a in (True, False):
    for b in (True, False):
        assert any([a, b]) == (not all([not a, not b]))
        assert all([a, b]) == (not any([not a, not b]))
```

One way or another, you should be able to find a way to minimize the amount of work being done by using any or all appropriately. There are also additional built-in modules for operating on iterators and generators in intelligent ways to maximize performance and efficiency (see Item 24: "Consider `itertools` for Working with Iterators and Generators").

Things to Remember

✦ The all built-in function returns True if all items provided are truthy. It stops processing input and returns False as soon as a falsey item is encountered.

✦ The any built-in function works similarly but with opposite logic: It returns False if all items are falsey and ends early with True as soon as it sees a truthy value.

✦ any and all always return the Boolean values True or False, unlike the or and and logical operators, which return the last item that needed to be tested.

✦ Using list comprehensions with any or all instead of generator expression undermines the efficiency benefits of these functions.

Item 24: Consider `itertools` for Working with Iterators and Generators

The `itertools` built-in module contains a large number of functions that are useful for organizing and interacting with iterators (see Item 43: "Consider Generators Instead of Returning Lists" and Item 21: "Be Defensive when Iterating over Arguments" for background):

```
import itertools
```

Whenever you find yourself dealing with tricky iteration code, it's worth looking at the `itertools` documentation again to see if there's anything in there for you to use (see https://docs.python.org/3/library/itertools.html). The following sections describe the most important functions that you should know in three primary categories.

Linking Iterators Together

The `itertools` built-in module includes a number of functions for linking iterators together.

chain

Use `chain` to combine multiple iterators into a single sequential iterator. Essentially this flattens the provided input iterators into one iterator of items:

```
it = itertools.chain([1, 2, 3], [4, 5, 6])
print(list(it))
```

```
>>>
[1, 2, 3, 4, 5, 6]
```

There's also an alternative version of this function, `chain.from_iterable`, that consumes an iterator of iterators and produces a single flattened output iterator that includes all of the contents of the iterators:

```
it1 = [i * 3 for i in ("a", "b", "c")]
it2 = [j * 2 for j in ("x", "y", "z")]
nested_it = [it1, it2]
output_it = itertools.chain.from_iterable(nested_it)
print(list(output_it))
```

```
>>>
['aaa', 'bbb', 'ccc', 'xx', 'yy', 'zz']
```

repeat

Use repeat to output a single value forever or use the second optional parameter to specify a maximum number of times:

```
it = itertools.repeat("hello", 3)
print(list(it))

>>>
['hello', 'hello', 'hello']
```

cycle

Use cycle to repeat an iterator's items forever:

```
it = itertools.cycle([1, 2])
result = [next(it) for _ in range(10)]
print(result)

>>>
[1, 2, 1, 2, 1, 2, 1, 2, 1, 2]
```

tee

Use tee to split a single iterator into the number of parallel iterators specified by the second parameter. The memory usage of this function will grow if the iterators don't progress at the same speed since buffering will be required to temporarily store the pending items:

```
it1, it2, it3 = itertools.tee(["first", "second"], 3)
print(list(it1))
print(list(it2))
print(list(it3))

>>>
['first', 'second']
['first', 'second']
['first', 'second']
```

zip_longest

This variant of the zip built-in function returns a placeholder value when an iterator is exhausted, which may happen if iterators have different lengths (see Item 18: "Use zip to Process Iterators in Parallel" for how the strict argument can provide similar behavior):

```
keys = ["one", "two", "three"]
values = [1, 2]
```

```
normal = list(zip(keys, values))
print("zip:          ", normal)

it = itertools.zip_longest(keys, values, fillvalue="nope")
longest = list(it)
print("zip_longest:", longest)

>>>
zip:          [('one', 1), ('two', 2)]
zip_longest: [('one', 1), ('two', 2), ('three', 'nope')]
```

Filtering Items from an Iterator

The itertools built-in module includes a number of functions for
filtering items from an iterator.

islice

Use islice to slice an iterator by numerical indexes without copying.
You can specify the end, start and end, or start, end, and step sizes.
The behavior of islice is similar to that of standard sequence slic-
ing and striding (see Item 14: "Know How to Slice Sequences" and
Item 15: "Avoid Striding and Slicing in a Single Expression"):

```
values = [1, 2, 3, 4, 5, 6, 7, 8, 9, 10]

first_five = itertools.islice(values, 5)
print("First five: ", list(first_five))

middle_odds = itertools.islice(values, 2, 8, 2)
print("Middle odds:", list(middle_odds))

>>>
First five:  [1, 2, 3, 4, 5]
Middle odds: [3, 5, 7]
```

takewhile

takewhile returns items from an iterator until a predicate function
returns False for an item, at which point all items from the iterator will
be consumed but not returned (see Item 39: "Prefer functools.partial
over lambda Expressions for Glue Functions" for more about defining
predicates):

```
values = [1, 2, 3, 4, 5, 6, 7, 8, 9, 10]
less_than_seven = lambda x: x < 7
it = itertools.takewhile(less_than_seven, values)
print(list(it))
```

```
>>>
[1, 2, 3, 4, 5, 6]
```

dropwhile

dropwhile, which is the opposite of takewhile, skips items from an iterator until the predicate function returns False for the first time, at which point all items from the iterator will be returned:

```
values = [1, 2, 3, 4, 5, 6, 7, 8, 9, 10]
less_than_seven = lambda x: x < 7
it = itertools.dropwhile(less_than_seven, values)
print(list(it))
```

```
>>>
[7, 8, 9, 10]
```

filterfalse

filterfalse, which is the opposite of the filter built-in function, returns all items from an iterator when a predicate function returns False:

```
values = [1, 2, 3, 4, 5, 6, 7, 8, 9, 10]
evens = lambda x: x % 2 == 0

filter_result = filter(evens, values)
print("Filter:      ", list(filter_result))

filter_false_result = itertools.filterfalse(evens, values)
print("Filter false:", list(filter_false_result))
```

```
>>>
Filter:        [2, 4, 6, 8, 10]
Filter false: [1, 3, 5, 7, 9]
```

Producing Combinations of Items from Iterators

The itertools built-in module includes a number of functions for producing combinations of items from iterators.

batched

Use batched to create an iterator that outputs fixed sized, non-overlapping groups of items from a single input iterator. The second argument is the batch size. This can be especially useful when processing data together for efficiency or satisfying other constraints, like data size limits:

```
it = itertools.batched([1, 2, 3, 4, 5, 6, 7, 8, 9], 3)
print(list(it))

>>>
[(1, 2, 3), (4, 5, 6), (7, 8, 9)]
```

The last group produced by the iterator might be smaller than the specified batch size if the items can't divide perfectly:

```
it = itertools.batched([1, 2, 3], 2)
print(list(it))

>>>
[(1, 2), (3,)]
```

pairwise

Use `pairwise` when you need to iterate through each pair of adjacent items in the input iterator. The pairs include overlaps, so each item except for the ends appears twice in the output iterator: once in the first position of a pair and another time in the second position. This can be helpful when writing graph-traversal algorithms that need to step through sequential sets of vertexes or endpoints:

```
route = ["Los Angeles", "Bakersfield", "Modesto", "Sacramento"]
it = itertools.pairwise(route)
print(list(it))

>>>
[('Los Angeles', 'Bakersfield'), ('Bakersfield', 'Modesto'),
➥('Modesto', 'Sacramento')]
```

accumulate

`accumulate` folds an item from the iterator into a running value by applying a function that takes two parameters. It outputs the current accumulated result for each input value:

```
values = [1, 2, 3, 4, 5, 6, 7, 8, 9, 10]
sum_reduce = itertools.accumulate(values)
print("Sum:   ", list(sum_reduce))

def sum_modulo_20(first, second):
    output = first + second
    return output % 20
```

```
modulo_reduce = itertools.accumulate(values, sum_modulo_20)
print("Modulo:", list(modulo_reduce))

>>>
Sum:    [1, 3, 6, 10, 15, 21, 28, 36, 45, 55]
Modulo: [1, 3, 6, 10, 15, 1, 8, 16, 5, 15]
```

This is essentially the same as the reduce function from the functools built-in module but with outputs yielded one step at a time. By default it sums the inputs if no binary function is specified.

product

product returns the Cartesian product of items from one or more iterators, which is a nice alternative to using deeply nested list comprehensions (see Item 41: "Avoid More Than Two Control Subexpressions in Comprehensions" for why to avoid those):

```
single = itertools.product([1, 2], repeat=2)
print("Single:  ", list(single))

multiple = itertools.product([1, 2], ["a", "b"])
print("Multiple:", list(multiple))

>>>
Single:   [(1, 1), (1, 2), (2, 1), (2, 2)]
Multiple: [(1, 'a'), (1, 'b'), (2, 'a'), (2, 'b')]
```

permutations

permutations returns the unique ordered permutations of length *N*—the second argument—with items from an iterator:

```
it = itertools.permutations([1, 2, 3, 4], 2)
print(list(it))

>>>
[(1, 2),
 (1, 3),
 (1, 4),
 (2, 1),
 (2, 3),
 (2, 4),
 (3, 1),
 (3, 2),
 (3, 4),
 (4, 1),
 (4, 2),
 (4, 3)]
```

combinations

combinations returns the unordered combinations of length *N*—the second argument—with unrepeated items from an iterator:

```
it = itertools.combinations([1, 2, 3, 4], 2)
print(list(it))
```

```
>>>
[(1, 2), (1, 3), (1, 4), (2, 3), (2, 4), (3, 4)]
```

combinations_with_replacement

combinations_with_replacement is the same as combinations, but repeated values are allowed. The difference between this and the permutations function is that this version allows the same input to be repeated multiple times in the output groups (i.e., see (1, 1) in the output below):

```
it = itertools.combinations_with_replacement([1, 2, 3, 4], 2)
print(list(it))
```

```
>>>
[(1, 1),
 (1, 2),
 (1, 3),
 (1, 4),
 (2, 2),
 (2, 3),
 (2, 4),
 (3, 3),
 (3, 4),
 (4, 4)]
```

Things to Remember

✦ The itertools functions fall into three main categories for working with iterators and generators: linking iterators together, filtering items they output, and producing combinations of items.

✦ There are more advanced functions, additional parameters, and useful recipes available in the official documentation.

Dictionaries

A natural complement to lists and sequences in Python is the dictionary type, which stores lookup keys mapped to corresponding values (in what is often called an *associative array* or a *hash table*). Their versatility makes dictionaries ideal for bookkeeping: dynamically keeping track of new and changing pieces of data and how they relate to each other. When writing a new program, using dictionaries is a great way to start before you're sure what other data structures or classes you might need.

Dictionaries provide constant time (amortized) performance for adding and removing items, which is far better than what simple lists can achieve on their own. Thus, it's understandable that dictionaries are the core data structure that Python uses to implement its object-oriented features. Python also has special syntax and related built-in modules that enhance dictionaries with additional capabilities beyond what you might expect from a simple hash table type in other languages.

Item 25: Be Cautious when Relying on Dictionary Insertion Ordering

In Python versions 3.5 and earlier, iterating over a dictionary instance would return its keys in arbitrary order. The order of iteration would not match the order in which the items were originally inserted into the dictionary. For example, here I use Python version 3.5 to create a dictionary that maps animal names to their corresponding baby names:

```
# Python 3.5
baby_names = {
    "cat": "kitten",
    "dog": "puppy",
}
print(baby_names)
```

```
>>>
{'dog': 'puppy', 'cat': 'kitten'}
```

When I created the dictionary, the keys were in the order "cat", "dog", but when I printed it, the keys were in the reverse order: "dog", "cat". This behavior is surprising, makes it harder to reproduce test cases, increases the difficulty of debugging, and is especially confusing to newcomers to Python.

This happened because the dictionary type in older versions of Python implements its hash table algorithm with a combination of the hash built-in function and a random seed that is assigned when the Python interpreter process starts executing. Together, these behaviors cause dictionary orderings to not match insertion order and to randomly shuffle between program executions.

Starting with Python 3.6, and officially part of the Python specification since version 3.7, dictionaries preserve insertion order. Now, this code always prints the dictionary in the same way it was originally created by the programmer:

```
baby_names = {
    "cat": "kitten",
    "dog": "puppy",
}
print(baby_names)
```

```
>>>
{'cat': 'kitten', 'dog': 'puppy'}
```

With Python 3.5 and earlier, all methods provided by dict that rely on iteration order—including keys, values, items, and popitem—similarly demonstrate this random-looking behavior:

```
# Python 3.5
print(list(baby_names.keys()))
print(list(baby_names.values()))
print(list(baby_names.items()))
print(baby_names.popitem())  # Randomly chooses an item
```

```
>>>
['dog', 'cat']
['puppy', 'kitten']
[('dog', 'puppy'), ('cat', 'kitten')]
('dog', 'puppy')
```

These methods now provide consistent insertion ordering that you can rely on when you write your programs:

```
print(list(baby_names.keys()))
print(list(baby_names.values()))
print(list(baby_names.items()))
print(baby_names.popitem())  # Last item inserted
```

```
>>>
['cat', 'dog']
['kitten', 'puppy']
[('cat', 'kitten'), ('dog', 'puppy')]
('dog', 'puppy')
```

There are many repercussions of this change on other Python features that are dependent on the dict type and its specific implementation.

Keyword arguments to functions—including the **kwargs catch-all parameter (see Item 35: "Provide Optional Behavior with Keyword Arguments" and Item 37: "Enforce Clarity with Keyword-Only and Positional-Only Arguments")— come through in seemingly random order in earlier versions of Python, which can make it harder to debug function calls:

```
# Python 3.5
def my_func(**kwargs):
    for key, value in kwargs.items():
        print("%s = %s" % (key, value))

my_func(goose="gosling", kangaroo="joey")
```

```
>>>
kangaroo = joey
goose = gosling
```

Now in the latest version of Python, the order of keyword arguments is always preserved to match how the programmer originally called the function:

```
def my_func(**kwargs):
    for key, value in kwargs.items():
        print(f"{key} = {value}")

my_func(goose="gosling", kangaroo="joey")
```

```
>>>
goose = gosling
kangaroo = joey
```

Classes also use the dict type for their instance dictionaries. In previous versions of Python, object fields show the randomizing behavior:

```
# Python 3.5
class MyClass:
    def __init__(self):
        self.alligator = "hatchling"
        self.elephant = "calf"

a = MyClass()
for key, value in a.__dict__.items():
    print("%s = %s" % (key, value))

>>>
elephant = calf
alligator = hatchling
```

Again, you can now assume that the order of assignment for these instance fields will be reflected in __dict__:

```
class MyClass:
    def __init__(self):
        self.alligator = "hatchling"
        self.elephant = "calf"

a = MyClass()
for key, value in a.__dict__.items():
    print(f"{key} = {value}")

>>>
alligator = hatchling
elephant = calf
```

The way that dictionaries preserve insertion ordering is now part of the Python language specification. For the language features above, you can rely on this behavior and even make it part of the APIs you design for your classes and functions (see Item 65: "Consider Class Body Definition Order to Establish Relationships Between Attributes" for an example).

Note

For a long time the collections built-in module has had an OrderedDict class that preserves insertion ordering. Although this class's behavior is similar to that of the standard dict type (since Python 3.7), the performance characteristics of OrderedDict are quite different. If you need to handle a high rate of key insertions and popitem calls (e.g., to implement a least-recently-used cache), OrderedDict may be a better fit than the standard Python dict type (see Item 92: "Profile Before Optimizing" on how to make sure you need this).

However, you shouldn't always assume that insertion ordering behavior will be present when you're handling dictionaries. Python makes it easy for programmers to define their own custom container types that emulate the standard *protocols* matching `list`, `dict`, and other types (see Item 57: "Inherit from `collections.abc` Classes for Custom Container Types"). Python is not statically typed, so most code relies on *duck typing*—where an object's behavior is its de facto type—instead of rigid class hierarchies (see Item 3: "Never Expect Python to Detect Errors at Compile Time"). This can result in surprising gotchas.

For example, say that I'm writing a program to show the results of a contest for the cutest baby animal. Here, I start with a dictionary containing the total vote count for each one:

```
votes = {
    "otter": 1281,
    "polar bear": 587,
    "fox": 863,
}
```

Now, I define a function to process this voting data and save the rank of each animal name into a provided empty dictionary. In this case, the dictionary could be the data model that powers a UI element:

```
def populate_ranks(votes, ranks):
    names = list(votes.keys())
    names.sort(key=votes.get, reverse=True)
    for i, name in enumerate(names, 1):
        ranks[name] = i
```

I also need a function that will tell me which animal won the contest. This function works by assuming that `populate_ranks` will assign the contents of the ranks dictionary in ascending order, meaning that the first key must be the winner:

```
def get_winner(ranks):
    return next(iter(ranks))
```

Here, I confirm that these functions work as designed and deliver the result that I expected:

```
ranks = {}
populate_ranks(votes, ranks)
print(ranks)
winner = get_winner(ranks)
print(winner)

>>>
{'otter': 1, 'fox': 2, 'polar bear': 3}
otter
```

Now, imagine that the requirements of this program have changed. The UI element that shows the results should be in alphabetical order instead of rank order. To accomplish this, I can use the collections.abc built-in module to define a new dictionary-like class that iterates its contents in alphabetical order:

```
from collections.abc import MutableMapping

class SortedDict(MutableMapping):
    def __init__(self):
        self.data = {}

    def __getitem__(self, key):
        return self.data[key]

    def __setitem__(self, key, value):
        self.data[key] = value

    def __delitem__(self, key):
        del self.data[key]

    def __iter__(self):
        keys = list(self.data.keys())
        keys.sort()
        for key in keys:
            yield key

    def __len__(self):
        return len(self.data)
```

I can use a SortedDict instance in place of a standard dict with the functions from before, and no errors will be raised since this class conforms to the protocol of a standard dictionary. However, the results are incorrect:

```
sorted_ranks = SortedDict()
populate_ranks(votes, sorted_ranks)
print(sorted_ranks.data)
winner = get_winner(sorted_ranks)
print(winner)

>>>
{'otter': 1, 'fox': 2, 'polar bear': 3}
fox
```

The problem here is that the implementation of get_winner assumes that the dictionary's iteration is in insertion order to match populate_ranks. This code is using SortedDict instead of dict, so that assumption is no longer true. Thus, the value returned for the winner is "fox", which is alphabetically first.

There are three ways to mitigate this problem. First, I can reimplement the get_winner function to no longer assume that the ranks dictionary has a specific iteration order. This is the most conservative and robust solution:

```
def get_winner(ranks):
    for name, rank in ranks.items():
        if rank == 1:
            return name

winner = get_winner(sorted_ranks)
print(winner)

>>>
otter
```

The second approach is to add an explicit check to the top of the function to ensure that the type of ranks matches my expectations and to raise an exception if not. This solution likely has better runtime performance than the more conservative approach:

```
def get_winner(ranks):
    if not isinstance(ranks, dict):
        raise TypeError("must provide a dict instance")
    return next(iter(ranks))


get_winner(sorted_ranks)

>>>
Traceback ...
TypeError: must provide a dict instance
```

The third alternative is to use type annotations to enforce that the value passed to get_winner is a dict instance and not a MutableMapping with dictionary-like behavior (see Item 124: "Consider Static Analysis via typing to Obviate Bugs"). Here, I run the mypy tool in strict mode on a type-annotated version of the code above:

```
from typing import Dict, MutableMapping

def populate_ranks(votes: Dict[str, int],
                   ranks: Dict[str, int]) -> None:
    names = list(votes.keys())
```

```
        names.sort(key=votes.__getitem__, reverse=True)
        for i, name in enumerate(names, 1):
            ranks[name] = i

def get_winner(ranks: Dict[str, int]) -> str:
    return next(iter(ranks))

class SortedDict(MutableMapping[str, int]):
    ...

votes = {
    "otter": 1281,
    "polar bear": 587,
    "fox": 863,
}

sorted_ranks = SortedDict()
populate_ranks(votes, sorted_ranks)
print(sorted_ranks.data)
winner = get_winner(sorted_ranks)
print(winner)

$ python3 -m mypy --strict example.py
.../example.py:48: error: Argument 2 to "populate_ranks" has
➥incompatible type "SortedDict"; expected "dict[str, int]"
➥[arg-type]
.../example.py:50: error: Argument 1 to "get_winner" has
➥incompatible type "SortedDict"; expected "dict[str, int]"
➥[arg-type]
Found 2 errors in 1 file (checked 1 source file)
```

This correctly detects the mismatch between the dict and SortedDict types and flags the incorrect usage as an error. This solution provides the best mix of static type safety and runtime performance.

Things to Remember

✦ Since Python 3.7, you can rely on the fact that iterating a dictionary instance's contents will occur in the same order in which the keys were initially added.

✦ Python makes it easy to define objects that act like dictionaries but that aren't dict instances. For these types, you can't assume that insertion ordering will be preserved.

✦ There are three ways to be careful about dictionary-like classes: Write code that doesn't rely on insertion ordering, explicitly check for the dict type at runtime, or require dict values using type annotations and static analysis.

Item 26: Prefer get over in and KeyError to Handle Missing Dictionary Keys

The three fundamental operations for interacting with dictionaries are accessing, assigning, and deleting keys and their associated values. The contents of dictionaries are dynamic, and thus it's entirely possible—even likely—that when you try to access or delete a key, it won't already be present.

For example, say that I'm trying to determine people's favorite type of bread to devise the menu for a sandwich shop. Here, I define a dictionary of counters with the current votes for each loaf's style:

```
counters = {
    "pumpernickel": 2,
    "sourdough": 1,
}
```

To increment the counter for a new vote, I need to see if the key exists, insert the key with a default counter value of zero if it's missing, and then increment the counter's value. This requires accessing the key two times and assigning it once. Here, I accomplish this task by using an if statement with an in operator that returns True when the key is present:

```
key = "wheat"

if key in counters:
    count = counters[key]
else:
    count = 0

counters[key] = count + 1
print(counters)

>>>
{'pumpernickel': 2, 'sourdough': 1, 'wheat': 1}
```

Another way to accomplish the same behavior is by relying on how dictionaries raise a KeyError exception when you try to get the value for a key that doesn't exist. Putting aside the cost of raising and catching exceptions (see Item 80: "Take Advantage of Each Block in try/except/else/finally"), this approach is more efficient, in theory, because it requires only one access and one assignment:

```
try:
    count = counters[key]
except KeyError:
    count = 0

counters[key] = count + 1
```

This flow of fetching a key that exists or returning a default value is so common that the dict built-in type provides the get method to accomplish this task. The second parameter to get is the default value to return in the case that the key—the first parameter—isn't present (see Item 32: "Prefer Raising Exceptions to Returning None" on whether that's a good interface). This approach also requires only one access and one assignment, but it's much shorter than the KeyError example and avoids the exception handling overhead:

```
count = counters.get(key, 0)
counters[key] = count + 1
```

It's possible to shorten the in operator and KeyError approaches in various ways, but all of these alternatives suffer from requiring code duplication for the assignments, which makes them less readable and worth avoiding:

```
if key not in counters:
    counters[key] = 0
counters[key] += 1

if key in counters:
    counters[key] += 1
else:
    counters[key] = 1

try:
    counters[key] += 1
except KeyError:
    counters[key] = 1
```

Thus, for a dictionary with simple types, using the get method is the shortest and clearest option.

Note

If you're maintaining dictionaries of counters like this, it's worth considering the Counter class from the collections built-in module, which provides most of the functionality you're likely to need.

What if the values in a dictionary are a more complex type, like a list? For example, say that instead of only counting votes, I also want to know who voted for each type of bread. Here, I do this by associating a list of names with each key:

```
votes = {
    "baguette": ["Bob", "Alice"],
    "ciabatta": ["Coco", "Deb"],
}

key = "brioche"
who = "Elmer"

if key in votes:
    names = votes[key]
else:
    votes[key] = names = []

names.append(who)
print(votes)

>>>
{'baguette': ['Bob', 'Alice'],
 'ciabatta': ['Coco', 'Deb'],
 'brioche': ['Elmer']}
```

Relying on the in operator requires two accesses if the key is present, or one access and one assignment if the key is missing. This example is different from the counters example above because the value for each key can be assigned blindly to the default value of an empty list if the key doesn't already exist. The triple assignment statement (votes[key] = names = []) populates the key in one line instead of two. Once the default value has been inserted into the dictionary, I don't need to assign it again because the list is modified by reference in the later call to append (see Item 30: "Know That Function Arguments Can Be Mutated" for background).

It's also possible to rely on the KeyError exception being raised when the dictionary value is a list. This approach requires one key access if the key is present, or one key access and one assignment if it's missing, which makes it more efficient than the in operator (ignoring the cost of the exception handling machinery):

```
try:
    names = votes[key]
except KeyError:
    votes[key] = names = []

names.append(who)
```

Similarly, I can use the get method to fetch a list value when the key is present, or do one fetch and one assignment if the key isn't present:

```
names = votes.get(key)
if names is None:
    votes[key] = names = []

names.append(who)
```

The approach that involves using get to fetch list values can further be shortened by one line if you use an assignment expression (introduced in Python 3.8; see Item 8: "Prevent Repetition with Assignment Expressions") in the if statement, which improves readability:

```
if (names := votes.get(key)) is None:
    votes[key] = names = []

names.append(who)
```

Notably, the dict type also provides the setdefault method to help shorten this pattern even further. setdefault tries to fetch the value of a key in the dictionary. If the key isn't present, the method assigns that key to the default value provided. And then the method returns the value for that key: either the originally present value or the newly inserted default value. Here, I use setdefault to implement the same logic as in the get example above:

```
names = votes.setdefault(key, [])
names.append(who)
```

This works as expected, and it is shorter than using get with an assignment expression. However, the readability of this approach isn't ideal. The method name setdefault doesn't make its purpose immediately obvious. Why is it set when what it's doing is getting a value? Why not call it get_or_set? I'm arguing about the color of the bike shed here, but the point is that if you were a new reader of the code and not completely familiar with Python, you might have trouble understanding what this code is trying to accomplish because setdefault isn't self-explanatory.

There's also one important gotcha: The default value passed to setdefault is assigned directly into the dictionary when the key is missing instead of being copied. Here, I demonstrate the effect of this when the value is a list:

```
data = {}
key = "foo"
value = []
```

```
data.setdefault(key, value)
print("Before:", data)
value.append("hello")
print("After: ", data)

>>>
Before: {'foo': []}
After:  {'foo': ['hello']}
```

So, I need to make sure I'm always constructing a new default value for each key I access with setdefault. This leads to a significant performance overhead in this example because I have to allocate a list instance for each call. If I reuse an object for the default value—which I might try to do to increase efficiency or readability—I might introduce strange behavior and bugs (see Item 36: "Use None and Docstrings to Specify Dynamic Default Arguments" for another example of this problem).

Going back to the earlier example that used counters for dictionary values instead of lists of who voted: Why not also use the setdefault method in that case? Here, I reimplement the same example using this approach:

```
count = counters.setdefault(key, 0)
counters[key] = count + 1
```

The problem here is that the call to setdefault is superfluous. You always need to assign the key in the dictionary to a new value after you increment the counter, so the extra assignment done by setdefault is unnecessary. The earlier approach of using get for counter updates requires only one access and one assignment, whereas using setdefault requires one access and two assignments.

There are only a few circumstances in which using setdefault is the shortest way to handle missing dictionary keys (e.g., for list instance default values that are cheap to construct and won't raise exceptions). In these very specific cases, it might seem worth accepting the confusing method name setdefault instead of having to write more characters and lines to use get. However, often what you really should do in these situations is use defaultdict instead (see Item 27: "Prefer defaultdict over setdefault to Handle Missing Items in Internal State").

Things to Remember

✦ There are four common ways to detect and handle missing keys in dictionaries: using in operators, KeyError exceptions, the get method, and the setdefault method.

✦ The get method is best for dictionaries that contain basic types like counters, and it is preferable along with assignment expressions when creating dictionary default values has a high cost or might raise exceptions.

✦ When the setdefault method of dict seems like the best fit for your problem, you should consider using defaultdict instead.

Item 27: Prefer defaultdict over setdefault to Handle Missing Items in Internal State

When working with a dictionary that you didn't create, there are a variety of ways to handle missing keys (see Item 26: "Prefer get over in and KeyError to Handle Missing Dictionary Keys"). Although using the get method is a better approach than using in operators and KeyError exceptions, for some use cases, setdefault appears to be the shortest option.

For example, say that I want to keep track of the cities I've visited in countries around the world. Here, I do this by using a dictionary that maps country names to a set instance containing corresponding city names:

```
visits = {
    "Mexico": {"Tulum", "Puerto Vallarta"},
    "Japan": {"Hakone"},
}
```

I can use the setdefault method to add new cities to the sets, whether the country name is already present in the dictionary or not. The code is much shorter than achieving the same behavior with the get method and an assignment expression:

```
# Short
visits.setdefault("France", set()).add("Arles")

# Long
if (japan := visits.get("Japan")) is None:
    visits["Japan"] = japan = set()

japan.add("Kyoto")
print(visits)

>>>
{'Mexico': {'Puerto Vallarta', 'Tulum'},
 'Japan': {'Kyoto', 'Hakone'},
 'France': {'Arles'}}
```

What about the situation when you *do* control creation of the dictionary being accessed? This is generally the case when you're using a dictionary instance to keep track of the internal state of an object, for example. Here, I wrap the example above in a class with helper methods to access its dynamic inner state that's stored in a dictionary:

```
class Visits:
    def __init__(self):
        self.data = {}

    def add(self, country, city):
        city_set = self.data.setdefault(country, set())
        city_set.add(city)
```

This new class hides the complexity of calling setdefault with the correct arguments, and it provides a nicer interface for the programmer:

```
visits = Visits()
visits.add("Russia", "Yekaterinburg")
visits.add("Tanzania", "Zanzibar")
print(visits.data)

>>>
{'Russia': {'Yekaterinburg'}, 'Tanzania': {'Zanzibar'}}
```

However, the implementation of the Visits.add method isn't ideal. The setdefault method is still confusingly named, which makes it more difficult for a new reader of the code to immediately understand what's happening. And the implementation isn't efficient because it constructs a new set instance on every call, regardless of whether the given country was already present in the data dictionary.

Luckily, the defaultdict class from the collections built-in module simplifies this common use case by automatically storing a default value when a key doesn't exist. All you have to do is provide a function that will return the default value to use each time a key is missing (an example of Item 48: "Accept Functions Instead of Classes for Simple Interfaces"). Here, I rewrite the Visits class to use defaultdict:

```
from collections import defaultdict

class Visits:
    def __init__(self):
        self.data = defaultdict(set)

    def add(self, country, city):
        self.data[country].add(city)
```

```
visits = Visits()
visits.add("England", "Bath")
visits.add("England", "London")
print(visits.data)

>>>
defaultdict(<class 'set'>, {'England': {'Bath', 'London'}})
```

Now, the implementation of add is short and simple. The code can assume that accessing any key in the data dictionary will always result in an existing set instance. No superfluous set instances will be allocated, which could be costly if the add method is called a large number of times.

Using defaultdict is much better than using setdefault for this type of situation (see Item 29: "Compose Classes Instead of Deeply Nesting Dictionaries, Lists, and Tuples" for another example). There are still cases in which defaultdict will fall short of solving your problems, but there are even more tools available in Python to work around those limitations (see Item 28: "Know How to Construct Key-Dependent Default Values with __missing__", Item 57: "Inherit from collections.abc Classes for Custom Container Types", and the collections.Counter built-in class).

Things to Remember

✦ If you're creating a dictionary to manage an arbitrary set of potential keys, then you should prefer using a defaultdict instance from the collections built-in module if it suits your problem.

✦ If a dictionary of arbitrary keys is passed to you, and you don't control its creation, then you should prefer the get method to access its items. However, it's worth considering using the setdefault method for the few situations in which it leads to shorter code and the default object allocation cost is low.

Item 28: Know How to Construct Key-Dependent Default Values with __missing__

The built-in dict type's setdefault method results in shorter code when handling missing keys in some specific circumstances (see Item 26: "Prefer get over in and KeyError to Handle Missing Dictionary Keys"). For many of those situations, the better tool for the job is the defaultdict type from the collections built-in module (see Item 27: "Prefer defaultdict over setdefault to Handle Missing Items in Internal State" for why). However, there are times when neither setdefault nor defaultdict is the right fit.

For example, say that I'm writing a program to manage social network profile pictures on the filesystem. I need a dictionary to map profile picture pathnames to open file handles so I can read and write those images as needed. Here, I do this by using a normal dict instance and checking for the presence of keys using the get method and an assignment expression (see Item 8: "Prevent Repetition with Assignment Expressions"):

```
pictures = {}
path = "profile_1234.png"

if (handle := pictures.get(path)) is None:
    try:
        handle = open(path, "a+b")
    except OSError:
        print(f"Failed to open path {path}")
        raise
    else:
        pictures[path] = handle

handle.seek(0)
image_data = handle.read()
```

When the file handle already exists in the dictionary, this code makes only a single dictionary access. In the case that the file handle doesn't exist, the dictionary is accessed once by get, and then it is assigned in the else clause of the try/except statement (see Item 80: "Take Advantage of Each Block in try/except/else/finally"). The call to the read method stands clearly separate from the code that calls open and handles exceptions.

Although it's possible to use the in operator or KeyError approaches to implement this same logic, those options require more dictionary accesses and levels of nesting. Given that these other options work, you might also assume that the setdefault method would work, too:

```
try:
    handle = pictures.setdefault(path, open(path, "a+b"))
except OSError:
    print(f"Failed to open path {path}")
    raise
else:
    handle.seek(0)
    image_data = handle.read()
```

This code has many problems. The open built-in function to create the file handle is always called, even when the path is already present in the dictionary. This results in an additional file handle that might conflict with existing open handles in the same program. Exceptions might be raised by the open call and need to be handled, but it may not be possible to differentiate them from exceptions that could be raised by the setdefault call on the same line (which is possible for other dictionary-like implementations; see Item 57: "Inherit from collections.abc Classes for Custom Container Types").

If you're trying to manage internal state, another assumption you might make is that a defaultdict could be used for keeping track of these profile pictures. Here, I attempt to implement the same logic as before but now using a helper function and the defaultdict class:

```
from collections import defaultdict

def open_picture(profile_path):
    try:
        return open(profile_path, "a+b")
    except OSError:
        print(f"Failed to open path {profile_path}")
        raise

pictures = defaultdict(open_picture)
handle = pictures[path]
handle.seek(0)
image_data = handle.read()

>>>
Traceback ...
TypeError: open_picture() missing 1 required positional
➥argument: 'profile_path'
```

The problem is that defaultdict expects that the function passed to its constructor doesn't require any arguments. This means that the helper function defaultdict calls doesn't know the specific key that's being accessed, which hinders my ability to call open. In this situation, both setdefault and defaultdict fall short of what I need.

Fortunately, this situation is common enough that Python has another built-in solution. You can subclass the dict type and implement the __missing__ special method to add custom logic for handling missing keys. Here, I do this by defining a new class that takes advantage of the same open_picture helper method defined above:

```
class Pictures(dict):
    def __missing__(self, key):
        value = open_picture(key)
```

```
        self[key] = value
        return value

pictures = Pictures()
handle = pictures[path]
handle.seek(0)
image_data = handle.read()
```

When the pictures[path] dictionary access finds that the path key isn't present in the dictionary, the __missing__ method is called. This method must create the new default value for the key, insert it into the dictionary, and return it to the caller. Subsequent accesses of the same path will not call __missing__ since the corresponding item is already present (similar to the behavior of __getattr__; see Item 61: "Use __getattr__, __getattribute__, and __setattr__ for Lazy Attributes").

Things to Remember

✦ The setdefault method of dict is a bad fit when creating the default value has high computational cost or might raise exceptions.

✦ The function passed to defaultdict must not require any arguments, which makes it impossible to have the default value depend on the key being accessed.

✦ You can define your own dict subclass with a __missing__ method in order to construct default values that must know which key was being accessed.

Item 29: Compose Classes Instead of Deeply Nesting Dictionaries, Lists, and Tuples

Python's built-in dictionary type is wonderful for maintaining dynamic internal state over the lifetime of an object. By *dynamic*, I mean situations in which you need to do bookkeeping for an unexpected set of identifiers. For example, say that I want to record the grades of a set of students whose names aren't known in advance. I can define a class to store the names in a dictionary instead of using a predefined attribute for each student:

```
class SimpleGradebook:
    def __init__(self):
        self._grades = {}

    def add_student(self, name):
        self._grades[name] = []
```

```
    def report_grade(self, name, score):
        self._grades[name].append(score)

    def average_grade(self, name):
        grades = self._grades[name]
        return sum(grades) / len(grades)
```

Using the class is simple:

```
book = SimpleGradebook()
book.add_student("Isaac Newton")
book.report_grade("Isaac Newton", 90)
book.report_grade("Isaac Newton", 95)
book.report_grade("Isaac Newton", 85)

print(book.average_grade("Isaac Newton"))
>>>
90.0
```

Dictionaries, lists, tuples, and sets are so easy to use that there's a danger they'll cause you to write brittle code. For example, say that I want to extend the SimpleGradebook class to keep a list of grades by subject, not just overall. I can do this by changing the _grades dictionary to map student names (its keys) to yet another dictionary (its values). The innermost dictionary will map subjects (its keys) to a list of grades (its values). Here, I do this by using a defaultdict instance for the inner dictionary to handle missing subjects (see Item 27: "Prefer defaultdict over setdefault to Handle Missing Items in Internal State" for background):

```
from collections import defaultdict

class BySubjectGradebook:
    def __init__(self):
        self._grades = {}                       # Outer dict

    def add_student(self, name):
        self._grades[name] = defaultdict(list)  # Inner dict

    def report_grade(self, name, subject, grade):
        by_subject = self._grades[name]
        grade_list = by_subject[subject]
        grade_list.append(grade)

    def average_grade(self, name):
        by_subject = self._grades[name]
```

```
    total, count = 0, 0
    for grades in by_subject.values():
        total += sum(grades)
        count += len(grades)
    return total / count
```

This is straightforward enough. The `report_grade` and `average_grade` methods gained quite a bit of complexity to deal with the multilevel dictionary, but it's seemingly manageable. Using the class remains simple:

```
book = BySubjectGradebook()
book.add_student("Albert Einstein")
book.report_grade("Albert Einstein", "Math", 75)
book.report_grade("Albert Einstein", "Math", 65)
book.report_grade("Albert Einstein", "Gym", 90)
book.report_grade("Albert Einstein", "Gym", 95)
print(book.average_grade("Albert Einstein"))
```

```
>>>
81.25
```

Now, imagine that the requirements change again. I also want to track the weight of each score toward the overall grade in the class so that midterm and final exams are more important than pop quizzes. One way to implement this feature is to change the innermost dictionary; instead of mapping subjects (its keys) to a list of grades (its values), I can use tuples of (score, weight) in each key's corresponding value list. Although the changes to `report_grade` seem simple—just make the `grade_list` store tuple instances—the `average_grade` method now has a loop within a loop and is difficult to read:

```
class WeightedGradebook:
    def __init__(self):
        self._grades = {}

    def add_student(self, name):
        self._grades[name] = defaultdict(list)

    def report_grade(self, name, subject, score, weight):
        by_subject = self._grades[name]
        grade_list = by_subject[subject]
        grade_list.append((score, weight))    # Changed

    def average_grade(self, name):
        by_subject = self._grades[name]
```

```
        score_sum, score_count = 0, 0
        for scores in by_subject.values():
            subject_avg, total_weight = 0, 0
            for score, weight in scores:        # Added inner loop
                subject_avg += score * weight
                total_weight += weight

            score_sum += subject_avg / total_weight
            score_count += 1

        return score_sum / score_count
```

Using the class has also gotten more difficult. It's unclear what all the numbers in the positional arguments mean:

```
book = WeightedGradebook()
book.add_student("Albert Einstein")
book.report_grade("Albert Einstein", "Math", 75, 0.05)
book.report_grade("Albert Einstein", "Math", 65, 0.15)
book.report_grade("Albert Einstein", "Math", 70, 0.80)
book.report_grade("Albert Einstein", "Gym", 100, 0.40)
book.report_grade("Albert Einstein", "Gym", 85, 0.60)
print(book.average_grade("Albert Einstein"))
```

```
>>>
80.25
```

When you see complexity like this, it's time to make the leap from built-in types like dictionaries, lists, tuples, and sets to a hierarchy of classes.

In the grades example, at first I didn't know I'd need to support weighted grades, so the complexity of creating other classes seemed unwarranted. Python's built-in dictionary and tuple types made it easy to keep going, adding layer after layer to the internal bookkeeping. But you should avoid doing this for more than one level of nesting; using dictionaries that contain dictionaries makes your code hard for other programmers to read and sets you up for a maintenance nightmare (see Item 9: "Consider match for Destructuring in Flow Control, Avoid When if Statements Are Sufficient" for another way to deal with this).

As soon as you realize that your bookkeeping is getting complicated, break it all out into classes. You can then provide well-defined interfaces that better encapsulate your data. This approach also enables you to create a layer of abstraction between your interfaces and your concrete implementations.

Refactoring to Classes

There are many approaches to refactoring (see Item 123: "Consider warnings to Refactor and Migrate Usage" for an example). In this case, I can start moving to classes at the bottom of the dependency tree: a single grade. A class seems too heavyweight for such simple information. A tuple, though, seems appropriate because grades are immutable. Here, I use a tuple of (score, weight) to track grades in a list:

```
grades = []
grades.append((95, 0.45))
grades.append((85, 0.55))
total = sum(score * weight for score, weight in grades)
total_weight = sum(weight for _, weight in grades)
average_grade = total / total_weight
```

I used _ (the underscore variable name, a Python convention for unused variables) to capture the first entry in each grade's tuple and ignore it when calculating total_weight.

The problem with this code is that tuple instances are positional. For example, if I want to associate more information with a grade, such as a set of notes from the teacher, I need to rewrite every usage of the two-tuple to be aware that there are now three items present instead of two, which means I need to use _ further to ignore certain indexes:

```
grades = []
grades.append((95, 0.45, "Great job"))
grades.append((85, 0.55, "Better next time"))
total = sum(score * weight for score, weight, _ in grades)
total_weight = sum(weight for _, weight, _ in grades)
average_grade = total / total_weight
```

This pattern of extending tuples longer and longer is similar to deepening layers of dictionaries. As soon as you find yourself going longer than a two-tuple, it's time to consider another approach. The dataclasses built-in module does exactly what I need in this case: It lets me easily define a small immutable class for storing values in attributes (see Item 56: "Prefer dataclasses for Creating Immutable Objects"):

```
from dataclasses import dataclass

@dataclass(frozen=True)
class Grade:
    score: int
    weight: float
```

Next, I can write a class to represent a single subject that contains a set of Grade instances:

```
class Subject:
    def __init__(self):
        self._grades = []

    def report_grade(self, score, weight):
        self._grades.append(Grade(score, weight))

    def average_grade(self):
        total, total_weight = 0, 0
        for grade in self._grades:
            total += grade.score * grade.weight
            total_weight += grade.weight
        return total / total_weight
```

Then, I write a class to hold the set of subjects that are being studied by a single student:

```
class Student:
    def __init__(self):
        self._subjects = defaultdict(Subject)

    def get_subject(self, name):
        return self._subjects[name]

    def average_grade(self):
        total, count = 0, 0
        for subject in self._subjects.values():
            total += subject.average_grade()
            count += 1
        return total / count
```

Finally, I write a container for all of the students, keyed dynamically by their names:

```
class Gradebook:
    def __init__(self):
        self._students = defaultdict(Student)

    def get_student(self, name):
        return self._students[name]
```

The line count of these classes is almost double the previous imple-mentation's size. But this code is much easier to read. The example driving the classes is also clearer and more extensible:

```
book = Gradebook()
albert = book.get_student("Albert Einstein")
math = albert.get_subject("Math")
math.report_grade(75, 0.05)
math.report_grade(65, 0.15)
math.report_grade(70, 0.80)
gym = albert.get_subject("Gym")
gym.report_grade(100, 0.40)
gym.report_grade(85, 0.60)
print(albert.average_grade())
```

```
>>>
80.25
```

It would also be possible to write backward-compatible methods to help migrate usage of the old API style to the new hierarchy of objects.

Things to Remember

+ Avoid making dictionaries with values that are dictionaries, long tuples, or complex nestings of other built-in types.

+ Use the dataclasses built-in module for lightweight, immutable data containers before you need the flexibility of a full class.

+ Move your bookkeeping code to using multiple classes when your internal state dictionaries get complicated.

5

Functions

The first organizational tool programmers use in Python is the *function*. As in other programming languages, functions enable you to break large programs into smaller, simpler components with names to represent their purpose. They improve readability and make code more approachable. They allow for reuse and refactoring.

Functions in Python have a variety of extra features that make a programmer's life easier. Some are similar to capabilities in other programming languages, but many are unique to Python. These extras can make a function's interface clearer. They can eliminate noise and reinforce the intention of callers. They can significantly reduce subtle bugs that are difficult to find.

Item 30: Know That Function Arguments Can Be Mutated

Python doesn't support pointer types (beyond interfacing with C; see Item 95: "Consider ctypes to Rapidly Integrate with Native Libraries"). But arguments passed to functions are all passed by reference. For simple types, like integers and strings, parameters appear to be passed by value because they're immutable objects. But more complex objects can be modified whenever they're passed to other functions, regardless of the caller's intent.

For example, if I pass a list to another function, that function has the ability to call mutation methods on the argument:

```
def my_func(items):
    items.append(4)

x = [1, 2, 3]
my_func(x)
print(x)  # 4 is now in the list
```

```
>>>
[1, 2, 3, 4]
```

In this case, you can't replace the original value of the variable x within the called function, as you might do with a C-style pointer type. But you can make modifications to the list assigned to x.

Similarly, when one variable is assigned to another, it stores a reference, or an *alias*, to the same underlying data structure. Thus, calling a function with what appears to be a separate variable actually allows for mutation of the original:

```
a = [7, 6, 5]
b = a              # Creates an alias
my_func(b)
print(a)           # 4 is now in the list
```

```
>>>
[7, 6, 5, 4]
```

For lists and dictionaries, you can work around this issue by passing a copy of the container to insulate you from the function's behavior. Here, I create a copy by using the slice operation with no starting or ending indexes (see Item 14: "Know How to Slice Sequences"):

```
def capitalize_items(items):
    for i in range(len(items)):
        items[i] = items[i].capitalize()

my_items = ["hello", "world"]
items_copy = my_items[:]  # Creates a copy
capitalize_items(items_copy)
print(items_copy)
```

```
>>>
['Hello', 'World']
```

The dictionary built-in type provides a copy method specifically for this purpose:

```
def concat_pairs(items):
    for key in items:
        items[key] = f"{key}={items[key]}"

my_pairs = {"foo": 1, "bar": 2}
pairs_copy = my_pairs.copy()  # Creates a copy
concat_pairs(pairs_copy)
print(pairs_copy)
```

```
>>>
{'foo': 'foo=1', 'bar': 'bar=2'}
```

User-defined classes (see Item 29: "Compose Classes Instead of Deeply Nesting Dictionaries, Lists, and Tuples") can also be modified by callers. Any of their internal properties can be accessed or assigned by any function they're passed to (see Item 55: "Prefer Public Attributes over Private Ones"):

```
class MyClass:
    def __init__(self, value):
        self.value = value

x = MyClass(10)

def my_func(obj):
    obj.value = 20   # Modifies the object

my_func(x)
print(x.value)

>>>
20
```

When implementing a function that others will call, you shouldn't modify any mutable value provided unless that behavior is mentioned explicitly in the function name, argument names, or documentation. You might also want to make a defensive copy of any arguments you receive to avoid various pitfalls with iteration (see Item 21: "Be Defensive when Iterating over Arguments" and Item 22: "Never Modify Containers While Iterating over Them; Use Copies or Caches Instead").

When calling a function, you should be careful about passing mutable arguments because your data might get modified, which can cause difficult-to-spot bugs. For complex objects you control, it can be useful to add helper functions and methods that make it easy to create defensive copies. Alternatively, you can use a more functional style and try to leverage immutable objects and pure functions (see Item 56: "Prefer dataclasses for Creating Immutable Objects").

Things to Remember

✦ Arguments in Python are passed by reference, meaning their attributes can be mutated by receiving functions and methods.

✦ Functions should make it clear (with naming and documentation) when they will modify input arguments and avoid modifying arguments otherwise.

✦ Creating copies of collections and objects you receive as input is a reliable way to ensure that your functions avoid inadvertently modifying data.

Item 31: Return Dedicated Result Objects Instead of Requiring Function Callers to Unpack More Than Three Variables

One effect of the unpacking syntax (see Item 5: "Prefer Multiple-Assignment Unpacking over Indexing") is that it allows a Python function to seemingly return more than one value. For example, say that I'm trying to determine various statistics for a population of alligators. Given a list of lengths, I need to calculate the minimum and maximum lengths in the population. Here, I do this in a single function that appears to return two values:

```
def get_stats(numbers):
    minimum = min(numbers)
    maximum = max(numbers)
    return minimum, maximum

lengths = [63, 73, 72, 60, 67, 66, 71, 61, 72, 70]

minimum, maximum = get_stats(lengths)  # Two return values

print(f"Min: {minimum}, Max: {maximum}")

>>>
Min: 60, Max: 73
```

The way this works is that multiple values are returned together in a two-item tuple. The calling code then unpacks the returned tuple by assigning two variables. Here, I use an even simpler example to show how an unpacking statement and multiple-return function work the same way:

```
first, second = 1, 2
assert first == 1
assert second == 2

def my_function():
    return 1, 2

first, second = my_function()
assert first == 1
assert second == 2
```

Multiple return values can also be received by starred expressions for catch-all unpacking (see Item 16: "Prefer Catch-All Unpacking over Slicing"). For example, say I need another function that calculates how big each alligator is relative to the population average. This function returns a list of ratios, but I can receive the longest and shortest items individually by using a starred expression for the middle portion of the list:

```
def get_avg_ratio(numbers):
    average = sum(numbers) / len(numbers)
    scaled = [x / average for x in numbers]
    scaled.sort(reverse=True)
    return scaled


longest, *middle, shortest = get_avg_ratio(lengths)

print(f"Longest:  {longest:>4.0%}")
print(f"Shortest: {shortest:>4.0%}")

>>>
Longest:  108%
Shortest:  89%
```

Now, imagine that the program's requirements change, and I need to also determine the average length, median length, and total population size of the alligators. I can do this by expanding the get_stats function to also calculate these statistics and return them in the result tuple that is unpacked by the caller:

```
def get_median(numbers):
    count = len(numbers)
    sorted_numbers = sorted(numbers)
    middle = count // 2
    if count % 2 == 0:
        lower = sorted_numbers[middle - 1]
        upper = sorted_numbers[middle]
        median = (lower + upper) / 2
    else:
        median = sorted_numbers[middle]
    return median


def get_stats_more(numbers):
    minimum = min(numbers)
    maximum = max(numbers)
    count = len(numbers)
    average = sum(numbers) / count
    median = get_median(numbers)
    return minimum, maximum, average, median, count
```

```
minimum, maximum, average, median, count =
➥get_stats_more(lengths)

print(f"Min: {minimum}, Max: {maximum}")
print(f"Average: {average}, Median: {median}, Count {count}")
>>>
Min: 60, Max: 73
Average: 67.5, Median: 68.5, Count 10
```

There are two problems with this code. First, all of the return values
are numeric, so it is all too easy to reorder them accidentally (e.g.,
swapping average and median), which can cause bugs that are hard
to spot later. Using a large number of return values is extremely error
prone:

```
# Correct:
minimum, maximum, average, median, count =
➥get_stats_more(lengths)

# Oops! Median and average swapped:
minimum, maximum, median, average, count =
➥get_stats_more(lengths)
```

Second, the line that calls the function and unpacks the values is
long, and it will likely need to be wrapped in one of a variety of ways
(due to PEP 8 style; see Item 2: "Follow the PEP 8 Style Guide"), which
hurts readability:

```
minimum, maximum, average, median, count = get_stats_more(
    lengths)

minimum, maximum, average, median, count =
    get_stats_more(lengths)

(minimum, maximum, average,
 median, count) = get_stats_more(lengths)

(minimum, maximum, average, median, count
  ) = get_stats_more(lengths)
```

To avoid these problems, you should never use more than three variables when unpacking the multiple return values from a function.
These could be individual values from a three-tuple, two variables
and one catch-all starred expression, or anything shorter.

If you need to unpack more return values than that, you're better off
defining a lightweight class (see Item 29: "Compose Classes Instead

of Deeply Nesting Dictionaries, Lists, and Tuples" and Item 51: "Prefer dataclasses for Defining Lightweight Classes") and having your function return an instance of that instead. Here, I write another version of the get_stats function that returns a result object instead of a tuple:

```
from dataclasses import dataclass

@dataclass
class Stats:
    minimum: float
    maximum: float
    average: float
    median: float
    count: int

def get_stats_obj(numbers):
    return Stats(
        minimum=min(numbers),
        maximum=max(numbers),
        count=len(numbers),
        average=sum(numbers) / count,
        median=get_median(numbers),
    )

result = get_stats_obj(lengths)
print(result)

>>>
Stats(minimum=60, maximum=73, average=67.5, median=68.5,
➥count=10)
```

The code is clearer, less error prone, and will be easier to refactor later.

Things to Remember

✦ You can have functions return multiple values by putting them in a tuple and having the caller take advantage of Python's unpacking syntax.

✦ Multiple return values from a function can also be unpacked by catch-all starred expressions.

✦ Unpacking into four or more variables is error prone and should be avoided; instead, return an instance of a lightweight class.

Item 32: Prefer Raising Exceptions to Returning None

When writing utility functions, there's a draw for Python programmers to give special meaning to the return value None. It seems to make sense in some cases (see Item 26: "Prefer get over in and KeyError to Handle Missing Dictionary Keys"). For example, say I want a helper function that divides one number by another. In the case of dividing by zero, returning None seems natural because the result is undefined:

```
def careful_divide(a, b):
    try:
        return a / b
    except ZeroDivisionError:
        return None
```

Code that uses this function can interpret the return value accordingly:

```
x, y = 1, 0
result = careful_divide(x, y)
if result is None:
    print("Invalid inputs")
```

What happens with the careful_divide function when the numerator is zero? If the denominator is not zero, then the function returns zero. The problem is that a zero return value can cause issues when you evaluate the result in a condition like an if statement. You might accidentally look for any falsey value to indicate errors instead of only looking for None (see Item 4: "Write Helper Functions Instead of Complex Expressions" and Item 7: "Consider Conditional Expressions for Simple Inline Logic"):

```
x, y = 0, 5
result = careful_divide(x, y)
if not result:                  # Changed
    print("Invalid inputs")  # This runs! But shouldn't

>>>
Invalid inputs
```

This misinterpretation of a False-equivalent return value is a common mistake in Python code when None has special meaning. This is why returning None from a function like careful_divide is error prone. There are two ways to reduce the chance of such errors.

The first way is to split the return value into a two-tuple (see Item 31: "Return Dedicated Result Objects Instead of Requiring Function Callers to Unpack More Than Three Variables" for background). The first part of the tuple indicates that the operation was a success or failure. The second part is the actual result that was computed:

```
def careful_divide(a, b):
    try:
        return True, a / b
    except ZeroDivisionError:
        return False, None
```

Callers of this function have to unpack the tuple. That forces them to consider the status part of the tuple instead of just looking at the result of division:

```
success, result = careful_divide(x, y)
if not success:
    print("Invalid inputs")
```

The problem is that callers can easily ignore the first part of the tuple (using the underscore variable name, which is a Python convention for unused variables). The resulting code doesn't look wrong at first glance, but this can be just as error prone as returning None:

```
_, result = careful_divide(x, y)
if not result:
    print("Invalid inputs")
```

The second, better way to reduce these errors is to never return None for special cases. Instead, raise an exception up to the caller and have the caller deal with it. Here, I turn ZeroDivisionError into ValueError to indicate to the caller that the input values are bad (see Item 88: "Consider Explicitly Chaining Exceptions to Clarify Tracebacks" and Item 121: "Define a Root Exception to Insulate Callers from APIs" for details):

```
def careful_divide(a, b):
    try:
        return a / b
    except ZeroDivisionError:
        raise ValueError("Invalid inputs")  # Changed
```

The caller no longer requires a condition on the return value of the function. Instead, it can assume that the return value is always valid and use the results immediately in the else block after try (see Item 80: "Take Advantage of Each Block in try/except/else/finally" for background):

```
x, y = 5, 2
try:
    result = careful_divide(x, y)
except ValueError:
    print("Invalid inputs")
else:
    print(f"Result is {result:.1f}")

>>>
Result is 2.5
```

This approach can be extended to code using type annotations (see Item 124: "Consider Static Analysis via typing to Obviate Bugs" for background). You can specify that a function's return value will always be a float and thus will never be None. However, Python's gradual typing purposely doesn't provide a way to indicate when exceptions are part of a function's interface (also known as *checked exceptions*). Instead, you have to document the exception-raising behavior and expect callers to rely on that in order to know which exceptions they should plan to catch (see Item 118: "Write Docstrings for Every Function, Class, and Module").

Pulling it all together, here's what this function should look like when using type annotations and docstrings:

```
def careful_divide(a: float, b: float) -> float:
    """Divides a by b.

    Raises:
        ValueError: When the inputs cannot be divided.
    """
    try:
        return a / b
    except ZeroDivisionError:
        raise ValueError("Invalid inputs")

try:
    result = careful_divide(1, 0)
except ValueError:
    print("Invalid inputs")  # Expected
else:
    print(f"Result is {result:.1f}")

>>>
$ python3 -m mypy --strict example.py
Success: no issues found in 1 source file
```

Now the inputs, outputs, and exceptional behavior are all clear, and the chance of a caller doing the wrong thing is extremely low.

Things to Remember

✦ Functions that return None to indicate special meaning are error prone because None and many other values, such as zero and empty strings, evaluate to False in Boolean expressions.

✦ Raise exceptions to indicate special situations instead of returning None. Expect the calling code to handle exceptions properly when they're documented.

✦ Type annotations can be used to make it clear that a function will never return the value None, even in special situations.

Item 33: Know How Closures Interact with Variable Scope and nonlocal

Imagine that I want to sort a list of numbers but prioritize one group of numbers to come first. This pattern is useful when you're rendering a user interface and want important messages or exceptional events to be displayed before everything else. A common way to do this is to pass a helper function as the key argument to a list's sort method (see Item 100: "Sort by Complex Criteria Using the key Parameter" for details). The helper's return value will be used as the value for sorting each item in the list. The helper can check whether the given item is in the important group and can vary the sorting value accordingly:

```
def sort_priority(values, group):
    def helper(x):
        if x in group:
            return (0, x)
        return (1, x)

    values.sort(key=helper)
```

This function works for simple inputs:

```
numbers = [8, 3, 1, 2, 5, 4, 7, 6]
group = {2, 3, 5, 7}
sort_priority(numbers, group)
print(numbers)

>>>
[2, 3, 5, 7, 1, 4, 6, 8]
```

There are three reasons this function operates as expected:

✦ Python supports *closures*—that is, functions that refer to variables from the scope in which they were defined. This is why the `helper` function is able to access the `group` argument for the `sort_priority` function.

✦ Functions are *first-class* objects in Python, which means you can refer to them directly, assign them to variables, pass them as arguments to other functions, compare them in expressions and if statements, and so on. This is how the `sort` method can accept a closure function as the `key` argument.

✦ Python has specific rules for comparing sequences (including tuples). It first compares items at index zero; then, if those are equal, it compares items at index one; if they are still equal, it compares items at index two, and so on. This is why the return value from the `helper` closure causes the sort order to have two distinct groups.

It'd be nice if this function returned whether higher-priority items were seen at all so the user interface code could act accordingly. Adding such behavior seems straightforward. There's already a closure function for deciding which group each number is in. Why not also use the closure to flip a flag when high-priority items are seen? Then, the function could return the flag value after it's modified by the closure.

Here, I try to do that in a seemingly obvious way:

```python
def sort_priority2(numbers, group):
    found = False          # Flag initial value

    def helper(x):
        if x in group:
            found = True   # Flip the flag
            return (0, x)
        return (1, x)

    numbers.sort(key=helper)
    return found           # Flag final value
```

I can run the function on the same inputs as before:

```python
found = sort_priority2(numbers, group)
print("Found:", found)
print(numbers)
```

```
>>>
Found: False
[2, 3, 5, 7, 1, 4, 6, 8]
```

The sorted results are correct, which means items from group were definitely found in numbers. However, the found result returned by the function is False when it should be True. How could this happen?

When you reference a variable in an expression, the Python interpreter traverses the nested scopes to resolve the reference in this order:

1. The current function's scope

2. Any enclosing scopes (such as other containing functions)

3. The scope of the module that contains the code (also called the *global scope*)

4. The built-in scope (that contains functions like len and str)

If none of these places has defined a variable with the referenced name, then a NameError exception is raised:

```
foo = does_not_exist * 5
```

```
>>>
Traceback ...
NameError: name 'does_not_exist' is not defined
```

Assigning a value to a variable works differently. If the variable is already defined in the current scope, that name will take on the new value in that scope. If the variable doesn't exist in the current scope, Python treats the assignment as a variable definition. Critically, the scope of the newly defined variable is the function that contains the assignment, not an enclosing scope with an earlier assignment.

This assignment behavior explains the wrong return value of the sort_priority2 function. The found variable is assigned to True in the helper closure. The closure's assignment is treated as a new variable definition within the scope of helper, not as an assignment within the scope of sort_priority2:

```
def sort_priority2(numbers, group):
    found = False          # Scope: 'sort_priority2'

    def helper(x):
        if x in group:
            found = True    # Scope: 'helper' -- Bad!
```

```
            return (0, x)
        return (1, x)

    numbers.sort(key=helper)
    return found
```

This problem is sometimes called the *scoping bug* because it can be so surprising to newbies. But this behavior is the intended result: It prevents local variables in a function from polluting the containing module. Otherwise, every assignment in a function would put garbage into the global module scope. Not only would that be noise, but the interplay of the resulting global variables could cause obscure bugs.

In Python, there is special syntax for assigning data outside of a closure's scope. The `nonlocal` statement is used to indicate that scope traversal should happen upon assignment for a specific variable name. The only limit is that `nonlocal` won't traverse up to the module-level scope (to avoid polluting globals).

Here, I define the same function again, now using `nonlocal`:

```
def sort_priority3(numbers, group):
    found = False

    def helper(x):
        nonlocal found  # Added
        if x in group:
            found = True
            return (0, x)
        return (1, x)

    numbers.sort(key=helper)
    return found
```

Now the found flag works as expected:

```
found = sort_priority3(numbers, group)
print("Found:", found)
print(numbers)

>>>
Found: True
[2, 3, 5, 7, 1, 4, 6, 8]
```

The `nonlocal` statement makes it clear when data is being assigned out of a closure and into another scope. It's complementary to the `global` statement, which indicates that a variable's assignment should go directly into the module scope.

However, much as with the anti-pattern of global variables, I caution against using nonlocal for anything beyond simple functions. The side effects of nonlocal can be hard to follow. It's especially hard to understand in long functions where the nonlocal statements and assignments to associated variables are far apart.

When your usage of nonlocal starts getting complicated, it's better to wrap your state in a helper class. Here, I define a class that can be called like a function; it achieves the same result as the nonlocal approach by assigning an object's attribute during sorting (see Item 55: "Prefer Public Attributes over Private Ones"):

```
class Sorter:
    def __init__(self, group):
        self.group = group
        self.found = False

    def __call__(self, x):
        if x in self.group:
            self.found = True
            return (0, x)
        return (1, x)
```

It's a little longer than before, but it's much easier to reason about and extend if needed (see Item 48: "Accept Functions Instead of Classes for Simple Interfaces" for details on the __call__ special method). I can access the found attribute on the Sorter instance to get the result:

```
sorter = Sorter(group)
numbers.sort(key=sorter)
print("Found:", sorter.found)
print(numbers)

>>>
Found: True
[2, 3, 5, 7, 1, 4, 6, 8]
```

Things to Remember

✦ Closure functions can refer to variables from any of the enclosing scopes in which they were defined.

✦ By default, closures can't affect enclosing scopes by assigning variables.

+ Use the `nonlocal` statement to indicate when a closure can modify a variable in its enclosing scopes. Use the `global` statement to do the same thing for module-level names.

+ Avoid using `nonlocal` statements for anything beyond simple functions.

Item 34: Reduce Visual Noise with Variable Positional Arguments

Accepting a variable number of positional arguments can make a function call clearer and reduce visual noise. These positional arguments are often called *varargs* for short, or *star args*, in reference to the conventional name for the parameter `*args`. For example, say that I want to log some debugging information. With a fixed number of arguments, I would need a function that takes a message and a list of values:

```
def log(message, values):
    if not values:
        print(message)
    else:
        values_str = ", ".join(str(x) for x in values)
        print(f"{message}: {values_str}")

log("My numbers are", [1, 2])
log("Hi there", [])

>>>
My numbers are: 1, 2
Hi there
```

Having to pass an empty list when I have no values to log is cumbersome and noisy. It'd be better to leave out the second argument entirely. I can do this in Python by prefixing the last positional parameter name with `*`. The first parameter for the log message is required, and any number of subsequent positional arguments are optional. The function body doesn't need to change; only the callers do:

```
def log(message, *values):    # Changed
    if not values:
        print(message)
    else:
        values_str = ", ".join(str(x) for x in values)
        print(f"{message}: {values_str}")
```

```
log("My numbers are", 1, 2)
log("Hi there")                    # Changed

>>>
My numbers are: 1, 2
Hi there
```

This syntax works very similarly to the starred expressions used in unpacking assignment statements (see Item 16: "Prefer Catch-All Unpacking over Slicing" and Item 9: "Consider match for Destructuring in Flow Control; Avoid When if Statements Are Sufficient" for more examples).

If I already have a sequence (like a list) and I want to call a variadic function like log, I can do this by using the * operator. This instructs Python to pass items from the sequence as positional arguments to the function:

```
favorites = [7, 33, 99]
log("Favorite colors", *favorites)

>>>
Favorite colors: 7, 33, 99
```

There are two problems with accepting a variable number of positional arguments.

The first issue is that these optional positional arguments are always turned into a tuple before they are passed to your function. This means that if the caller of your function uses the * operator on a generator, it will be iterated until it's exhausted (see Item 43: "Consider Generators Instead of Returning Lists" for background). The resulting tuple includes every value from the generator, which could consume a lot of memory and cause the program to crash:

```
def my_generator():
    for i in range(10):
        yield i

def my_func(*args):
    print(args)

it = my_generator()
my_func(*it)

>>>
(0, 1, 2, 3, 4, 5, 6, 7, 8, 9)
```

Functions that accept *args are best for situations where you know the number of inputs in the argument list will be reasonably small. *args is ideal for function calls that pass many literals or variable names together. It's primarily for the convenience of the programmer who calls the function and the readability of the calling code.

The second issue with *args is that you can't add new positional arguments to a function in the future without migrating every caller. If you try to add a positional argument in the front of the argument list, existing callers will subtly break if they aren't updated. For example, here I add sequence as the first argument of the function and use it to render the log messages:

```
def log_seq(sequence, message, *values):
    if not values:
        print(f"{sequence} - {message}")
    else:
        values_str = ", ".join(str(x) for x in values)
        print(f"{sequence} - {message}: {values_str}")

log_seq(1, "Favorites", 7, 33)       # New with *args OK
log_seq(1, "Hi there")               # New message only OK
log_seq("Favorite numbers", 7, 33)   # Old usage breaks

>>>
1 - Favorites: 7, 33
1 - Hi there
Favorite numbers - 7: 33
```

The problem with the code above is that the third call to log used 7 as the message parameter because a sequence argument wasn't provided. Bugs like this are hard to track down because the code still runs without raising any exceptions. To avoid this possibility entirely, you should use keyword-only arguments when you want to extend functions that accept *args (see Item 37: "Enforce Clarity with Keyword-Only and Positional-Only Arguments"). To be even more defensive, you could also consider using type annotations (see Item 124: "Consider Static Analysis via typing to Obviate Bugs").

Things to Remember

✦ You can have functions accept a variable number of positional arguments by using *args in the def statement.

✦ You can use the items from a sequence as the positional arguments for a function with the * operator.

✦ Using the * operator with a generator may cause a program to run out of memory and crash.

✦ Adding new positional arguments to functions that accept *args can introduce hard-to-detect bugs.

Item 35: Provide Optional Behavior with Keyword Arguments

As in most other programming languages, in Python you may pass arguments by position when calling a function:

```
def remainder(number, divisor):
    return number % divisor

assert remainder(20, 7) == 6
```

All normal arguments to Python functions can also be passed by keyword, where the name of the argument is used in an assignment within the parentheses of a function call. Keyword arguments can be passed in any order, as long as all of the required positional arguments are specified. You can mix and match keyword and positional arguments. These calls are equivalent:

```
remainder(20, 7)
remainder(20, divisor=7)
remainder(number=20, divisor=7)
remainder(divisor=7, number=20)
```

Positional arguments must be specified before keyword arguments:

```
remainder(number=20, 7)

>>>
Traceback ...
SyntaxError: positional argument follows keyword argument
```

Each argument can be specified only once:

```
remainder(20, number=7)

>>>
Traceback ...
TypeError: remainder() got multiple values for argument
➥'number'
```

If you already have a dictionary object, and you want to use its contents to call a function like remainder, you can do this by using the ** operator. This instructs Python to pass the key-value pairs

from the dictionary as the corresponding keyword arguments of the
function:

```
my_kwargs = {
    "number": 20,
    "divisor": 7,
}
assert remainder(**my_kwargs) == 6
```

You can mix the ** operator with positional arguments or keyword
arguments in the function call as long as no argument is repeated:

```
my_kwargs = {
    "divisor": 7,
}
assert remainder(number=20, **my_kwargs) == 6
```

You can also use the ** operator multiple times if you know that the
dictionaries don't contain overlapping keys:

```
my_kwargs = {
    "number": 20,
}
other_kwargs = {
    "divisor": 7,
}
assert remainder(**my_kwargs, **other_kwargs) == 6
```

And if you'd like for a function to receive any named keyword argument, you can use the **kwargs catch-all parameter to collect those
arguments into a dict that you can then process (see Item 38: "Define
Function Decorators with functools.wraps" for when this is especially
useful):

```
def print_parameters(**kwargs):
    for key, value in kwargs.items():
        print(f"{key} = {value}")

print_parameters(alpha=1.5, beta=9, gamma=4)

>>>
alpha = 1.5
beta = 9
gamma = 4
```

The flexibility of keyword arguments provides three significant
benefits.

The first benefit is that keyword arguments make the function call clearer to new readers of the code. With the call remainder(20, 7), it's not evident which argument is number and which is divisor unless you look at the implementation of the remainder method. In the call with keyword arguments, number=20 and divisor=7 make it immediately obvious which parameter is being used for each purpose.

The second benefit of keyword arguments is that they can have default values specified in the function definition. This allows a function to provide additional capabilities when you need them, but you can accept the default behavior most of the time. This eliminates repetitive code and reduces noise.

For example, say that I want to compute the rate of fluid flowing into a vat. If the vat is also on a scale to measure its weight, then I could use the difference between two weight measurements at two different times to determine the flow rate:

```
def flow_rate(weight_diff, time_diff):
    return weight_diff / time_diff


weight_a = 2.5
weight_b = 3
time_a = 1
time_b = 4
weight_diff = weight_b - weight_a
time_diff = time_b - time_a
flow = flow_rate(weight_diff, time_diff)
print(f"{flow:.3} kg per second")

>>>
0.167 kg per second
```

In the typical case, it's useful to know the flow rate in kilograms per second. Other times, it'd be helpful to use the last sensor measurements to approximate larger time scales, like hours or days. I can provide this behavior in the same function by adding an argument for the time period scaling factor:

```
def flow_rate(weight_diff, time_diff, period):
    return (weight_diff / time_diff) * period
```

The problem is that now I need to specify the period argument every time I call the function, even in the common case of flow rate per second (where the period is 1):

```
flow_per_second = flow_rate(weight_diff, time_diff, 1)
```

To make this less noisy, I can give the `period` argument a default value:

```
def flow_rate(weight_diff, time_diff, period=1):  # Changed
    return (weight_diff / time_diff) * period
```

The `period` argument is now optional:

```
flow_per_second = flow_rate(weight_diff, time_diff)
flow_per_hour = flow_rate(weight_diff, time_diff, period=3600)
```

This works well for simple default values that are immutable; it gets tricky for complex default values like `list` instances and user-defined objects (see Item 36: "Use None and Docstrings to Specify Dynamic Default Arguments" for details).

The third reason to use keyword arguments is that they provide a powerful way to extend a function's parameters while remaining backward compatible with existing callers. This means you can provide additional functionality without having to migrate a lot of existing code, which reduces the chance of introducing bugs.

For example, say that I want to extend the `flow_rate` function above to calculate flow rates in weight units besides kilograms. I can do this by adding a new optional parameter that provides a conversion rate to alternative measurement units:

```
def flow_rate(weight_diff, time_diff,
              period=1, units_per_kg=1):
    return ((weight_diff * units_per_kg) / time_diff) * period
```

The default argument value for `units_per_kg` is 1, which makes the returned weight units remain kilograms. This means that all existing callers will see no change in behavior. New callers to `flow_rate` can specify the new keyword argument to see the new behavior:

```
pounds_per_hour = flow_rate(
    weight_diff,
    time_diff,
    period=3600,
    units_per_kg=2.2,
)
```

Providing backward compatibility using optional keyword arguments like this is also crucial for functions that accept `*args` (see Item 34: "Reduce Visual Noise with Variable Positional Arguments").

The only problem with this approach is that optional keyword arguments like `period` and `units_per_kg` may still be specified as positional arguments:

```
pounds_per_hour = flow_rate(weight_diff, time_diff, 3600, 2.2)
```

Supplying optional arguments positionally can be confusing because it isn't clear what the values 3600 and 2.2 correspond to. The best practice is to always specify optional arguments using the keyword names and never pass them as positional arguments. As a function author, you can also require that all callers use this more explicit keyword style to minimize potential errors (see Item 37: "Enforce Clarity with Keyword-Only and Positional-Only Arguments").

Things to Remember

✦ Function arguments can be specified by position or by keyword.

✦ Keywords make it clear what the purpose of each argument is when it would be confusing with only positional arguments.

✦ Keyword arguments with default values make it easy to add new behaviors to a function without needing to migrate all existing callers.

✦ Optional keyword arguments should always be passed by keyword instead of by position.

Item 36: Use None and Docstrings to Specify Dynamic Default Arguments

Sometimes it can be helpful to use a function call, a newly created object, or a container type (like an empty list) as a keyword argument's default value. For example, say that I want to print logging messages that are marked with the time of the logged event. In the default case, I want the message to include the time when the function was called. I might try the following approach, which assumes that the default value for the `when` keyword argument is reevaluated each time the function is called:

```
from time import sleep
from datetime import datetime

def log(message, when=datetime.now()):
    print(f"{when}: {message}")
```

```
log("Hi there!")
sleep(0.1)
log("Hello again!")

>>>
2024-06-28 22:44:32.157132: Hi there!
2024-06-28 22:44:32.157132: Hello again!
```

This doesn't work as expected. The timestamps are the same because datetime.now is executed only a single time: when the function is defined at module import time. A default argument value is evaluated only once per module load, which usually happens when a program starts up (see Item 98: "Lazy-Load Modules with Dynamic Imports to Reduce Startup Time" for details). After the module containing this code is loaded, the datetime.now() default argument expression will never be evaluated again.

The convention for achieving the desired result in Python is to provide a default value of None and to document the actual behavior in the docstring (see Item 118: "Write Docstrings for Every Function, Class, and Module" for background). When your code sees that the argument value is None, you allocate the default value accordingly:

```
def log(message, when=None):
    """Log a message with a timestamp.

    Args:
        message: Message to print.
        when: datetime of when the message occurred.
            Defaults to the present time.
    """
    if when is None:
        when = datetime.now()
    print(f"{when}: {message}")
```

Now the timestamps will be different:

```
log("Hi there!")
sleep(0.1)
log("Hello again!")

>>>
2024-06-28 22:44:32.446842: Hi there!
2024-06-28 22:44:32.551912: Hello again!
```

Using None for default argument values is especially important when the arguments are mutable. For example, say that I want to load a value that's encoded as JSON data; if decoding the data fails, I want an empty dictionary to be returned by default:

```
import json

def decode(data, default={}):
    try:
        return json.loads(data)
    except ValueError:
        return default
```

The problem here is similar to the problem in the `datetime.now` example above. The dictionary specified for `default` will be shared by all calls to decode because default argument values are evaluated only once (at module load time). This can cause extremely surprising behavior:

```
foo = decode("bad data")
foo["stuff"] = 5
bar = decode("also bad")
bar["meep"] = 1
print("Foo:", foo)
print("Bar:", bar)

>>>
Foo: {'stuff': 5, 'meep': 1}
Bar: {'stuff': 5, 'meep': 1}
```

You might expect two different dictionaries, each with a single key and value. But modifying one seems to also modify the other. The culprit is that foo and bar are both equal to the `default` parameter to the decode function. They are the same dictionary object:

```
assert foo is bar
```

The fix is to set the keyword argument default value to `None`, document the actual default value in the function's docstring, and act accordingly in the function body when the argument has the value `None`:

```
def decode(data, default=None):
    """Load JSON data from a string.

    Args:
        data: JSON data to decode.
        default: Value to return if decoding fails.
            Defaults to an empty dictionary.
    """
```

```
try:
    return json.loads(data)
except ValueError:
    if default is None:  # Check here
        default = {}
    return default
```

Now, running the same test code as before produces the expected result:

```
foo = decode("bad data")
foo["stuff"] = 5
bar = decode("also bad")
bar["meep"] = 1
print("Foo:", foo)
print("Bar:", bar)
assert foo is not bar
```

```
>>>
Foo: {'stuff': 5}
Bar: {'meep': 1}
```

This approach also works with type annotations (see Item 124: "Consider Static Analysis via typing to Obviate Bugs"). Here, the when argument is marked as having an optional value that is a datetime. Thus, the only two valid choices for when are None or a datetime object:

```
def log_typed(message: str, when: datetime | None = None) ->
            None:
    """Log a message with a timestamp.

    Args:
        message: Message to print.
        when: datetime of when the message occurred.
            Defaults to the present time.
    """
    if when is None:
        when = datetime.now()
    print(f"{when}: {message}")
```

Things to Remember

✦ A default argument value is evaluated only once: during function definition at module load time. This can cause odd behaviors for dynamic values (like function calls, newly created objects, and container types).

✦ Use None as a placeholder default value for a keyword argument that must have its actual default value initialized dynamically.

Document the intended default for the argument in the function's docstring. Check for the None argument value in the function body to trigger the correct default behavior.

✦ Using None to represent keyword argument default values also works correctly with type annotations.

Item 37: Enforce Clarity with Keyword-Only and Positional-Only Arguments

Passing arguments by keyword is a powerful feature of Python functions (see Item 35: "Provide Optional Behavior with Keyword Arguments"). Keyword arguments enable you to write flexible functions that will be clear to new readers of your code for many use cases.

For example, say that I want to divide one number by another while being very careful about special cases. Sometimes, I want to ignore ZeroDivisionError exceptions and return infinity instead. Other times, I want to ignore OverflowError exceptions and return zero instead. Here, I define a function with these options:

```python
def safe_division(
    number,
    divisor,
    ignore_overflow,
    ignore_zero_division,
):
    try:
        return number / divisor
    except OverflowError:
        if ignore_overflow:
            return 0
        else:
            raise
    except ZeroDivisionError:
        if ignore_zero_division:
            return float("inf")
        else:
            raise
```

Using this function is straightforward. This call ignores the float overflow from division and returns zero:

```python
result = safe_division(1.0, 10**500, True, False)
print(result)
>>>
0
```

This call ignores the error from dividing by zero and returns infinity:

```
result = safe_division(1.0, 0, False, True)
print(result)
```

```
>>>
inf
```

The problem is that it's easy to confuse the position of the two Boolean arguments that control the exception handling behavior. This can easily cause bugs that are hard to track down. One way to improve the readability of this code is to use keyword arguments. Using default keyword arguments (see Item 36: "Use None and Docstrings to Specify Dynamic Default Arguments"), the function can be overly cautious and can always re-raise exceptions:

```
def safe_division_b(
    number,
    divisor,
    ignore_overflow=False,        # Changed
    ignore_zero_division=False,   # Changed
):
    ...
```

Then, callers can use keyword arguments to specify which of the ignore flags they want to set for specific operations, overriding the default behavior:

```
result = safe_division_b(1.0, 10**500, ignore_overflow=True)
print(result)

result = safe_division_b(1.0, 0, ignore_zero_division=True)
print(result)
```

```
>>>
0
inf
```

The problem is, because these keyword arguments are optional behavior, there's nothing forcing callers of your functions to use keyword arguments for clarity. Even with the new definition of safe_division_b, I can still call it the old way with positional arguments:

```
assert safe_division_b(1.0, 10**500, True, False) == 0
```

With complex functions like this, it's better to require that callers are clear about their intentions by defining your functions with *keyword-only arguments*. These arguments can only be supplied by keyword, never by position.

Here, I redefine the `safe_division` function to accept keyword-only arguments. The `*` symbol in the argument list indicates the end of positional arguments and the beginning of keyword-only arguments (`*args` has the same effect; see Item 34: "Reduce Visual Noise with Variable Positional Arguments"):

```
def safe_division_c(
    number,
    divisor,
    *,   # Added
    ignore_overflow=False,
    ignore_zero_division=False,
):
    ...
```

Now, calling the function with positional arguments that correspond to the keyword arguments won't work:

```
safe_division_c(1.0, 10**500, True, False)
```

```
>>>
Traceback ...
TypeError: safe_division_c() takes 2 positional arguments but 4
➥were given
```

But keyword arguments and their default values will work as expected (ignoring an exception in one case and raising it in another):

```
result = safe_division_c(1.0, 0, ignore_zero_division=True)
assert result == float("inf")

try:
    result = safe_division_c(1.0, 0)
except ZeroDivisionError:
    pass  # Expected
```

However, a problem still remains with the `safe_division_c` version of this function: Callers may specify the first two required arguments (`number` and `divisor`) with a mix of positions and keywords:

```
assert safe_division_c(number=2, divisor=5) == 0.4
assert safe_division_c(divisor=5, number=2) == 0.4
assert safe_division_c(2, divisor=5) == 0.4
```

Later, I may decide to change the names of these first two arguments because of expanding needs or even just because my style preferences change:

```
def safe_division_d(
    numerator,     # Changed
    denominator,   # Changed
    *,
    ignore_overflow=False,
    ignore_zero_division=False
):
    ...
```

Unfortunately, this seemingly superficial change breaks all of the existing callers that specified the `number` or `divisor` arguments using keywords:

```
safe_division_d(number=2, divisor=5)
```

```
>>>
Traceback ...
TypeError: safe_division_d() got an unexpected keyword argument
➥'number'
```

This is especially problematic because I never intended for the keywords `number` and `divisor` to be part of an explicit interface for this function. These were just convenient parameter names that I chose for the implementation, and I didn't expect anyone to rely on them explicitly.

Python 3.8 introduces a solution to this problem, called *positional-only arguments*. These arguments can be supplied only by position and never by keyword (the opposite of the keyword-only arguments demonstrated above).

Here, I redefine the `safe_division` function to use positional-only arguments for the first two required parameters. The / symbol in the argument list indicates where positional-only arguments end:

```
def safe_division_e(
    numerator,
    denominator,
    /,  # Added
    *,
    ignore_overflow=False,
    ignore_zero_division=False,
):
    ...
```

I can verify that this function works when the required arguments are provided positionally:

```
assert safe_division_e(2, 5) == 0.4
```

But an exception is raised if keywords are used for the positional-only parameters:

```
safe_division_e(numerator=2, denominator=5)
```

```
>>>
Traceback ...
TypeError: safe_division_e() got some positional-only arguments
➥passed as keyword arguments: 'numerator, denominator'
```

Now, I can be sure that the first two required positional arguments in the definition of the safe_division_e function are decoupled from callers. I won't break anyone if I change the parameters' names again.

One notable consequence of keyword- and positional-only arguments is that any parameter name between the / and * symbols in the argument list may be passed either by position or by keyword (which is the default for all function arguments in Python). Depending on your API's style and needs, allowing both argument passing styles can increase readability and reduce noise. For example, here I've added another optional parameter to safe_division that allows callers to specify how many digits to use in rounding the result:

```
def safe_division_f(
    numerator,
    denominator,
    /,
    ndigits=10,   # Changed
    *,
    ignore_overflow=False,
    ignore_zero_division=False,
):
    try:
        fraction = numerator / denominator  # Changed
        return round(fraction, ndigits)     # Changed
    except OverflowError:
        if ignore_overflow:
            return 0
        else:
            raise
    except ZeroDivisionError:
        if ignore_zero_division:
            return float("inf")
        else:
            raise
```

Now, I can call this new version of the function in all of these different ways, since ndigits is an optional parameter that may be passed either by position or by keyword:

```
result = safe_division_f(22, 7)
print(result)

result = safe_division_f(22, 7, 5)
print(result)

result = safe_division_f(22, 7, ndigits=2)
print(result)

>>>
3.1428571429
3.14286
3.14
```

Things to Remember

✦ Keyword-only arguments force callers to supply certain arguments by keyword (instead of by position), which makes the intention of a function call clearer. Keyword-only arguments are defined after a * in the argument list (whether on its own or as part of variable arguments like *args).

✦ Positional-only arguments ensure that callers can't supply certain parameters using keywords, which helps reduce coupling. Positional-only arguments are defined before a single / in the argument list.

✦ Parameters between the / and * characters in the argument list may be supplied by position or keyword, which is the default for Python parameters.

Item 38: Define Function Decorators with functools.wraps

Python has special syntax for *decorators* that can be applied to functions. A decorator has the ability to run additional code before and after each call to a function it wraps. This means decorators can access and modify input arguments, return values, and raised exceptions. These capabilities can be useful for enforcing semantics, debugging, registering functions, and more.

For example, say that I want to print the arguments and return value of a function call. This can be especially helpful when debugging the stack of nested function calls from a recursive function. (Logging exceptions could be useful too; see Item 86: "Understand the Difference Between Exception and BaseException"). Here, I define such a decorator by using *args and **kwargs (see Item 34: "Reduce Visual Noise with Variable Positional Arguments" and Item 35: "Provide Optional Behavior with Keyword Arguments") to pass through all parameters to the wrapped function:

```
def trace(func):
    def wrapper(*args, **kwargs):
        args_repr = repr(args)
        kwargs_repr = repr(kwargs)
        result = func(*args, **kwargs)
        print(f"{func.__name__}"
              f"({args_repr}, {kwargs_repr}) "
              f"-> {result!r}")
        return result

    return wrapper
```

I can apply this decorator to a function by using the @ symbol:

```
@trace
def fibonacci(n):
    """Return the n-th Fibonacci number"""
    if n in (0, 1):
        return n
    return fibonacci(n - 2) + fibonacci(n - 1)
```

Using the @ symbol is equivalent to calling the decorator on the function it wraps and assigning the return value to the original name in the same scope:

```
fibonacci = trace(fibonacci)
```

The decorated function runs the `wrapper` code before and after fibonacci runs. It prints the arguments and return value at each level in the recursive stack:

```
fibonacci(4)

>>>
fibonacci((0,), {}) -> 0
fibonacci((1,), {}) -> 1
fibonacci((2,), {}) -> 1
fibonacci((1,), {}) -> 1
fibonacci((0,), {}) -> 0
fibonacci((1,), {}) -> 1
fibonacci((2,), {}) -> 1
fibonacci((3,), {}) -> 2
fibonacci((4,), {}) -> 3
```

This works well, but it has an unintended side effect. The value returned by the decorator—the function that's called above—doesn't think it's named `fibonacci`:

```
print(fibonacci)
```

```
>>>
<function trace.<locals>.wrapper at 0x104a179c0>
```

The cause of this isn't hard to see. The `trace` function returns the `wrapper` defined within its body. The `wrapper` function is what's assigned to the `fibonacci` name in the containing module because of the decorator. This behavior is problematic because it undermines tools that do introspection, such as debuggers (see Item 114: "Consider Interactive Debugging with pdb").

For example, the `help` built-in function is useless when called on the decorated `fibonacci` function. It should print out the docstring defined above (`"""Return the n-th Fibonacci number"""`), but it doesn't:

```
help(fibonacci)
```

```
>>>
Help on function wrapper in module __main__:

wrapper(*args, **kwargs)
```

Another problem is that object serializers (see Item 107: "Make pickle Serialization Maintainable with copyreg") break because they can't determine the location of the original function that was decorated:

```
import pickle
```

```
pickle.dumps(fibonacci)
```

```
>>>
Traceback ...
AttributeError: Can't pickle local object 'trace.<locals>.
➥wrapper'
```

The solution is to use the `wraps` helper function from the `functools` built-in module. This is a decorator that helps you write decorators. When you apply it to the `wrapper` function, it copies all of the important metadata about the inner function to the outer function. Here, I redefine the `trace` decorator using `wraps`:

```
from functools import wraps
```

```
def trace(func):
    @wraps(func)   # Changed
```

```
    def wrapper(*args, **kwargs):
        ...

    return wrapper

@trace
def fibonacci(n):
    ...
```

Now, running the `help` function produces the expected result, even though the function is decorated:

```
help(fibonacci)
>>>
Help on function fibonacci in module __main__:

fibonacci(n)
    Return the n-th Fibonacci number
```

The `pickle` object serializer also works:

```
print(pickle.dumps(fibonacci))

>>>
b'\x80\x04\x95\x1a\x00\x00\x00\x00\x00\x00\x00\x8c\x08__main__\
➡x94\x8c\tfibonacci\x94\x93\x94.'
```

Beyond these examples, Python functions have many other standard attributes (e.g., `__name__`, `__module__`, `__annotations__`) that must be preserved to maintain the interface of functions in the language. Using `wraps` ensures that you'll always get the correct behavior.

Things to Remember

✦ Decorators in Python are syntax to allow one function to modify another function at runtime.

✦ Using decorators can cause strange behaviors in tools that do introspection, such as debuggers.

✦ Use the `wraps` decorator from the `functools` built-in module when you define your own decorators to avoid any issues.

Item 39: Prefer `functools.partial` over `lambda` Expressions for Glue Functions

Many APIs in Python accept simple functions as part of their interface (see Item 100: "Sort by Complex Criteria Using the `key` Parameter,"

Item 27: "Prefer `defaultdict` over `setdefault` to Handle Missing Items in Internal State," and Item 24: "Consider `itertools` for Working with Iterators and Generators"). However, these interfaces can cause friction because they might fall short of your needs.

For example, the `reduce` function from the `functools` built-in module allows you to calculate one result from a near-limitless iterable of values. Here, I use `reduce` to calculate the sum of many log-scaled numbers (which effectively multiplies them):

```
def log_sum(log_total, value):
    log_value = math.log(value)
    return log_total + log_value

result = functools.reduce(log_sum, [10, 20, 40], 0)
print(math.exp(result))

>>>
8000.0
```

The problem is that you don't always have a function like `log_sum` that exactly matches the function signature required by `reduce`. For example, imagine that you simply had the parameters reversed—since it's an arbitrary choice anyway—with `value` first and `log_total` second. How could you easily fit this function to the required interface?

```
def log_sum_alt(value, log_total):   # Changed
    ...
```

One solution is to define a `lambda` function in an expression to reorder the input arguments to match what's required by `reduce`:

```
result = functools.reduce(
    lambda total, value: log_sum_alt(value, total),   # Reordered
    [10, 20, 40],
    0,
)
```

For one-offs, creating a `lambda` like this is fine. But if you find yourself doing this repeatedly and copying code, it's worth defining another helper function with reordered arguments that you can call multiple times:

```
def log_sum_for_reduce(total, value):
    return log_sum_alt(value, total)
```

Another situation where function interfaces are mismatched is when you need to pass along some additional information for use in

processing. For example, say I want to choose the base for the logarithm instead of always using natural log:

```
def logn_sum(base, logn_total, value):   # New first parameter
    logn_value = math.log(value, base)
    return logn_total + logn_value
```

In order to pass this function to reduce, I need to somehow provide
the base argument for every call. But reduce doesn't give me a way to
do this easily. Again, lambda can help here by allowing me to specify one parameter and pass through the rest. Here, I always provide
10 as the first argument to logn_sum in order to calculate a base-10
logarithm:

```
result = functools.reduce(
    lambda total, value: logn_sum(10, total, value),   # Changed
    [10, 20, 40],
    0,
)
print(math.pow(10, result))
```

```
>>>
8000.000000000004
```

This pattern of pinning some arguments to specific values while
allowing the rest of them to be passed normally is quite common with
functional-style code. This technique is often called *Currying* or *partial application*. The functools built-in module provides the partial
function to make this easy and more readable. It takes the function to
partially apply as the first argument followed by the pinned positional
arguments:

```
result = functools.reduce(
    functools.partial(logn_sum, 10),   # Changed
    [10, 20, 40],
    0,
)
```

partial also allows you to easily pin keyword arguments (see Item 35:
"Provide Optional Behavior with Keyword Arguments" and Item 37:
"Enforce Clarity with Keyword-Only and Positional-Only Arguments"
for background). For example, imagine that the logn_sum function
accepts base as a keyword-only argument, like this:

```
def logn_sum_last(logn_total, value, *, base=10):   # New kwarg
    logn_value = math.log(value, base)
    return logn_total + logn_value
```

Here, I use `partial` to pin the value of `base` to Euler's number:

```
import math

log_sum_e = functools.partial(logn_sum_last,
                              base=math.e)  # Pinned `base`
print(log_sum_e(3, math.e**10))
>>>
13.0
```

Achieving the same behavior is possible with a `lambda` expression, but it's verbose and error prone:

```
log_sum_e_alt = lambda *a, base=math.e, **kw: \
    logn_sum_last(*a, base=base, **kw)
```

`partial` also allows you to inspect which arguments have already been supplied, and the function being wrapped, which can be helpful for debugging:

```
print(log_sum_e.args, log_sum_e.keywords, log_sum_e.func)
>>>
() {'base': 2.718281828459045} <function logn_sum_last at
➥0x1033534c0>
```

In general, you should prefer using `partial` when it satisfies your use case because of these extra niceties. However, `partial` can't be used to reorder the parameters altogether, so that's one situation where `lambda` is preferable.

In many cases, a `lambda` or `partial` instance is still not enough, especially if you need to access or modify state as part of a simple function interface. Luckily, Python provides additional facilities, including closures, to make this possible (see Item 33: "Know How Closures Interact with Variable Scope and `nonlocal`" and Item 48: "Accept Functions Instead of Classes for Simple Interfaces").

Things to Remember

✦ `lambda` expressions can succinctly make two function interfaces compatible by reordering arguments or pinning certain parameter values.

✦ The `partial` function from the `functools` built-in is a general tool for creating functions with pinned positional and keyword arguments.

✦ Use `lambda` instead of `partial` if you need to reorder the arguments of a wrapped function.

Comprehensions and Generators

Many programs are built around processing lists, dictionary key/value pairs, and sets. Python provides a special syntax, called *comprehensions*, for succinctly iterating through these types and creating derivative data structures. Comprehensions can significantly increase the readability of code performing these common tasks and provide a number of other benefits.

This style of processing is extended to functions with *generators*, which enable a stream of values to be incrementally returned by a function. The result of a call to a generator function can be used anywhere an iterator is appropriate (e.g., for loops, starred unpacking expressions). Generators can improve performance, reduce memory usage, increase readability, and simplify implementations.

Item 40: Use Comprehensions Instead of `map` and `filter`

Python provides compact syntax for deriving a new list from another sequence or iterable. These expressions are called *list comprehensions*. For example, say that I want to compute the square of each number in a list. Here, I do this by using a simple for loop:

```
a = [1, 2, 3, 4, 5, 6, 7, 8, 9, 10]
squares = []
for x in a:
    squares.append(x**2)
print(squares)

>>>
[1, 4, 9, 16, 25, 36, 49, 64, 81, 100]
```

With a list comprehension, I can achieve the same outcome in a single line by specifying the expression for my computation along with the input sequence variable to loop over:

```
squares = [x**2 for x in a]  # List comprehension
print(squares)
```

```
>>>
[1, 4, 9, 16, 25, 36, 49, 64, 81, 100]
```

Unless you're applying a single-argument function, list comprehensions are clearer than the map built-in function for simple cases. map requires the creation of a lambda function for the computation (see Item 39: "Prefer functools.partial over lambda Expressions for Glue Functions"), which is visually noisy in comparison:

```
alt = map(lambda x: x**2, a)
```

Unlike map, list comprehensions let you easily filter items from the input list to remove corresponding outputs from the result. For example, say that I want to compute the squares of the numbers that are divisible by 2. Here, I do this by adding an if clause to the list comprehension after the loop:

```
even_squares = [x**2 for x in a if x % 2 == 0]
print(even_squares)
```

```
>>>
[4, 16, 36, 64, 100]
```

The filter built-in function can be used along with map to achieve the same outcome, but it is much harder to read due to nesting and boilerplate:

```
alt = map(lambda x: x**2, filter(lambda x: x % 2 == 0, a))
assert even_squares == list(alt)
```

Dictionaries and sets have their own equivalents of list comprehensions (called *dictionary comprehensions* and *set comprehensions*, respectively). These make it easy to create other types of derivative data structures when writing algorithms:

```
even_squares_dict = {x: x**2 for x in a if x % 2 == 0}
threes_cubed_set = {x**3 for x in a if x % 3 == 0}
print(even_squares_dict)
print(threes_cubed_set)
```

```
>>>
{2: 4, 4: 16, 6: 36, 8: 64, 10: 100}
{216, 729, 27}
```

Achieving the same outcome is possible with map and filter if you wrap each call with a corresponding constructor. These statements get so long that you have to break them up across multiple lines, which is even noisier and should be avoided:

```
alt_dict = dict(
    map(
        lambda x: (x, x**2),
        filter(lambda x: x % 2 == 0, a),
    )
)
alt_set = set(
    map(
        lambda x: x**3,
        filter(lambda x: x % 3 == 0, a),
    )
)
```

However, one benefit of the map and filter built-in functions is that they return iterators that incrementally produce one result at a time. This enables these functions to be composed together efficiently with minimal memory usage (see Item 43: "Consider Generators Instead of Returning Lists" and Item 24: "Consider itertools for Working with Iterators and Generators" for background). List comprehensions, in contrast, materialize the entire result upon evaluation, which consumes much more memory. Luckily, Python also provides a syntax that's very similar to list comprehensions that can create infinitely long, memory-efficient streams of values (see Item 44: "Consider Generator Expressions for Large List Comprehensions").

Things to Remember

✦ List comprehensions are clearer than the map and filter built-in functions because they don't require lambda expressions.

✦ List comprehensions allow you to easily skip items from the input list by using if clauses, a behavior that map doesn't support without help from filter.

✦ Dictionaries and sets may also be created using comprehensions.

✦ List comprehensions materialize the full result when evaluated, which can use a significant amount of memory compared to an iterator that produces each output incrementally.

Item 41: Avoid More Than Two Control Subexpressions in Comprehensions

Beyond basic usage (see Item 40: "Use Comprehensions Instead of `map` and `filter`"), comprehensions also support multiple levels of looping. For example, say that I want to simplify a matrix (a list containing other list instances) into one flat list of all items. Here, I do this with a list comprehension by including two `for` subexpressions. These subexpressions run in the order provided, from left to right:

```
matrix = [
    [1, 2, 3],
    [4, 5, 6],
    [7, 8, 9],
]
flat = [x for row in matrix for x in row]
print(flat)

>>>
[1, 2, 3, 4, 5, 6, 7, 8, 9]
```

This example is simple, readable, and a reasonable usage of multiple loops in a comprehension. Another reasonable usage of multiple loops involves replicating the two-level-deep layout of the input list. For example, say that I want to square the value in each cell of a two-dimensional matrix. This comprehension is noisier because of the extra [] characters, but it's still relatively easy to read:

```
squared = [[x**2 for x in row] for row in matrix]
print(squared)

>>>
[[1, 4, 9], [16, 25, 36], [49, 64, 81]]
```

If this comprehension included another loop, it would get so long that I'd have to split it over multiple lines:

```
my_lists = [
    [[1, 2, 3], [4, 5, 6]],
    ...
]
flat = [x for sublist1 in my_lists
        for sublist2 in sublist1
        for x in sublist2]
```

At this point, the multiline comprehension isn't much shorter than the alternative. Here, I produce the same result using normal loop statements. The indentation of this version makes the looping clearer than the three-level-list comprehension above:

```
flat = []
for sublist1 in my_lists:
    for sublist2 in sublist1:
        flat.extend(sublist2)
```

Comprehensions support multiple if conditions. Multiple conditions at the same loop level have an implicit and expression. For example, say that I want to filter a list of numbers to only even values greater than 4. These two list comprehensions are equivalent:

```
a = [1, 2, 3, 4, 5, 6, 7, 8, 9, 10]
b = [x for x in a if x > 4 if x % 2 == 0]
c = [x for x in a if x > 4 and x % 2 == 0]
```

Conditions can be specified at each level of looping after the for subexpression. For example, say that I want to filter a matrix so the only cells remaining are those divisible by 4 in rows that sum to 10 or higher. Expressing this with a list comprehension does not require a lot of code, but it is extremely difficult to read:

```
matrix = [
    [1, 2, 3],
    [4, 5, 6],
    [7, 8, 9],
]
filtered = [[x for x in row if x % 4 == 0]
            for row in matrix if sum(row) >= 10]
print(filtered)

>>>
[[4], [8]]
```

Although this example is a bit convoluted, in practice you'll see situations arise where such comprehensions seem like a good fit. I strongly encourage you to avoid using list, dictionary, or set comprehensions that look like this. The resulting code is very difficult for new readers to understand. The potential for confusion is especially great with a dictionary comprehension since it already needs an extra parameter to represent both the key and the value for each item.

The rule of thumb is to avoid using more than two control subexpressions in a comprehension. This could be two conditions, two loops, or one condition and one loop. As soon as it gets more complicated than that, you should use normal if and for statements and write a helper function (see Item 43: "Consider Generators Instead of Returning Lists").

Things to Remember

✦ Comprehensions support multiple levels of loops and multiple conditions per loop level.

✦ Comprehensions with more than two control subexpressions are very difficult to read and should be avoided.

Item 42: Reduce Repetition in Comprehensions with Assignment Expressions

A common pattern with comprehensions—including list, dictionary, and set variants—is the need to reference the same computation in multiple places. For example, say that I'm writing a program to manage orders for a fastener company. As new orders come in from customers, I need to be able to tell them whether or not I can fulfill their orders. Concretely, imagine that I need to verify that a request is sufficiently in stock and above the minimum threshold for shipping (e.g., in batches of 8), like this:

```
stock = {
    "nails": 125,
    "screws": 35,
    "wingnuts": 8,
    "washers": 24,
}

order = ["screws", "wingnuts", "clips"]

def get_batches(count, size):
    return count // size

result = {}
for name in order:
    count = stock.get(name, 0)
    batches = get_batches(count, 8)
    if batches:
        result[name] = batches

print(result)

>>>
{'screws': 4, 'wingnuts': 1}
```

Here, I implement this looping logic more succinctly by using a dictionary comprehension (see Item 40: "Use Comprehensions Instead of map and filter" for best practices):

```
found = {name: get_batches(stock.get(name, 0), 8)
         for name in order
         if get_batches(stock.get(name, 0), 8)}
print(found)

>>>
{'screws': 4, 'wingnuts': 1}
```

Although this code is more compact, the problem with it is that the get_batches(stock.get(name, 0), 8) expression is repeated. This hurts readability by adding visual noise and is technically unnecessary. The duplication also increases the likelihood of introducing a bug if the two expressions aren't kept in sync. For example, here I've changed the first get_batches call to have 4 as its second parameter instead of 8, which causes the results to be different:

```
has_bug = {name: get_batches(stock.get(name, 0), 4)   # Wrong
           for name in order
           if get_batches(stock.get(name, 0), 8)}

print("Expected:", found)
print("Found:    ", has_bug)

>>>
Expected: {'screws': 4, 'wingnuts': 1}
Found:    {'screws': 8, 'wingnuts': 2}
```

An easy solution to these problems is to use an assignment expression—often called the walrus operator—as part of the comprehension (see Item 8: "Prevent Repetition with Assignment Expressions" for background):

```
found = {name: batches for name in order
         if (batches := get_batches(stock.get(name, 0), 8))}
```

The assignment expression (batches := get_batches(...)) allows me to look up the value for each order key in the stock dictionary a single time, call get_batches once, and then store its corresponding value in the batches variable. I can then reference that variable elsewhere in the comprehension to construct the dictionary's contents instead of having to call get_batches a second time. Eliminating the redundant calls to get and get_batches may also improve performance by avoiding unnecessary computations for each item in order.

It's valid syntax to define an assignment expression in the value expression for a comprehension. But if you try to reference the variable it defines (tenth) in other parts of the comprehension, you might get an exception at runtime because of the order in which comprehensions are evaluated:

```
result = {name: (tenth := count // 10)
          for name, count in stock.items() if tenth > 0}
```

```
>>>
Traceback ...
NameError: name 'tenth' is not defined
```

You can fix this example by moving the assignment expression into the condition and then referencing the variable name it defined (tenth) in the comprehension's value expression:

```
result = {name: tenth for name, count in stock.items()
          if (tenth := count // 10) > 0}
print(result)
```

```
>>>
{'nails': 12, 'screws': 3, 'washers': 2}
```

When a comprehension uses walrus operators, any corresponding variable names will be leaked into the containing scope (see Item 33: "Know How Closures Interact with Variable Scope and nonlocal" for background):

```
half = [(squared := last**2)
        for count in stock.values()
        if (last := count // 2) > 10]
print(f"Last item of {half} is {last} ** 2 = {squared}")
```

```
>>>
Last item of [3844, 289, 144] is 12 ** 2 = 144
```

The leakage of these variable names is similar to what happens with a normal for loop:

```
for count in stock.values():
    last = count // 2
    squared = last**2

print(f"{count} // 2 = {last}; {last} ** 2 = {squared}")
```

```
>>>
24 // 2 = 12; 12 ** 2 = 144
```

However, this leakage behavior can be surprising because when comprehensions don't use assignment expressions, the loop variable names won't leak like that (see Item 20: "Never Use for Loop Variables After the Loop Ends" and Item 84: "Beware of Exception Variables Disappearing" for more background):

```
half = [count // 2 for count in stock.values()]
print(half)    # Works
print(count)   # Exception because loop variable didn't leak
```

```
>>>
[62, 17, 4, 12]
Traceback ...
NameError: name 'count' is not defined
```

Using an assignment expression also works the same way in generator expressions (see Item 44: "Consider Generator Expressions for Large List Comprehensions"). Here, I create an iterator of pairs containing the item name and the current count in stock instead of a dict instance:

```
found = ((name, batches) for name in order
         if (batches := get_batches(stock.get(name, 0), 8)))
print(next(found))
print(next(found))
```

```
>>>
('screws', 4)
('wingnuts', 1)
```

Things to Remember

✦ Assignment expressions make it possible for comprehensions and generator expressions to reuse the value from one condition elsewhere in the same comprehension, which can improve readability and performance.

✦ Although it's possible to use an assignment expression outside of a comprehension or generator expression's condition, you should avoid doing so because it doesn't work reliably.

✦ In comprehensions, variables from assignment expressions will leak into the enclosing scope; in contrast, comprehension loop variables don't leak.

Item 43: Consider Generators Instead of Returning Lists

The simplest choice for a function that produces a sequence of results is to return a list of items. For example, say that I want to find the index of every word in a string. Here, I accumulate results in a list by using the append method and return it at the end of the function:

```
def index_words(text):
    result = []
    if text:
        result.append(0)
    for index, letter in enumerate(text):
        if letter == " ":
            result.append(index + 1)
    return result
```

This works as expected for some sample input:

```
address = "Four score and seven years ago..."
result = index_words(address)
print(result[:10])

>>>
[0, 5, 11, 15, 21, 27, 31, 35, 43, 51]
```

There are two problems with the index_words function above.

The first problem is that the code is a bit dense and noisy. Each time a new result is found, I call the append method. The method call's bulk (result.append) deemphasizes the value being added to the list (index + 1). There is one line for creating the result list and another for returning it. While the function body contains around 130 characters (without whitespace), only around 75 characters are important.

A better way to write this function is by using a *generator*, which is a function that uses yield expressions to incrementally produce outputs. Here, I define a generator version of the function that achieves the same result as before:

```
def index_words_iter(text):
    if text:
        yield 0
    for index, letter in enumerate(text):
        if letter == " ":
            yield index + 1
```

When called, a generator function does not actually run but instead immediately returns an iterator. With each call to the next built-in function, the iterator advances the generator to its next yield expression. Each value passed to yield by the generator is returned by the iterator to the caller of next:

```
it = index_words_iter(address)
print(next(it))
print(next(it))
```

```
>>>
0
5
```

The index_words_iter function is significantly easier to read because all interactions with the result list have been eliminated. Results are passed to yield expressions instead. I can easily convert the iterator returned by the generator to a list by passing it to the list built-in function if necessary (see Item 44: "Consider Generator Expressions for Large List Comprehensions" for how this works):

```
result = list(index_words_iter(address))
print(result[:10])
```

```
>>>
[0, 5, 11, 15, 21, 27, 31, 35, 43, 51]
```

The second problem with index_words is that it requires all results to be stored in the list before being returned. For huge inputs, this can cause a program to run out of memory and crash.

In contrast, a generator version of this function can easily be adapted to take inputs of arbitrary length due to its bounded memory requirements. For example, here I define a generator that streams input from a file one line at a time and yields outputs one word at a time:

```
def index_file(handle):
    offset = 0
    for line in handle:
        if line:
            yield offset
        for letter in line:
            offset += 1
            if letter == " ":
                yield offset
```

The working memory for this function is limited to the maximum length of one line of input instead of the entire input file's contents. Here, I show that running the generator on a file input produces the same results (see Item 24: "Consider itertools for Working with Iterators and Generators" for more about the islice function):

```
with open("address.txt", "r") as f:
    it = index_file(f)
    results = itertools.islice(it, 0, 10)
    print(list(results))
```

```
>>>
[0, 5, 11, 15, 21, 27, 31, 35, 43, 51]
```

The only gotcha with defining generators like this is that the callers must be aware that the iterators returned are stateful and can't be reused (see Item 21: "Be Defensive when Iterating over Arguments").

Things to Remember

✦ Using generators can be clearer than the alternative of having a function return a list of accumulated results.

✦ The iterator returned by a generator produces the set of values passed to yield expressions within the generator function's body.

✦ A generator can produce a sequence of outputs for arbitrarily large inputs because its working memory doesn't include a materialization of all prior inputs and outputs.

Item 44: Consider Generator Expressions for Large List Comprehensions

One problem with list comprehensions (see Item 40: "Use Comprehensions Instead of map and filter") is that they create new list instances that may potentially contain an item for each value in their input sequences. This is fine for small inputs, but for large inputs, this behavior might consume significant amounts of memory and cause a program to crash.

For example, say that I want to read a file and return the number of characters on each line. Here, I use a list comprehension to implement this logic:

```
value = [len(x) for x in open("my_file.txt")]
print(value)
```

```
>>>
[100, 57, 15, 1, 12, 75, 5, 86, 89, 11]
```

This code requires holding the length of every line of the file in memory. If the file is absolutely enormous or perhaps a never-ending network socket, it won't work. To solve this issue, Python provides *generator expressions*, which build on the syntax of list comprehensions and the behavior of generators. Generator expressions don't materialize the whole output sequence when they're run. Instead, generator expressions evaluate to an iterator that yields one item at a time from the expression.

You create a generator expression by putting list-comprehension-like syntax between () characters. Here, I use a generator expression that is equivalent to the code above. However, the generator expression immediately evaluates to an iterator, doesn't make any forward progress, and has little memory overhead:

```
it = (len(x) for x in open("my_file.txt"))
print(it)
```

```
>>>
<generator object <genexpr> at 0x104f37510>
```

The returned iterator can be advanced one step at a time to produce the next output from the generator expression, as needed (using the next built-in function). I can consume as much of the generator expression as I want without risking a blowup in memory usage:

```
print(next(it))
print(next(it))
```

```
>>>
100
57
```

Another powerful outcome of generator expressions is that they can be composed together. Here, I take the iterator returned by the generator expression above and use it as the input for another generator expression:

```
roots = ((x, x**0.5) for x in it)
```

Each time I advance this iterator, it also advances the interior iterator, creating a domino effect of looping, evaluating expressions, and passing around inputs and outputs, all while being as memory efficient as possible:

```
print(next(roots))
```

```
>>>
(15, 3.872983346207417)
```

Code that chains generators together like this executes very quickly in Python. When you're looking for a way to compose functionality that's operating on a large stream of input, generator expressions are the best tool for the job (see Item 23: "Pass Iterators to any and all for Efficient Short-Circuiting Logic" and Item 24: "Consider `itertools` for Working with Iterators and Generators" for more examples). The only gotcha is that the iterators returned by generator expressions are stateful, so you must be careful not to use such an iterator more than once (see Item 21: "Be Defensive when Iterating over Arguments").

Things to Remember

✦ List comprehensions can cause problems for large inputs by using too much memory.

✦ Generator expressions avoid memory issues by producing outputs one at a time as iterators.

✦ Generator expressions can be composed by passing the iterator from one generator expression into the `for` subexpression of another.

✦ Generator expressions execute very quickly when chained together and are memory efficient.

Item 45: Compose Multiple Generators with `yield` `from`

Generators provide a variety of benefits (see Item 43: "Consider Generators Instead of Returning Lists") and solutions to common problems (see Item 21: "Be Defensive when Iterating over Arguments"). Generators are so useful that many programs start to look like layers of generators strung together.

For example, say that I have a graphical program that's using generators to animate the movement of images onscreen. To get the visual effect I'm looking for, I need the images to move quickly at first, pause temporarily, and then continue moving at a slower pace. Here, I define two generators that yield the expected onscreen deltas for each part of this animation:

```
def move(period, speed):
    for _ in range(period):
        yield speed

def pause(delay):
    for _ in range(delay):
        yield 0
```

To create the final animation, I need to combine `move` and `pause` together to produce a single sequence of onscreen deltas. Here, I do this by calling a generator for each step of the animation, iterating over each generator in turn, and then yielding the deltas from all of them in sequence:

```
def animate():
    for delta in move(4, 5.0):
        yield delta
    for delta in pause(3):
        yield delta
    for delta in move(2, 3.0):
        yield delta
```

Now, I can render those deltas onscreen as they're produced by the single animation generator:

```
def render(delta):
    print(f"Delta: {delta:.1f}")
    # Move the images onscreen
    ...

def run(func):
    for delta in func():
        render(delta)

run(animate)

>>>
Delta: 5.0
Delta: 5.0
Delta: 5.0
Delta: 5.0
Delta: 0.0
Delta: 0.0
Delta: 0.0
Delta: 3.0
Delta: 3.0
```

The problem with this code is the repetitive nature of the animate function. The redundancy of the for statements and yield expressions for each generator adds noise and reduces readability. This example includes only three nested generators, and it's already hurting clarity; a complex animation with a dozen phases or more would be extremely difficult to follow.

The solution to this problem is to use the yield from expression. This advanced generator feature allows you to yield all values from a nested generator before returning control to the parent generator. Here, I reimplement the animation function by using yield from:

```
def animate_composed():
    yield from move(4, 5.0)
    yield from pause(3)
    yield from move(2, 3.0)

run(animate_composed)
```

```
>>>
Delta: 5.0
Delta: 5.0
Delta: 5.0
Delta: 5.0
Delta: 0.0
Delta: 0.0
Delta: 0.0
Delta: 3.0
Delta: 3.0
```

The result is the same as before, but now the code is clearer and more intuitive. yield from essentially instructs the Python interpreter to do the nested for loop and yield expressions for you, resulting in slightly faster execution as well. If you find yourself composing generators, I strongly encourage you to use yield from when possible.

Things to Remember

✦ The yield from expression allows you to compose multiple nested generators together into a single combined generator.

✦ yield from eliminates the boilerplate required for manually iterating nested generators and yielding their outputs.

Item 46: Pass Iterators into Generators as Arguments Instead of Calling the send Method

yield expressions provide generator functions with a simple way to produce an iterable series of output values (see Item 43: "Consider Generators Instead of Returning Lists"). However, this channel appears to be unidirectional: There's no immediately obvious way to simultaneously stream data in and out of a generator as it runs. Having such bidirectional communication could be valuable in a variety of situations.

For example, say that I'm writing a program to transmit signals using a software-defined radio. Here, I use a function to generate an approximation of a sine wave with a given number of points:

```
import math

def wave(amplitude, steps):
    step_size = 2 * math.pi / steps
    for step in range(steps):
        radians = step * step_size
        fraction = math.sin(radians)
        output = amplitude * fraction
        yield output
```

Now, I can transmit the wave signal at a single specified amplitude by iterating over the wave generator:

```
def transmit(output):
    if output is None:
        print(f"Output is None")
    else:
        print(f"Output: {output:>5.1f}")

def run(it):
    for output in it:
        transmit(output)

run(wave(3.0, 8))

>>>
Output:    0.0
Output:    2.1
Output:    3.0
Output:    2.1
Output:    0.0
Output:   -2.1
Output:   -3.0
Output:   -2.1
```

This works fine for producing basic waveforms, but it can't be used to constantly vary the amplitude of the wave based on a separate input (i.e., as required to broadcast AM radio signals). I need a way to modulate the amplitude on each iteration of the generator.

Python generators support the send method, which upgrades yield expressions into a two-way channel. The send method can be used to provide streaming inputs to a generator at the same time it's yielding outputs. Normally, when iterating a generator, the value of the yield expression is None:

```
def my_generator():
    received = yield 1
    print(f"{received=}")

it = my_generator()
output = next(it)  # Get first generator output
print(f"{output=}")

try:
    next(it)         # Run generator until it exits
except StopIteration:
    pass

>>>
output=1
received=None
```

When I call the send method instead of iterating the generator with a for loop or the next built-in function, the supplied parameter becomes the value of the yield expression when the generator is resumed. However, when the generator first starts, a yield expression has not been encountered yet, so the only valid value for calling send initially is None. (Any other argument would raise an exception at runtime.) Here, I run the same generators as above but using send instead of next to progress them forward:

```
it = my_generator()
output = it.send(None)  # Get first generator output
print(f"{output=}")

try:
    it.send("hello!")    # Send value into the generator
except StopIteration:
    pass

>>>
output=1
received='hello!'
```

I can take advantage of this behavior in order to modulate the amplitude of the sine wave based on an input signal. First, I need to change the wave generator to save the amplitude returned by the yield expression and use it to calculate the next generated output:

```
def wave_modulating(steps):
    step_size = 2 * math.pi / steps
    amplitude = yield              # Receive initial amplitude
    for step in range(steps):
        radians = step * step_size
        fraction = math.sin(radians)
        output = amplitude * fraction
        amplitude = yield output   # Receive next amplitude
```

Then, I need to update the run function to stream the modulating amplitude into the wave_modulating generator on each iteration. The first input to send must be None since a yield expression would not have occurred within the generator yet:

```
def run_modulating(it):
    amplitudes = [None, 7, 7, 7, 2, 2, 2, 2, 10, 10, 10, 10, 10]
    for amplitude in amplitudes:
        output = it.send(amplitude)
        transmit(output)

run_modulating(wave_modulating(12))

>>>
Output is None
Output:    0.0
Output:    3.5
Output:    6.1
Output:    2.0
Output:    1.7
Output:    1.0
Output:    0.0
Output:   -5.0
Output:   -8.7
Output:  -10.0
Output:   -8.7
Output:   -5.0
```

This works; it properly varies the output amplitude based on the input signal. The first output is None, as expected, because a value for amplitude wasn't received by the generator until after the initial yield expression.

One problem with this code is that it's difficult for new readers to understand: Using `yield` on the right side of an assignment statement isn't intuitive, and it's hard to see the connection between `yield` and send without already knowing the details of this advanced generator feature.

Now, imagine that the program's requirements get more complicated. Instead of using a simple sine wave as my carrier, I need to use a complex waveform consisting of multiple signals in sequence. One way to implement this behavior is by composing multiple generators together with the `yield from` expression (see Item 45: "Compose Multiple Generators with `yield from`"). Here, I confirm that this works as expected in the simpler case where the amplitude is fixed:

```
def complex_wave():
    yield from wave(7.0, 3)
    yield from wave(2.0, 4)
    yield from wave(10.0, 5)

run(complex_wave())

>>>
Output:    0.0
Output:    6.1
Output:   -6.1
Output:    0.0
Output:    2.0
Output:    0.0
Output:   -2.0
Output:    0.0
Output:    9.5
Output:    5.9
Output:   -5.9
Output:   -9.5
```

Given that the `yield from` expression handles the simpler case, you may expect it to also work properly along with the generator send method. Here, I try to use `yield from` to compose multiple calls to the wave_modulating generator (that uses send):

```
def complex_wave_modulating():
    yield from wave_modulating(3)
    yield from wave_modulating(4)
    yield from wave_modulating(5)

run_modulating(complex_wave_modulating())
```

```
>>>
Output is None
Output:    0.0
Output:    6.1
Output:   -6.1
Output is None
Output:    0.0
Output:    2.0
Output:    0.0
Output:  -10.0
Output is None
Output:    0.0
Output:    9.5
Output:    5.9
```

This works to some extent, but the result contains a big surprise: There are many None values in the output! Why does this happen? When each yield from expression finishes iterating over a nested generator, it moves on to the next one. Each nested generator starts with a bare yield expression—one without a value—in order to receive the initial amplitude from a generator send method call. This causes the parent generator to output a None value when it transitions between child generators.

This means that your assumptions about how the yield from and send features behave individually will be broken if you try to use them together. Although it's possible to work around this None problem by increasing the complexity of the run_modulating function, it's not worth the trouble. It's already difficult for new readers of the code to understand how send works. This surprising gotcha with yield from makes it even worse. My advice is to avoid the send method entirely and go with a simpler approach.

The easiest solution is to pass an iterator into the wave function. The iterator should return an input amplitude each time the next built-in function is called on it. This arrangement ensures that each generator is progressed in a cascade as inputs and outputs are processed (see Item 44: "Consider Generator Expressions for Large List Comprehensions" and Item 23: "Pass Iterators to any and all for Efficient Short-Circuiting Logic" for other examples):

```
def wave_cascading(amplitude_it, steps):
    step_size = 2 * math.pi / steps
    for step in range(steps):
        radians = step * step_size
        fraction = math.sin(radians)
```

```
            amplitude = next(amplitude_it)  # Get next input
            output = amplitude * fraction
            yield output
```

I can pass the same iterator into each of the generator functions that I'm trying to compose together with yield from. Iterators are stateful, and thus each of the nested generators picks up where the previous generator left off (see Item 21: "Be Defensive when Iterating over Arguments" for background):

```
def complex_wave_cascading(amplitude_it):
    yield from wave_cascading(amplitude_it, 3)
    yield from wave_cascading(amplitude_it, 4)
    yield from wave_cascading(amplitude_it, 5)
```

Now, I can run the composed generator by simply passing in an iterator from the amplitudes list:

```
def run_cascading():
    amplitudes = [7, 7, 7, 2, 2, 2, 2, 10, 10, 10, 10, 10]
    it = complex_wave_cascading(iter(amplitudes))  # Iterator
    for amplitude in amplitudes:
        output = next(it)
        transmit(output)


run_cascading()

>>>
Output:    0.0
Output:    6.1
Output:   -6.1
Output:    0.0
Output:    2.0
Output:    0.0
Output:   -2.0
Output:    0.0
Output:    9.5
Output:    5.9
Output:   -5.9
Output:   -9.5
```

The best part about this approach is that the input iterator can come from anywhere and could be completely dynamic (e.g., implemented using a generator function or composed; see Item 24: "Consider itertools for Working with Iterators and Generators"). The only downside is that this code assumes that the input generator is thread safe, which may not be the case. If you need to cross thread boundaries, async functions may be a better fit (see Item 77: "Mix Threads and Coroutines to Ease the Transition to asyncio").

Things to Remember

✦ The send method can be used to inject data into a generator by giving the yield expression a value that can be assigned to a variable.

✦ Using send with yield from expressions may cause surprising behavior, such as None values appearing at unexpected times in the generator output.

✦ Providing an input iterator to a set of composed generators is a better approach than using the send method, which should be avoided.

Item 47: Manage Iterative State Transitions with a Class Instead of the Generator throw Method

In addition to yield from expressions (see Item 45: "Compose Multiple Generators with yield from") and the send method (see Item 46: "Pass Iterators into Generators as Arguments Instead of Calling the send Method"), another advanced generator feature is the throw method for re-raising Exception instances within generator functions. The way throw works is simple: When the method is called, the next occurrence of a yield expression inside the generator re-raises the provided Exception instance after its output is received instead of continuing normally. Here, I show a simple example of this behavior in action:

```
class MyError(Exception):
    pass

def my_generator():
    yield 1
    yield 2
    yield 3

it = my_generator()
print(next(it))                          # Yields 1
print(next(it))                          # Yields 2
print(it.throw(MyError("test error")))   # Raises

>>>
1
2
Traceback ...
MyError: test error
```

When you call throw, the generator function may catch the injected exception with a standard try/except compound statement that surrounds the last yield expression that was executed (see Item 80: "Take Advantage of Each Block in try/except/else/finally" for more about exception handling):

```
def my_generator():
    yield 1

    try:
        yield 2
    except MyError:
        print("Got MyError!")
    else:
        yield 3

    yield 4

it = my_generator()
print(next(it))                         # Yields 1
print(next(it))                         # Yields 2
print(it.throw(MyError("test error")))  # Yields 4

>>>
1
2
Got MyError!
4
```

This functionality provides a two-way communication channel between a generator and its caller that can be useful in certain situations. For example, imagine that I need a timer program that supports sporadic resets. Here, I implement this behavior by defining a generator that relies on Reset exceptions to be raised when the yield expression is evaluated:

```
class Reset(Exception):
    pass

def timer(period):
    current = period
    while current:
        try:
            yield current
        except Reset:
```

```
        print("Resetting")
        current = period
    else:
        current -= 1
```

Whenever the throw method is called on the generator with a Reset exception, the counter is restarted in the except block. Here, I define a driver function that iterates the timer generator, announces progress at each step, and injects reset events that might be caused by an externally polled input (such as a button):

```
def check_for_reset():
    # Poll for external event
    ...

def announce(remaining):
    print(f"{remaining} ticks remaining")

def run():
    it = timer(4)
    while True:
        try:
            if check_for_reset():
                current = it.throw(Reset())
            else:
                current = next(it)
        except StopIteration:
            break
        else:
            announce(current)

run()

>>>
4 ticks remaining
3 ticks remaining
2 ticks remaining
Resetting
4 ticks remaining
3 ticks remaining
Resetting
4 ticks remaining
3 ticks remaining
2 ticks remaining
1 ticks remaining
```

This code works as expected, but it's much harder to read than necessary. The various levels of nesting required to catch StopIteration exceptions or decide which function to call make the code noisy.

A simpler approach to implementing this functionality is to create a basic class to manage the timer's state and enable state transitions. Here, I define a class with a tick method to step the timer, a reset method to restart the clock, and the __bool__ special method to check whether the timer has elapsed (see Item 57: "Inherit from collections.abc Classes for Custom Container Types" for background):

```
class Timer:
    def __init__(self, period):
        self.current = period
        self.period = period

    def reset(self):
        print("Resetting")
        self.current = self.period

    def tick(self):
        before = self.current
        self.current -= 1
        return before

    def __bool__(self):
        return self.current > 0
```

Now, the run method can use the Timer object as the test expression in the while statement; the code in the loop body is much easier to follow because of the reduction in the levels of nesting:

```
def run():
    timer = Timer(4)
    while timer:
        if check_for_reset():
            timer.reset()

        announce(timer.tick())

run()

>>>
4 ticks remaining
3 ticks remaining
2 ticks remaining
```

```
Resetting
4 ticks remaining
3 ticks remaining
Resetting
4 ticks remaining
3 ticks remaining
2 ticks remaining
1 ticks remaining
```

The output matches the earlier version using throw, but this implementation is much easier to understand, especially for new readers of the code. I suggest that you avoid using throw entirely and instead use a stateful class if you need this type of exceptional behavior (see Item 89: "Always Pass Resources into Generators and Have Callers Clean Them Up Outside" for another reason). Otherwise, if you really need more advanced cooperation between generator-like functions, it's worth considering Python's asynchronous features (see Item 75: "Achieve Highly Concurrent I/O with Coroutines").

Things to Remember

✦ The throw method can be used to re-raise an exception within a generator at the position of the most recently executed yield expression.

✦ Using throw harms readability because it requires additional nesting and boilerplate in order to raise and catch exceptions.

✦ A better approach is to simply define a stateful class that provides methods for iteration and state transitions.

Classes and Interfaces

As an object-oriented programming language, Python supports a full range of features, such as inheritance, polymorphism, and encapsulation. Getting things done in Python often requires writing new classes and defining how they interact through their interfaces and relationships.

Classes and inheritance make it easy to express a Python program's intended behaviors with objects. They allow you to improve and expand functionality over time. They provide flexibility in an environment of changing requirements. Knowing how to use classes and inheritance well enables you to write maintainable code.

Python is also a multi-paradigm language that encourages functional-style programming. Function objects are first class, meaning they can be passed around like normal variables. Python also allows you to use a mix of object-oriented-style and functional-style features in the same program, which can be even more powerful than each style on its own.

Item 48: Accept Functions Instead of Classes for Simple Interfaces

Many of Python's built-in APIs allow you to customize behavior by passing in a function. These *hooks* are used by APIs to call back your code while they execute. For example, the list type's sort method takes an optional key argument that's used to determine each index's value for sorting (see Item 100: "Sort by Complex Criteria Using the key Parameter" for details). Here I sort a list of names based on their lengths by providing the len built-in function as the key hook:

```
names = ["Socrates", "Archimedes", "Plato", "Aristotle"]
names.sort(key=len)
print(names)
```

```
>>>
['Plato', 'Socrates', 'Aristotle', 'Archimedes']
```

In other languages, you might expect hooks to be defined by an abstract class. In Python, many hooks are just stateless functions with well-documented arguments and return values. Functions are ideal for hooks because they are easier to describe and simpler to implement than classes. Functions work as hooks because Python has *first-class* functions: Functions and methods can be passed around and referenced like any other value in the language.

For example, say that I want to customize the behavior of the defaultdict class (see Item 27: "Prefer defaultdict over setdefault to Handle Missing Items in Internal State" for background). This data structure allows you to supply a function that will be called with no arguments each time a missing key is accessed. The function must return the default value that the missing key should have in the dictionary. Here I define a hook that logs each time a key is missing and returns 0 for the default value:

```
def log_missing():
    print("Key added")
    return 0
```

Given an initial dictionary and a set of desired increments, I can cause the log_missing function to run and print twice (for "red" and "orange"):

```
from collections import defaultdict

current = {"green": 12, "blue": 3}
increments = [
    ("red", 5),
    ("blue", 17),
    ("orange", 9),
]
result = defaultdict(log_missing, current)
print("Before:", dict(result))
for key, amount in increments:
    result[key] += amount
print("After: ", dict(result))
```

```
>>>
Before: {'green': 12, 'blue': 3}
Key added
Key added
After:  {'green': 12, 'blue': 20, 'red': 5, 'orange': 9}
```

Enabling functions like `log_missing` to be supplied helps APIs separate side effects from deterministic behavior. For example, say that I now want the default value hook passed to `defaultdict` to count the total number of missing keys. One way to achieve this is by using a stateful closure (see Item 33: "Know How Closures Interact with Variable Scope and `nonlocal`" for details). Here I define a helper function that uses such a closure as the default value hook:

```
def increment_with_report(current, increments):
    added_count = 0

    def missing():
        nonlocal added_count  # Stateful closure
        added_count += 1
        return 0

    result = defaultdict(missing, current)
    for key, amount in increments:
        result[key] += amount

    return result, added_count
```

Running this function produces the expected result (2), even though the `defaultdict` instance has no idea that the `missing` hook maintains state in the added_count closure variable:

```
result, count = increment_with_report(current, increments)
assert count == 2
```

The problem with defining a closure for stateful hooks is that it's harder to read than the stateless function example. Another approach is to define a small class that encapsulates the state you want to track:

```
class CountMissing:
    def __init__(self):
        self.added = 0

    def missing(self):
        self.added += 1
        return 0
```

In other languages, you might expect that now `defaultdict` would have to be modified to accommodate the interface of `CountMissing`. But in Python, thanks to first-class functions, you can reference the `CountMissing.missing` method directly on an object and pass it to defaultdict as the default value hook. It's trivial to have an object instance's method satisfy a function interface:

```
counter = CountMissing()
result = defaultdict(counter.missing, current)  # Method ref
for key, amount in increments:
    result[key] += amount
assert counter.added == 2
```

Using a helper class like this to provide the behavior of a stateful closure is clearer than using the increment_with_report function, as above. However, in isolation, it's still not immediately obvious what the purpose of the CountMissing class is. Who constructs a CountMissing object? Who calls the missing method? Will the class need other public methods to be added in the future? Until you see its usage with defaultdict, the class is a bit of a mystery.

To clarify this situation, Python classes can define the __call__ special method. __call__ allows an object to be called just like a function. It also causes the callable built-in function to return True for such an instance, just like a normal function or method. All objects that can be executed in this manner are referred to as *callables*:

```
class BetterCountMissing:
    def __init__(self):
        self.added = 0

    def __call__(self):
        self.added += 1
        return 0

counter = BetterCountMissing()
assert counter() == 0
assert callable(counter)
```

Here I use a BetterCountMissing instance as the default value hook for a defaultdict to track the number of missing keys that were added:

```
counter = BetterCountMissing()
result = defaultdict(counter, current)  # Relies on __call__
for key, amount in increments:
    result[key] += amount
assert counter.added == 2
```

This is much clearer than the CountMissing.missing example. The __call__ method indicates that a class's instances will be used somewhere a function argument would also be suitable (like API hooks). It directs new readers of the code to the entry point that's responsible for the class's primary behavior. It provides a strong hint that the goal of the class is to act as a stateful closure.

Best of all, defaultdict still has no view into what's going on when you use __call__. All that defaultdict requires is a callable for the default value hook. Python provides many different ways to satisfy a simple function interface, and you can choose the one that works best for what you need to accomplish.

Things to Remember

✦ Instead of defining and instantiating classes, you can often simply use functions for simple interfaces between components in Python.

✦ References to functions and methods in Python are first class, meaning they can be used in expressions (like any other type).

✦ The __call__ special method enables instances of a class to be called like plain Python functions and pass callable checks.

✦ When you need a function to maintain state, consider defining a class that provides the __call__ method instead of implementing a stateful closure function.

Item 49: Prefer Object-Oriented Polymorphism over Functions with isinstance Checks

Imagine that I want to create a pocket calculator that receives simple formulas as input and computes the solution. To do this, I would normally tokenize and parse the provided text and create an *abstract syntax tree* (AST) to represent the operations to perform, similar to what the Python compiler does when it's loading programs. For example, here I define three AST classes for the addition and multiplication of two integers:

```
class Integer:
    def __init__(self, value):
        self.value = value


class Add:
    def __init__(self, left, right):
        self.left = left
        self.right = right


class Multiply:
    def __init__(self, left, right):
        self.left = left
        self.right = right
```

For a basic equation like 2 + 9, I can create the AST (bypassing tokenization and parsing) by directly instantiating objects:

```
tree = Add(
    Integer(2),
    Integer(9),
)
```

A recursive function can be used to evaluate an AST like this. For each type of operation it might encounter, I need to add another branch to one compound `if` statement. I can use the `isinstance` built-in function to direct control flow based on the type of AST object being evaluated (see Item 9: "Consider `match` for Destructuring in Flow Control; Avoid When `if` Statements Are Sufficient" for another way to do this):

```
def evaluate(node):
    if isinstance(node, Integer):
        return node.value
    elif isinstance(node, Add):
        return evaluate(node.left) + evaluate(node.right)
    elif isinstance(node, Multiply):
        return evaluate(node.left) * evaluate(node.right)
    else:
        raise NotImplementedError
```

And indeed, this approach to interpreting the AST—often called *tree walking*—works as expected:

```
print(evaluate(tree))
>>>
11
```

By calling the same evaluate function for every type of node, the system can support arbitrary nesting without additional complexity. For example, here I define an AST for the equation (3 + 5) * (4 + 7) and evaluate it without having to make any other code changes:

```
tree = Multiply(
    Add(Integer(3), Integer(5)),
    Add(Integer(4), Integer(7)),
)
print(evaluate(tree))

>>>
88
```

Now, imagine that the number of nodes I need to consider in the tree is significantly more than three. I need to handle subtraction, division, logarithms, and on and on. Mathematics has an enormous surface

area, and there could be hundreds of node types. If I need to do everything in this one evaluate function, it's going to get extremely long.
Even if I add helper functions and call them inside the elif blocks,
the overall if compound statement would be huge. There must be a
better way.

One common approach to solving this problem is *object-oriented programming (OOP)*. Instead of having one function that does everything
for all types of objects, you encapsulate the functionality for each type
right next to its data (in methods). Then you rely on *polymorphism* to
dynamically dispatch method calls to the right subclass implementation at runtime. This has the same effect as the if compound statement and isinstance checks but does it in a way that doesn't require
defining everything in one gigantic function.

For this pocket calculator example, using OOP would begin with
defining a superclass (see Item 53: "Initialize Parent Classes with
super" for background) with the methods that should be common
among all objects in the AST:

```
class Node:
    def evaluate(self):
        raise NotImplementedError
```

Each type of node would need to implement the evaluate method to
compute the result that corresponds to the data contained within the
object. Here I define this method for integers:

```
class IntegerNode(Node):
    def __init__(self, value):
        self.value = value

    def evaluate(self):
        return self.value
```

And here's the implementation of evaluate for addition and multiplication operations:

```
class AddNode(Node):
    def __init__(self, left, right):
        self.left = left
        self.right = right

    def evaluate(self):
        left = self.left.evaluate()
        right = self.right.evaluate()
        return left + right
```

```
class MultiplyNode(Node):
    def __init__(self, left, right):
        self.left = left
        self.right = right

    def evaluate(self):
        left = self.left.evaluate()
        right = self.right.evaluate()
        return left * right
```

Creating objects representing the AST is straightforward, as before, but this time I can directly call the evaluate method on the tree object instead of having to use a separate helper function:

```
tree = MultiplyNode(
    AddNode(IntegerNode(3), IntegerNode(5)),
    AddNode(IntegerNode(4), IntegerNode(7)),
)
print(tree.evaluate())

>>>
88
```

The way this works is that the call to tree.evaluate will call the MultiplyNode.evaluate method with the tree instance. Then the AddNode.evaluate method will be called for the left node, which in turn calls IntegerNode.evaluate for values 3 and 5. After that, the AddNode.evaluate method is called for the right node, which similarly calls IntegerNode.evaluate for values 4 and 7. Critically, all of the decisions on which evaluate method implementation to call for each Node subclass occur at runtime. This is the key benefit of object-oriented polymorphism.

Later, I might need to extend the pocket calculator with more features. For example, I could add the ability for the calculator to print the formula that was inputted but with pretty formatting that's consistent and easy to read. With OOP, I'd accomplish this by adding another abstract method to the superclass and implement it in each of the subclasses. Here I add the pretty method for this new purpose:

```
class NodeAlt:
    def evaluate(self):
        raise NotImplementedError

    def pretty(self):
        raise NotImplementedError
```

The implementation for integers is very simple:

```
class IntegerNodeAlt(NodeAlt):
    ...

    def pretty(self):
        return repr(self.value)
```

The add and multiply operations descend into their left and right branches to produce a formatted result:

```
class AddNodeAlt(NodeAlt):
    ...

    def pretty(self):
        left_str = self.left.pretty()
        right_str = self.right.pretty()
        return f"({left_str} + {right_str})"


class MultiplyNodeAlt(NodeAlt):
    ...

    def pretty(self):
        left_str = self.left.pretty()
        right_str = self.right.pretty()
        return f"({left_str} * {right_str})"
```

Much as with the evaluate method above, I can call the pretty method on the tree root in order to format the whole AST as a string:

```
tree = MultiplyNodeAlt(
    AddNodeAlt(IntegerNodeAlt(3), IntegerNodeAlt(5)),
    AddNodeAlt(IntegerNodeAlt(4), IntegerNodeAlt(7)),
)
print(tree.pretty())

>>>
((3 + 5) * (4 + 7))
```

With OOP you can add more and more AST methods and subclasses as the needs of your program grow. It's not necessary to maintain one enormous function with dozens of isinstance checks. Each of the types can have its own self-contained implementation, which makes the code relatively easy to organize, extend, and test. Python also provides many additional features to make polymorphic code more useful (see Item 52: "Use @classmethod Polymorphism to Construct Objects Generically" and Item 57: "Inherit from collections.abc Classes for Custom Container Types").

However, it's also important to understand that OOP has serious limitations when solving certain types of problems, especially in large programs (see Item 50: "Consider functtools.singledispatch for Functional-Style Programming Instead of Object-Oriented Polymorphism").

Things to Remember

✦ Python programs can use the isinstance built-in function to alter behavior at runtime based on the type of objects.

✦ Polymorphism is an object-oriented programming (OOP) technique for dispatching a method call to the most specific subclass implementation at runtime.

✦ Code that uses polymorphism among many classes instead of isinstance checks can be much easier to read, maintain, extend, and test.

Item 50: Consider functools.singledispatch for Functional-Style Programming Instead of Object-Oriented Polymorphism

In the pocket calculator example from Item 49: "Prefer Object-Oriented Polymorphism over Functions with isinstance Checks," I showed how object-oriented programming (OOP) can make it easier to vary behavior based on the type of an object. At the end, I had a hierarchy of classes with different method implementations, like this:

```
class NodeAlt:
    def evaluate(self):
        raise NotImplementedError

    def pretty(self):
        raise NotImplementedError

class IntegerNodeAlt(NodeAlt):
    def __init__(self, value):
        self.value = value

    def evaluate(self):
        return self.value

    def pretty(self):
        return repr(self.value)
```

```
class AddNodeAlt(NodeAlt):
    ...


class MultiplyNodeAlt(NodeAlt):
    ...
```

This made it possible to call the recursive methods evaluate and pretty on the root of an *abstract syntax tree* (*AST*) that represents the calculation to perform:

```
tree = MultiplyNodeAlt(
    AddNodeAlt(IntegerNodeAlt(3), IntegerNodeAlt(5)),
    AddNodeAlt(IntegerNodeAlt(4), IntegerNodeAlt(7)),
)
print(tree.evaluate())
print(tree.pretty())

>>>
19
((3 + 5) * (4 + 7))
```

Now, imagine that instead of there being 2 methods required by the superclass, there were 25 of them: One method might simplify an equation; another would check for undefined variables; yet another could calculate the derivative; still another would produce LaTeX syntax; and so on. In the typical approach to OOP, I would add 25 new methods to each class that contains a node type's data. This would make the class definition very large, especially considering all of the helper functions and supporting data structures that might be required. With so much code, I'd want to split these node class definitions across multiple modules (e.g., one file per node type) to improve code organization:

```
class NodeAlt2:
    def evaluate(self):
        ...

    def pretty(self):
        ...

    def solve(self):
        ...

    def error_check(self):
        ...
```

```
def derivative(self):
    ...

# And 20 more methods...
```

Unfortunately, this type of module-per-class code organization can cause serious maintainability problems in production systems. The critical issue is that all of the 25 new methods might actually be quite different from one other, even though they are somehow related to a pocket calculator. When you're editing and debugging code, the view you need is within each of the larger, independent systems (e.g., solving, error checking), but with OOP these systems must be implemented across all of the classes. That means that in practice, for this hypothetical example, the OOP approach could cause you to jump between 25 different files in order to accomplish simple programming tasks. The code appears to be organized along the wrong axis. You'll almost never need to look at two independent systems for a single class at the same time, but that's how the source files are laid out.

Making matters worse, OOP code organization also conflates dependencies. For this example, the LaTeX-generating methods might need to import a native library for handling that format, the formula-solving methods might need a heavy-weight symbolic math module, and so on. If your code organization is class-centric, that means each module defining a class needs to import all of the dependencies for all of the methods (see Item 98: "Lazy-Load Modules with Dynamic Imports to Reduce Startup Time" for background). This prevents you from creating self-contained, well-factored systems of functionality, thus hampering extensibility, refactoring, and testability. Fortunately, OOP is not the only option.

Single dispatch is a functional-style programming technique in which a program decides which version of a function to call based on the type of one of its arguments. It behaves similarly to polymorphism, but it can also avoid many of OOP's pitfalls. You can use single dispatch to essentially add methods to a class without modifying it. Python provides the `singledispatch` decorator in the `functools` built-in module for this purpose.

To use `singledispatch`, first I need to define the function that will do the dispatching. Here I create a function for custom object printing:

```
import functools


@functools.singledispatch
def my_print(value):
    raise NotImplementedError
```

This initial version of the function will be called as a last resort if no better option is found for the type of the first argument (value). I can specialize the implementation for a particular type by using the dispatching function's register method as a decorator. Here I add implementations for the int and float built-in types:

```
@my_print.register(int)
def _(value):
    print("Integer!", value)

@my_print.register(float)
def _(value):
    print("Float!", value)
```

These functions use the underscore (_) to indicate that their names don't matter and they won't be called directly; all dispatching will occur through the my_print function. Here I show this working for the types I've registered so far:

```
my_print(20)
my_print(1.23)

>>>
Integer! 20
Float! 1.23
```

Going back to the pocket calculator example, I can use singledispatch to implement the evaluate functionality without OOP. First, I define a new dispatching function:

```
@functools.singledispatch
def my_evaluate(node):
    raise NotImplementedError
```

Then I add a type-specific implementation for the simple integer data structure:

```
class Integer:
    def __init__(self, value):
        self.value = value

@my_evaluate.register(Integer)
def _(node):
    return node.value
```

And I provide similar implementations for the simple operation data structures. Note how none of the data structures define any additional methods:

```
class Add:
    def __init__(self, left, right):
        self.left = left
        self.right = right

@my_evaluate.register(Add)
def _(node):
    left = my_evaluate(node.left)
    right = my_evaluate(node.right)
    return left + right

class Multiply:
    def __init__(self, left, right):
        self.left = left
        self.right = right

@my_evaluate.register(Multiply)
def _(node):
    left = my_evaluate(node.left)
    right = my_evaluate(node.right)
    return left * right
```

These functions work as expected when I call my_evaluate:

```
tree = Multiply(
    Add(Integer(3), Integer(5)),
    Add(Integer(4), Integer(7)),
)
result = my_evaluate(tree)
print(result)

>>>
88
```

Now, say that I want to implement equation pretty printing, as in Item 49: "Prefer Object-Oriented Polymorphism over Functions with isinstance Checks," but without using OOP. I can do this simply by defining another singledispatch function and decorating implementation functions for each type I want to handle:

```
@functools.singledispatch
def my_pretty(node):
    raise NotImplementedError
```

```
@my_pretty.register(Integer)
def _(node):
    return repr(node.value)

@my_pretty.register(Add)
def _(node):
    left_str = my_pretty(node.left)
    right_str = my_pretty(node.right)
    return f"({left_str} + {right_str})"

@my_pretty.register(Multiply)
def _(node):
    left_str = my_pretty(node.left)
    right_str = my_pretty(node.right)
    return f"({left_str} * {right_str})"
```

And again, this works as expected without using OOP:

```
print(my_pretty(tree))

>>>
((3 + 5) * (4 + 7))
```

If I create a new type that is a subclass of a type I've already registered, it will immediately work with my_pretty without additional code changes because it follows method-resolution order, like inheritance (see Item 53: "Initialize Parent Classes with super"). For example, here I add a subclass of the Integer type and show that it can pretty print:

```
class PositiveInteger(Integer):
    ...

print(my_pretty(PositiveInteger(1234)))

>>>
1234
```

The difficulty with singledispatch arises when I create a new class. For example, calling the my_pretty function with a new type of object will raise a NotImplementedError exception because there's no implementation registered to handle the new type:

```
class Float:
    ...

print(my_pretty(Float(5.678)))

>>>
Traceback ...
NotImplementedError
```

This is the fundamental trade-off in using function-style single dispatch: When you add a new type to the code, you need to add a corresponding implementation for every dispatch function you want to support. That might require modifying many or all of the independent modules in your program. In contrast, with object-oriented polymorphism, new classes might seem easier to add—just implement the required methods—but adding a new method to the system requires updating every class. Although there's some friction with either approach, in my view, the burden with single dispatch is lower, and the benefits are numerous.

With single dispatch, you can have thousands of data structures and hundreds of behaviors in the program without polluting the class definitions with methods. This allows you to create independent systems of behavior in completely separate modules with no interdependencies on each other and a narrow set of external dependencies. Simple data structures can live at the bottom of your program's dependency tree and be shared across the whole codebase without high coupling. Using the single dispatch approach like this organizes the code on the correct axis: All of the related behaviors are together instead of spread across countless modules where OOP classes reside. Ultimately, this makes it easier to maintain, debug, extend, refactor, and test your code. That said, OOP can still be a good choice when your classes share common functionality and the larger systems are more interconnected.

The choice between these code structures comes down to how independent the program's components are and how much common data or behavior they share. You can also mix OOP and single dispatch together to benefit from the best attributes of both styles. For example, you could add utility methods to the simple classes that are common across all of the independent systems.

Things to Remember

✦ Object-oriented programming leads to class-centric code organization, which can make it difficult to build and maintain large programs because behavior is spread out across many modules.

✦ Single dispatch is an alternative approach for achieving dynamic dispatch using functions instead of method polymorphism, making it possible to bring related functionality closer together in source code.

✦ Python's functools built-in module has a singledispatch decorator that can be used to implement single dispatch behaviors.

✦ Programs with highly independent systems that operate on the same underlying data might benefit from the functional style of single dispatch instead of OOP.

Item 51: Prefer dataclasses for Defining Lightweight Classes

It's easy to start writing Python programs by using built-in data types (such as strings and dictionaries) and defining functions that interact with them. At some point, your code will get complex enough that creating your own types of objects to contain data and encapsulate behavior is warranted (see Item 29: "Compose Classes Instead of Deeply Nesting Dictionaries, Lists, and Tuples" for an example).

However, Python's vast set of object-oriented capabilities can be overwhelming, especially for beginners. To help make these features more approachable, Python provides a variety of built-in modules (see Item 57: "Inherit from collections.abc Classes for Custom Container Types"), and there are many community-built packages as well (such as attrs and pydantic—see Item 116: "Know Where to Find Community-Built Modules").

One especially valuable built-in module is dataclasses, which you can use to greatly reduce the amount of repetitive code in class definitions. The cost of using the module is a small performance overhead at import time due to how its implementation uses exec (see Item 91: "Avoid exec and eval Unless You're Building a Developer Tool"). But it's well worth it, especially for classes with few or no methods that exist primarily to store data in attributes.

The potential benefits of dataclasses become most clear when you consider how much effort it takes to build each of its features yourself (see Item 56: "Prefer dataclasses for Creating Immutable Objects" for more examples). Understanding how these common object-oriented idioms work under the hood is also important so you can migrate your code away from dataclasses when you inevitably need more flexibility or customization.

Avoiding __init__ Boilerplate

The first thing to do with objects is to create them. The __init__ special method is called to construct an object when a class name is invoked like a function call. For example, here I define a simple class to store an RGB (red, green, blue) color value:

```
class RGB:
    def __init__(self, red, green, blue):
        self.red = red
```

```
        self.green = green
        self.blue = blue
```

This code is verbose, repeating the name of each attribute three times. It's also error prone because there are many opportunities to insert typos or accidentally assign an attribute to the wrong argument of __init__:

```
class BadRGB:
    def __init__(self, green, red, blue):   # Bad: Order swapped
        self.red = red
        self.green = green
        self.bloe = blue                   # Bad: Typo
```

The dataclasses module includes a class decorator (see Item 66: "Prefer Class Decorators over Metaclasses for Composable Class Extensions") that provides better default behaviors for simple classes like this. Here I define a new class similar to the one above, but I wrap it in the @dataclass decorator:

```
from dataclasses import dataclass


@dataclass
class DataclassRGB:
    red: int
    green: int
    blue: int
```

To use the dataclass decorator, I list each attribute of the object in the class body with its corresponding type hint (see Item 124: "Consider Static Analysis via typing to Obviate Bugs"). I only have to identify each attribute a single time, so I avoid the risk of typos. If I reorder the attributes, I only need to update the callers instead of making sure the class is consistent within itself.

With these type annotations present, I can also use a static type checking tool to detect errors before the program is executed. For example, here I provide the wrong types when constructing an object and modifying it:

```
from dataclasses import dataclass


@dataclass
class DataclassRGB:
    red: int
    green: int
    blue: int
```

```
obj = DataclassRGB(1, "bad", 3)
obj.red = "also bad"
```

The type checker is able to report these problems without needing more code in the class definition:

```
>>>
$ python3 -m mypy --strict example.py
.../example.py:9: error: Argument 2 to "DataclassRGB" has
➡incompatible type "str"; expected "int"  [arg-type]
.../example.py:10: error: Incompatible types in assignment
➡(expression has type "str", variable has type "int")
➡[assignment]
Found 2 errors in 1 file (checked 1 source file)
```

It's possible to enable the same type checking with a standard class by putting type information to the __init__ method, but this location is cramped and visually noisy in comparison to the class body:

```
class RGB:
    def __init__(
        self, red: int, green: int, blue: int
    ) -> None:  # Changed
        self.red = red
        self.green = green
        self.blue = blue
```

If you don't want type annotations in your project (see Item 3: "Never Expect Python to Detect Errors at Compile Time"), or if you need your class's attributes to be totally flexible, you can still use the dataclass decorator. Simply provide the Any type from the built-in typing module for the fields:

```
from typing import Any

@dataclass
class DataclassRGB:
    red: Any
    green: Any
    blue: Any
```

Requiring Initialization Arguments to Be Passed by Keyword

Arguments are supplied to __init__ just as they would be for any other function call, meaning both positional arguments and keyword arguments are allowed (see Item 35: "Provide Optional Behavior with

Keyword Arguments" for background). For example, here I initialize
the RGB class three different ways:

```
color1 = RGB(red=1, green=2, blue=3)
color2 = RGB(1, 2, 3)
color3 = RGB(1, 2, blue=3)
```

However, this flexibility is error prone because I can too easily mix up
the different color component values. To address this, I can use the
* symbol in the argument list to require that arguments to __init__
are always supplied by keyword (see Item 37: "Enforce Clarity with
Keyword-Only and Positional-Only Arguments" for details):

```
class RGB:
    def __init__(self, *, red, green, blue):  # Changed
        self.red = red
        self.green = green
        self.blue = blue
```

Now using keyword arguments is the only way to create these objects:

```
color4 = RGB(red=1, green=2, blue=3)
```

Initializing the class with positional arguments will fail:

```
RGB(1, 2, 3)
```

```
>>>
Traceback ...
TypeError: RGB.__init__() takes 1 positional argument but 4
➥were given
```

By default, classes wrapped by the dataclass decorator will also
accept a mix of positional and keyword arguments. I can achieve the
same keyword-only behavior as above by simply passing the kw_only
flag to the decorator:

```
@dataclass(kw_only=True)
class DataclassRGB:
    red: int
    green: int
    blue: int
```

Now this class must be initialized with keyword arguments:

```
color5 = DataclassRGB(red=1, green=2, blue=3)
```

Passing any positional arguments will fail, just like the standard class implementation:

```
DataclassRGB(1, 2, 3)
```

```
>>>
Traceback ...
TypeError: DataclassRGB.__init__() takes 1 positional argument
➥but 4 were given
```

Providing Default Attribute Values

For classes that are focused on storing data, it can be useful to have default values for some attributes so they don't need to be specified every time an object is constructed.

For example, say that I want to extend the RGB class to allow for an alpha field to represent the color's level of transparency on a scale of 0 to 1. By default, I want the color to be opaque with an alpha of 1. Here I achieve this by providing a default value for the corresponding argument in the __init__ constructor:

```
class RGBA:
    def __init__(self, *, red, green, blue, alpha=1.0):
        self.red = red
        self.green = green
        self.blue = blue
        self.alpha = alpha
```

Now I can omit the alpha argument, and the default value will be assigned anyway:

```
color1 = RGBA(red=1, green=2, blue=3)
print(
    color1.red,
    color1.green,
    color1.blue,
    color1.alpha,
)
```

```
>>>
1 2 3 1.0
```

To enable the same behavior with the dataclass decorator, I simply assign a default value to the attribute in the class body:

```
@dataclass(kw_only=True)
class DataclassRGBA:
    red: int
    green: int
```

```
    blue: int
    alpha: int = 1.0
```

Creating an object with this new constructor will assign the correct default value for the alpha attribute:

```
color2 = DataclassRGBA(red=1, green=2, blue=3)
print(color2)
```

```
>>>
DataclassRGBA(red=1, green=2, blue=3, alpha=1.0)
```

However, neither of these approaches will work correctly when the default value is mutable (see Item 26: "Prefer get over in and KeyError to Handle Missing Dictionary Keys" for a similar problem and Item 30: "Know That Function Arguments Can Be Mutated" for background). For example, if the default value provided is a list, a single object reference will be shared between all instances of a class, causing weird behaviors like this:

```
class BadContainer:
    def __init__(self, *, value=[]):
        self.value = value


obj1 = BadContainer()
obj2 = BadContainer()
obj1.value.append(1)
print(obj2.value)  # Should be empty, but isn't
```

```
>>>
[1]
```

For standard classes, you can solve this problem by providing a default value of None in the __init__ method and then dynamically allocating the real default value (see Item 36: "Use None and Docstrings to Specify Dynamic Default Arguments" for background):

```
class MyContainer:
    def __init__(self, *, value=None):
        if value is None:
            value = []   # Create when not supplied
        self.value = value
```

Now each object will have a different list allocated by default:

```
obj1 = MyContainer()
obj2 = MyContainer()
obj1.value.append(1)
assert obj1.value == [1]
assert obj2.value == []
```

To achieve the same behavior with the dataclass decorator, I can use the field helper function from the dataclasses module. It accepts a default_factory argument that is the function to call in order to allocate a default value for that attribute:

```
from dataclasses import field

@dataclass
class DataclassContainer:
    value: list = field(default_factory=list)
```

This similarly fixes the implementation to ensure that each new object has its own separate list instance:

```
obj1 = DataclassContainer()
obj2 = DataclassContainer()
obj1.value.append(1)
assert obj1.value == [1]
assert obj2.value == []
```

The dataclasses module provides many other helpful features like this, which are covered in detail in the official documentation (https://docs.python.org/3/library/dataclasses.html).

Representing Objects as Strings

When you define a new class in Python using the standard approach, even a basic feature like print doesn't seem to work correctly. Instead of seeing a nice list of attributes and their values, you get the memory address of the object, which is practically useless:

```
color1 = RGB(red=1, green=2, blue=3)
print(color1)

>>>
<__main__.RGB object at 0x1029a0b90>
```

To fix this, I can implement the __repr__ special method (see Item 12: "Understand the Difference Between repr and str when Printing Objects" for background). Here I add such a method to a standard Python class using one big format string (see Item 11: "Prefer Interpolated F-Strings over C-Style Format Strings and str.format" for background):

```
class RGB:
    ...

    def __repr__(self):
        return (
```

```
            f"{type(self).__module__}"
            f".{type(self).__name__}("
            f"red={self.red!r}, "
            f"green={self.green!r}, "
            f"blue={self.blue!r})"
        )
```

Now these objects will look good when they're printed:

```
color1 = RGB(red=1, green=2, blue=3)
print(color1)

>>>
__main__.RGB(red=1, green=2, blue=3)
```

However, there are two problems with implementing __repr__ your-self. First, it's repetitive and verbose boilerplate that needs to be added to every class. Second, it's error prone because I could easily forget to add new attributes, misspell attribute names, put attribute names in the wrong order for positional construction, or incorrectly insert separating commas and whitespace.

The dataclass decorator provides an implementation of the __repr__ special method by default, increasing productivity and avoiding these potential bugs:

```
color2 = DataclassRGB(red=1, green=2, blue=3)
print(color2)

>>>
DataclassRGB(red=1, green=2, blue=3)
```

Converting Objects into Tuples

To help with equality testing, indexing, and sorting, it can be useful to convert an object into a tuple. To do this with a standard Python class, here I define a new method that packs an object's attributes together:

```
class RGB:
    ...

    def _astuple(self):
        return (self.red, self.green, self.blue)
```

Using this method is simple:

```
color1 = RGB(1, 2, 3)
print(color1._astuple())

>>>
(1, 2, 3)
```

The _astuple method also allows me to copy an object by using the return value as positional arguments for the constructor using the * operator (see Item 34: "Reduce Visual Noise with Variable Positional Arguments" and Item 16: "Prefer Catch-All Unpacking over Slicing" for background):

```
color2 = RGB(*color1._astuple())
print(color2.red, color2.green, color2.blue)
```

```
>>>
1 2 3
```

However, like the __repr__ implementation for standard Python classes, the _astuple method requires error-prone boilerplate with all of the same pitfalls. In contrast, I can use the astuple function from the dataclasses module to achieve the same behavior for any dataclass-decorated class:

```
from dataclasses import astuple

color3 = DataclassRGB(1, 2, 3)
print(astuple(color3))
```

```
>>>
(1, 2, 3)
```

Converting Objects into Dictionaries

To help with data serialization, it can be useful to convert an object into a dictionary containing its attributes. I can achieve this with a standard Python class by defining a new method:

```
class RGB:
    ...

    def _asdict(self):
        return dict(
            red=self.red,
            green=self.green,
            blue=self.blue,
        )
```

The return value of this method can be passed to the dumps function from the json built-in module to produce a serialized representation:

```
import json

color1 = RGB(red=1, green=2, blue=3)
data = json.dumps(color1._asdict())
print(data)
```

```
>>>
{"red": 1, "green": 2, "blue": 3}
```

The _asdict method also lets you create a copy of an object using a dictionary of keyword arguments with the ** operator, similar to how _astuple works for positional arguments:

```
color2 = RGB(**color1._asdict())
print(color2)
```

```
>>>
__main__.RGB(red=1, green=2, blue=3)
```

To get the same behavior using the dataclasses module, I can use the asdict function, which avoids all of the boilerplate:

```
from dataclasses import asdict
```

```
color3 = DataclassRGB(red=1, green=2, blue=3)
print(asdict(color3))
```

```
>>>
{'red': 1, 'green': 2, 'blue': 3}
```

The asdict function from dataclasses is also superior to my hand-built _asdict method; it will automatically transform data nested in attributes, including basic container types and other dataclass objects. To achieve the same effect using a standard class requires much more work (see Item 54: "Consider Composing Functionality with Mix-in Classes" for details).

Checking Whether Objects Are Equivalent

With a standard Python class, two objects that look like they're equivalent actually aren't:

```
color1 = RGB(1, 2, 3)
color2 = RGB(1, 2, 3)
print(color1 == color2)
```

```
>>>
False
```

The reason for this behavior is that the default implementation of the __eq__ special method uses the is operator, which tests whether the two operands have the same identity (i.e., whether they occupy the same location in memory):

```
assert color1 == color1
assert color1 is color1
assert color1 != color2
assert color1 is not color2
```

For simple classes, it's a lot more useful when two objects of the same type with the same attribute values are considered equivalent. Here I implement this behavior for a standard Python class by using the _astuple method:

```
class RGB:
    ...

    def __eq__(self, other):
        return (
            type(self) == type(other)
            and self._astuple() == other._astuple()
        )
```

Now the == and != operators work as expected:

```
color1 = RGB(1, 2, 3)
color2 = RGB(1, 2, 3)
color3 = RGB(5, 6, 7)
assert color1 == color1
assert color1 == color2
assert color1 is not color2
assert color1 != color3
```

When a class is created using the dataclass decorator, you get this functionality automatically and don't need to implement __eq__ yourself:

```
color4 = DataclassRGB(1, 2, 3)
color5 = DataclassRGB(1, 2, 3)
color6 = DataclassRGB(5, 6, 7)
assert color4 == color4
assert color4 == color5
assert color4 is not color5
assert color4 != color6
```

Enabling Objects to Be Compared

Beyond equivalence, it can be useful to compare two objects to see which one is bigger or smaller. For example, here I define a standard class to represent the size of a planet in the universe and its distance from Earth:

```
class Planet:
    def __init__(self, distance, size):
        self.distance = distance
        self.size = size
```

```
def __repr__(self):
    return (
        f"{type(self).__module__}"
        f"{type(self).__name__}("
        f"distance={self.distance}, "
        f"size={self.size})"
    )
```

If I try to sort these planets, an exception will be raised because Python doesn't know how to order the objects:

```
far = Planet(10, 5)
near = Planet(1, 2)
data = [far, near]
data.sort()
```

```
>>>
Traceback ...
TypeError: '<' not supported between instances of 'Planet' and
➥'Planet'
```

There are work-arounds for this limitation that are sufficient in many cases (see Item 100: "Sort by Complex Criteria Using the key Parameter"). However, there are other situations in which you need an object to have its own natural ordering (see Item 104: "Know How to Use heapq for Priority Queues" for an example).

To support this behavior in a standard class, I use the _astuple helper method, as described above, to fill in all of the special methods that Python needs to compare objects:

```
class Planet:
    ...

    def _astuple(self):
        return (self.distance, self.size)

    def __eq__(self, other):
        return (
            type(self) == type(other)
            and self._astuple() == other._astuple()
        )

    def __lt__(self, other):
        if type(self) != type(other):
            return NotImplemented
        return self._astuple() < other._astuple()
```

```
    def __le__(self, other):
        if type(self) != type(other):
            return NotImplemented
        return self._astuple() <= other._astuple()

    def __gt__(self, other):
        if type(self) != type(other):
            return NotImplemented
        return self._astuple() > other._astuple()

    def __ge__(self, other):
        if type(self) != type(other):
            return NotImplemented
        return self._astuple() >= other._astuple()
```

Python will allow comparisons between different types, so I need to return the NotImplemented singleton—which is not the same as the NotImplementedError exception class—to indicate when objects are not comparable.

Now these objects have a natural ordering given by the value returned from _astuple, and they can be sorted (first by distance from Earth, then by size) without any additional boilerplate:

```
far = Planet(10, 2)
near = Planet(1, 5)
data = [far, near]
data.sort()
print(data)
```

```
>>>
[__main__Planet(distance=1, size=5), __main__
➥Planet(distance=10, size=2)]
```

One alternative that reduces the number of special method implementations needed is the total_ordering class decorator from the functools built-in module. But achieving the same behavior with dataclass is even easier. Simply pass the order flag:

```
@dataclass(order=True)
class DataclassPlanet:
    distance: float
    size: float
```

These objects will be comparable using their attributes in the order they're declared in the class body:

```
far2 = DataclassPlanet(10, 2)
near2 = DataclassPlanet(1, 5)
assert far2 > near2
assert near2 < far2
```

Things to remember

✦ The dataclass decorator from the dataclasses built-in module can be used to define versatile, lightweight classes without the boilerplate typically required by standard Python syntax.

✦ Using the dataclasses module can help you avoid pitfalls caused by the verbose and error-prone nature of Python's standard object-oriented features.

✦ The dataclasses module provides additional helper functions for conversions (e.g., asdict, astuple) and advanced attribute behavior (e.g., field).

✦ It's important to know how to implement object-oriented idioms yourself so you can migrate away from the dataclasses module once you need more customization than it allows.

Item 52: Use @classmethod Polymorphism to Construct Objects Generically

In Python, not only do objects support polymorphism, but classes do as well. What does this mean, and what is it good for?

Polymorphism enables multiple classes in a hierarchy to implement their own unique versions of a method. This means that many classes can fulfill the same interface or abstract base class while providing different functionality (see Item 49: "Prefer Object-Oriented Polymorphism over Functions with isinstance Checks" and Item 57: "Inherit from collections.abc Classes for Custom Container Types" for background).

For example, say that I'm writing a map-reduce implementation, and I want a common class to represent the input data. Here I define such a class with a read method that must be defined by subclasses:

```
class InputData:
    def read(self):
        raise NotImplementedError
```

I also have a concrete subclass of InputData that reads data from a file on disk:

```
class PathInputData(InputData):
    def __init__(self, path):
        super().__init__()
        self.path = path

    def read(self):
        with open(self.path) as f:
            return f.read()
```

I could have any number of InputData subclasses, like PathInputData, and each of them could implement the standard interface for read to return the data to process. Other InputData subclasses could read from the network, decompress data transparently, and so on.

I'd want a similar abstract interface for the map-reduce worker that consumes the input data in a standard way:

```
class Worker:
    def __init__(self, input_data):
        self.input_data = input_data
        self.result = None

    def map(self):
        raise NotImplementedError

    def reduce(self, other):
        raise NotImplementedError
```

Here I define the concrete subclass Worker to implement the specific map-reduce function I want to apply—a simple newline counter:

```
class LineCountWorker(Worker):
    def map(self):
        data = self.input_data.read()
        self.result = data.count("\n")

    def reduce(self, other):
        self.result += other.result
```

It might look like this implementation is going great, but I've reached the biggest hurdle in all of this: What connects all of these pieces? I have a nice set of classes with reasonable interfaces and abstractions, but that's only useful once the objects are constructed. What component is responsible for building the objects and orchestrating the map-reduce?

The simplest approach is to manually build and connect the objects with some helper functions. Here I list the contents of a directory and construct a `PathInputData` instance for each file it contains:

```python
import os

def generate_inputs(data_dir):
    for name in os.listdir(data_dir):
        yield PathInputData(os.path.join(data_dir, name))
```

Next, I create the `LineCountWorker` instances by using the `InputData` instances returned by `generate_inputs`:

```python
def create_workers(input_list):
    workers = []
    for input_data in input_list:
        workers.append(LineCountWorker(input_data))
    return workers
```

I execute these `Worker` instances by fanning out the `map` step to multiple threads (see Item 68: "Use Threads for Blocking I/O; Avoid for Parallelism" for background). Then, I call `reduce` repeatedly to combine the results into one final value:

```python
from threading import Thread

def execute(workers):
    threads = [Thread(target=w.map) for w in workers]
    for thread in threads:
        thread.start()
    for thread in threads:
        thread.join()

    first, *rest = workers
    for worker in rest:
        first.reduce(worker)
    return first.result
```

Finally, I connect all of the pieces together in a function that runs each step:

```python
def mapreduce(data_dir):
    inputs = generate_inputs(data_dir)
    workers = create_workers(inputs)
    return execute(workers)
```

Calling this function with a set of test input files works great:

```
import os
import random

def write_test_files(tmpdir):
    os.makedirs(tmpdir)
    for i in range(100):
        with open(os.path.join(tmpdir, str(i)), "w") as f:
            f.write("\n" * random.randint(0, 100))

tmpdir = "test_inputs"
write_test_files(tmpdir)

result = mapreduce(tmpdir)
print(f"There are {result} lines")

>>>
There are 4360 lines
```

What's the problem? The huge issue is that the mapreduce function is not generic at all. If I wanted to write another InputData or Worker subclass, I would also have to rewrite the generate_inputs, create_workers, and mapreduce functions to match.

This problem boils down to needing a generic way to construct objects. In other languages, you'd solve this problem with constructor polymorphism, requiring that each InputData subclass provides a special constructor that can be used generically by the helper methods that orchestrate the map-reduce (similar to the factory pattern). The trouble is that Python only allows for the single constructor method (__init__). It's unreasonable to require every InputData subclass to have a compatible constructor.

The best way to solve this problem is with *class method* polymorphism. This is exactly like the instance method polymorphism I used for InputData.read, except that it's for whole classes instead of their constructed objects.

Let me apply this idea to the map-reduce classes. Here I extend the InputData class with a generic @classmethod that's responsible for creating new InputData instances using a common interface:

```
class GenericInputData:
    def read(self):
        raise NotImplementedError
```

```
@classmethod
def generate_inputs(cls, config):
    raise NotImplementedError
```

I have generate_inputs take a dictionary with a set of configuration parameters that the GenericInputData concrete subclass needs to interpret. Here I use the config argument to find the directory to list for input files:

```
class PathInputData(GenericInputData):
    ...

    @classmethod
    def generate_inputs(cls, config):
        data_dir = config["data_dir"]
        for name in os.listdir(data_dir):
            yield cls(os.path.join(data_dir, name))
```

Similarly, I can make the create_workers helper part of the GenericWorker class. Here I use the input_class parameter, which must be a subclass of GenericInputData, to generate the necessary inputs:

```
class GenericWorker:
    def __init__(self, input_data):
        self.input_data = input_data
        self.result = None

    def map(self):
        raise NotImplementedError

    def reduce(self, other):
        raise NotImplementedError

    @classmethod
    def create_workers(cls, input_class, config):
        workers = []
        for input_data in input_class.generate_inputs(config):
            workers.append(cls(input_data))
        return workers
```

Note that the call to input_class.generate_inputs above is the class polymorphism that I'm trying to show. You can also see how create_workers calling cls provides an alternative way to construct GenericWorker objects besides using the __init__ method directly.

The effect on my concrete GenericWorker subclass is nothing more than changing its parent class:

```
class LineCountWorker(GenericWorker):   # Changed
    ...
```

Finally, I can rewrite the mapreduce function to be completely generic by calling the create_workers class method:

```
def mapreduce(worker_class, input_class, config):
    workers = worker_class.create_workers(input_class, config)
    return execute(workers)
```

Running the new worker on a set of test files produces the same result as the old implementation. The difference is that the mapreduce function requires more parameters so that it can operate generically:

```
config = {"data_dir": tmpdir}
result = mapreduce(LineCountWorker, PathInputData, config)
print(f"There are {result} lines")
```

```
>>>
There are 4360 lines
```

Now I can write other GenericInputData and GenericWorker subclasses as I wish, without having to rewrite any of the glue code.

Things to Remember

✦ Python only supports a single constructor per class: the __init__ method.

✦ Use @classmethod to define alternative constructors for your classes.

✦ Use class method polymorphism to provide generic ways to build and connect many concrete subclasses.

Item 53: Initialize Parent Classes with super

The old, simple way to initialize a parent class from a child class is to directly call the parent class's __init__ method with the child instance:

```
class MyBaseClass:
    def __init__(self, value):
        self.value = value


class MyChildClass(MyBaseClass):
    def __init__(self):
        MyBaseClass.__init__(self, 5)
```

This approach works fine for basic class hierarchies but breaks in many cases.

If a class is affected by multiple inheritance (something to avoid in general; see Item 54: "Consider Composing Functionality with Mix-in Classes"), calling the superclasses' __init__ methods directly can lead to unpredictable behavior.

One problem is that the __init__ call order isn't specified across all subclasses. For example, here I define two parent classes that operate on the instance's value field:

```
class TimesTwo:
    def __init__(self):
        self.value *= 2


class PlusFive:
    def __init__(self):
        self.value += 5
```

This class defines its parent classes in one ordering:

```
class OneWay(MyBaseClass, TimesTwo, PlusFive):
    def __init__(self, value):
        MyBaseClass.__init__(self, value)
        TimesTwo.__init__(self)
        PlusFive.__init__(self)
```

And constructing it produces a result that matches the parent class ordering:

```
foo = OneWay(5)
print("First ordering value is (5 * 2) + 5 =", foo.value)

>>>
First ordering value is (5 * 2) + 5 = 15
```

Here's another class that defines the same parent classes but in a different ordering (PlusFive followed by TimesTwo instead of the other way around):

```
class AnotherWay(MyBaseClass, PlusFive, TimesTwo):
    def __init__(self, value):
        MyBaseClass.__init__(self, value)
        TimesTwo.__init__(self)
        PlusFive.__init__(self)
```

However, I left the calls to the parent class constructors—PlusFive.__init__ and TimesTwo.__init__—in the same order as before, which means this class's behavior doesn't match the order of the parent classes in its definition. The conflict here between the ordering of the inheritance base classes and the __init__ calls is hard to spot, which makes this especially difficult for new readers of the code to understand:

```
bar = AnotherWay(5)
print("Second ordering should be (5 + 5) * 2, but is", bar.value)

>>>
Second ordering should be (5 + 5) * 2, but is 15
```

Another problem occurs with diamond inheritance. Diamond inheritance happens when a subclass inherits from two separate classes that have the same superclass somewhere in the hierarchy. Diamond inheritance causes the common superclass's __init__ method to run multiple times, leading to unexpected behavior. For example, here I define two child classes that inherit from MyBaseClass:

```
class TimesSeven(MyBaseClass):
    def __init__(self, value):
        MyBaseClass.__init__(self, value)
        self.value *= 7

class PlusNine(MyBaseClass):
    def __init__(self, value):
        MyBaseClass.__init__(self, value)
        self.value += 9
```

Then I define a child class that inherits from both of these classes, making MyBaseClass the top of the diamond:

```
class ThisWay(TimesSeven, PlusNine):
    def __init__(self, value):
        TimesSeven.__init__(self, value)
        PlusNine.__init__(self, value)

foo = ThisWay(5)
print("Should be (5 * 7) + 9 = 44 but is", foo.value)

>>>
Should be (5 * 7) + 9 = 44 but is 14
```

The call to the second parent class's constructor, PlusNine.__init__, causes self.value to be reset back to 5 when MyBaseClass.__init__ gets called a second time. That results in the calculation of self.value to be 5 + 9 = 14, completely ignoring the effect of the TimesSeven.__init__ constructor. This behavior is surprising and can be very difficult to debug in more complex cases.

To solve these problems, Python has the super built-in function and standard method resolution order (MRO). super ensures that common superclasses in diamond hierarchies are run only once (see Item 62: "Validate Subclasses with __init_subclass__" for another example). The MRO defines the ordering in which superclasses are initialized, following an algorithm called *C3 linearization*.

Here I create a diamond-shaped class hierarchy again, but this time I use super to initialize the parent class:

```
class TimesSevenCorrect(MyBaseClass):
    def __init__(self, value):
        super().__init__(value)
        self.value *= 7


class PlusNineCorrect(MyBaseClass):
    def __init__(self, value):
        super().__init__(value)
        self.value += 9
```

Now the top part of the diamond, MyBaseClass.__init__, is run only a single time. The other parent classes are run in the order specified in the class statement:

```
class GoodWay(TimesSevenCorrect, PlusNineCorrect):
    def __init__(self, value):
        super().__init__(value)


foo = GoodWay(5)
print("Should be 7 * (5 + 9) = 98 and is", foo.value)

>>>
Should be 7 * (5 + 9) = 98 and is 98
```

This order might seem backward. Shouldn't TimesSevenCorrect. __init__ have run first? Shouldn't the result be (5 * 7) + 9 = 44? The answer is no. This ordering matches what the MRO defines for this class. The MRO ordering is available via a class method called mro or cached in a class attribute called __mro__:

```
mro_str = "\n".join(repr(cls) for cls in GoodWay.__mro__)
print(mro_str)

>>>
<class '__main__.GoodWay'>
<class '__main__.TimesSevenCorrect'>
<class '__main__.PlusNineCorrect'>
<class '__main__.MyBaseClass'>
<class 'object'>
```

When I call GoodWay(5), it in turn calls TimesSevenCorrect.__init__, which calls PlusNineCorrect.__init__, which calls MyBaseClass.__init__. Once this reaches the top of the diamond, all of the initialization methods actually do their work in the opposite order from how their __init__ functions were called. MyBaseClass.__init__ assigns value to 5. PlusNineCorrect.__init__ adds 9 to make value equal 14. TimesSevenCorrect.__init__ multiplies it by 7 to make value equal 98.

Besides making multiple inheritance robust, the call to super().__init__ is also much more maintainable than calling MyBaseClass.__init__ directly from within the subclasses. I could later rename MyBaseClass to something else or have TimesSevenCorrect and PlusNineCorrect inherit from another superclass without having to update their __init__ methods to match.

The super function can also be called with two parameters: first the type of the class whose MRO parent view you're trying to access and then the instance on which to access that view. Using these optional parameters within the constructor looks like this:

```
class ExplicitTrisect(MyBaseClass):
    def __init__(self, value):
        super(ExplicitTrisect, self).__init__(value)
        self.value /= 3
```

However, these parameters are not required for object instance initialization. Python's compiler automatically provides the correct parameters (__class__ and self) for you when super is called with zero arguments within a class definition. This means all three of these usages are equivalent:

```
class AutomaticTrisect(MyBaseClass):
    def __init__(self, value):
        super(__class__, self).__init__(value)
        self.value /= 3

class ImplicitTrisect(MyBaseClass):
    def __init__(self, value):
        super().__init__(value)
        self.value /= 3

assert ExplicitTrisect(9).value == 3
assert AutomaticTrisect(9).value == 3
assert ImplicitTrisect(9).value == 3
```

The only time you should provide parameters to super is in situations where you need to access the specific functionality of a superclass's implementation from a child class (e.g., in order to wrap or reuse functionality).

Things to Remember

✦ Python's standard MRO solves the problems of superclass initialization order and diamond inheritance.

✦ Use the super built-in function with zero arguments to initialize parent classes and call parent methods.

Item 54: Consider Composing Functionality with Mix-in Classes

Python is an object-oriented language with built-in facilities for making multiple inheritance tractable (see Item 53: "Initialize Parent Classes with super"). However, it's better to avoid multiple inheritance altogether.

If you find yourself desiring the convenience and encapsulation that come with multiple inheritance but wanting to avoid the potential headaches, consider writing a mix-in instead. A *mix-in* is a class that defines only a small set of additional methods for its child classes to provide. Mix-in classes don't define their own instance attributes or require their __init__ constructor to be called.

Writing mix-ins is easy because Python makes it trivial to inspect the current state of any object, regardless of its type. Dynamic inspection means you can write generic functionality just once, in a mix-in, and it can then be applied to many other classes. Mix-ins can be composed and layered to minimize repetitive code and maximize reuse.

For example, say that I want to have the ability to convert a Python object from its in-memory representation to a dictionary that's ready for serialization. Why not write this functionality generically so I can use it with all of my classes?

Here I define an example mix-in that accomplishes this with a new public method that's added to any class that inherits from it. The implementation details are straightforward and rely on dynamic attribute access using hasattr, dynamic type inspection with isinstance, and accessing the instance dictionary __dict__:

```
class ToDictMixin:
    def to_dict(self):
        return self._traverse_dict(self.__dict__)
```

```
    def _traverse_dict(self, instance_dict):
        output = {}
        for key, value in instance_dict.items():
            output[key] = self._traverse(key, value)
        return output

    def _traverse(self, key, value):
        if isinstance(value, ToDictMixin):
            return value.to_dict()
        elif isinstance(value, dict):
            return self._traverse_dict(value)
        elif isinstance(value, list):
            return [self._traverse(key, i) for i in value]
        elif hasattr(value, "__dict__"):
            return self._traverse_dict(value.__dict__)
        else:
            return value
```

Here I define an example class that uses the mix-in to make a dictionary representation of a binary tree:

```
class BinaryTree(ToDictMixin):
    def __init__(self, value, left=None, right=None):
        self.value = value
        self.left = left
        self.right = right
```

Translating a large number of related Python objects into a dictionary becomes easy:

```
tree = BinaryTree(
    10,
    left=BinaryTree(7, right=BinaryTree(9)),
    right=BinaryTree(13, left=BinaryTree(11)),
)
print(tree.to_dict())

>>>
{'value': 10,
 'left': {'value': 7,
          'left': None,
          'right': {'value': 9, 'left': None, 'right': None}},
 'right': {'value': 13,
           'left': {'value': 11, 'left': None, 'right': None},
           'right': None}}
```

The best part about mix-ins is that you can make their generic functionality pluggable so behaviors can be overridden when required. For example, here I define a subclass of BinaryTree that holds a reference to its parent. This circular reference would cause the default implementation of ToDictMixin.to_dict to loop forever. The solution is to override the BinaryTreeWithParent._traverse method to only process values that matter, preventing cycles encountered by the mix-in. Here the _traverse override inserts the parent's numerical value and otherwise defers to the mix-in's default implementation by using the super built-in function:

```python
class BinaryTreeWithParent(BinaryTree):
    def __init__(
        self,
        value,
        left=None,
        right=None,
        parent=None,
    ):
        super().__init__(value, left=left, right=right)
        self.parent = parent

    def _traverse(self, key, value):
        if (
            isinstance(value, BinaryTreeWithParent)
            and key == "parent"
        ):
            return value.value  # Prevent cycles
        else:
            return super()._traverse(key, value)
```

Calling BinaryTreeWithParent.to_dict works without issue because the circular referencing properties aren't followed:

```python
root = BinaryTreeWithParent(10)
root.left = BinaryTreeWithParent(7, parent=root)
root.left.right = BinaryTreeWithParent(9, parent=root.left)
print(root.to_dict())

>>>
{'value': 10,
 'left': {'value': 7,
          'left': None,
          'right': {'value': 9,
                    'left': None,
                    'right': None,
```

```
                      'parent': 7},
               'parent': 10},
 'right': None,
 'parent': None}
```

By defining BinaryTreeWithParent._traverse, I've also enabled any class that has an attribute of type BinaryTreeWithParent to automatically work with ToDictMixin:

```
class NamedSubTree(ToDictMixin):
    def __init__(self, name, tree_with_parent):
        self.name = name
        self.tree_with_parent = tree_with_parent


my_tree = NamedSubTree("foobar", root.left.right)
print(my_tree.to_dict())  # No infinite loop

>>>
{'name': 'foobar',
 'tree_with_parent': {'value': 9,
                      'left': None,
                      'right': None,
                      'parent': 7}}
```

Mix-ins can also be composed together. For example, say I want a mix-in that provides generic JSON serialization for any class. I can do this by assuming that a class provides a to_dict method (which may or may not be provided by the ToDictMixin class):

```
import json


class JsonMixin:
    @classmethod
    def from_json(cls, data):
        kwargs = json.loads(data)
        return cls(**kwargs)

    def to_json(self):
        return json.dumps(self.to_dict())
```

Note how the JsonMixin class defines both instance methods and class methods. Mix-ins let you add either kind of behavior to subclasses (see Item 52: "Use @classmethod Polymorphism to Construct Objects Generically" for similar functionality). In this example, the only requirements of a JsonMixin subclass are providing a to_dict method and taking keyword arguments for the __init__ method (see Item 35: "Provide Optional Behavior with Keyword Arguments" for background).

This mix-in makes it simple to create hierarchies of utility classes that can be serialized to and from JSON with little boilerplate. For example, here I have a hierarchy of classes representing parts of a datacenter topology:

```
class DatacenterRack(ToDictMixin, JsonMixin):
    def __init__(self, switch=None, machines=None):
        self.switch = Switch(**switch)
        self.machines = [
            Machine(**kwargs) for kwargs in machines]

class Switch(ToDictMixin, JsonMixin):
    def __init__(self, ports=None, speed=None):
        self.ports = ports
        self.speed = speed

class Machine(ToDictMixin, JsonMixin):
    def __init__(self, cores=None, ram=None, disk=None):
        self.cores = cores
        self.ram = ram
        self.disk = disk
```

Serializing these classes to and from JSON is simple. Here I verify that the data is able to be sent round-trip through serializing and deserializing:

```
serialized = """{
    "switch": {"ports": 5, "speed": 1e9},
    "machines": [
        {"cores": 8, "ram": 32e9, "disk": 5e12},
        {"cores": 4, "ram": 16e9, "disk": 1e12},
        {"cores": 2, "ram": 4e9, "disk": 500e9}
    ]
}"""

deserialized = DatacenterRack.from_json(serialized)
roundtrip = deserialized.to_json()
assert json.loads(serialized) == json.loads(roundtrip)
```

When you use mix-ins like this, it's fine if the class you apply JsonMixin to already inherits from JsonMixin higher up in the class hierarchy. The resulting class will behave the same way, thanks to the behavior of super.

Things to Remember

◆ Avoid using multiple inheritance with instance attributes and
  __init__ if mix-in classes can achieve the same outcome.

◆ Use pluggable behaviors at the instance level to provide per-class
  customization when mix-in classes may require it.

◆ Mix-ins can include instance methods or class methods, depending
  on your needs.

◆ Compose mix-ins to create complex functionality from simple
  behaviors.

Item 55: Prefer Public Attributes over Private Ones

In Python, there are only two types of visibility for a class's attributes:
public and *private*:

```
class MyObject:
    def __init__(self):
        self.public_field = 5
        self.__private_field = 10

    def get_private_field(self):
        return self.__private_field
```

Public attributes can be accessed by anyone using the dot operator on
an object:

```
foo = MyObject()
assert foo.public_field == 5
```

Private fields are specified by prefixing an attribute's name with a
double underscore. They can be accessed directly by methods of the
containing class:

```
assert foo.get_private_field() == 10
```

However, directly accessing private fields from outside the class raises
an exception:

```
foo.__private_field

>>>
Traceback ...
AttributeError: 'MyObject' object has no attribute
➡'__private_field'
```

Class methods also have access to private attributes because they are declared within the surrounding class block:

```
class MyOtherObject:
    def __init__(self):
        self.__private_field = 71

    @classmethod
    def get_private_field_of_instance(cls, instance):
        return instance.__private_field

bar = MyOtherObject()
assert MyOtherObject.get_private_field_of_instance(bar) == 71
```

As you'd expect with private fields, a subclass can't access its parent class's private fields:

```
class MyParentObject:
    def __init__(self):
        self.__private_field = 71

class MyChildObject(MyParentObject):
    def get_private_field(self):
        return self.__private_field

baz = MyChildObject()
baz.get_private_field()

>>>
Traceback ...
AttributeError: 'MyChildObject' object has no attribute
➥'_MyChildObject__private_field'
```

The private attribute behavior is implemented with a simple transformation of the attribute name. When the Python compiler sees private attribute access in methods like MyChildObject.get_private_field, it translates the __private_field attribute access to use the name _MyChildObject__private_field instead. In the example above, __private_field is only defined in MyParentObject.__init__, which means the private attribute's real name is _MyParentObject__private_field. Accessing the parent's private attribute from the child class fails simply because the transformed attribute name doesn't exist (_MyChildObject__private_field instead of _MyParentObject__private_field).

Knowing this scheme, you can easily access the private attributes of any class—from a subclass or externally—without asking for permission:

```
assert baz._MyParentObject__private_field == 71
```

If you look in the object's attribute dictionary, you can see that private attributes are actually stored with the names as they appear after the transformation:

```
print(baz.__dict__)
```

```
>>>
{'_MyParentObject__private_field': 71}
```

Why doesn't the syntax for private attributes actually enforce strict visibility? The simplest answer is one often-quoted motto of Python: "We are all consenting adults here." What this means is that we don't need the language to prevent us from doing what we want to do. It's our individual choice to extend functionality as we wish and to take responsibility for the consequences of such a risk. Python programmers believe that the benefits of being open—permitting unplanned extension of classes by default—outweigh the downsides.

Beyond that, having the ability to hook language features like attribute access (see Item 61: "Use __getattr__, __getattribute__, and __setattr__ for Lazy Attributes") enables you to mess around with the internals of objects whenever you wish. If you can do that, what is the value of Python trying to prevent private attribute access otherwise?

To minimize damage caused by accessing internals unknowingly, Python programmers follow a naming convention defined in the style guide (see Item 2: "Follow the PEP 8 Style Guide"). Any field whose name is prefixed by a single underscore (like _protected_field) is *protected* by convention, meaning external users of the class should proceed with caution.

However, programmers who are new to Python might consider using private fields to indicate an internal API that shouldn't be accessed by subclasses or externally:

```
class MyStringClass:
    def __init__(self, value):
        self.__value = value

    def get_value(self):
        return str(self.__value)

foo = MyStringClass(5)
assert foo.get_value() == "5"
```

This is the wrong approach. Inevitably someone—maybe even you—will want to subclass your class to add new behavior or to work around deficiencies in existing methods (e.g., the way that MyStringClass.get_value always returns a string). By choosing private attributes, you're only making subclass overrides and extensions cumbersome and brittle. Your potential subclassers will still access the private fields when they absolutely need to do so:

```
class MyIntegerSubclass(MyStringClass):
    def get_value(self):
        return int(self._MyStringClass__value)


foo = MyIntegerSubclass("5")
assert foo.get_value() == 5
```

But if the class hierarchy above you changes, these classes will break because the private attribute references are no longer valid. Here the MyIntegerSubclass class's immediate parent, MyStringClass, has had another parent class, called MyBaseClass, added:

```
class MyBaseClass:
    def __init__(self, value):
        self.__value = value

    def get_value(self):
        return self.__value

class MyStringClass(MyBaseClass):
    def get_value(self):
        return str(super().get_value())         # Updated

class MyIntegerSubclass(MyStringClass):
    def get_value(self):
        return int(self._MyStringClass__value)  # Not updated
```

The __value attribute is now assigned in the MyBaseClass parent class, not the MyStringClass parent. This causes the private variable reference self._MyStringClass__value to break in MyIntegerSubclass:

```
foo = MyIntegerSubclass(5)
foo.get_value()

>>>
Traceback ...
AttributeError: 'MyIntegerSubclass' object has no attribute
➥'_MyStringClass__value'
```

In general, it's better to err on the side of allowing subclasses to do more by using protected attributes. Document each protected field and explain which fields are internal APIs available to subclasses and which should be left alone entirely. This is as much advice to other programmers as it is guidance for your future self on how to extend your own code safely:

```
class MyStringClass:
    def __init__(self, value):
        # This stores the user-supplied value for the object.
        # It should be coercible to a string. Once assigned in
        # the object it should be treated as immutable.
        self._value = value

    ...
```

The only time to seriously consider using private attributes is when you're worried about naming conflicts between subclasses. This problem occurs when a child class unwittingly defines an attribute that was already defined by its parent class:

```
class ApiClass:
    def __init__(self):
        self._value = 5

    def get(self):
        return self._value

class Child(ApiClass):
    def __init__(self):
        super().__init__()
        self._value = "hello"  # Conflicts

a = Child()
print(f"{a.get()} and {a._value} should be different")

>>>
hello and hello should be different
```

This is primarily a concern with classes that are part of a public API; the subclasses are out of your control, so you can't refactor to fix the problem. Such a conflict is especially possible with attribute names that are very common (like value). To reduce the risk of this issue occurring, you can use a private attribute in the parent class to ensure that there are no attribute names that overlap with child classes:

```
class ApiClass:
    def __init__(self):
        self.__value = 5        # Double underscore

    def get(self):
        return self.__value     # Double underscore

class Child(ApiClass):
    def __init__(self):
        super().__init__()
        self._value = "hello"  # OK!

a = Child()
print(f"{a.get()} and {a._value} are different")

>>>
5 and hello are different
```

Things to Remember

✦ Private attributes aren't rigorously enforced by the Python compiler.

✦ Plan from the beginning to allow subclasses to do more with your internal APIs and attributes instead of choosing to lock them out.

✦ Use documentation of protected fields to guide subclasses instead of trying to force access control with private attributes.

✦ Only consider using private attributes to avoid naming conflicts with subclasses that are out of your control.

Item 56: Prefer dataclasses for Creating Immutable Objects

Nearly everything in Python can be modified at runtime, which is a fundamental part of the language's philosophy (see Item 55: "Prefer Public Attributes over Private Ones" and Item 3: "Never Expect Python to Detect Errors at Compile Time"). However, this flexibility often causes problems that are difficult to debug.

One way to reduce the scope of what can go wrong is to not allow changes to objects after they're created. This requirement forces code to be written in a *functional style*, where the primary purpose of functions and methods is to consistently map inputs to outputs, kind of like mathematical equations.

A function written in this style is easy to test. You only need to consider the equivalence of arguments and return values instead of worrying about object references and identities. It's straightforward to reason about and modify a function that doesn't make mutable state transitions or cause external side effects. And by returning values that can't be modified later, functions can avoid downstream surprises.

You can benefit from these advantages with your own data types by creating *immutable objects*. The dataclasses built-in module (see Item 51: "Prefer dataclasses for Defining Lightweight Classes" for background) provides a way to define such classes that is far more productive than using Python's standard object-oriented features. dataclasses also enables other functionality out of the box, such as the ability to use value objects as keys in dictionaries and members in sets.

Preventing Objects from Being Modified

In Python, all arguments to functions are passed by reference, which, unfortunately, enables a caller's data to be changed by any callee (see Item 30: "Know That Function Arguments Can Be Mutated" for details). This behavior can cause all kinds of confusing bugs. For example, here I define a standard class that represents the location of a labeled point in two-dimensional space:

```
class Point:
    def __init__(self, name, x, y):
        self.name = name
        self.x = x
        self.y = y
```

I can define a well-behaved helper function that calculates the distance between two points and doesn't modify the inputs:

```
def distance(left, right):
    return ((left.x - right.x) ** 2 +
            (left.y - right.y) ** 2) ** 0.5

origin1 = Point("source", 0, 0)
point1 = Point("destination", 3, 4)
print(distance(origin1, point1))

>>>
5.0
```

I can also define a poorly behaved function that overwrites the value of the x attribute for the first parameter:

```
def bad_distance(left, right):
    left.x = -3
    return distance(left, right)
```

This modification causes the wrong calculation to be made and permanently changes the state of the origin object so subsequent calculations will also be incorrect:

```
print(bad_distance(origin1, point1))
print(origin1.x)

>>>
7.211102550927978
-3
```

I can prevent these types of modifications in a standard class by implementing the __setattr__ and __delattr__ special methods and having them raise an AttributeError exception (see Item 61: "Use __getattr__, __getattribute__, and __setattr__ for Lazy Attributes" for background). To set the initial attribute values, I directly assign keys in the __dict__ instance dictionary:

```
class ImmutablePoint:
    def __init__(self, name, x, y):
        self.__dict__.update(name=name, x=x, y=y)

    def __setattr__(self, key, value):
        raise AttributeError("Immutable object: set not allowed")

    def __delattr__(self, key):
        raise AttributeError("Immutable object: del not allowed")
```

Now I can do the same distance calculation as before and get the right answer:

```
origin2 = ImmutablePoint("source", 0, 0)
assert distance(origin2, point1) == 5
```

But using the poorly behaved function that modifies its inputs will raise an exception:

```
bad_distance(origin2, point1)

>>>
Traceback ...
AttributeError: Immutable object: set not allowed
```

To achieve the same behavior with the dataclasses built-in module, all I have to do is pass the frozen flag to the dataclass decorator:

```
from dataclasses import dataclass

@dataclass(frozen=True)
class DataclassImmutablePoint:
    name: str
    x: float
    y: float

origin3 = DataclassImmutablePoint("origin", 0, 0)
assert distance(origin3, point1) == 5
```

Trying to modify the attributes of this new dataclass will raise a similar AttributeError error at runtime:

```
bad_distance(origin3, point1)

>>>
Traceback ...
FrozenInstanceError: cannot assign to field 'x'
```

As an added benefit, the dataclass approach also enables static analysis tools to detect this problem before program execution (see Item 124: "Consider Static Analysis via typing to Obviate Bugs" for details):

```
from dataclasses import dataclass

@dataclass(frozen=True)
class DataclassImmutablePoint:
    name: str
    x: float
    y: float

origin = DataclassImmutablePoint("origin", 0, 0)
origin.x = -3

>>>
$ python3 -m mypy --strict example.py
.../example.py:10: error: Property "x" defined in
➥"DataclassImmutablePoint" is read-only  [misc]
Found 1 error in 1 file (checked 1 source file)
```

You can also use the Final and Never annotations from the typing built-in module to make standard classes similarly fail static analysis, but much more code is required:

```
from typing import Any, Final, Never

class ImmutablePoint:
    name: Final[str]
    x: Final[int]
    y: Final[int]

    def __init__(self, name: str, x: int, y: int) -> None:
        self.name = name
        self.x = x
        self.y = y

    def __setattr__(self, key: str, value: Any) -> None:
        if key in self.__annotations__ and key not in dir(self):
            # Allow the very first assignment to happen
            super().__setattr__(key, value)
        else:
            raise AttributeError("Immutable object")

    def __delattr__(self, key: str) -> Never:
        raise AttributeError("Immutable object")
```

Creating Copies of Objects with Replaced Attributes

When objects are immutable, a natural question arises: How are you supposed to write code that accomplishes anything when modifications to data structures aren't possible? For example, here I have another helper function that moves a Point object by a relative amount:

```
def translate(point, delta_x, delta_y):
    point.x += delta_x
    point.y += delta_y
```

As expected, it fails when the input object is immutable:

```
point1 = ImmutablePoint("destination", 5, 3)
translate(point1, 10, 20)

>>>
Traceback ...
AttributeError: Immutable object: set not allowed
```

One way to work around this limitation is to return a copy of the given argument with updated attribute values:

```
def translate_copy(point, delta_x, delta_y):
    return ImmutablePoint(
        name=point.name,
        x=point.x + delta_x,
        y=point.y + delta_y,
    )
```

However, this is error prone because you need to copy all of the attributes that you're not trying to modify, such as name in this case. Over time, as the class adds, removes, or changes attributes, this copying code might get out of sync and cause mysterious bugs in your program.

To reduce the risk of such errors in a standard class, here I add a method that knows how to create copies of an object with a given set of attribute overrides:

```
class ImmutablePoint:
    ...

    def _replace(self, **overrides):
        fields = dict(
            name=self.name,
            x=self.x,
            y=self.y,
        )
        fields.update(overrides)
        cls = type(self)
        return cls(**fields)
```

Now code can rely on the _replace method to ensure that all attributes are properly accounted for. Here I define another version of the translate function that uses this method:

```
def translate_replace(point, delta_x, delta_y):
    return point._replace(  # Changed
        x=point.x + delta_x,
        y=point.y + delta_y,
    )
```

Note how the name attribute is no longer mentioned.

But this approach still isn't ideal. Although I've centralized the field copying code to one location inside the class, it's still possible for the _replace method to get out of sync because it needs to be manually maintained. Further, each class that needs this functionality must define its own _replace method, which leads to more boilerplate code to manage.

To accomplish the same behavior with dataclass, I can simply use the replace helper function from the dataclasses module; no changes to the class definition are required, no custom _replace method needs to be defined, and there's no chance for the method to get out of sync:

```
import dataclasses

def translate_dataclass(point, delta_x, delta_y):
    return dataclasses.replace(  # Changed
        point,
        x=point.x + delta_x,
        y=point.y + delta_y,
    )
```

Using Immutable Objects in Dictionaries and Sets

When you assign the same key to different values in a dict, you expect only the final mapping to be preserved:

```
my_dict = {}
my_dict["a"] = 123
my_dict["a"] = 456
print(my_dict)

>>>
{'a': 456}
```

Similarly, when you add a value to a set, you expect that all subsequent additions of the same value will result in no changes to the set because the item is already present:

```
my_set = set()
my_set.add("b")
my_set.add("b")
print(my_set)

>>>
{'b'}
```

These stable mapping and deduplication behaviors are critical expectations for how these data structures work. Surprisingly, by default, user-defined objects can't be used as dictionary keys or set values in the same way the simple values "a" and "b" were in the code above.

For example, say that I want to write a program that simulates the physics of electricity. Here I create a dictionary that maps Point objects to the amount of charge at that location (there could be other dictionaries that map the same `Point` objects to other quantities like magnetic flux, etc).:

```
point1 = Point("A", 5, 10)
point2 = Point("B", -7, 4)
charges = {
    point1: 1.5,
    point2: 3.5,
}
```

Retrieving the value for a given `Point` in the dictionary seems to work:

```
print(charges[point1])
```

```
>>>
1.5
```

But if I create another `Point` object that appears equivalent to the first one—the same coordinates and name—a `KeyError` exception is raised by dictionary lookup:

```
point3 = Point("A", 5, 10)
charges[point3]
```

```
>>>
Traceback ...
KeyError: <__main__.Point object at 0x100e85eb0>
```

Upon further inspection, the `Point` objects aren't considered equivalent because I haven't implemented the `__eq__` special method for the class:

```
assert point1 != point3
```

The default implementation of the `==` operator for objects is the same as the `is` operator that only compares their identities. Here I implement the `__eq__` special method so it compares the values of the objects' attributes instead:

```
class Point:
    ...

    def __eq__(self, other):
        return (
            type(self) == type(other)
            and self.name == other.name
            and self.x == other.x
            and self.y == other.y
        )
```

Now, two Point objects that appear equivalent will also be treated as such by the == operator:

```
point4 = Point("A", 5, 10)
point5 = Point("A", 5, 10)
assert point4 == point5
```

However, even with these new equivalent objects, the dictionary lookup from earlier still fails:

```
other_charges = {
    point4: 1.5,
}
other_charges[point5]
```

```
>>>
Traceback ...
TypeError: unhashable type: 'Point'
```

The issue is that the Point class doesn't implement the __hash__ special method. Python's implementation of the dictionary type relies on the integer value returned by the __hash__ method to maintain its internal lookup table. In order for dictionaries to work properly, this hash value must be stable and unchanging for individual objects, and it must be the same for equivalent objects. Here I implement the __hash__ method by putting the object's attributes in a tuple and passing it to the hash built-in function:

```
class Point:
    ...

    def __hash__(self):
        return hash((self.name, self.x, self.y))
```

Now the dictionary lookup works as expected:

```
point6 = Point("A", 5, 10)
point7 = Point("A", 5, 10)

more_charges = {
    point6: 1.5,
}
value = more_charges[point7]
assert value == 1.5
```

With dataclasses, none of this effort is required in order to use an immutable object as a key in a dictionary. When you provide the frozen flag to the dataclass decorator, you get all these behaviors (e.g., __eq__, __hash__) automatically:

```
point8 = DataclassImmutablePoint("A", 5, 10)
point9 = DataclassImmutablePoint("A", 5, 10)

easy_charges = {
    point8: 1.5,
}
assert easy_charges[point9] == 1.5
```

These immutable objects can also be used as values in a set and will properly deduplicate:

```
my_set = {point8, point9}
assert my_set == {point8}
```

What about namedtuple?

Before dataclasses was added to the Python standard library (in version 3.7), a good choice for creating immutable objects was the namedtuple function from the collections built-in module. namedtuple provides many of the same benefits as the dataclass decorator using the frozen flag, including:

+ Construction of objects with positional or keyword arguments, default values provided when attributes are unspecified.

+ Automatic definition of object-oriented special methods (e.g., __init__, __repr__, __eq__, __hash__, __lt__).

+ Built-in helper methods _replace and _dict, runtime introspection with the _fields and _field_defaults class attributes.

+ Support for static type checking when using the NamedTuple class from the typing built-in module.

+ Low memory usage by avoiding __dict__ instance dictionaries (i.e., similar to using dataclasses with slots=True).

In addition, all fields of a namedtuple are accessible by positional index, which can be ideal for wrapping sequential data structures like lines from a CSV (comma-separated values) file or rows from database query results—with a dataclass you must call the _astuple method. However, the sequential nature of namedtuple can lead to unintentional usage (i.e., numerical indexing and iteration) that can cause bugs and make it difficult to migrate to a standard class later, especially for external APIs (see Item 119: "Use Packages to Organize Modules and Provide Stable APIs"). If your data structure is sequential, then namedtuple might be a good choice, but otherwise it's best to go with dataclasses or a standard class (see Item 65: "Consider Class Body Definition Order to Establish Relationships Between Attributes").

Things to remember

✦ Functional-style code that uses immutable objects is often more robust than imperative-style code that modifies state and causes side effects.

✦ The easiest way to make your own immutable objects is by using the dataclasses built-in module; simply apply the dataclass decorator when defining a class and pass the frozen=True argument.

✦ The replace helper function from the dataclasses module allows you to create copies of immutable objects with some attributes changed, making it easier to write functional-style code.

✦ Immutable objects created with dataclass are comparable for equivalence by value and have stable hashes, which allows them to be used as keys in dictionaries and as values in sets.

Item 57: Inherit from collections.abc Classes for Custom Container Types

Much of programming in Python involves defining classes that contain data and describing how such objects relate to each other. Every Python class is a container of some kind, encapsulating attributes and functionality together. Python also provides built-in container types for managing data: lists, tuples, sets, and dictionaries.

When you're designing classes for simple use cases like sequences, it's natural to want to subclass Python's built-in list type directly. For example, say that I want to create my own custom list type that has additional methods for counting the frequency of its members:

```python
class FrequencyList(list):
    def __init__(self, members):
        super().__init__(members)

    def frequency(self):
        counts = {}
        for item in self:
            counts[item] = counts.get(item, 0) + 1
        return counts
```

By subclassing list, I get all of list's standard functionality and preserve the semantics familiar to all Python programmers. I can define additional methods to provide any custom behaviors that I need:

```python
foo = FrequencyList(["a", "b", "a", "c", "b", "a", "d"])
print("Length is", len(foo))
```

```
foo.pop()  # Removes "d"
print("After pop:", repr(foo))
print("Frequency:", foo.frequency())

>>>
Length is 7
After pop: ['a', 'b', 'a', 'c', 'b', 'a']
Frequency: {'a': 3, 'b': 2, 'c': 1}
```

Now, imagine that I need to define an object that feels like a list and allows indexing but isn't a list subclass. For example, say that I want to provide sequence semantics (like list or tuple; see Item 14: "Know How to Slice Sequences" for background) for a binary tree class:

```
class BinaryNode:
    def __init__(self, value, left=None, right=None):
        self.value = value
        self.left = left
        self.right = right
```

How do you make this class act like a sequence type? Python implements its container behaviors with instance methods that have special names. When you access a sequence item by index:

```
bar = [1, 2, 3]
bar[0]
```

it will be interpreted as:

```
bar.__getitem__(0)
```

To make the BinaryNode class act like a sequence, you can provide a custom implementation of __getitem__ (often pronounced "dunder getitem" as an abbreviation for "double underscore getitem") that traverses the object tree depth-first:

```
class IndexableNode(BinaryNode):
    def _traverse(self):
        if self.left is not None:
            yield from self.left._traverse()
        yield self
        if self.right is not None:
            yield from self.right._traverse()

    def __getitem__(self, index):
        for i, item in enumerate(self._traverse()):
            if i == index:
                return item.value
        raise IndexError(f"Index {index} is out of range")
```

Here I construct a binary tree with normal object initialization:

```
tree = IndexableNode(
    10,
    left=IndexableNode(
        5,
        left=IndexableNode(2),
        right=IndexableNode(6, right=IndexableNode(7)),
    ),
    right=IndexableNode(15, left=IndexableNode(11)),
)
```

But I can also access it like a list in addition to being able to traverse the tree with the `left` and `right` attributes:

```
print("LRR is", tree.left.right.right.value)
print("Index 0 is", tree[0])
print("Index 1 is", tree[1])
print("11 in the tree?", 11 in tree)
print("17 in the tree?", 17 in tree)
print("Tree is", list(tree))
```

```
>>>
LRR is 7
Index 0 is 2
Index 1 is 5
11 in the tree? True
17 in the tree? False
Tree is [2, 5, 6, 7, 10, 11, 15]
```

The problem is that implementing `__getitem__` isn't enough to provide all of the sequence semantics Python expects from a `list` instance:

```
len(tree)
```

```
>>>
Traceback ...
TypeError: object of type 'IndexableNode' has no len()
```

The `len` built-in function requires another special method, `__len__`, that must have an implementation for a custom sequence type:

```
class SequenceNode(IndexableNode):
    def __len__(self):
        count = 0
        for _ in self._traverse():
            count += 1
        return count
```

```
tree = SequenceNode(
    10,
    left=SequenceNode(
        5,
        left=SequenceNode(2),
        right=SequenceNode(6, right=SequenceNode(7)),
    ),
    right=SequenceNode(15, left=SequenceNode(11)),
)

print("Tree length is", len(tree))

>>>
Tree length is 7
```

Unfortunately, this still isn't enough for the class to fully act as a valid sequence. Also missing are the count and index methods that a Python programmer would expect to see on a sequence like list or tuple. It turns out that defining your own container types is much harder than it seems.

To avoid this difficulty throughout the Python universe, the collections.abc built-in module defines a set of abstract base classes that provide all of the typical methods for each container type. When you subclass from these abstract base classes and forget to implement required methods, the module tells you something is wrong:

```
from collections.abc import Sequence

class BadType(Sequence):
    pass

foo = BadType()

>>>
Traceback ...
TypeError: Can't instantiate abstract class BadType without an
➥implementation for abstract methods '__getitem__', '__len__'
```

When you implement all of the methods required by an abstract base class from collections.abc, as I did above with SequenceNode, it provides all of the additional methods, like index and count, for free:

```
class BetterNode(SequenceNode, Sequence):
    pass
```

```
tree = BetterNode(
    10,
    left=BetterNode(
        5,
        left=BetterNode(2),
        right=BetterNode(6, right=BetterNode(7)),
    ),
    right=BetterNode(15, left=BetterNode(11)),
)

print("Index of 7 is", tree.index(7))
print("Count of 10 is", tree.count(10))

>>>
Index of 7 is 3
Count of 10 is 1
```

The benefit of using these abstract base classes is even greater for more complex container types such as Set and MutableMapping, which have a large number of special methods that need to be implemented to match Python conventions.

Beyond the collections.abc module, Python also uses a variety of special methods for object comparisons and sorting, which may be provided by container classes and non-container classes alike (see Item 104: "Know How to Use heapq for Priority Queues" and Item 51: "Prefer dataclasses for Defining Lightweight Classes" for examples).

Things to Remember

◆ For simple use cases, it's fine to inherit directly from Python's container types (like list or dict) to utilize their fundamental behavior.

◆ Beware of the large number of methods required to implement custom container types correctly when not inheriting from a built-in type.

◆ To ensure that your custom container classes match the required behaviors, have them inherit from the interfaces defined in collections.abc.

Metaclasses and Attributes

Metaclasses are often mentioned in lists of Python's unique features, but few understand what they accomplish in practice. The name *metaclass* vaguely implies a concept above and beyond a class. Simply put, metaclasses let you intercept Python's class statement and provide special behavior each time a class is defined.

Similarly mysterious are Python's built-in features for dynamically customizing attribute accesses. Along with Python's object-oriented constructs, these facilities provide powerful tools to ease the transition from simple classes to complex ones.

However, with these capabilities come many pitfalls. Dynamic attributes enable you to override objects and cause unexpected side effects. Metaclasses can create extremely bizarre behaviors that are unapproachable to newcomers. It's important that you follow the *rule of least surprise* and only use these mechanisms to implement well-understood idioms.

Item 58: Use Plain Attributes Instead of Setter and Getter Methods

Programmers coming to Python from other languages might naturally try to implement explicit getter and setter methods in their classes to access protected attributes (see Item 55: "Prefer Public Attributes over Private Ones" for background):

```python
class OldResistor:
    def __init__(self, ohms):
        self._ohms = ohms

    def get_ohms(self):
        return self._ohms
```

```
    def set_ohms(self, ohms):
        self._ohms = ohms
```

Using these setters and getters is simple, but it's not Pythonic:

```
r0 = OldResistor(50e3)
print("Before:", r0.get_ohms())
r0.set_ohms(10e3)
print("After: ", r0.get_ohms())

>>>
Before: 50000.0
After:   10000.0
```

Such methods are especially clumsy for operations like incrementing in place:

```
r0.set_ohms(r0.get_ohms() - 4e3)
assert r0.get_ohms() == 6e3
```

These utility methods do, however, help define the interface for a class, making it easier to encapsulate functionality, validate usage, and define boundaries. Those are important goals when designing a class to ensure that you don't break callers as the class evolves over time.

In Python, however, you never need to implement explicit setter or getter methods like this. Instead, you should always start your implementations with simple public attributes, as I do here:

```
class Resistor:
    def __init__(self, ohms):
        self.ohms = ohms
        self.voltage = 0
        self.current = 0

r1 = Resistor(50e3)
r1.ohms = 10e3
```

These attributes make operations like incrementing in place natural and clear:

```
r1.ohms += 5e3
```

Later, if I decide I need special behavior when an attribute is set, I can migrate to the @property decorator (see Item 38: "Define Function Decorators with functools.wraps" for background) and its corresponding setter attribute. Here, I define a new subclass of Resistor that lets me vary current by assigning the voltage property. Note that in order for this code to work properly, the names of both the setter and the getter methods must match the intended property name (voltage):

```python
class VoltageResistance(Resistor):
    def __init__(self, ohms):
        super().__init__(ohms)
        self._voltage = 0

    @property
    def voltage(self):
        return self._voltage

    @voltage.setter
    def voltage(self, voltage):
        self._voltage = voltage
        self.current = self._voltage / self.ohms
```

Now, assigning the voltage property will run the voltage setter method, which in turn will update the current attribute of the object to match:

```python
r2 = VoltageResistance(1e2)
print(f"Before: {r2.current:.2f} amps")
r2.voltage = 10
print(f"After:  {r2.current:.2f} amps")
```

```
>>>
Before: 0.00 amps
After:  0.10 amps
```

Specifying the setter for a property also enables me to perform type checking and validation on values passed to the class. Here I define a class that ensures all resistance values are above zero ohms:

```python
class BoundedResistance(Resistor):
    def __init__(self, ohms):
        super().__init__(ohms)

    @property
    def ohms(self):
        return self._ohms

    @ohms.setter
    def ohms(self, ohms):
        if ohms <= 0:
            raise ValueError(f"ohms must be > 0; got {ohms}")
        self._ohms = ohms
```

Assigning an invalid resistance to the attribute now raises an exception:

```
r3 = BoundedResistance(1e3)
r3.ohms = 0
```

```
>>>
Traceback ...
ValueError: ohms must be > 0; got 0
```

An exception is also raised if I pass an invalid value to the constructor:

```
BoundedResistance(-5)
```

```
>>>
Traceback ...
ValueError: ohms must be > 0; got -5
```

This happens because BoundedResistance.__init__ calls Resistor. __init__, which assigns self.ohms = -5. That assignment causes the @ohms.setter method from BoundedResistance to be called, and it immediately runs the validation code before object construction has completed.

I can even use @property to make attributes from parent classes immutable (see Item 56: "Prefer dataclasses for Creating Immutable Objects" for another approach):

```
class FixedResistance(Resistor):
    def __init__(self, ohms):
        super().__init__(ohms)

    @property
    def ohms(self):
        return self._ohms

    @ohms.setter
    def ohms(self, ohms):
        if hasattr(self, "_ohms"):
            raise AttributeError("Ohms is immutable")
        self._ohms = ohms
```

Trying to assign to the property after construction raises an exception:

```
r4 = FixedResistance(1e3)
r4.ohms = 2e3
```

```
>>>
Traceback ...
AttributeError: Ohms is immutable
```

When you use @property methods to implement setters and getters, be sure that the behavior you implement is not surprising. For example, don't set other attributes in getter property methods:

```python
class MysteriousResistor(Resistor):
    @property
    def ohms(self):
        self.voltage = self._ohms * self.current
        return self._ohms

    @ohms.setter
    def ohms(self, ohms):
        self._ohms = ohms
```

Setting other attributes in getter property methods leads to extremely bizarre behavior:

```python
r7 = MysteriousResistor(10)
r7.current = 0.1
print(f"Before: {r7.voltage:.2f}")
r7.ohms
print(f"After:  {r7.voltage:.2f}")
```

```
>>>
Before: 0.00
After:  1.00
```

The best policy is to modify only related object state in @property.setter methods. Be sure to also avoid any other side effects that the caller may not expect beyond the object, such as importing modules dynamically, running slow helper functions, doing I/O, or making expensive database queries. Users of a class will expect its attributes to be like any other Python object: quick and easy. Use normal methods to do anything more complex or slow.

The biggest shortcoming of @property is that the methods for an attribute can only be shared by subclasses. Unrelated classes can't share the same implementation. However, Python also supports *descriptors* (see Item 60: "Use Descriptors for Reusable @property Methods") that enable reusable property logic and many other use cases.

Things to Remember

◆ Define new class interfaces using simple public attributes and avoid defining setter and getter methods.

◆ Use @property to define special behavior when attributes are accessed on your objects.

+ Follow the rule of least surprise and avoid odd side effects in your `@property` methods.

+ Ensure that `@property` methods are fast; for slow or complex work—especially involving I/O or causing side effects—use normal methods instead.

Item 59: Consider `@property` Instead of Refactoring Attributes

The built-in `@property` decorator makes it easy for simple accesses of an instance's attributes to act more intelligently (see Item 58: "Use Plain Attributes Instead of Setter and Getter Methods"). One advanced but common use of `@property` is transitioning what was once a simple numerical attribute into an on-the-fly calculation. This is extremely helpful because it lets you migrate all existing usage of a class to have new behaviors without requiring any of the call sites to be rewritten (which is especially important if there's calling code that you don't control). `@property` also provides an important stopgap for improving interfaces over time.

For example, say that I want to implement a leaky-bucket rate-limiting quota system using plain Python objects. Here, the `Bucket` class represents how much quota remains and the duration for which the quota will be available:

```python
from datetime import datetime, timedelta

class Bucket:
    def __init__(self, period):
        self.period_delta = timedelta(seconds=period)
        self.reset_time = datetime.now()
        self.quota = 0

    def __repr__(self):
        return f"Bucket(quota={self.quota})"
```

The leaky-bucket algorithm works by ensuring that, whenever the bucket is filled, the amount of quota does not carry over from one period to the next:

```python
def fill(bucket, amount):
    now = datetime.now()
    if (now - bucket.reset_time) > bucket.period_delta:
        bucket.quota = 0
        bucket.reset_time = now
    bucket.quota += amount
```

Each time a quota consumer wants to do something, it must first ensure that it can deduct the amount of quota it needs to use:

```
def deduct(bucket, amount):
    now = datetime.now()
    if (now - bucket.reset_time) > bucket.period_delta:
        return False  # Bucket hasn't been filled this period
    if bucket.quota - amount < 0:
        return False  # Bucket was filled, but not enough
    bucket.quota -= amount
    return True       # Bucket had enough, quota consumed
```

To use this class, first I fill up the bucket:

```
bucket = Bucket(60)
fill(bucket, 100)
print(bucket)

>>>
Bucket(quota=100)
```

Then, I deduct the quota that I need:

```
if deduct(bucket, 99):
    print("Had 99 quota")
else:
    print("Not enough for 99 quota")

print(bucket)

>>>
Had 99 quota
Bucket(quota=1)
```

Eventually, I'm prevented from making progress because I try to deduct more quota than is available. In this case, the bucket's quota level remains unchanged:

```
if deduct(bucket, 3):
    print("Had 3 quota")
else:
    print("Not enough for 3 quota")

print(bucket)

>>>
Not enough for 3 quota
Bucket(quota=1)
```

The problem with this implementation is that I never know what quota level the bucket started with. The quota is deducted over the course of the period until it reaches zero. At that point, deduct will always return False until the bucket is refilled. When that happens, it would be useful to know whether callers to deduct are being blocked because the Bucket ran out of quota or because the Bucket never had quota during this period in the first place.

To fix this, I can change the class to keep track of the max_quota issued in the period and the quota_consumed in the same period:

```
class NewBucket:
    def __init__(self, period):
        self.period_delta = timedelta(seconds=period)
        self.reset_time = datetime.now()
        self.max_quota = 0
        self.quota_consumed = 0

    def __repr__(self):
        return (
            f"NewBucket(max_quota={self.max_quota}, "
            f"quota_consumed={self.quota_consumed})"
        )
```

To match the previous interface of the original Bucket class, I use a @property method to compute the current level of quota on-the-fly using these new attributes:

```
    @property
    def quota(self):
        return self.max_quota - self.quota_consumed
```

When the quota attribute is assigned, I take special action to be compatible with the current usage of the class by the fill and deduct functions:

```
    @quota.setter
    def quota(self, amount):
        delta = self.max_quota - amount
        if amount == 0:
            # Quota being reset for a new period
            self.quota_consumed = 0
            self.max_quota = 0
        elif delta < 0:
            # Quota being filled during the period
            self.max_quota = amount + self.quota_consumed
        else:
            # Quota being consumed during the period
            self.quota_consumed = delta
```

Rerunning the demo code from above produces the same results:

```
bucket = NewBucket(60)
print("Initial", bucket)
fill(bucket, 100)
print("Filled", bucket)

if deduct(bucket, 99):
    print("Had 99 quota")
else:
    print("Not enough for 99 quota")

print("Now", bucket)

if deduct(bucket, 3):
    print("Had 3 quota")
else:
    print("Not enough for 3 quota")

print("Still", bucket)

>>>
Initial NewBucket(max_quota=0, quota_consumed=0)
Filled NewBucket(max_quota=100, quota_consumed=0)
Had 99 quota
Now NewBucket(max_quota=100, quota_consumed=99)
Not enough for 3 quota
Still NewBucket(max_quota=100, quota_consumed=99)
```

The best part is that the code using Bucket.quota doesn't have to change or know that the class has changed. New usage of Bucket can do the right thing and access max_quota and quota_consumed directly.

I especially like @property because it lets you make incremental progress toward a better data model over time. Reading the Bucket example above, you might have thought that fill and deduct should have been implemented as instance methods in the first place. Although you're probably right, in practice there are many situations in which objects start with poorly defined interfaces or act as dumb data containers (see Item 51: "Prefer dataclasses for Defining Lightweight Classes" for examples). This happens when code grows over time, scope increases, multiple authors contribute without anyone considering long-term hygiene, and so on.

@property is a tool to help you address problems you'll come across in real-world code. Don't overuse it. When you find yourself repeatedly extending @property methods, it's probably time to refactor your class instead of further paving over your code's poor design.

Things to Remember

✦ Use `@property` to give existing instance attributes new functionality.

✦ Make incremental progress toward better data models by using `@property`.

✦ Consider refactoring a class and all call sites when you find yourself using `@property` too heavily.

Item 60: Use Descriptors for Reusable `@property` Methods

The big problem with the `@property` built-in (see Item 58: "Use Plain Attributes Instead of Setter and Getter Methods" and Item 59: "Consider `@property` Instead of Refactoring Attributes") is reuse. The methods it decorates can't be reused for multiple attributes of the same class. They also can't be reused by unrelated classes.

For example, say that I want a class to validate that the grade received by a student on a homework assignment is a percentage:

```
class Homework:
    def __init__(self):
        self._grade = 0

    @property
    def grade(self):
        return self._grade

    @grade.setter
    def grade(self, value):
        if not (0 <= value <= 100):
            raise ValueError("Grade must be between 0 and 100")
        self._grade = value
```

Using `@property` makes this class easy to use:

```
galileo = Homework()
galileo.grade = 95
```

Say that I also want to give the student a grade for an exam, where the exam has multiple subjects, each with a separate grade:

```
class Exam:
    def __init__(self):
        self._writing_grade = 0
        self._math_grade = 0
```

```
@staticmethod
def _check_grade(value):
    if not (0 <= value <= 100):
        raise ValueError("Grade must be between 0 and 100")
```

This quickly gets tedious. For each section of the exam, I need to add a new @property and related validation:

```
@property
def writing_grade(self):
    return self._writing_grade

@writing_grade.setter
def writing_grade(self, value):
    self._check_grade(value)
    self._writing_grade = value

@property
def math_grade(self):
    return self._math_grade

@math_grade.setter
def math_grade(self, value):
    self._check_grade(value)
    self._math_grade = value
```

Also, this approach is not general. If I want to reuse this percentage validation in other classes beyond homework and exams, I'll need to write the @property boilerplate and _check_grade method over and over again.

The better way to do this in Python is to use a *descriptor*. The *descriptor protocol* defines how attribute access is interpreted by the language. A descriptor class can provide __get__ and __set__ methods that let you reuse the grade validation behavior without any boilerplate. For this purpose, descriptors are also better than mix-ins (see Item 54: "Consider Composing Functionality with Mix-in Classes") because they let you reuse the same logic for many different attributes in a single class.

Here I define a new class called Exam with class attributes that are Grade instances. The Grade class implements the descriptor protocol:

```
class Grade:
    def __get__(self, instance, instance_type):
        ...
```

```
    def __set__(self, instance, value):
        ...

class Exam:
    # Class attributes
    math_grade = Grade()
    writing_grade = Grade()
    science_grade = Grade()
```

Before I explain how the Grade class works, it's important to understand what Python will do when such descriptor attributes are accessed on an Exam instance. When I assign a property:

```
exam = Exam()
exam.writing_grade = 40
```

it is interpreted as:

```
Exam.__dict__["writing_grade"].__set__(exam, 40)
```

When I retrieve a property:

```
exam.writing_grade
```

it is interpreted as:

```
Exam.__dict__["writing_grade"].__get__(exam, Exam)
```

What drives this behavior is the __getattribute__ method of object (see Item 61: "Use __getattr__, __getattribute__, and __setattr__ for Lazy Attributes" for background). In short, when an Exam instance doesn't have an attribute named writing_grade, Python falls back to the Exam class's attribute instead. If this class attribute is an object that has __get__ and __set__ methods, Python assumes that you want to follow the descriptor protocol.

Knowing this behavior and how I used @property for grade validation in the Homework class, here's a reasonable first attempt at implementing the Grade descriptor:

```
class Grade:
    def __init__(self):
        self._value = 0

    def __get__(self, instance, instance_type):
        return self._value

    def __set__(self, instance, value):
        if not (0 <= value <= 100):
            raise ValueError("Grade must be between 0 and 100")
        self._value = value
```

Unfortunately, this is wrong and results in broken behavior. Accessing multiple attributes on a single Exam instance works as expected:

```
class Exam:
    math_grade = Grade()
    writing_grade = Grade()
    science_grade = Grade()

first_exam = Exam()
first_exam.writing_grade = 82
first_exam.science_grade = 99
print("Writing", first_exam.writing_grade)
print("Science", first_exam.science_grade)

>>>
Writing 82
Science 99
```

But accessing these attributes on multiple Exam instances results in surprising behavior:

```
second_exam = Exam()
second_exam.writing_grade = 75
print(f"Second {second_exam.writing_grade} is right")
print(f"First  {first_exam.writing_grade} is wrong; "
      f"should be 82")

>>>
Second 75 is right
First  75 is wrong; should be 82
```

The problem is that a single Grade instance is shared across all Exam instances for the class attribute writing_grade. The Grade instance for this attribute is constructed once in the program lifetime, when the Exam class is first defined, not each time an Exam instance is created.

To solve this, I need the Grade class to keep track of its value for each unique Exam instance. I can do this by saving the per-instance state in a dictionary:

```
class DictGrade:
    def __init__(self):
        self._values = {}

    def __get__(self, instance, instance_type):
        if instance is None:
            return self
        return self._values.get(instance, 0)
```

```
def __set__(self, instance, value):
    if not (0 <= value <= 100):
        raise ValueError("Grade must be between 0 and 100")
    self._values[instance] = value
```

This implementation is simple and works well, but there's still one gotcha: It leaks memory. The _values dictionary holds a reference to every instance of Exam ever passed to __set__ over the lifetime of the program. This causes instances to never have their reference count go to zero, preventing cleanup by the garbage collector (see Item 115: "Use tracemalloc to Understand Memory Usage and Leaks" for how to detect this type of problem).

Instead, you should rely on Python's __set_name__ special method for descriptors (see Item 64: "Annotate Class Attributes with __set_name__" for background). This method is called on each descriptor instance after a class is defined. Critically, the name of the class attribute assigned to the descriptor instance is supplied by Python. This allows you to compute a string to use for the per-object attribute name (in this case, a protected field that starts with "_"):

```
class NamedGrade:
    def __set_name__(self, owner, name):
        self.internal_name = "_" + name
```

I can call setattr and getattr on the object with the internal_name from the descriptor to store and retrieve the corresponding attribute data:

```
    def __get__(self, instance, instance_type):
        if instance is None:
            return self
        return getattr(instance, self.internal_name)

    def __set__(self, instance, value):
        if not (0 <= value <= 100):
            raise ValueError("Grade must be between 0 and 100")
        setattr(instance, self.internal_name, value)
```

Now I can define a new class with this improved descriptor and see how the attribute data for the descriptor resides inside the object's instance dictionary (__dict__):

```
class NamedExam:
    math_grade = NamedGrade()
    writing_grade = NamedGrade()
    science_grade = NamedGrade()
```

```
first_exam = NamedExam()
first_exam.math_grade = 78
first_exam.writing_grade = 89
first_exam.science_grade = 94
print(first_exam.__dict__)

>>>
{'_math_grade': 78, '_writing_grade': 89, '_science_grade': 94}
```

Unlike the earlier implementation, this won't leak memory because when a NamedExam object is garbage collected, all of its attribute data, including values assigned by descriptors, will be freed too.

Things to Remember

✦ Reuse the behavior and validation of @property methods by defining your own descriptor classes.

✦ Use __set_name__ along with setattr and getattr to store the data needed by descriptors in object instance dictionaries in order to avoid memory leaks.

✦ Don't get bogged down trying to understand exactly how __getattribute__ uses the descriptor protocol for getting and setting attributes.

Item 61: Use __getattr__, __getattribute__, and __setattr__ for Lazy Attributes

Python's object base class provides hooks that make it easy to write generic code for gluing systems together. For example, say that I want to represent the records in a database as Python objects. I assume that the database has its schema already defined elsewhere. In most languages, I'd need to explicitly specify in code how the database schema maps to classes and objects in my program. However, in Python, I can do this object-relational mapping generically at run-time, so no boilerplate is required.

How is that possible? Plain instance attributes, @property methods, and descriptors can't do this because they all need to be defined in advance. Python enables this dynamic behavior with the __getattr__ special method. If a class defines __getattr__, that method is called every time an attribute can't be found in an object's instance dictionary. Here, I define a __getattr__ hook that will insert an attribute into the object's instance dictionary to prove that it ran:

```
class LazyRecord:
    def __init__(self):
        self.exists = 5

    def __getattr__(self, name):
        value = f"Value for {name}"
        setattr(self, name, value)
        return value
```

When I access the missing object attribute foo, for example, Python calls the __getattr__ method above, which mutates the instance dictionary __dict__:

```
data = LazyRecord()
print("Before:", data.__dict__)
print("foo:   ", data.foo)
print("After: ", data.__dict__)
```

```
>>>
Before: {'exists': 5}
foo:    Value for foo
After:  {'exists': 5, 'foo': 'Value for foo'}
```

I can add logging to LazyRecord to show when __getattr__ is actually called. Note how in this implementation I call super().__getattr__() to use the superclass's implementation of __getattr__ in order to fetch the real property value and avoid infinite recursion (see Item 53: "Initialize Parent Classes with super" for background):

```
class LoggingLazyRecord(LazyRecord):
    def __getattr__(self, name):
        print(
            f"* Called __getattr__({name!r}), "
            f"populating instance dictionary"
        )
        result = super().__getattr__(name)
        print(f"* Returning {result!r}")
        return result

data = LoggingLazyRecord()
print("exists:     ", data.exists)
print("First foo:  ", data.foo)
print("Second foo: ", data.foo)
```

```
>>>
exists:      5
* Called __getattr__('foo'), populating instance dictionary
* Returning 'Value for foo'
First foo:   Value for foo
Second foo:  Value for foo
```

The exists attribute is present in the instance dictionary, so `__getattr__` is never called for it. The foo attribute is not in the instance dictionary initially, so `__getattr__` is called the first time. But the call to `__getattr__` for foo also does a setattr, which populates foo in the instance dictionary. This is why the second time I access foo, it doesn't log a call to `__getattr__`.

This behavior is especially helpful for use cases like lazily accessing schemaless data. `__getattr__` runs once to do the hard work of loading a property; all subsequent accesses retrieve the existing result.

Now imagine that I also want transactions in this database system. The next time the user accesses a dynamic attribute, I want to know whether the corresponding record in the database is still valid and whether the transaction is still open. The `__getattr__` hook won't get called every time the attribute is accessed because it will use the object's instance dictionary as the fast path for existing attributes.

To enable this more advanced use case, Python has another object hook called `__getattribute__`. This special method is called every time an attribute is accessed on an object, even in cases where it *does* exist in the attribute dictionary. This enables me to do things like check global transaction state on every property access. It's important to note that such an operation can incur significant overhead and negatively impact performance, but sometimes it's worth it. Here, I define ValidatingRecord to log each time `__getattribute__` is called:

```python
class ValidatingRecord:
    def __init__(self):
        self.exists = 5

    def __getattribute__(self, name):
        print(f"* Called __getattribute__({name!r})")
        try:
            value = super().__getattribute__(name)
            print(f"* Found {name!r}, returning {value!r}")
            return value
        except AttributeError:
            value = f"Value for {name}"
            print(f"* Setting {name!r} to {value!r}")
```

```
                setattr(self, name, value)
                return value

data = ValidatingRecord()
print("exists:      ", data.exists)
print("First foo:  ", data.foo)
print("Second foo: ", data.foo)

>>>
* Called __getattribute__('exists')
* Found 'exists', returning 5
exists:       5
* Called __getattribute__('foo')
* Setting 'foo' to 'Value for foo'
First foo:    Value for foo
* Called __getattribute__('foo')
* Found 'foo', returning 'Value for foo'
Second foo:  Value for foo
```

In the event that a dynamically accessed property shouldn't exist, you can raise an AttributeError to cause Python's standard missing property behavior for both __getattr__ and __getattribute__:

```
class MissingPropertyRecord:
    def __getattr__(self, name):
        if name == "bad_name":
            raise AttributeError(f"{name} is missing")
        ...

data = MissingPropertyRecord()
data.bad_name

>>>
Traceback ...
AttributeError: bad_name is missing
```

Python code implementing generic functionality often relies on the hasattr built-in function to determine when properties exist and the getattr built-in function to retrieve property values. These functions also look in the instance dictionary for an attribute name before calling __getattr__:

```
data = LoggingLazyRecord()  # Implements __getattr__
print("Before:         ", data.__dict__)
print("Has first foo:  ", hasattr(data, "foo"))
print("After:          ", data.__dict__)
print("Has second foo: ", hasattr(data, "foo"))
```

```
>>>
Before:           {'exists': 5}
* Called __getattr__('foo'), populating instance dictionary
* Returning 'Value for foo'
Has first foo:    True
After:            {'exists': 5, 'foo': 'Value for foo'}
Has second foo:   True
```

In the example above, __getattr__ is called only once (for the first
hasattr call). In contrast, classes that implement __getattribute__
have that method called each time hasattr or getattr is used with an
instance:

```
data = ValidatingRecord()  # Implements __getattribute__
print("Has first foo:  ", hasattr(data, "foo"))
print("Has second foo: ", hasattr(data, "foo"))

>>>
* Called __getattribute__('foo')
* Setting 'foo' to 'Value for foo'
Has first foo:    True
* Called __getattribute__('foo')
* Found 'foo', returning 'Value for foo'
Has second foo:   True
```

Now, say that I want to lazily push data back to the database
when values are assigned to my Python object. I can do this with
__setattr__, a similar object hook that lets you intercept arbitrary
attribute assignments. Unlike when retrieving an attribute with
__getattr__ and __getattribute__, there's no need for two separate
methods. The __setattr__ method is always called every time an
attribute is assigned on an instance (either directly or through the
setattr built-in function):

```
class SavingRecord:
    def __setattr__(self, name, value):
        # Save some data for the record
        ...
        super().__setattr__(name, value)
```

Here, I define a logging subclass of SavingRecord. Its __setattr__
method is always called on each attribute assignment:

```
class LoggingSavingRecord(SavingRecord):
    def __setattr__(self, name, value):
        print(f"* Called __setattr__({name!r}, {value!r})")
        super().__setattr__(name, value)
```

```
data = LoggingSavingRecord()
print("Before: ", data.__dict__)
data.foo = 5
print("After:  ", data.__dict__)
data.foo = 7
print("Finally:", data.__dict__)

>>>
Before:  {}
* Called __setattr__('foo', 5)
After:   {'foo': 5}
* Called __setattr__('foo', 7)
Finally: {'foo': 7}
```

The problem with __getattribute__ and __setattr__ is that they're called on every attribute access for an object—even when you might not want that to happen. For example, say that attribute accesses on my object should actually look up keys in an associated dictionary:

```
class BrokenDictionaryRecord:
    def __init__(self, data):
        self._data = data

    def __getattribute__(self, name):
        print(f"* Called __getattribute__({name!r})")
        return self._data[name]
```

This requires accessing self._data from the __getattribute__ method. However, if I actually try to do that, Python will recurse until it reaches its stack limit, and then the program will crash:

```
data = BrokenDictionaryRecord({"foo": 3})
data.foo

>>>
* Called __getattribute__('foo')
* Called __getattribute__('_data')
* Called __getattribute__('_data')
* Called __getattribute__('_data')
...
Traceback ...
RecursionError: maximum recursion depth exceeded while calling
➥a Python object
```

The problem is that __getattribute__ accesses self._data, which causes __getattribute__ to run again, which accesses self._data again, and so on. The solution is to use the super().__getattribute__ method to fetch values from the instance attribute dictionary; this avoids the accidental recursion:

```
class DictionaryRecord:
    def __init__(self, data):
        self._data = data

    def __getattribute__(self, name):
        print(f"* Called __getattribute__({name!r})")
        data_dict = super().__getattribute__("_data")
        return data_dict[name]

data = DictionaryRecord({"foo": 3})
print("foo: ", data.foo)

>>>
* Called __getattribute__('foo')
foo:  3
```

__setattr__ methods that modify attributes on an object similarly need to use super().__setattr__.

Things to Remember

✦ Use __getattr__ and __setattr__ to lazily load and save attributes for an object.

✦ Understand that __getattr__ only gets called when accessing a missing attribute, whereas __getattribute__ gets called every time any attribute is accessed.

✦ Avoid infinite recursion in __getattribute__ and __setattr__ method implementations by calling super().__getattribute__ and super().__getattr__ to access object attributes.

Item 62: Validate Subclasses with __init_subclass__

One of the simplest applications of metaclasses is verifying that a class was defined correctly. When you're building a complex class hierarchy, you may want to enforce style, require overriding methods, or have strict relationships between class attributes. Metaclasses enable these use cases by providing a reliable way to run your validation code each time a new subclass is defined.

Often a class's validation code runs in the __init__ method when an object of the class's type is constructed at runtime (see Item 58: "Use Plain Attributes Instead of Setter and Getter Methods" for an example). Using metaclasses for validation can raise errors much earlier, such as when the module containing the class is first imported at program startup.

Before I get into how to define a metaclass for validating subclasses, it's important to understand what a metaclass does for standard objects. A metaclass is defined by inheriting from type. A class indicates its metaclass with the metaclass keyword argument in its inheritance argument list. In the typical case, a metaclass has its __new__ method called with the contents of any associated class statements when they occur. Here, I use a basic metaclass to inspect a class's information before the type is actually constructed:

```python
class Meta(type):
    def __new__(meta, name, bases, class_dict):
        print(f"* Running {meta}.__new__ for {name}")
        print("Bases:", bases)
        print(class_dict)
        return type.__new__(meta, name, bases, class_dict)

class MyClass(metaclass=Meta):
    stuff = 123

    def foo(self):
        pass

class MySubclass(MyClass):
    other = 567

    def bar(self):
        pass

>>>
* Running <class '__main__.Meta'>.__new__ for MyClass
Bases: ()
{'__module__': '__main__',
 '__qualname__': 'MyClass',
 'stuff': 123,
 'foo': <function MyClass.foo at 0x104a63a60>}
* Running <class '__main__.Meta'>.__new__ for MySubclass
Bases: (<class '__main__.MyClass'>,)
{'__module__': '__main__',
 '__qualname__': 'MySubclass',
 'other': 567,
 'bar': <function MySubclass.bar at 0x104a63b00>}
```

The metaclass has access to the name of the class, the parent classes it inherits from (bases), and all of the class attributes that were defined in the class's body. All classes inherit from object, so it's not explicitly listed in the tuple of base classes.

I can add functionality to the Meta.__new__ method in order to validate all of the parameters of an associated subclass before it's defined. For example, say that I want to represent any type of multisided polygon. I can do this by defining a special validating metaclass and using it in the base class of my polygon class hierarchy. Note that it's important not to apply the same validation to the base class:

```
class ValidatePolygon(type):
    def __new__(meta, name, bases, class_dict):
        # Only validate subclasses of the Polygon class
        if bases:
            if class_dict["sides"] < 3:
                raise ValueError("Polygons need 3+ sides")
        return type.__new__(meta, name, bases, class_dict)

class Polygon(metaclass=ValidatePolygon):
    sides = None  # Must be specified by subclasses

    @classmethod
    def interior_angles(cls):
        return (cls.sides - 2) * 180

class Triangle(Polygon):
    sides = 3

class Rectangle(Polygon):
    sides = 4

class Nonagon(Polygon):
    sides = 9

assert Triangle.interior_angles() == 180
assert Rectangle.interior_angles() == 360
assert Nonagon.interior_angles() == 1260
```

If I try to define a polygon with fewer than three sides, the validation logic will cause the class statement to fail immediately after the class statement body. This means the program will not even be able to start running when I define such a class (unless it's defined in a dynamically imported module; see Item 98: "Lazy-Load Modules with Dynamic Imports to Reduce Startup Time" for how this can happen):

```
print("Before class")

class Line(Polygon):
    print("Before sides")
    sides = 2
    print("After sides")

print("After class")

>>>
Before class
Before sides
After sides
Traceback ...
ValueError: Polygons need 3+ sides
```

This seems like quite a lot of machinery in order to get Python to accomplish such a basic task. Luckily, Python 3.6 introduced simplified syntax—the __init_subclass__ special class method—for achieving the same behavior and avoiding metaclasses entirely. Here, I use this mechanism to provide the same level of validation as before:

```
class BetterPolygon:
    sides = None  # Must be specified by subclasses

    def __init_subclass__(cls):
        super().__init_subclass__()
        if cls.sides < 3:
            raise ValueError("Polygons need 3+ sides")

    @classmethod
    def interior_angles(cls):
        return (cls.sides - 2) * 180

class Hexagon(BetterPolygon):
    sides = 6

assert Hexagon.interior_angles() == 720
```

The code is much shorter now, and the ValidatePolygon metaclass is gone entirely. It's also easier to follow since I can access the sides attribute directly on the cls instance in __init_subclass__ instead of having to go into the class's dictionary with class_dict["sides"].

If I define an invalid subclass of BetterPolygon, the same exception as before is raised:

```
print("Before class")

class Point(BetterPolygon):
    sides = 1

print("After class")
>>>
Before class
Traceback ...
ValueError: Polygons need 3+ sides
```

Another problem with the standard Python metaclass machinery is that you can only specify a single metaclass per class definition. Here, I define a second metaclass that I'd like to use for validating the fill color used for a region (not necessarily just polygons):

```
class ValidateFilled(type):
    def __new__(meta, name, bases, class_dict):
        # Only validate subclasses of the Filled class
        if bases:
            if class_dict["color"] not in ("red", "green"):
                raise ValueError("Fill color must be supported")
        return type.__new__(meta, name, bases, class_dict)

class Filled(metaclass=ValidateFilled):
    color = None  # Must be specified by subclasses
```

When I try to use the Polygon metaclass and Filled metaclass together, I get a cryptic error message:

```
class RedPentagon(Filled, Polygon):
    color = "blue"
    sides = 5
>>>
Traceback ...
TypeError: metaclass conflict: the metaclass of a derived class
➥must be a (non-strict) subclass of the metaclasses of all its
➥bases
```

It's possible to fix this by creating a complex hierarchy of metaclass type definitions to layer validation:

```
class ValidatePolygon(type):
    def __new__(meta, name, bases, class_dict):
        # Only validate non-root classes
        if not class_dict.get("is_root"):
            if class_dict["sides"] < 3:
                raise ValueError("Polygons need 3+ sides")
        return type.__new__(meta, name, bases, class_dict)

class Polygon(metaclass=ValidatePolygon):
    is_root = True
    sides = None  # Must be specified by subclasses

class ValidateFilledPolygon(ValidatePolygon):
    def __new__(meta, name, bases, class_dict):
        # Only validate non-root classes
        if not class_dict.get("is_root"):
            if class_dict["color"] not in ("red", "green"):
                raise ValueError("Fill color must be supported")
        return super().__new__(meta, name, bases, class_dict)

class FilledPolygon(Polygon, metaclass=ValidateFilledPolygon):
    is_root = True
    color = None  # Must be specified by subclasses
```

This requires every FilledPolygon instance to be a Polygon instance:

```
class GreenPentagon(FilledPolygon):
    color = "green"
    sides = 5

greenie = GreenPentagon()
assert isinstance(greenie, Polygon)
```

Validation works for colors:

```
class OrangePentagon(FilledPolygon):
    color = "orange"
    sides = 5

>>>
Traceback ...
ValueError: Fill color must be supported
```

Validation also works for number of sides:

```
class RedLine(FilledPolygon):
    color = "red"
    sides = 2

>>>
Traceback ...
ValueError: Polygons need 3+ sides
```

However, this approach ruins composability, which is often the purpose of class validation like this (similar to mix-ins; see Item 54: "Consider Composing Functionality with Mix-in Classes"). If I want to apply the color validation logic from ValidateFilledPolygon to another hierarchy of classes, I'll have to duplicate all of the logic again, which reduces code reuse and increases boilerplate.

The __init_subclass__ special class method can also be used to solve this problem. It can be defined by multiple levels of a class hierarchy as long as the super built-in function is used to call any parent or sibling __init_subclass__ definitions. Here, I define a class to represent a region's fill color that can be composed with the BetterPolygon class from before:

```
class Filled:
    color = None  # Must be specified by subclasses

    def __init_subclass__(cls):
        super().__init_subclass__()
        if cls.color not in ("red", "green", "blue"):
            raise ValueError("Fills need a valid color")
```

I can inherit from both classes to define a new class. Both classes call super().__init_subclass__(), causing their corresponding validation logic to run when the subclass is created:

```
class RedTriangle(Filled, BetterPolygon):
    color = "red"
    sides = 3

ruddy = RedTriangle()
assert isinstance(ruddy, Filled)
assert isinstance(ruddy, BetterPolygon)
```

If I specify the number of sides incorrectly, I get a validation error:

```
print("Before class")

class BlueLine(Filled, BetterPolygon):
    color = "blue"
    sides = 2

print("After class")

>>>
Before class
Traceback ...
ValueError: Polygons need 3+ sides
```

If I specify the color incorrectly, I also get a validation error:

```
print("Before class")

class BeigeSquare(Filled, BetterPolygon):
    color = "beige"
    sides = 4

print("After class")

>>>
Before class
Traceback ...
ValueError: Fills need a valid color
```

You can even use __init_subclass__ in complex cases like multiple inheritance and diamond inheritance (see Item 53: "Initialize Parent Classes with super" for background). Here, I define a basic diamond hierarchy to show this in action:

```
class Top:
    def __init_subclass__(cls):
        super().__init_subclass__()
        print(f"Top for {cls}")

class Left(Top):
    def __init_subclass__(cls):
        super().__init_subclass__()
        print(f"Left for {cls}")

class Right(Top):
    def __init_subclass__(cls):
        super().__init_subclass__()
        print(f"Right for {cls}")
```

```
class Bottom(Left, Right):
    def __init_subclass__(cls):
        super().__init_subclass__()
        print(f"Bottom for {cls}")

>>>
Top for <class '__main__.Left'>
Top for <class '__main__.Right'>
Top for <class '__main__.Bottom'>
Right for <class '__main__.Bottom'>
Left for <class '__main__.Bottom'>
```

As expected, Top.__init_subclass__ is called only a single time for each class, even though there are two paths to it for the Bottom class through its Left and Right parent classes.

Things to Remember

✦ The __new__ method of metaclasses is run after the class statement's entire body has been processed.

✦ Metaclasses can be used to inspect or modify a class after it's defined but before it's created, but they're often more heavyweight than you need.

✦ Use __init_subclass__ to ensure that subclasses are well formed at the time they are defined, before objects of their type are constructed.

✦ Be sure to call super().__init_subclass__ from within your class's __init_subclass__ definition to enable composable validation in multiple layers of classes and multiple inheritance.

Item 63: Register Class Existence with __init_subclass__

Another common use of metaclasses (see Item 62: "Validate Subclasses with __init_subclass__" for background) is to automatically register types in a program. Registration is useful for doing reverse lookups, where you need to map an identifier back to a corresponding class.

For example, say that I want to implement my own serialized representation of a Python object using JSON. I need a way to turn an object into a JSON string. Here, I do this generically by defining a base class that records the constructor parameters and turns them into a JSON dictionary (see Item 54: "Consider Composing Function-ality with Mix-in Classes" for another approach):

```
import json

class Serializable:
    def __init__(self, *args):
        self.args = args

    def serialize(self):
        return json.dumps({"args": self.args})
```

This class makes it easy to serialize simple data structures to a string, like this one:

```
class Point2D(Serializable):
    def __init__(self, x, y):
        super().__init__(x, y)
        self.x = x
        self.y = y

    def __repr__(self):
        return f"Point2D({self.x}, {self.y})"


point = Point2D(5, 3)
print("Object:    ", point)
print("Serialized:", point.serialize())

>>>
Object:     Point2D(5, 3)
Serialized: {"args": [5, 3]}
```

Now I need to deserialize this JSON string and construct the `Point2D` object it represents. Here I define another class that can deseri-alize the data from its `Serializable` parent class (see Item 52: "Use `@classmethod` Polymorphism to Construct Objects Generically" for background):

```
class Deserializable(Serializable):
    @classmethod
    def deserialize(cls, json_data):
        params = json.loads(json_data)
        return cls(*params["args"])
```

Using Deserializable as a parent class makes it easy to serialize and deserialize simple objects in a generic way:

```python
class BetterPoint2D(Deserializable):
    def __init__(self, x, y):
        super().__init__(x, y)
        self.x = x
        self.y = y

    def __repr__(self):
        return f"Point2D({self.x}, {self.y})"


before = BetterPoint2D(5, 3)
print("Before:    ", before)
data = before.serialize()
print("Serialized:", data)
after = BetterPoint2D.deserialize(data)
print("After:     ", after)

>>>
Before:     Point2D(5, 3)
Serialized: {"args": [5, 3]}
After:      Point2D(5, 3)
```

The problem with this approach is that it works only if you know the intended type of the serialized data ahead of time (e.g., Point2D, BetterPoint2D). Ideally, you'd have a large number of classes serializing to JSON and one common function that could deserialize any of them back to a corresponding Python object (see Item 50: "Consider functools.singledispatch for Functional-Style Programming Instead of Object-Oriented Polymorphism" for a similar example).

To do this, I can include the serialized object's class name in the JSON data:

```python
class BetterSerializable:
    def __init__(self, *args):
        self.args = args

    def serialize(self):
        return json.dumps(
            {
                "class": self.__class__.__name__,
                "args": self.args,
            }
        )
```

```
def __repr__(self):
    name = self.__class__.__name__
    args_str = ", ".join(str(x) for x in self.args)
    return f"{name}({args_str})"
```

Then I can maintain a mapping of class names back to constructors for those objects. The general deserialize function works for any classes passed to register_class:

```
REGISTRY = {}

def register_class(target_class):
    REGISTRY[target_class.__name__] = target_class

def deserialize(data):
    params = json.loads(data)
    name = params["class"]
    target_class = REGISTRY[name]
    return target_class(*params["args"])
```

To ensure that deserialize always works properly, I must call register_class for every class I might want to deserialize in the future:

```
class EvenBetterPoint2D(BetterSerializable):
    def __init__(self, x, y):
        super().__init__(x, y)
        self.x = x
        self.y = y

register_class(EvenBetterPoint2D)
```

Now I can deserialize an arbitrary JSON string without having to know which class it contains:

```
before = EvenBetterPoint2D(5, 3)
print("Before:   ", before)
data = before.serialize()
print("Serialized:", data)
after = deserialize(data)
print("After:    ", after)

>>>
Before:    EvenBetterPoint2D(5, 3)
Serialized: {"class": "EvenBetterPoint2D", "args": [5, 3]}
After:     EvenBetterPoint2D(5, 3)
```

The problem with this approach is that it's possible to forget to call register_class:

```
class Point3D(BetterSerializable):
    def __init__(self, x, y, z):
        super().__init__(x, y, z)
        self.x = x
        self.y = y
        self.z = z


# Forgot to call register_class! Whoops!
```

The code breaks at runtime when I try to deserialize an object of a class I forgot to register:

```
point = Point3D(5, 9, -4)
data = point.serialize()
deserialize(data)

>>>
Traceback ...
KeyError: 'Point3D'
```

Even though I chose to subclass BetterSerializable, I don't actually get all of its features if I forget to call register_class after the class statement body. This approach is error prone and especially challenging for beginners to debug. The same omission can happen with *class decorators* (see Item 66: "Prefer Class Decorators over Metaclasses for Composable Class Extensions" for when those are appropriate).

What if I could somehow act on the programmer's intent to use BetterSerializable and ensure that register_class is called in all cases? Metaclasses enable this by intercepting the class statement when subclasses are defined. Here I use a metaclass and corresponding superclass to register any child classes immediately after their class statements end:

```
class Meta(type):
    def __new__(meta, name, bases, class_dict):
        cls = type.__new__(meta, name, bases, class_dict)
        register_class(cls)
        return cls


class RegisteredSerializable(BetterSerializable, metaclass=Meta):
    pass
```

When I define a subclass of `RegisteredSerializable`, I can be confident
that the call to `register_class` happens and `deserialize` will always
work as expected:

```
class Vector3D(RegisteredSerializable):
    def __init__(self, x, y, z):
        super().__init__(x, y, z)
        self.x, self.y, self.z = x, y, z


before = Vector3D(10, -7, 3)
print("Before:    ", before)
data = before.serialize()
print("Serialized:", data)
print("After:     ", deserialize(data))

>>>
Before:     Vector3D(10, -7, 3)
Serialized: {"class": "Vector3D", "args": [10, -7, 3]}
After:      Vector3D(10, -7, 3)
```

An even better approach is to use the `__init_subclass__` special class
method. This simplified syntax, introduced in Python 3.6, reduces
the visual noise of applying custom logic when a class is defined. It
also makes it more approachable to beginners who may be confused
by the complexity of metaclass syntax. Here I implement a new superclass to automatically call `register_class` and a subclass that uses it:

```
class BetterRegisteredSerializable(BetterSerializable):
    def __init_subclass__(cls):
        super().__init_subclass__()
        register_class(cls)


class Vector1D(BetterRegisteredSerializable):
    def __init__(self, magnitude):
        super().__init__(magnitude)
        self.magnitude = magnitude
```

Serialization and deserialization work as expected for this new class:

```
before = Vector1D(6)
print("Before:    ", before)
data = before.serialize()
print("Serialized:", data)
print("After:     ", deserialize(data))

>>>
Before:     Vector1D(6)
Serialized: {"class": "Vector1D", "args": [6]}
After:      Vector1D(6)
```

By using __init_subclass__ (or metaclasses) for class registration, you can ensure that you'll never miss registering a class as long as the inheritance tree is right. This works well for serialization, as I've shown, and also applies to database object-relational mappings (ORMs), extensible plug-in systems, and callback hooks.

Things to Remember

✦ Class registration is a helpful pattern for building modular Python programs.

✦ Metaclasses let you run registration code automatically each time your base class is subclassed in a program.

✦ Using metaclasses for class registration helps you avoid errors by ensuring that you never miss a registration call.

✦ Prefer __init_subclass__ over standard metaclass machinery because it's clearer and easier for beginners to understand.

Item 64: Annotate Class Attributes with __set_name__

One more useful feature enabled by metaclasses (see Item 62: "Validate Subclasses with __init_subclass__" for background) is the ability to modify or annotate properties after a class is defined but before the class is actually used. This approach is commonly used with descriptors (see Item 60: "Use Descriptors for Reusable @property Methods" for details) to give these attributes more introspection into how they're being used within their containing class.

For example, say that I want to define a new class that represents a row in a customer database. I'd like to have a corresponding property on the class for each column in the database table. Here I define a descriptor class to connect attributes to column names:

```
class Field:
    def __init__(self, column_name):
        self.column_name = column_name
        self.internal_name = "_" + self.column_name
```

I can use the column name to save all of the per-instance state directly in the instance dictionary as protected fields by using the setattr built-in function, and later I can load state with getattr (see Item 61: "Use __getattr__, __getattribute__, and __setattr__ for Lazy Attributes" for background):

```
    def __get__(self, instance, instance_type):
        if instance is None:
            return self
        return getattr(instance, self.internal_name, "")
```

```
def __set__(self, instance, value):
    setattr(instance, self.internal_name, value)
```

Defining the class representing a row requires supplying the database table's column name for each descriptor attribute:

```
class Customer:
    # Class attributes
    first_name = Field("first_name")
    last_name = Field("last_name")
    prefix = Field("prefix")
    suffix = Field("suffix")
```

Using the row class is simple. Here, the Field descriptors modify the instance dictionary __dict__ as expected:

```
cust = Customer()
print(f"Before: {cust.first_name!r} {cust.__dict__}")
cust.first_name = "Euclid"
print(f"After:  {cust.first_name!r} {cust.__dict__}")

>>>
Before: '' {}
After:  'Euclid' {'_first_name': 'Euclid'}
```

But the code for this class definition seems redundant. I already declared the name of the field for the class on the left (field_name =). Why do I also have to pass a string containing the same information to the Field constructor (Field("first_name")) on the right?

```
class Customer:
    # Left side is redundant with right side
    first_name = Field("first_name")
    ...
```

The problem is that the order of evaluation for the Customer class definition is the opposite of how it reads from left to right. First, the Field constructor is called as Field("first_name"). Then, the return value of that is assigned to the Customer.first_name class attribute. There's no way for a Field instance to know upfront which class attribute it will be assigned to.

To eliminate this redundancy, I can use a metaclass. A metaclass lets you hook the class statement directly and take action as soon as a class body is finished. In this case, I can use the metaclass to assign Field.column_name and Field.internal_name on the descriptor automatically instead of manually specifying the field name multiple times:

```
class Meta(type):
    def __new__(meta, name, bases, class_dict):
        for key, value in class_dict.items():
            if isinstance(value, Field):
                value.column_name = key
                value.internal_name = "_" + key
        cls = type.__new__(meta, name, bases, class_dict)
        return cls
```

Here I define a base class that uses the metaclass. All classes representing database rows should inherit from this class to ensure that they use the metaclass:

```
class DatabaseRow(metaclass=Meta):
    pass
```

To work with the metaclass, the field descriptor is largely unchanged. The only difference is that it no longer requires any arguments to be passed to its constructor. Instead, its attributes are set by the Meta.__new__ method above:

```
class Field:
    def __init__(self):
        # These will be assigned by the metaclass.
        self.column_name = None
        self.internal_name = None

    def __get__(self, instance, instance_type):
        if instance is None:
            return self
        return getattr(instance, self.internal_name, "")

    def __set__(self, instance, value):
        setattr(instance, self.internal_name, value)
```

When I use the metaclass, the new DatabaseRow base class, and the new Field descriptor, the class definition for a database row no longer has the redundancy from before:

```
class BetterCustomer(DatabaseRow):
    first_name = Field()
    last_name = Field()
    prefix = Field()
    suffix = Field()
```

The behavior of the new class is identical to the behavior of the old one:

```
cust = BetterCustomer()
print(f"Before: {cust.first_name!r} {cust.__dict__}")
cust.first_name = "Euler"
print(f"After:  {cust.first_name!r} {cust.__dict__}")

>>>
Before: '' {}
After:  'Euler' {'_first_name': 'Euler'}
```

The trouble with this approach is that you can't use the Field class for properties unless you also inherit from DatabaseRow. If you somehow forget to subclass DatabaseRow, or if you don't want to due to other structural requirements of the class hierarchy, the code will break:

```
class BrokenCustomer:  # Missing inheritance
    first_name = Field()
    last_name = Field()
    prefix = Field()
    suffix = Field()


cust = BrokenCustomer()
cust.first_name = "Mersenne"

>>>
Traceback ...
TypeError: attribute name must be string, not 'NoneType'
```

The solution to this problem is to use the __set_name__ special method for descriptors. This method, introduced in Python 3.6, is called on every descriptor instance when its containing class is defined. It receives as parameters the owning class that contains the descriptor instance and the attribute name to which the descriptor instance was assigned. Here I avoid defining a metaclass entirely and move what the Meta.__new__ method from above was doing into the __set_name__ method:

```
class Field:
    def __init__(self):
        self.column_name = None
        self.internal_name = None

    def __set_name__(self, owner, column_name):
        # Called on class creation for each descriptor
        self.column_name = column_name
        self.internal_name = "_" + column_name
```

```
    def __get__(self, instance, instance_type):
        if instance is None:
            return self
        return getattr(instance, self.internal_name, "")

    def __set__(self, instance, value):
        setattr(instance, self.internal_name, value)
```

Now, I can get the benefits of the Field descriptor without having to inherit from a specific parent class or having to use a metaclass:

```
class FixedCustomer:  # No parent class
    first_name = Field()
    last_name = Field()
    prefix = Field()
    suffix = Field()

cust = FixedCustomer()
print(f"Before: {cust.first_name!r} {cust.__dict__}")
cust.first_name = "Mersenne"
print(f"After:  {cust.first_name!r} {cust.__dict__}")

>>>
Before: '' {}
After:  'Mersenne' {'_first_name': 'Mersenne'}
```

Things to Remember

✦ A metaclass enables you to modify a class's attributes before the class is fully defined.

✦ Descriptors and metaclasses make a powerful combination for declarative behavior and runtime introspection.

✦ Define __set_name__ on your descriptor classes to allow them to take into account their surrounding class and its property names.

Item 65: Consider Class Body Definition Order to Establish Relationships Between Attributes

The purpose of many classes defined in Python programs is to represent external data that is created and maintained elsewhere. For example, say that I have a CSV (comma-separated values) file containing a list of freight deliveries where each row includes the destination city, method of travel, and shipment weight. Here, I read in this data using the `csv` built-in module:

```
import csv


with open("packages.csv") as f:
    for row in csv.reader(f):
        print(row)
```

```
>>>
['Sydney', 'truck', '25']
['Melbourne', 'boat', '6']
['Brisbane', 'plane', '12']
['Perth', 'road train', '90']
['Adelaide', 'truck', '17']
...
```

I can define a new class to store this data and a helper function that creates an object, given a CSV row (see Item 52: "Use @classmethod Polymorphism to Construct Objects Generically" for background):

```
class Delivery:
    def __init__(self, destination, method, weight):
        self.destination = destination
        self.method = method
        self.weight = weight

    @classmethod
    def from_row(cls, row):
        return cls(row[0], row[1], row[2])
```

This works as expected when provided a list of values, one for each column:

```
row1 = ["Sydney", "truck", "25"]
obj1 = Delivery.from_row(row1)
print(obj1.__dict__)
```

```
>>>
{'destination': 'Sydney', 'method': 'truck', 'weight': '25'}
```

If more columns are added to the CSV file or if the columns are reordered, with a small amount of effort, I can make corresponding adjustments to the __init__ and from_row methods to maintain compatibility with the file format. Now imagine that there are many kinds of CSV files that I want to process, each with different numbers of columns and types of cell values. It would be better if I could more efficiently define a new class for each CSV file without much boilerplate.

Here I try to accomplish this by implementing a base class that uses the `fields` class attribute to map CSV columns (in the order they appear in the file) to object attribute names (see Item 64: "Annotate Class Attributes with __set_name__" for another approach):

```python
class RowMapper:
    fields = ()  # Must be in CSV column order

    def __init__(self, **kwargs):
        for key, value in kwargs.items():
            if key not in type(self).fields:
                raise TypeError(f"Invalid field: {key}")
            setattr(self, key, value)

    @classmethod
    def from_row(cls, row):
        if len(row) != len(cls.fields):
            raise ValueError("Wrong number of fields")
        kwargs = dict(pair for pair in zip(cls.fields, row))
        return cls(**kwargs)
```

Now I can create a concrete child class for the freight CSV file format:

```python
class DeliveryMapper(RowMapper):
    fields = ("destination", "method", "weight")

obj2 = DeliveryMapper.from_row(row1)
assert obj2.destination == "Sydney"
assert obj2.method == "truck"
assert obj2.weight == "25"
```

If I had another CSV format to support—say, for moving-van logistics—I could quickly create another child by providing the column names:

```python
class MovingMapper(RowMapper):
    fields = ("source", "destination", "square_feet")
```

Although this works, it's not Pythonic. The attributes are specified using strings instead of variable names, which makes the code difficult to read and flummoxes tools (see Item 124: "Consider Static Analysis via typing to Obviate Bugs" and Item 3: "Never Expect Python to Detect Errors at Compile Time"). More importantly, the `fields` tuple feels redundant with the body of the class: It's a list of attributes nested inside a list of attributes.

What would be better is if I could put the names of the CSV columns in the body of the class, like this:

```
class BetterMovingMapper:
    source = ...
    destination = ...
    square_feet = ...
```

It turns out this is possible using three features of Python together (see Item 51: "Prefer dataclasses for Defining Lightweight Classes" for another approach). The first feature is the __init_subclass__ special class method, which allows you to run code when a subclass is defined (see Item 62: "Validate Subclasses with __init_subclass__"). The second feature is how Python class attributes can be inspected at runtime using the __dict__ instance dictionary of a class object (see Item 54: "Consider Composing Functionality with Mix-in Classes"). The third feature is how Python dictionaries preserve the insertion order of key/value pairs (see Item 25: "Be Cautious when Relying on Dictionary Insertion Ordering").

Here I create a class that finds child attributes assigned to ... and stores their names in the fields class attribute for the RowMapper parent class to use:

```
class BetterRowMapper(RowMapper):
    def __init_subclass__(cls):
        fields = []
        for key, value in cls.__dict__.items():
            if value is Ellipsis:
                fields.append(key)
        cls.fields = tuple(fields)
```

Now I can declare a concrete class like before, but using the class body with ellipses to indicate the columns of the CSV file:

```
class BetterDeliveryMapper(BetterRowMapper):
    destination = ...
    method = ...
    weight = ...


obj3 = BetterDeliveryMapper.from_row(row1)
assert obj3.destination == "Sydney"
assert obj3.method == "truck"
assert obj3.weight == "25"
```

If the order of the columns in the CSV file changes, I can just change the attribute definition order to compensate. For example, here I move the `destination` field to the end:

```
class ReorderedDeliveryMapper(BetterRowMapper):
    method = ...
    weight = ...
    destination = ...   # Moved

row4 = ["road train", "90", "Perth"]  # Different order
obj4 = ReorderedDeliveryMapper.from_row(row4)
print(obj4.__dict__)

>>>
{'method': 'road train', 'weight': '90', 'destination':
➥'Perth'}
```

In a real program, I would use a descriptor class instead of ellipses when declaring the fields to enable use cases like attribute validation and data conversion (see Item 60: "Use Descriptors for Reusable @property Methods" for background). For example, say that I want the weight column to be parsed into a floating point number instead of remaining as a string.

Here I implement a descriptor class that intercepts attribute accesses and converts assigned values as needed:

```
class Field:
    def __init__(self):
        self.internal_name = None

    def __set_name__(self, owner, column_name):
        self.internal_name = "_" + column_name

    def __get__(self, instance, instance_type):
        if instance is None:
            return self
        return getattr(instance, self.internal_name, "")

    def __set__(self, instance, value):
        adjusted_value = self.convert(value)
        setattr(instance, self.internal_name, adjusted_value)

    def convert(self, value):
        raise NotImplementedError
```

I can implement two concrete `Field` subclasses—one for strings and another for floating point numbers:

```
class StringField(Field):
    def convert(self, value):
        if not isinstance(value, str):
            raise ValueError
        return value


class FloatField(Field):
    def convert(self, value):
        return float(value)
```

Another new base class for representing CSV files can look for `Field` instances instead of `Ellipsis` instances to discover the ordered CSV columns and populate the `fields` class attribute accordingly:

```
class DescriptorRowMapper(RowMapper):
    def __init_subclass__(cls):
        fields = []
        for key, value in cls.__dict__.items():
            if isinstance(value, Field):  # Changed
                fields.append(key)
        cls.fields = tuple(fields)
```

Now I can declare a concrete subclass for my specific CSV format, and the `weight` field will be converted to a floating point, as expected:

```
class ConvertingDeliveryMapper(DescriptorRowMapper):
    destination = StringField()
    method = StringField()
    weight = FloatField()


obj5 = ConvertingDeliveryMapper.from_row(row1)
assert obj5.destination == "Sydney"
assert obj5.method == "truck"
assert obj5.weight == 25.0  # Number, not string
```

Inspecting class attributes can also be used to discover methods. In a completely different example from the CSV use-case above, imagine that I want to create a class that describes a sequential workflow of methods that need to run in definition order, like this:

```
class HypotheticalWorkflow:
    def start_engine(self):
        ...
```

```
    def release_brake(self):
        ...

    def run(self):
        # Runs `start_engine` then `release_brake`
        ...
```

I can make this work by first creating a simple function decorator (see Item 38: "Define Function Decorators with `functools.wraps`") that indicates which methods should be considered for the workflow:

```
def step(func):
    func._is_step = True
    return func
```

A new base class can then look for callable class attributes (see Item 48: "Accept Functions Instead of Classes for Simple Interfaces" for background) with the _is_step attribute present to discover which methods should be included in the workflow and the order in which they should be called:

```
class Workflow:
    def __init_subclass__(cls):
        steps = []
        for key, value in cls.__dict__.items():
            if callable(value) and hasattr(value, "_is_step"):
                steps.append(key)
        cls.steps = tuple(steps)
```

The run method only needs to iterate through the list of steps and call the methods in the saved sequence. No other boilerplate is required:

```
    def run(self):
        for step_name in type(self).steps:
            func = getattr(self, step_name)
            func()
```

Putting it together, here I define a simple workflow for starting a car, which includes a helper method that should be ignored by the base class:

```
class MyWorkflow(Workflow):
    @step
    def start_engine(self):
        print("Engine is on!")
        ...
```

```
def my_helper_function(self):
    raise RuntimeError("Should not be called")

@step
def release_brake(self):
    print("Brake is off!")
    ...

...
```

The workflow runs successfully and doesn't call the bad method:

```
workflow = MyWorkflow()
workflow.run()

>>>
Engine is on!
Brake is off!
...
```

Things to Remember

✦ You can examine the attributes and methods defined in a class body at runtime by inspecting the corresponding class object's __dict__ instance dictionary.

✦ The definition order of class bodies is preserved in a class object's __dict__, enabling code to consider the relative positions of a class's attributes and methods. This is especially useful for use cases like mapping object fields to CSV column indexes.

✦ Descriptors and method decorators can be used to further enhance the power of using the definition order of class bodies to control program behavior.

Item 66: Prefer Class Decorators over Metaclasses for Composable Class Extensions

Although metaclasses allow you to customize class creation in multiple ways (see Item 62: "Validate Subclasses with __init_subclass__" and Item 63: "Register Class Existence with __init_subclass__"), they still fall short of handling every situation that may arise.

For example, say that I want to decorate all of the methods of a class with a helper function that prints arguments, return values, and any exceptions that were raised. Here, I define such a debugging decorator (see Item 38: "Define Function Decorators with `functools.wraps`" for background):

```
from functools import wraps

def trace_func(func):
    if hasattr(func, "tracing"):  # Only decorate once
        return func

    @wraps(func)
    def wrapper(*args, **kwargs):
        args_repr = repr(args)
        kwargs_repr = repr(kwargs)
        result = None
        try:
            result = func(*args, **kwargs)
            return result
        except Exception as e:
            result = e
            raise
        finally:
            print(
                f"{func.__name__}"
                f"({args_repr}, {kwargs_repr}) -> "
                f"{result!r}"
            )

    wrapper.tracing = True
    return wrapper
```

I can apply this decorator to various special methods in my new dict subclass (see Item 57: "Inherit from `collections.abc` Classes for Custom Container Types"):

```
class TraceDict(dict):
    @trace_func
    def __init__(self, *args, **kwargs):
        return super().__init__(*args, **kwargs)

    @trace_func
    def __setitem__(self, *args, **kwargs):
        return super().__setitem__(*args, **kwargs)

    @trace_func
    def __getitem__(self, *args, **kwargs):
        return super().__getitem__(*args, **kwargs)

    ...
```

And I can verify that these methods are decorated by interacting with an instance of the class:

```
trace_dict = TraceDict([("hi", 1)])
trace_dict["there"] = 2
trace_dict["hi"]
try:
    trace_dict["does not exist"]
except KeyError:
    pass  # Expected

>>>
__init__(({}, [('hi', 1)]), {}) -> None
__setitem__(({'hi': 1}, 'there', 2), {}) -> None
__getitem__(({'hi': 1, 'there': 2}, 'hi'), {}) -> 1
__getitem__(({'hi': 1, 'there': 2}, 'does not exist'),
➥{}) -> KeyError('does not exist')
```

The problem with this code is that I had to redefine all the methods that I wanted to decorate with @trace_func. This is redundant boiler-plate that's hard to read and error prone. Further, if a new method is later added to the dict superclass, it won't be decorated unless I also define it in TraceDict.

One way to solve this problem is to use a metaclass to automatically decorate all methods of a class. Here I implement this behavior by wrapping each function or method in the new type with the trace_func decorator:

```
import types

TRACE_TYPES = (
    types.MethodType,
    types.FunctionType,
    types.BuiltinFunctionType,
    types.BuiltinMethodType,
    types.MethodDescriptorType,
    types.ClassMethodDescriptorType,
    types.WrapperDescriptorType,
)

IGNORE_METHODS = (
    "__repr__",
    "__str__",
)
```

```
class TraceMeta(type):
    def __new__(meta, name, bases, class_dict):
        klass = super().__new__(meta, name, bases, class_dict)

        for key in dir(klass):
            if key in IGNORE_METHODS:
                continue

            value = getattr(klass, key)
            if not isinstance(value, TRACE_TYPES):
                continue

            wrapped = trace_func(value)
            setattr(klass, key, wrapped)

        return klass
```

Now I can declare my dict subclass by using the TraceMeta metaclass and verify that it works as expected:

```
class TraceDict(dict, metaclass=TraceMeta):
    pass

trace_dict = TraceDict([("hi", 1)])
trace_dict["there"] = 2
trace_dict["hi"]
try:
    trace_dict["does not exist"]
except KeyError:
    pass  # Expected
```

```
>>>
__new__((<class '__main__.TraceDict'>, [('hi', 1)]), {}) -> {}
__init__(({}, [('hi', 1)]), {}) -> None
__setitem__(({'hi': 1}, 'there', 2), {}) -> None
__getitem__(({'hi': 1, 'there': 2}, 'hi'), {}) -> 1
__getitem__(({'hi': 1, 'there': 2}, 'does not exist'),
➥{}) -> KeyError('does not exist')
```

This works, and it even prints out a call to __new__ that was missing from my earlier implementation. What happens if I try to use TraceMeta when a superclass already has specified a metaclass?

```
class OtherMeta(type):
    pass

class SimpleDict(dict, metaclass=OtherMeta):
    pass
```

```
class ChildTraceDict(SimpleDict, metaclass=TraceMeta):
    pass

>>>
Traceback ...
TypeError: metaclass conflict: the metaclass of a derived class
➥must be a (non-strict) subclass of the metaclasses of all its
➥bases
```

This fails because TraceMeta does not inherit from OtherMeta. In theory, I can use metaclass inheritance to solve this problem by having OtherMeta inherit from TraceMeta:

```
class TraceMeta(type):
    ...

class OtherMeta(TraceMeta):
    pass

class SimpleDict(dict, metaclass=OtherMeta):
    pass

class ChildTraceDict(SimpleDict, metaclass=TraceMeta):
    pass

trace_dict = ChildTraceDict([("hi", 1)])
trace_dict["there"] = 2
trace_dict["hi"]
try:
    trace_dict["does not exist"]
except KeyError:
    pass  # Expected

>>>
__init_subclass__((), {}) -> None
__new__((<class '__main__.ChildTraceDict'>, [('hi', 1)]),
➥{}) -> {}
__init__(({}, [('hi', 1)]), {}) -> None
__setitem__(({'hi': 1}, 'there', 2), {}) -> None
__getitem__(({'hi': 1, 'there': 2}, 'hi'), {}) -> 1
__getitem__(({'hi': 1, 'there': 2}, 'does not exist'),
➥{}) -> KeyError('does not exist')
```

But this won't work if the metaclass is from a library that I can't modify or if I want to use multiple utility metaclasses like TraceMeta at the same time. The metaclass approach puts too many constraints on the class that's being modified.

To solve this problem, Python supports class decorators. *Class decorators* work just like function decorators: They're applied with the @ symbol prefixing a function before the class declaration. The function is expected to modify or re-create the class accordingly and then return it, like this:

```
def my_class_decorator(klass):
    klass.extra_param = "hello"
    return klass

@my_class_decorator
class MyClass:
    pass

print(MyClass)
print(MyClass.extra_param)

>>>
<class '__main__.MyClass'>
hello
```

I can implement a class decorator to apply the trace_func function decorator to all methods of a class by moving the core of the TraceMeta.__new__ method above into a stand-alone function. This implementation is much shorter than the metaclass version:

```
def trace(klass):
    for key in dir(klass):
        if key in IGNORE_METHODS:
            continue

        value = getattr(klass, key)
        if not isinstance(value, TRACE_TYPES):
            continue

        wrapped = trace_func(value)
        setattr(klass, key, wrapped)

    return klass
```

I can apply this decorator to my dict subclass to get the same behavior that I get by using the metaclass approach above:

```
@trace
class DecoratedTraceDict(dict):
    pass
```

```
trace_dict = DecoratedTraceDict([("hi", 1)])
trace_dict["there"] = 2
trace_dict["hi"]
try:
    trace_dict["does not exist"]
except KeyError:
    pass  # Expected

>>>
__new__((<class '__main__.DecoratedTraceDict'>, [('hi', 1)]),
➥{}) -> {}
__init__(({}, [('hi', 1)]), {}) -> None
__setitem__(({'hi': 1}, 'there', 2), {}) -> None
__getitem__(({'hi': 1, 'there': 2}, 'hi'), {}) -> 1
__getitem__(({'hi': 1, 'there': 2}, 'does not exist'),
➥{}) -> KeyError('does not exist')
```

Class decorators also work when the class being decorated already has a metaclass:

```
class OtherMeta(type):
    pass

@trace
class HasMetaTraceDict(dict, metaclass=OtherMeta):
    pass

trace_dict = HasMetaTraceDict([("hi", 1)])
trace_dict["there"] = 2
trace_dict["hi"]
try:
    trace_dict["does not exist"]
except KeyError:
    pass  # Expected

>>>
__new__((<class '__main__.HasMetaTraceDict'>, [('hi', 1)]),
➥{}) -> {}
__init__(({}, [('hi', 1)]), {}) -> None
__setitem__(({'hi': 1}, 'there', 2), {}) -> None
__getitem__(({'hi': 1, 'there': 2}, 'hi'), {}) -> 1
__getitem__(({'hi': 1, 'there': 2}, 'does not exist'),
➥{}) -> KeyError('does not exist')
```

When you're looking for composable ways to extend classes, class decorators are the best tool for the job. (See Item 104: "Know How to Use `heapq` for Priority Queues" for an example class decorator called `functools.total_ordering`.)

Things to Remember

✦ A class decorator is a simple function that receives a class instance as a parameter and returns either a new class or a modified version of the original class.

✦ Class decorators are useful when you want to modify every method or attribute of a class with minimal boilerplate.

✦ Metaclasses can't be composed together easily, although many class decorators can be used to extend the same class without conflicts.

Concurrency and Parallelism

Concurrency enables a computer to do many different things *seemingly* at the same time. For example, on a computer with one CPU core, the operating system rapidly changes which program is running on the single processor. In doing so, it interleaves execution of the programs, providing the illusion that the programs are running simultaneously.

Parallelism, in contrast, involves *actually* doing many different things at the same time. Computers with multiple CPU cores can execute multiple programs simultaneously. Each CPU core runs the instructions of a separate program, allowing each program to make forward progress during the same instant.

Within a single program, concurrency is a tool that makes it easier for programmers to solve certain types of problems. Concurrent programs enable many distinct paths of execution, including separate streams of I/O, to make forward progress in a way that seems to be both simultaneous and independent.

The key difference between parallelism and concurrency is *speedup*. When two distinct paths of execution in a program make forward progress in parallel, the time it takes to do the total work is cut in half; the speed of execution is faster by a factor of two. In contrast, concurrent programs may run thousands of separate paths of execution seemingly in parallel but provide no speedup for the total work.

Python makes it easy to write concurrent programs in a variety of styles. Threads support a relatively small amount of concurrency, while asynchronous coroutines enable vast numbers of concurrent functions. Python can also be used to do parallel work through system calls, subprocesses, and C extensions. But it can be very difficult to make concurrent Python code truly run in parallel. It's important to understand how to best utilize Python in these different situations.

Item 67: Use subprocess to Manage Child Processes

Python has battle-hardened libraries for running and managing child processes. This makes Python a great language for gluing together other tools, such as command-line utilities. When existing shell scripts get complicated, as they often do over time, graduating them to a rewrite in Python for the sake of readability and maintainability is a natural choice.

Child processes started by Python are able to run in parallel, enabling you to use Python to consume all of the CPU cores of your machine and maximize the throughput of your programs. Although Python itself may be CPU bound (see Item 68: "Use Threads for Blocking I/O; Avoid for Parallelism"), it's easy to use Python to drive and coordinate CPU-intensive workloads.

Python has many ways to run subprocesses (e.g., os.popen, os.exec*), but the best choice for managing child processes is to use the subprocess built-in module. Running a child process with subprocess is simple. Here I use the module's run convenience function to start a process, read its output, and verify that it terminated cleanly:

```
import subprocess

result = subprocess.run(
    ["echo", "Hello from the child!"],
    capture_output=True,
    encoding="utf-8",
)

result.check_returncode()  # No exception means it exited cleanly
print(result.stdout)

>>>
Hello from the child!
```

Note

The examples in this item assume that your system has the echo, sleep, and openssl commands available. On Windows, this may not be the case. Please refer to the full example code for this item online to see specific directions on how to run these snippets on Windows.

Child processes run independently from their parent process, the Python interpreter. If you create a subprocess using the Popen class instead of the run function, you can poll child process status periodically while Python does other work:

```
proc = subprocess.Popen(["sleep", "1"])
while proc.poll() is None:
    print("Working...")
    # Some time-consuming work here
    ...

print("Exit status", proc.poll())

>>>
Working...
Working...
Working...
Working...
Exit status 0
```

Decoupling the child process from the parent frees up the parent process to run many child processes in parallel. Here I do this by starting all the child processes together with Popen upfront:

```
import time

start = time.perf_counter()
sleep_procs = []
for _ in range(10):
    proc = subprocess.Popen(["sleep", "1"])
    sleep_procs.append(proc)
```

Later, I can wait for them to finish their I/O and terminate with the communicate method:

```
for proc in sleep_procs:
    proc.communicate()

end = time.perf_counter()
delta = end - start
print(f"Finished in {delta:.3} seconds")

>>>
Finished in 1.01 seconds
```

If these processes ran in sequence, the total delay would be 10 seconds or more rather than the ~1 second that I measured.

You can also pipe data from a Python program into a subprocess and retrieve its output. This allows you to utilize many other programs to do work in parallel. For example, say that I want to use the openssl command-line tool to encrypt some data. Starting the child process with command-line arguments and I/O pipes is easy:

```
import os

def run_encrypt(data):
    env = os.environ.copy()
    env["password"] = "zf7ShyBhZOraQDdE/FiZpm/m/8f9X+M1"
    proc = subprocess.Popen(
        ["openssl", "enc", "-des3", "-pass", "env:password"],
        env=env,
        stdin=subprocess.PIPE,
        stdout=subprocess.PIPE,
    )
    proc.stdin.write(data)
    proc.stdin.flush()  # Ensure that the child gets input
    return proc
```

Here I pipe random bytes into the encryption function, but in practice this input pipe would be fed data from user input, a file handle, a network socket, and so on:

```
procs = []
for _ in range(3):
    data = os.urandom(10)
    proc = run_encrypt(data)
    procs.append(proc)
```

The child processes run in parallel and consume their input. Here I wait for them to finish and then retrieve their final output. The output is random encrypted bytes, as expected:

```
for proc in procs:
    out, _ = proc.communicate()
    print(out[-10:])
```

```
>>>
b'\x02a_\xd3\xd3\x9a\xd0\x8f\x14|'
b'S\x9c\x1a\x919\x9a-P\x0c\x1f'
b'\x1a\x7f\x1e\xbf\xac\xe5A>\xa3\xdd'
```

It's also possible to create chains of parallel processes, just like UNIX pipelines, connecting the output of one child process to the input of another, and so on. Here's a function that starts the openssl command-line tool as a subprocess to generate a Whirlpool hash of the input stream:

```
def run_hash(input_stdin):
    return subprocess.Popen(
        ["openssl", "dgst", "-whirlpool", "-binary"],
        stdin=input_stdin,
        stdout=subprocess.PIPE,
    )
```

Now I can kick off one set of processes to encrypt some data and another set of processes to subsequently hash their encrypted output. Note that I have to be careful with how the stdout instance of the upstream process is retained by the Python interpreter process that's starting this pipeline of child processes:

```
encrypt_procs = []
hash_procs = []
for _ in range(3):
    data = os.urandom(100)

    encrypt_proc = run_encrypt(data)
    encrypt_procs.append(encrypt_proc)

    hash_proc = run_hash(encrypt_proc.stdout)
    hash_procs.append(hash_proc)

    # Ensure that the child consumes the input stream and
    # the communicate() method doesn't inadvertently steal
    # input from the child. Also lets SIGPIPE propagate to
    # the upstream process if the downstream process dies.
    encrypt_proc.stdout.close()
    encrypt_proc.stdout = None
```

The I/O between the child processes happens automatically once they are started. All I need to do is wait for them to finish and print the final output:

```
for proc in encrypt_procs:
    proc.communicate()
    assert proc.returncode == 0

for proc in hash_procs:
    out, _ = proc.communicate()
    print(out[-10:])
    assert proc.returncode == 0
```

```
>>>
b'\xc6\n\x8a"cg\x85\xd2\x81|'
b'\x14\r\xc6J\xb0\xb0\xbf\x0c2X'
b'@\x90$\xcc\xc7\xf4\x08\x19Y\x0b'
```

If I'm worried about the child processes never finishing or somehow blocking on input or output pipes, I can pass the `timeout` parameter to the `communicate` method. This causes an exception to be raised if the child process hasn't finished within the time period, giving me a chance to terminate the misbehaving subprocess:

```
proc = subprocess.Popen(["sleep", "10"])
try:
    proc.communicate(timeout=0.1)
except subprocess.TimeoutExpired:
    proc.terminate()
    proc.wait()

print("Exit status", proc.poll())
```

```
>>>
Exit status -15
```

Things to Remember

✦ Use the `subprocess` module to run child processes and manage their input and output streams.

✦ Child processes run in parallel with the Python interpreter, enabling you to maximize your usage of CPU cores.

✦ Use the `run` convenience function for simple usage and the `Popen` class for advanced usage like UNIX-style pipelines.

✦ Use the `timeout` parameter of the `communicate` method to avoid deadlocks and hanging child processes.

Item 68: Use Threads for Blocking I/O; Avoid for Parallelism

The standard implementation of Python is called CPython. CPython runs a Python program in two steps. First, it parses and compiles the source text into *bytecode*, which is a low-level representation of the program as 8-bit instructions (see Item 97: "Rely on Precompiled Bytecode and File System Caching to Improve Startup Time" for background). (As of Python 3.6, it's technically *wordcode* with 16-bit instructions, but the idea is the same.) Then, CPython runs the bytecode using a stack-based interpreter. The bytecode interpreter has state that must be maintained and coherent while the Python program executes. CPython enforces coherence with a mechanism called the *global interpreter lock* (GIL).

Essentially, the GIL is a mutual-exclusion lock (mutex) that prevents CPython from being affected by preemptive multithreading, where one thread takes control of a program by interrupting another thread. Such an interruption could corrupt the interpreter state (e.g., garbage collection reference counts) if it comes at an unexpected time. The GIL prevents these interruptions and ensures that every bytecode instruction works correctly with the CPython implementation and its C-extension modules (see Item 96: "Consider Extension Modules to Maximize Performance and Ergonomics" for background).

The GIL has an important negative side effect. With programs written in languages like C++ or Java, having multiple threads of execution means that a program can utilize multiple CPU cores at the same time. Although Python supports multiple threads of execution, the GIL causes only one of them to ever make forward progress at a time. This means that when you reach for threads to do parallel computation and speed up your Python programs, you will be sorely disappointed.

For example, say that I want to do something computationally intensive with Python. Here I use a naive number factorization algorithm as a proxy:

```
def factorize(number):
    for i in range(1, number + 1):
        if number % i == 0:
            yield i
```

Factoring a list of 16 numbers in serial takes quite a long time:

```
import time

numbers = [7775876, 6694411, 5038540, 5426782,
           9934740, 9168996, 5271226, 8288002,
           9403196, 6678888, 6776096, 9582542,
           7107467, 9633726, 5747908, 7613918]
start = time.perf_counter()

for number in numbers:
    list(factorize(number))

end = time.perf_counter()
delta = end - start
```

```
print(f"Took {delta:.3f} seconds")
```

```
>>>
Took 3.304 seconds
```

Using multiple threads to do this computation would make sense in other languages because I could take advantage of all the CPU cores of my computer. Let me try that in Python. Here I define a Python thread for doing the same computation as before:

```
from threading import Thread

class FactorizeThread(Thread):
    def __init__(self, number):
        super().__init__()
        self.number = number

    def run(self):
        self.factors = list(factorize(self.number))
```

Then, I start a thread for each number to factorize in parallel:

```
start = time.perf_counter()

threads = []
for number in numbers:
    thread = FactorizeThread(number)
    thread.start()
    threads.append(thread)
```

Finally, I wait for all of the threads to finish:

```
for thread in threads:
    thread.join()

end = time.perf_counter()
delta = end - start
print(f"Took {delta:.3f} seconds")
```

```
>>>
Took 3.293 seconds
```

Surprisingly, this takes almost exactly the same amount of time as running factorize in serial. With one thread per number—again, 16 threads in total for this example—you might expect less than a 16x speedup in other languages due to the overhead of creating threads and coordinating with them. You might also expect only an

8x speedup on the 8-core machine I used to run this code. But you wouldn't expect the performance of these threads to appear no better when there are multiple CPUs to utilize. This demonstrates the effect of the GIL (e.g., lock contention, scheduling overhead) on programs running in the standard CPython interpreter.

There are ways to get CPython to utilize multiple cores, but they don't work with the standard Thread class (see Item 79: "Consider concurrent.futures for True Parallelism" and Item 94: "Know When and How to Replace Python with Another Programming Language"), and they can require substantial effort.

Note

Starting in CPython version 3.13, there is an experimental option to compile Python without the GIL, thus enabling programs to avoid its constraints. This can improve parallel performance with multiple threads, but there are significant downsides: Many C-extension modules and common libraries aren't yet compatible with this behavior; and the straight-line performance of individual threads is reduced because of synchronization overhead. It will be interesting to see how this experiment develops in subsequent releases.

Given these limitations, why does Python support threads at all? There are two good reasons.

First, multiple threads make it easy for a program to seem like it's doing multiple things at the same time. Managing the juggling act of simultaneous tasks is difficult to implement yourself (see Item 71: "Know How to Recognize When Concurrency Is Necessary" for an example). With threads, you can leave it to Python to run your functions concurrently. This works because CPython ensures a level of fairness between Python threads of execution, even though only one of them makes forward progress at a time due to the GIL.

The second reason Python supports threads is to deal with blocking I/O, which happens when Python does certain types of system calls. A Python program uses system calls to ask the computer's operating system to interact with the external environment on its behalf. Blocking I/O includes things like reading and writing files, interacting with networks, communicating with devices like displays, and so on. Threads help handle blocking I/O by insulating a program from the delay required for the operating system to respond to requests.

For example, say that I want to send a signal to a radio-controlled helicopter through a serial port. I'll use a slow system call (select) as a proxy for this activity. This function asks the operating system to block for 0.1 seconds and then return control to my program, which is similar to what would happen when using a synchronous serial port:

```
import select
import socket

def slow_systemcall():
    select.select([socket.socket()], [], [], 0.1)
```

Running this system call in serial requires a linearly increasing amount of time—5 calls takes about 0.5 seconds:

```
start = time.perf_counter()

for _ in range(5):
    slow_systemcall()

end = time.perf_counter()
delta = end - start
print(f"Took {delta:.3f} seconds")

>>>
Took 0.525 seconds
```

The problem is that while the slow_systemcall function is running, my program can't make any other progress. My program's main thread of execution is blocked on the select system call. This situation is awful in practice. I need to be able to compute my helicopter's next move while I'm sending it a signal; otherwise, it'll crash. When you find yourself needing to do blocking I/O and computation simultaneously like this, it's time to consider moving your system calls to threads.

Here I run multiple invocations of the slow_systemcall function in separate threads. This allows me to communicate with multiple serial ports (and helicopters) at the same time while leaving the main thread to do whatever computation is required:

```
start = time.perf_counter()

threads = []
for _ in range(5):
    thread = Thread(target=slow_systemcall)
    thread.start()
    threads.append(thread)
```

With the threads started, here I do some work to calculate the next helicopter move before waiting for the system call threads to finish:

```
def compute_helicopter_location(index):
    ...

for i in range(5):
    compute_helicopter_location(i)

for thread in threads:
    thread.join()

end = time.perf_counter()
delta = end - start
print(f"Took {delta:.3f} seconds")

>>>
Took 0.106 seconds
```

The parallel time is ~5x less than the serial time from the example code earlier. This shows that all the system calls will run in parallel from multiple Python threads even though they're limited by the GIL. The GIL prevents my Python code from running in parallel, but it doesn't have an effect on system calls. Python threads release the GIL just before they make system calls, and they reacquire the GIL as soon as the system calls are done.

There are many other ways to deal with blocking I/O besides using threads, such as using the `asyncio` built-in module, and these alternatives have important benefits. But those options might require extra work in refactoring your code to fit a different model of execution (see Item 75: "Achieve Highly Concurrent I/O with Coroutines" and Item 77: "Mix Threads and Coroutines to Ease the Transition to asyncio"). Using threads is the simplest way to do blocking I/O in parallel with minimal changes to your program.

Things to Remember

✦ Python threads can't run in parallel on multiple CPU cores because of the global interpreter lock (GIL).

✦ Python threads are still useful despite the GIL because they provide an easy way to do multiple things seemingly at the same time.

✦ You can use Python threads to make multiple system calls in parallel, allowing you to do blocking I/O at the same time as computation.

Item 69: Use Lock to Prevent Data Races in Threads

After learning about the global interpreter lock (GIL) (see Item 68: "Use Threads for Blocking I/O; Avoid for Parallelism"), many new Python programmers assume that they can forgo using mutual-exclusion locks (also called *mutexes*) in their code altogether. If the GIL is already preventing Python threads from running on multiple CPU cores in parallel, it must also act as a lock for a program's data structures, right? Some testing on types like lists and dictionaries may even show that this assumption appears to hold.

But beware: This is not truly the case. The GIL will not protect you. Although only one Python thread runs at a time, a thread's operations on data structures can be interrupted between any two byte-code instructions in the Python interpreter. This is dangerous if you access the same objects from multiple threads simultaneously. The invariants of your data structures could be violated at practically any time because of these interruptions, potentially putting your program in a corrupted state.

For example, say that I want to write a program that counts many things in parallel, like sampling light levels from a network of sensors. Imagine that each sensor has its own worker thread because reading from the sensor requires blocking I/O. After each sensor measurement, the worker thread increments a shared counter variable with the number of photons received:

```
counter = 0

def read_sensor(sensor_index):
    # Returns sensor data or raises an exception
    ...

def get_offset(data):
    # Always returns 1 or greater
    ...

def worker(sensor_index, how_many):
    global counter
    for _ in range(how_many):
        data = read_sensor(sensor_index)
        counter += get_offset(data)
```

Here I run one worker thread for each sensor in parallel and wait for them all to finish their readings:

```
from threading import Thread
```

```
how_many = 10**6
sensor_count = 4

threads = []
for i in range(sensor_count):
    thread = Thread(target=worker, args=(i, how_many))
    threads.append(thread)
    thread.start()

for thread in threads:
    thread.join()

expected = how_many * sensor_count
print(f"Counter should be {expected}, got {counter}")

>>>
Counter should be 4000000, got 1980032
```

Given how get_offset always returns 1 or more, it appears that the result is way off! What happened here? How could something so simple go so wrong, especially since only one Python interpreter thread can run at a time due to the GIL?

The answer is preemption. The Python interpreter enforces fairness between all of the threads that are executing to ensure they get a roughly equal amount of processing time. To do this, Python suspends a thread as it's running and resumes another thread in turn. The problem is that you don't know exactly when Python will suspend your threads. A thread can even be paused seemingly halfway through what looks like an atomic operation.

That's what happened in this case, on this line in the worker function from above:

```
counter += get_offset(data)
```

The += operator used on the counter variable actually instructs Python to do three separate operations behind the scenes. The statement above is equivalent to this:

```
value = counter
delta = get_offset(data)
result = value + delta
counter = result
```

Python threads incrementing the counter might be suspended between any two of these operations. This is problematic if the way the operations interleave causes old versions of value to be assigned to the counter. Here's an example of bad interaction between two threads, A and B:

```
# Running in Thread A
value_a = counter
delta_a = get_offset(data_a)
# Context switch to Thread B
value_b = counter
delta_b = get_offset(data_b)
result_b = value_b + delta_b
counter = result_b
# Context switch back to Thread A
result_a = value_a + delta_a
counter = result_a
```

Thread B interrupted thread A before it had completely finished. Thread B ran and finished, but then thread A resumed mid-execution, overwriting all of thread B's progress in incrementing the counter. This is exactly what happened in the light sensor example above.

To prevent data races like these, and other forms of data structure corruption, Python includes a robust set of tools in the `threading` built-in module. The simplest and most useful of them is the `Lock` class, a mutual-exclusion lock (mutex).

By using a lock, I can have the `Counter` class protect its current value against simultaneous accesses from multiple threads. Only one thread will be able to acquire the lock at a time. Here I use a `with` statement to acquire and release the lock; the extra level of indentation makes it easier to see which code is executing while the lock is held (see Item 82: "Consider `contextlib` and `with` Statements for Reusable `try/finally` Behavior" for background):

```
from threading import Lock

counter = 0
counter_lock = Lock()

def locking_worker(sensor_index, how_many):
    global counter
    for _ in range(how_many):
        data = read_sensor(sensor_index)
        with counter_lock:                      # Added
            counter += get_offset(data)
```

Now I run the sensor threads as before but use a `locking_worker` instead:

```
for i in range(sensor_count):
    thread = Thread(target=locking_worker, args=(i, how_many))
    threads.append(thread)
    thread.start()

for thread in threads:
    thread.join()

expected = how_many * sensor_count
print(f"Counter should be {expected}, got {counter}")

>>>
Counter should be 4000000, got 4000000
```

The result is exactly what I expect. The Lock solved the problem.

Things to Remember

◆ Even though Python has a global interpreter lock, you're still responsible for protecting against data races between the threads in your programs.

◆ Your programs will corrupt their data structures if you allow multiple threads to modify the same objects without mutual exclusion locks (mutexes).

◆ Use the Lock class from the threading built-in module to enforce your program's invariants between multiple threads.

Item 70: Use Queue to Coordinate Work Between Threads

Python programs that do many things concurrently often need to coordinate their work. One of the most useful arrangements for concurrent work is a pipeline of functions.

A pipeline works like an assembly line used in manufacturing. Pipelines have many phases in serial, with a specific function for each phase. New pieces of work are constantly added to the beginning of the pipeline. The functions can operate concurrently, each processing the piece of work in its phase. The work moves forward as each function completes until there are no phases remaining. This approach is especially good for work that includes blocking I/O or subprocesses—activities that can easily be parallelized using Python (see

Item 67: "Use subprocess to Manage Child Processes" and Item 68: "Use Threads for Blocking I/O; Avoid for Parallelism").

For example, say that I want to build a system that will take a constant stream of images from my digital camera, resize them, and then add them to a photo gallery online. Such a program could be split into three phases of a pipeline. New images are retrieved in the first phase. The downloaded images are passed through the resize function in the second phase. The resized images are consumed by the upload function in the final phase.

Imagine that I've already written Python functions that execute the phases: download, resize, and upload. How do I assemble a pipeline to do the work concurrently?

```
def download(item):
    ...

def resize(item):
    ...

def upload(item):
    ...
```

The first thing I need is a way to hand off work between the pipeline phases. This can be modeled as a thread-safe producer–consumer queue (see Item 69: "Use Lock to Prevent Data Races in Threads" to understand the importance of thread safety in Python; see Item 103: "Prefer deque for Producer–Consumer Queues" to understand queue performance):

```
from collections import deque
from threading import Lock

class MyQueue:
    def __init__(self):
        self.items = deque()
        self.lock = Lock()
```

The producer, my digital camera, adds new images to the end of the deque of pending items:

```
    def put(self, item):
        with self.lock:
            self.items.append(item)
```

The consumer, the first phase of the processing pipeline, removes images from the front of the deque of pending items:

```
def get(self):
    with self.lock:
        return self.items.popleft()
```

Here I represent each phase of the pipeline as a Python thread that takes work from one queue like this, runs a function on it, and puts the result on another queue. I also track how many times the worker has checked for new input and how much work it's completed:

```
from threading import Thread
import time

class Worker(Thread):
    def __init__(self, func, in_queue, out_queue):
        super().__init__()
        self.func = func
        self.in_queue = in_queue
        self.out_queue = out_queue
        self.polled_count = 0
        self.work_done = 0
```

The trickiest part is that the worker thread must properly handle the case where the input queue is empty because the previous phase hasn't completed its work yet. This happens where I catch the IndexError exception below. You can think of this as a holdup in the assembly line:

```
def run(self):
    while True:
        self.polled_count += 1
        try:
            item = self.in_queue.get()
        except IndexError:
            time.sleep(0.01)  # No work to do
        else:
            result = self.func(item)
            self.out_queue.put(result)
            self.work_done += 1
```

Now I can connect the three phases together by creating the queues for their coordination points and the corresponding worker threads:

```
download_queue = MyQueue()
resize_queue = MyQueue()
```

```
upload_queue = MyQueue()
done_queue  = MyQueue()
threads = [
    Worker(download, download_queue, resize_queue),
    Worker(resize, resize_queue, upload_queue),
    Worker(upload, upload_queue, done_queue),
]
```

I can start the threads and then inject a bunch of work into the first phase of the pipeline. Here I use a plain object instance as a proxy for the real data required by the download function:

```
for thread in threads:
    thread.start()

for _ in range(1000):
    download_queue.put(object())
```

Now I wait for all of the items to be processed by the pipeline and end up in the done_queue:

```
while len(done_queue.items) < 1000:
    # Do something useful while waiting
    ...
```

This runs properly, but there's an interesting side effect caused by the threads polling their input queues for new work. The tricky part, where I catch IndexError exceptions in the run method, executes a large number of times:

```
processed = len(done_queue.items)
polled = sum(t.polled_count for t in threads)
print(f"Processed {processed} items after "
      f"polling {polled} times")
```

```
>>>
Processed 1000 items after polling 3033 times
```

When the worker functions vary in their respective speeds, an earlier phase can prevent progress in later phases, causing the pipeline to back up. This causes later phases to starve and constantly check their input queues for new work in a tight loop. The outcome is that worker threads waste CPU time doing nothing useful; they're constantly raising and catching IndexError exceptions.

But that's just the beginning of what's wrong with this implementation. There are three more problems that you should also avoid. First, determining that all of the input work is complete requires yet another busy wait on the done_queue. Second, in Worker, the run method will execute forever in its busy loop. There's no obvious way to signal to a worker thread that it's time to exit.

Third, and worst of all, a backup in the pipeline can cause the program to crash arbitrarily. If the first phase makes rapid progress but the second phase makes slow progress, then the queue connecting the first phase to the second phase will constantly increase in size. The second phase won't be able to keep up. Given enough time and input data, the program will eventually run out of memory and terminate.

The lesson here isn't that pipelines are bad; it's that it's hard to build a good producer–consumer queue yourself. So why even try?

Queue to the Rescue

The Queue class from the queue built-in module provides all the functionality you need to solve the problems outlined above.

Queue eliminates busy waiting for new items by making the get method block the calling thread until data is available. For example, here I start a thread that waits for some input data on a queue:

```
from queue import Queue

my_queue = Queue()

def consumer():
    print("Consumer waiting")
    my_queue.get()  # Runs after put() below
    print("Consumer done")

thread = Thread(target=consumer)
thread.start()
```

Even though the consumer thread is running first, it won't finish until the put method adds an item to the Queue instance and the get method has something to return:

```
print("Producer putting")
my_queue.put(object())  # Runs before get() above
print("Producer done")
thread.join()

>>>
Consumer waiting
Producer putting
Producer done
Consumer done
```

To solve the pipeline backup issue and avoid out-of-memory errors, the Queue class lets you specify the maximum amount of pending work to allow between two phases. This buffer size causes calls to put to block when the queue is already full. (Sometimes this behavior is called *back pressure*.) For example, here I define a thread that waits for a while before consuming a queue:

```
my_queue = Queue(1)  # Buffer size of 1

def consumer():
    time.sleep(0.1)  # Wait
    my_queue.get()   # Runs second
    print("Consumer got 1")
    my_queue.get()   # Runs fourth
    print("Consumer got 2")
    print("Consumer done")

thread = Thread(target=consumer)
thread.start()
```

The wait should allow the producer thread to call the queue's put method for both objects before the consumer thread ever calls get. But the queue's size is 1. This means that the producer adding items to the queue will have to wait for the consumer thread to call get at least once before the second call to put will stop blocking and actually add the second item to the queue:

```
my_queue.put(object())  # Runs first
print("Producer put 1")
my_queue.put(object())  # Runs third
print("Producer put 2")
print("Producer done")
thread.join()

>>>
Producer put 1
Consumer got 1
Producer put 2
Producer done
Consumer got 2
Consumer done
```

The Queue class can also track the progress of work using the task_done method. This lets you wait for a phase's input queue to drain (using the join method) and eliminates the need to poll for the last phase of a pipeline (as with done_queue in the section above). For example, here I define a consumer thread that calls task_done when it finishes working on an item:

```
in_queue = Queue()

def consumer():
    print("Consumer waiting")
    work = in_queue.get()        # Runs second
    print("Consumer working")
    # Doing work
    ...
    print("Consumer done")
    in_queue.task_done()         # Runs third

thread = Thread(target=consumer)
thread.start()
```

Now the producer code doesn't have to call join on the consumer thread or poll. The producer can just wait for in_queue to finish by calling join on the Queue instance. Even once it's empty, in_queue won't be joinable until after task_done is called for every item that was ever enqueued:

```
print("Producer putting")
in_queue.put(object())          # Runs first
print("Producer waiting")
in_queue.join()                 # Runs fourth
print("Producer done")
thread.join()

>>>
Consumer waiting
Producer putting
Producer waiting
Consumer working
Consumer done
Producer done
```

The Queue class also allows for easy termination of worker threads by calling the shutdown method (a feature added in Python version 3.13). After the shutdown signal is received, any call to put on the queue will raise an exception, but the queue will permit get calls to drain the queue and complete pending work. Once the queue is fully empty, a ShutDown exception will be raised by get in the worker thread, giving it a chance to clean up and exit (see Item 80: "Take Advantage of Each Block in try/except/else/finally" for background). For example, here I show how a thread continues to process work after `shutdown` is called:

```python
from queue import ShutDown

my_queue2 = Queue()

def consumer():
    while True:
        try:
            item = my_queue2.get()
        except ShutDown:
            print("Terminating!")
            return
        else:
            print("Got item", item)
            my_queue2.task_done()

thread = Thread(target=consumer)
my_queue2.put(1)
my_queue2.put(2)
my_queue2.put(3)
my_queue2.shutdown()

thread.start()

my_queue2.join()
thread.join()
print("Done")

>>>
Got item 1
Got item 2
Got item 3
Terminating!
Done
```

I can bring all of these behaviors together into a new worker thread class that processes input items one at a time, puts the results on an output queue, marks the input items as done, and terminates when the `ShutDown` exception is raised:

```python
class StoppableWorker(Thread):
    def __init__(self, func, in_queue, out_queue):
        super().__init__()
        self.func = func
```

```
        self.in_queue = in_queue
        self.out_queue = out_queue

    def run(self):
        while True:
            try:
                item = self.in_queue.get()
            except ShutDown:
                return
            else:
                result = self.func(item)
                self.out_queue.put(result)
                self.in_queue.task_done()
```

Now I can create a set of pipeline threads and queues using the new worker class; the resize and upload phases have a maximum number of items specified to prevent the program from running out of memory:

```
download_queue = Queue()
resize_queue = Queue(100)
upload_queue = Queue(100)
done_queue = Queue()

threads = [
    StoppableWorker(download, download_queue, resize_queue),
    StoppableWorker(resize, resize_queue, upload_queue),
    StoppableWorker(upload, upload_queue, done_queue),
]

for thread in threads:
    thread.start()
```

To start processing, I inject all of the input work into the beginning of the pipeline:

```
for _ in range(1000):
    download_queue.put(object())
```

Then I wait for the work in each phase to finish. I'm careful to call shutdown for each queue in the pipeline only after all work for that phase has been added to the corresponding queue. I use the join method to ensure that I wait for all of the work in the queue to be completed before sending the termination signal for the next phase:

```
download_queue.shutdown()
download_queue.join()
```

```
resize_queue.shutdown()
resize_queue.join()

upload_queue.shutdown()
upload_queue.join()
```

Once the prior phases are complete, I send the shutdown signal to the final queue, receive each of the output items in the main thread, and wait for the worker threads to terminate:

```
done_queue.shutdown()

counter = 0

while True:
    try:
        item = done_queue.get()
    except ShutDown:
        break
    else:
        # Process the item
        ...
        done_queue.task_done()
        counter += 1

done_queue.join()

for thread in threads:
    thread.join()

print(counter, "items finished")

>>>
1000 items finished
```

This approach can be extended to use multiple worker threads per phase, which can increase I/O parallelism and speed up this type of program significantly. To do this, first I define helper functions for starting replicas of worker threads and draining the final queue:

```
def start_threads(count, *args):
    threads = [StoppableWorker(*args) for _ in range(count)]
    for thread in threads:
        thread.start()
    return threads
```

```
def drain_queue(input_queue):
    input_queue.shutdown()

    counter = 0

    while True:
        try:
            item = input_queue.get()
        except ShutDown:
            break
        else:
            input_queue.task_done()
            counter += 1

    input_queue.join()

    return counter
```

Then I connect the queues together as before and start the workers:

```
download_queue = Queue()
resize_queue = Queue(100)
upload_queue = Queue(100)
done_queue = Queue()

threads = (
    start_threads(3, download, download_queue, resize_queue)
    + start_threads(4, resize, resize_queue, upload_queue)
    + start_threads(5, upload, upload_queue, done_queue)
)
```

Following the same order of calls to put, shutdown, get, and join as in the example above, I can drive the work through the pipeline—but this time using multiple workers for each intermediate phase:

```
for _ in range(2000):
    download_queue.put(object())

download_queue.shutdown()
download_queue.join()

resize_queue.shutdown()
resize_queue.join()

upload_queue.shutdown()
upload_queue.join()
```

```
counter = drain_queue(done_queue)

for thread in threads:
    thread.join()

print(counter, "items finished")

>>>
2000 items finished
```

Although Queue works well with a linear pipeline, there are other tools that you should consider using in different situations (see Item 75: "Achieve Highly Concurrent I/O with Coroutines" for an example).

Things to Remember

✦ Pipelines allow you to organize sequences of work—especially I/O-bound programs—that run concurrently using multiple Python threads.

✦ Be aware of the many problems in building concurrent pipelines: busy waiting, telling workers to stop, knowing when work is done, and memory explosion.

✦ The Queue class has all the facilities you need to build robust pipelines: blocking operations, buffer sizes, joining, and shutdown.

Item 71: Know How to Recognize When Concurrency Is Necessary

Inevitably, as the scope of a program grows, so does its complexity. Dealing with expanding requirements in a way that maintains clarity, testability, and efficiency is one of the most difficult parts of programming. Perhaps the hardest type of change to handle is moving from a single-threaded program to a program that needs multiple concurrent lines of execution.

Let me demonstrate how you might encounter this problem with an example. Say that I want to implement Conway's Game of Life, a classic illustration of finite state automata. The rules of the game are simple: There's a two-dimensional grid of an arbitrary size, and each cell in the grid can either be alive or empty:

```
ALIVE = "*"
EMPTY = "-"
```

The game progresses one tick of the clock at a time. Every tick, each cell counts how many of its neighboring eight cells are still alive. Based on its neighbor count, a cell decides if it will keep living, die, or regenerate. (I'll explain the specific rules further below.) Here's an example of a 5 × 5 Game of Life grid after four generations with time going to the right:

```
  0    |   1   |   2   |   3   |   4
-----  | ----- | ----- | ----- | -----
_*___  | __*__ | __**_ | __*__ | -----
__**_  | __**_ | _*___ | _*___ | _**__
___*_  | __**_ | __**_ | __*__ | -----
-----  | ----- | ----- | ----- | -----
```

I can represent the state of each cell with a simple container class. The class must have methods that allow me to get and set the value of any coordinate. Coordinates that are out of bounds should wrap around, making the grid act like an infinite looping space:

```python
class Grid:
    def __init__(self, height, width):
        self.height = height
        self.width = width
        self.rows = []
        for _ in range(self.height):
            self.rows.append([EMPTY] * self.width)

    def get(self, y, x):
        return self.rows[y % self.height][x % self.width]

    def set(self, y, x, state):
        self.rows[y % self.height][x % self.width] = state

    def __str__(self):
        ...
```

To see this class in action, I can create a Grid instance and set its initial state to a classic shape called a glider:

```python
grid = Grid(5, 9)
grid.set(0, 3, ALIVE)
grid.set(1, 4, ALIVE)
grid.set(2, 2, ALIVE)
grid.set(2, 3, ALIVE)
grid.set(2, 4, ALIVE)
print(grid)
```

```
>>>
---*-----
----*----
--***----
---------
---------
```

Now I need a way to retrieve the status of neighboring cells. I can do this with a helper function that queries the grid for information about its surrounding environment and returns the count of living neighbors. I use a simple function for the get_cell parameter instead of passing in a whole Grid instance in order to reduce coupling (see Item 48: "Accept Functions Instead of Classes for Simple Interfaces" for more about this approach):

```
def count_neighbors(y, x, get_cell):
    n_ = get_cell(y - 1, x + 0)  # North
    ne = get_cell(y - 1, x + 1)  # Northeast
    e_ = get_cell(y + 0, x + 1)  # East
    se = get_cell(y + 1, x + 1)  # Southeast
    s_ = get_cell(y + 1, x + 0)  # South
    sw = get_cell(y + 1, x - 1)  # Southwest
    w_ = get_cell(y + 0, x - 1)  # West
    nw = get_cell(y - 1, x - 1)  # Northwest
    neighbor_states = [n_, ne, e_, se, s_, sw, w_, nw]
    count = 0
    for state in neighbor_states:
        if state == ALIVE:
            count += 1
    return count
```

Now I define the simple logic for Conway's Game of Life based on the game's three rules: Die if a cell has fewer than two neighbors, die if a cell has more than three neighbors, or become alive if an empty cell has exactly three neighbors:

```
def game_logic(state, neighbors):
    if state == ALIVE:
        if neighbors < 2:
            return EMPTY        # Die: Too few
        elif neighbors > 3:
            return EMPTY        # Die: Too many
    else:
        if neighbors == 3:
            return ALIVE        # Regenerate
    return state
```

I can connect count_neighbors and game_logic together in another function that transitions the state of a cell. This function will be called each generation to figure out a cell's current state, inspect the neighboring cells around it, determine what its next state should be, and update the resulting grid accordingly. Again, I use a function interface for set_cell instead of passing in the Grid instance to make this code more decoupled:

```
def step_cell(y, x, get_cell, set_cell):
    state = get_cell(y, x)
    neighbors = count_neighbors(y, x, get_cell)
    next_state = game_logic(state, neighbors)
    set_cell(y, x, next_state)
```

Finally, I can define a function that progresses the whole grid of cells forward by a single step and then returns a new grid containing the state for the next generation. The important detail here is that I need all dependent functions to call the get_cell method on the previous generation's Grid instance and to call the set method on the next generation's Grid instance. This is how I ensure that all of the cells move in lockstep, which is an essential part of how the game works. This is easy to achieve because I used function interfaces for get_cell and set_cell instead of passing Grid instances:

```
def simulate(grid):
    next_grid = Grid(grid.height, grid.width)
    for y in range(grid.height):
        for x in range(grid.width):
            step_cell(y, x, grid.get, next_grid.set)
    return next_grid
```

Now I can progress the grid forward one generation at a time. You can see how the glider moves down and to the right on the grid based on the simple rules from the game_logic function:

```
class ColumnPrinter:
    ...

columns = ColumnPrinter()
for i in range(5):
    columns.append(str(grid))
    grid = simulate(grid)

print(columns)
```

```
>>>
    0      |     1      |     2      |     3      |     4
---*----- | --------- | --------- | --------- | ---------
----*---- | --*-*---- | ----*---- | ---*----- | ----*----
--***---- | ---**---- | --*-*---- | ----**--- | -----*---
--------- | ---*----- | ---**---- | ---**---- | ---***---
--------- | --------- | --------- | --------- | ---------
```

This works great for a program that can run in one thread on a single machine. But imagine that the program's requirements have changed—as I alluded to above—and now I need to do some I/O (e.g., with a network socket) from within the game_logic function. For example, this might be required if I'm trying to build a massively multiplayer online game where the state transitions are determined by a combination of the grid state and communication with other players over the Internet.

How can I extend this implementation to support such functionality? The simplest thing to do is to add blocking I/O directly into the game_logic function:

```
def game_logic(state, neighbors):
    ...
    # Do some blocking input/output in here:
    data = my_socket.recv(100)
    ...
```

The problem with this approach is that it's going to slow down the whole program. If the latency of the I/O required is 100 milliseconds (which is a reasonably good cross-continent, round-trip latency on the Internet), and there are 45 cells in the grid, then each generation will take a minimum of 4.5 seconds to evaluate because each cell is processed serially in the simulate function. That's far too slow and will make the game unplayable. It also scales poorly: If I later wanted to expand the grid to 10,000 cells, I would need over 15 minutes to evaluate each generation.

The solution is to do the I/O in parallel so each generation takes roughly 100 milliseconds, regardless of how big the grid is. The process of spawning a concurrent line of execution for each unit of work—a cell in this case—is called *fan-out*. Waiting for all of those concurrent units of work to finish before moving on to the next phase in a coordinated process—a generation in this case—is called *fan-in*.

Python provides many built-in tools for achieving fan-out and fan-in with various trade-offs. You should understand the pros and cons of each approach and choose the best tool for the job, depending on the situation. See the following items for details: Item 72: "Avoid Creating New Thread Instances for On-Demand Fan-out," Item 73: "Understand How Using Queue for Concurrency Requires Refactoring," Item 74: "Consider ThreadPoolExecutor When Threads Are Necessary for Concurrency," and Item 75: "Achieve Highly Concurrent I/O with Coroutines").

Things to Remember

✦ As a program's scope and complexity increase, it often starts requiring support for multiple concurrent lines of execution.

✦ The most common types of concurrency coordination are fan-out (generating new units of concurrency) and fan-in (waiting for existing units of concurrency to complete).

✦ Python has many different ways of achieving fan-out and fan-in.

Item 72: Avoid Creating New Thread Instances for On-Demand Fan-out

Threads are the natural first tool to reach for in order to do parallel I/O in Python (see Item 68: "Use Threads for Blocking I/O; Avoid for Parallelism"). However, they have significant downsides when you try to use them for fanning out to many concurrent lines of execution.

To demonstrate this, I'll continue with the Game of Life example from before (see Item 71: "Know How to Recognize When Concurrency Is Necessary" for background and the implementations of various functions and classes below). I'll use threads to solve the latency problem caused by doing I/O in the game_logic function. To begin, threads will require coordination using locks to ensure that assumptions within data structures are maintained properly (see Item 69: "Use Lock to Prevent Data Races in Threads" for details). I can create a subclass of the Grid class that adds locking behavior so an instance can be used by multiple threads simultaneously:

```
from threading import Lock

ALIVE = "*"
EMPTY = "-"

class Grid:
    ...

class LockingGrid(Grid):
    def __init__(self, height, width):
```

```
        super().__init__(height, width)
        self.lock = Lock()

    def __str__(self):
        with self.lock:
            return super().__str__()

    def get(self, y, x):
        with self.lock:
            return super().get(y, x)

    def set(self, y, x, state):
        with self.lock:
            return super().set(y, x, state)
```

Then, I can reimplement the simulate function to *fan out* by creating a thread for each call to step_cell. The threads will run in parallel and won't have to wait on each other's I/O. I can then *fan in* by waiting for all of the threads to complete before moving on to the next generation:

```
from threading import Thread

def count_neighbors(y, x, get_cell):
    ...

def game_logic(state, neighbors):
    ...
    # Do some blocking input/output in here:
    data = my_socket.recv(100)
    ...

def step_cell(y, x, get_cell, set_cell):
    state = get_cell(y, x)
    neighbors = count_neighbors(y, x, get_cell)
    next_state = game_logic(state, neighbors)
    set_cell(y, x, next_state)

def simulate_threaded(grid):
    next_grid = LockingGrid(grid.height, grid.width)

    threads = []
    for y in range(grid.height):
        for x in range(grid.width):
            args = (y, x, grid.get, next_grid.set)
            thread = Thread(target=step_cell, args=args)
```

```
        thread.start()   # Fan-out
        threads.append(thread)

    for thread in threads:
        thread.join()   # Fan-in

    return next_grid
```

I can run this code using the same implementation of step_cell and the same driving code as before with only two lines changed to use the LockingGrid and simulate_threaded implementations:

```
class ColumnPrinter:
    ...

grid = LockingGrid(5, 9)   # Changed
grid.set(0, 3, ALIVE)
grid.set(1, 4, ALIVE)
grid.set(2, 2, ALIVE)
grid.set(2, 3, ALIVE)
grid.set(2, 4, ALIVE)

columns = ColumnPrinter()
for i in range(5):
    columns.append(str(grid))
    grid = simulate_threaded(grid)   # Changed

print(columns)
```

```
>>>
    0     |     1     |     2     |     3     |     4
---*----- | --------- | --------- | --------- | ---------
----*---- | --*-*---- | ----*---- | ---*----- | ----*----
--***---- | ---**---- | --*-*---- | ----**--- | -----*---
--------- | ---*----- | ---**---- | ---**---- | ---***---
--------- | --------- | --------- | --------- | ---------
```

This works as expected, and the I/O is now parallelized between the threads. However, this code has three big problems:

+ The Thread instances require special tools (i.e., Lock objects) to coordinate with each other safely. This makes the code that uses threads harder to reason about in comparison to the procedural, single-threaded code from before. This complexity makes threaded code more difficult to extend and maintain over time.

+ Threads require a lot of memory—about 8 MB per executing thread. On many computers, that amount of memory doesn't matter for the 45 threads I'd need in this example. But if the game grid had to grow to 10,000 cells, I would need to create that many threads, which is so much memory (80 GB) that the program won't fit on my machine. Although some operating systems play tricks to delay a thread's full memory allocation until its execution stack is sufficiently deep, there's still a risk that running one thread per concurrent activity won't work reliably.

+ Starting a thread is costly, and threads have a negative performance impact when they run due to the overhead of context switching between them. In the code above, all of the threads are started and stopped each generation of the game, which has so much overhead it will increase latency beyond the expected I/O time of 100 milliseconds.

This code would also be very difficult to debug if something went wrong. For example, imagine that the game_logic function raises an exception, which is highly likely due to the generally flaky nature of I/O:

```
def game_logic(state, neighbors):
    ...
    raise OSError("Problem with I/O")
    ...
```

I can test what this would do by running a Thread instance pointed at this function and redirecting the sys.stderr output from the program to an in-memory StringIO buffer:

```
import contextlib
import io

fake_stderr = io.StringIO()
with contextlib.redirect_stderr(fake_stderr):
    thread = Thread(target=game_logic, args=(ALIVE, 3))
    thread.start()
    thread.join()

print(fake_stderr.getvalue())

>>>
Exception in thread Thread-226 (game_logic):
Traceback (most recent call last):
  File "threading.py", line 1039, in _bootstrap_inner
    self.run()
```

```
    ~~~~~~~~^^
  File "threading.py", line 990, in run
    self._target(*self._args, **self._kwargs)
    ~~~~~~~~~~~~^^^^^^^^^^^^^^^^^^^^^^^^^^^^^^
  File "example.py", line 205, in game_logic
    raise OSError('Problem with I/O')
OSError: Problem with I/O
```

An OSError exception is expected, but somehow the code that created the thread and called join on it is unaffected. How can this be? The reason is that the Thread class will independently catch any exceptions that are raised by the target function and then write their traceback to sys.stderr. Such exceptions are never re-raised to the caller that started the thread in the first place.

Given all these issues, it's clear that threads are not the solution if you need to constantly create and finish new concurrent functions. Python provides other solutions that are a better fit (see Item 73: "Understand How Using Queue for Concurrency Requires Refactoring," Item 74: "Consider ThreadPoolExecutor When Threads Are Necessary for Concurrency," and Item 75: "Achieve Highly Concurrent I/O with Coroutines").

Things to Remember

+ Threads have many downsides: They're costly to start and run if you need a lot of them, they each require a significant amount of memory, and they require special tools like Lock instances for coordination.

+ A Thread doesn't have a built-in way to raise exceptions back in the code that started it or in a separate thread that is waiting for it to finish, which greatly hampers debugging.

Item 73: Understand How Using Queue for Concurrency Requires Refactoring

In the previous item (see Item 72: "Avoid Creating New Thread Instances for On-Demand Fan-out") I covered the downsides of using Thread to solve the parallel I/O problem in the Game of Life example from earlier (see Item 71: "Know How to Recognize When Concurrency Is Necessary" for background and the implementations of various functions and classes below).

The next approach to try is implementing a threaded pipeline using the Queue class from the queue built-in module (see Item 70: "Use Queue to Coordinate Work Between Threads" for background; I rely on the implementation of StoppableWorker from that item in the example code below).

Here's the general approach: Instead of creating one thread per cell per generation of the Game of Life, I can create a fixed number of worker threads upfront and have them do parallelized I/O as needed. This will keep my resource usage under control and eliminate the overhead of frequently starting new threads.

To do this, I need two Queue instances to use for communicating to and from the worker threads that execute the game_logic function:

```
from queue import Queue

in_queue = Queue()
out_queue = Queue()
```

I can start multiple threads that will consume items from in_queue, process them by calling game_logic, and put the results on out_queue. These threads will run concurrently, allowing for parallel I/O and reduced latency for each generation:

```
from threading import Thread

class StoppableWorker(Thread):
    ...

def game_logic(state, neighbors):
    ...
    # Do some blocking input/output in here:
    data = my_socket.recv(100)
    ...

def game_logic_thread(item):
    y, x, state, neighbors = item
    try:
        next_state = game_logic(state, neighbors)
    except Exception as e:
        next_state = e
    return (y, x, next_state)
```

```
# Start the threads upfront
threads = []
for _ in range(5):
    thread = StoppableWorker(
        game_logic_thread, in_queue, out_queue)
    thread.start()
    threads.append(thread)
```

Now I can redefine the `simulate` function to interact with these queues to request state transition decisions and receive corresponding responses. Adding items to in_queue is what causes *fan-out*, and consuming items from the out_queue until it's empty is what causes *fan-in*:

```
ALIVE = "*"
EMPTY = "-"

class SimulationError(Exception):
    pass

class Grid:
    ...

def count_neighbors(y, x, get_cell):
    ...

def simulate_pipeline(grid, in_queue, out_queue):
    for y in range(grid.height):
        for x in range(grid.width):
            state = grid.get(y, x)
            neighbors = count_neighbors(y, x, grid.get)
            in_queue.put((y, x, state, neighbors))  # Fan-out

    in_queue.join()
    item_count = out_queue.qsize()

    next_grid = Grid(grid.height, grid.width)
    for _ in range(item_count):
        item = out_queue.get()                      # Fan-in
        y, x, next_state = item
        if isinstance(next_state, Exception):
            raise SimulationError(y, x) from next_state
        next_grid.set(y, x, next_state)

    return next_grid
```

The calls to Grid.get and Grid.set both happen within this new simulate_pipeline function, which means I can use the single-threaded implementation of Grid instead of the implementation that requires Lock instances for synchronization (see Item 69: "Use Lock to Prevent Data Races in Threads" for background).

This code is also easier to debug than the Thread approach used in the previous item. If an exception occurs while doing I/O in the game_logic function, it will be caught by the surrounding game_logic_thread function, propagated to the out_queue, and then re-raised in the main thread:

```
def game_logic(state, neighbors):
    ...
    raise OSError("Problem with I/O in game_logic")
    ...


simulate_pipeline(Grid(1, 1), in_queue, out_queue)

>>>
Traceback ...
OSError: Problem with I/O in game_logic

The above exception was the direct cause of the following
exception:

Traceback ...
SimulationError: (0, 0)
```

I can drive this multithreaded pipeline for repeated generations by calling simulate_pipeline in a loop:

```
class ColumnPrinter:
    ...


grid = Grid(5, 9)
grid.set(0, 3, ALIVE)
grid.set(1, 4, ALIVE)
grid.set(2, 2, ALIVE)
grid.set(2, 3, ALIVE)
grid.set(2, 4, ALIVE)

columns = ColumnPrinter()
for i in range(5):
    columns.append(str(grid))
    grid = simulate_pipeline(grid, in_queue, out_queue)
```

```
print(columns)

in_queue.shutdown()
in_queue.join()

for thread in threads:
    thread.join()
>>>
```

```
    0     |     1     |     2     |     3     |     4
---*----- | --------- | --------- | --------- | ---------
----*---- | --*-*---- | ----*---- | ---*----- | ----*----
--***---- | ---**---- | --*-*---- | ----**--- | -----*---
--------- | ---*----- | ---**---- | ---**---- | ---***---
--------- | --------- | --------- | --------- | ---------
```

The results are the same as before. Although I've addressed the memory explosion problem, startup costs, and debugging issues related to using threads on their own, many issues remain:

- The `simulate_pipeline` function is even harder to follow than the `simulate_threaded` approach from the previous item.

- Extra support functionality is required (e.g., `StoppableWorker`) to make the code easier to read, at the expense of increased complexity.

- I have to specify the amount of potential parallelism—the number of threads running `game_logic_thread`—upfront based on my expectations of the workload instead of having the system automatically scale up parallelism as needed.

- In order to enable debugging, I have to manually catch exceptions in worker threads, propagate them on a queue, and then re-raise them in the main thread.

However, the biggest problem with this code is apparent if the requirements change again. Imagine that later I needed to do I/O within the `count_neighbors` function in addition to the I/O that was needed within `game_logic`:

```
def count_neighbors(y, x, get_cell):
    ...
    # Do some blocking input/output in here:
    data = my_socket.recv(100)
    ...
```

In order to make this parallelizable, I need to add another stage to the pipeline that runs count_neighbors in a thread. I need to make sure that exceptions propagate correctly between the worker threads and the main thread. And I need to use a lock for the Grid class in order to ensure safe synchronization between the worker threads (see Item 72: "Avoid Creating New Thread Instances for On-Demand Fan-out" for background and for the implementation of LockingGrid):

```
def count_neighbors_thread(item):
    y, x, state, get_cell = item
    try:
        neighbors = count_neighbors(y, x, get_cell)
    except Exception as e:
        neighbors = e
    return (y, x, state, neighbors)

def game_logic_thread(item):
    y, x, state, neighbors = item
    if isinstance(neighbors, Exception):
        next_state = neighbors
    else:
        try:
            next_state = game_logic(state, neighbors)
        except Exception as e:
            next_state = e
    return (y, x, next_state)

class LockingGrid(Grid):
    ...
```

I have to create another set of Queue instances for the count_neighbors_thread workers and the corresponding Thread instances:

```
in_queue = Queue()
logic_queue = Queue()
out_queue = Queue()

threads = []

for _ in range(5):
    thread = StoppableWorker(
        count_neighbors_thread, in_queue, logic_queue
    )
```

```
        thread.start()
        threads.append(thread)

    for _ in range(5):
        thread = StoppableWorker(
            game_logic_thread, logic_queue, out_queue
        )
        thread.start()
        threads.append(thread)
```

Finally, I need to update simulate_pipeline to coordinate the multiple phases in the pipeline and ensure that work fans out and back in correctly:

```
def simulate_phased_pipeline(grid, in_queue, logic_queue,
out_queue):
    for y in range(grid.height):
        for x in range(grid.width):
            state = grid.get(y, x)
            item = (y, x, state, grid.get)
            in_queue.put(item)                # Fan-out

    in_queue.join()
    logic_queue.join()                        # Pipeline sequencing
    item_count = out_queue.qsize()

    next_grid = LockingGrid(grid.height, grid.width)
    for _ in range(item_count):
        y, x, next_state = out_queue.get()  # Fan-in
        if isinstance(next_state, Exception):
            raise SimulationError(y, x) from next_state
        next_grid.set(y, x, next_state)

    return next_grid
```

With these updated implementations, now I can run the multiphase pipeline end-to-end:

```
grid = LockingGrid(5, 9)
grid.set(0, 3, ALIVE)
grid.set(1, 4, ALIVE)
grid.set(2, 2, ALIVE)
grid.set(2, 3, ALIVE)
grid.set(2, 4, ALIVE)
```

```
columns = ColumnPrinter()
for i in range(5):
    columns.append(str(grid))
    grid = simulate_phased_pipeline(
        grid, in_queue, logic_queue, out_queue
    )

print(columns)

in_queue.shutdown()
in_queue.join()

logic_queue.shutdown()
logic_queue.join()

for thread in threads:
    thread.join()
```

```
>>>
    0      |     1     |     2     |     3     |     4
---*----- | --------- | --------- | --------- | ---------
----*---- | --*-*---- | ----*---- | ---*----- | ----*----
--***---- | ---**---- | --*-*---- | ----**--- | -----*---
--------- | ---*----- | ---**---- | ---**---- | ---***---
--------- | --------- | --------- | --------- | ---------
```

Again, this works as expected, but it required a lot of changes and boilerplate. The point here is that Queue does make it possible to solve fan-out and fan-in problems, but the complexity is very high. Although using Queue is a better approach than using Thread instances on their own, it's still not nearly as good as using some of the other tools provided by Python (see Item 74: "Consider ThreadPoolExecutor When Threads Are Necessary for Concurrency" and Item 75: "Achieve Highly Concurrent I/O with Coroutines").

Things to Remember

✦ Using Queue instances with a fixed number of worker threads improves the scalability of fan-out and fan-in using threads.

✦ It takes a significant amount of work to refactor existing code to use Queue, especially when multiple stages of a pipeline are required.

✦ Using Queue with a fixed number of worker threads fundamentally limits the total amount of I/O parallelism a program can leverage compared to alternative approaches provided by other built-in Python features and modules that are more dynamic.

Item 74: Consider ThreadPoolExecutor When Threads Are Necessary for Concurrency

Python includes the concurrent.futures built-in module, which provides the ThreadPoolExecutor class. It combines the best of the Thread (see Item 72: "Avoid Creating New Thread Instances for On-Demand Fan-out") and Queue (see Item 73: "Understand How Using Queue for Concurrency Requires Refactoring") approaches to solving the parallel I/O problem from the Game of Life example (see Item 71: "Know How to Recognize When Concurrency Is Necessary" for background and the implementations of various functions and classes below):

```
ALIVE = "*"
EMPTY = "-"

class Grid:
    ...

class LockingGrid(Grid):
    ...

def count_neighbors(y, x, get_cell):
    ...

def game_logic(state, neighbors):
    ...
    # Do some blocking input/output in here:
    data = my_socket.recv(100)
    ...

def step_cell(y, x, get_cell, set_cell):
    state = get_cell(y, x)
    neighbors = count_neighbors(y, x, get_cell)
    next_state = game_logic(state, neighbors)
    set_cell(y, x, next_state)
```

Instead of starting a new Thread instance for each Grid square, I can *fan out* by submitting a function to an executor that will be run in a separate thread. Later, I can wait for the result of all tasks in order to *fan in*:

```python
from concurrent.futures import ThreadPoolExecutor

def simulate_pool(pool, grid):
    next_grid = LockingGrid(grid.height, grid.width)

    futures = []
    for y in range(grid.height):
        for x in range(grid.width):
            args = (y, x, grid.get, next_grid.set)
            future = pool.submit(step_cell, *args)   # Fan-out
            futures.append(future)

    for future in futures:
        future.result()                              # Fan-in

    return next_grid
```

The threads used for the executor can be allocated in advance, which means I don't have to pay the startup cost on each execution of simulate_pool. I can also specify the maximum number of threads to use for the pool—using the max_workers parameter—to prevent the memory blow-up issues associated with the naive Thread solution to the parallel I/O problem (i.e., one thread per cell):

```python
class ColumnPrinter:
    ...

grid = LockingGrid(5, 9)
grid.set(0, 3, ALIVE)
grid.set(1, 4, ALIVE)
grid.set(2, 2, ALIVE)
grid.set(2, 3, ALIVE)
grid.set(2, 4, ALIVE)

columns = ColumnPrinter()
with ThreadPoolExecutor(max_workers=10) as pool:
    for i in range(5):
        columns.append(str(grid))
        grid = simulate_pool(pool, grid)
```

```
print(columns)

>>>
    0      |     1     |     2     |     3     |     4
---*----- | --------- | --------- | --------- | ---------
----*---- | --*-*---- | ----*---- | ---*----- | ----*----
--***---- | ---**---- | --*-*---- | ----**--- | -----*---
--------- | ---*----- | ---**---- | ---**---- | ---***---
--------- | --------- | --------- | --------- | ---------
```

The best part about the ThreadPoolExecutor class is that it automatically propagates exceptions back to the caller when the result method is called on the Future instance returned by the submit method:

```
def game_logic(state, neighbors):
    ...
    raise OSError("Problem with I/O")
    ...


with ThreadPoolExecutor(max_workers=10) as pool:
    task = pool.submit(game_logic, ALIVE, 3)
    task.result()

>>>
Traceback ...
OSError: Problem with I/O
```

If I need to provide I/O parallelism for the count_neighbors function in addition to game_logic, no modifications to the program are required because ThreadPoolExecutor already runs these functions concurrently as part of step_cell. It's even possible to achieve CPU parallelism by using the same interface if necessary (see Item 79: "Consider concurrent.futures for True Parallelism").

However, the big problem that remains is the limited amount of I/O parallelism that ThreadPoolExecutor provides. Even if I use a max_workers parameter of 100, this solution still won't scale if I need 10,000+ cells in the grid that require simultaneous I/O. ThreadPoolExecutor is a good choice for situations where there is no asynchronous solution (e.g., blocking file system operations), but there are better ways to maximize I/O parallelism in many cases (see Item 75: "Achieve Highly Concurrent I/O with Coroutines").

Things to Remember

✦ ThreadPoolExecutor enables simple I/O parallelism with limited refactoring required.

✦ You can use `ThreadPoolExecutor` to avoid the cost of thread startup each time fan-out concurrency is required.

✦ `ThreadPoolExecutor` makes threaded code easier to debug by automatically propagating exceptions across thread boundaries.

✦ Although `ThreadPoolExecutor` eliminates the potential memory blow-up issues of using threads directly, it also limits I/O parallelism by requiring `max_workers` to be specified upfront.

Item 75: Achieve Highly Concurrent I/O with Coroutines

The previous items have tried to solve the parallel I/O problem for the Game of Life example with varying degrees of success (see Item 71: "Know How to Recognize When Concurrency Is Necessary" for background and the implementations of various functions and classes below). All of the other approaches fall short in their ability to handle thousands of simultaneously concurrent functions (see Item 72: "Avoid Creating New Thread Instances for On-Demand Fan-out," Item 73: "Understand How Using `Queue` for Concurrency Requires Refactoring," and Item 74: "Consider `ThreadPoolExecutor` When Threads Are Necessary for Concurrency").

Python addresses the need for highly concurrent I/O with coroutines. *Coroutines* let you have a very large number of seemingly simultaneously executing functions in your Python programs. They're implemented using the `async` and `await` keywords along with the same infrastructure that powers generators (see Item 43: "Consider Generators Instead of Returning Lists," Item 46: "Pass Iterators into Generators as Arguments Instead of Calling the `send` Method," and Item 47: "Manage Iterative State Transitions with a Class Instead of the Generator `throw` Method").

The cost of starting a coroutine is a function call. Once a coroutine is active, it uses less than 1 KB of memory until it's exhausted. Like threads, coroutines are independent functions that can consume inputs from their environment and produce resulting outputs. The difference is that coroutines pause at each `await` expression and resume executing an `async` function after the pending *awaitable* is resolved (similarly to how `yield` behaves in generators).

When many separate `async` functions are advanced in lockstep, they all seem to be running simultaneously, mimicking the concurrent behavior of Python threads. However, coroutines do this without the memory overhead, startup and context switching costs, and complex locking and synchronization code required for threads. The magical mechanism powering coroutines is the *event loop*, which can do highly concurrent I/O efficiently while rapidly interleaving execution between appropriately written functions.

I can use coroutines to implement the Game of Life. My goal is to allow for I/O to occur within the game_logic function while overcoming the problems from the Thread, Queue, and ThreadPoolExecutor approaches in the previous items. To do this, first I indicate that the game_logic function is a coroutine by defining it using async def instead of def. This will allow me to use the await syntax for I/O, such as an asynchronous read from a socket:

```python
ALIVE = "*"
EMPTY = "-"

class Grid:
    ...

def count_neighbors(y, x, get_cell):
    ...

async def game_logic(state, neighbors):
    ...
    # Do some input/output in here:
    data = await my_socket.read(50)
    ...
```

Similarly, I can turn step_cell into a coroutine by adding async to its definition and using await for the call to the game_logic function:

```python
async def step_cell(y, x, get_cell, set_cell):
    state = get_cell(y, x)
    neighbors = count_neighbors(y, x, get_cell)
    next_state = await game_logic(state, neighbors)
    set_cell(y, x, next_state)
```

The simulate function also needs to become a coroutine:

```python
import asyncio

async def simulate(grid):
    next_grid = Grid(grid.height, grid.width)

    tasks = []
    for y in range(grid.height):
        for x in range(grid.width):
```

```
            task = step_cell(
                y, x, grid.get, next_grid.set)          # Fan-out
            tasks.append(task)

    await asyncio.gather(*tasks)                          # Fan-in

    return next_grid
```

The coroutine version of the simulate function requires some explanation:

- Calling step_cell doesn't immediately run that function. Instead, it returns a coroutine instance that can be used with an await expression at a later time. This is similar to how a generator function that uses yield returns a generator instance when it's called instead of executing immediately. Deferring execution like this is the mechanism that causes *fan-out*.

- The gather function from the asyncio built-in library is what causes *fan-in*. The await expression on gather instructs the event loop to run the step_cell coroutines concurrently and resume execution of the simulate coroutine when all the coroutines have been completed (see Item 77: "Mix Threads and Coroutines to Ease the Transition to asyncio" for another approach using asyncio.TaskGroup).

- No locks are required for the Grid instance since all execution occurs within a single thread. The I/O becomes parallelized as part of the event loop that's provided by asyncio.

Finally, I can drive this code with a one-line change to the original example. This relies on the asyncio.run function to execute the simulate coroutine in an event loop and carry out its dependent I/O:

```
class ColumnPrinter:
    ...

grid = Grid(5, 9)
grid.set(0, 3, ALIVE)
grid.set(1, 4, ALIVE)
grid.set(2, 2, ALIVE)
grid.set(2, 3, ALIVE)
grid.set(2, 4, ALIVE)

columns = ColumnPrinter()
for i in range(5):
```

```
        columns.append(str(grid))
        grid = asyncio.run(simulate(grid))  # Run the event loop

print(columns)

>>>
    0      |     1      |     2      |     3      |     4
---*----- | --------- | --------- | --------- | ---------
----*---- | --*-*---- | ----*---- | ---*----- | ----*----
--*****--- | ---**---- | --*-*---- | ----**--- | -----*---
--------- | ---*----- | ---**---- | ---**---- | ---***---
--------- | --------- | --------- | --------- | ---------
```

The result is the same as before. All the overhead associated with threads has been eliminated. Whereas the Queue and ThreadPoolExecutor approaches are limited in their exception handling—merely re-raising exceptions across thread boundaries—with coroutines I can even use the interactive debugger to step through the exception handling code line by line (see Item 114: "Consider Interactive Debugging with pdb").

Later, if my requirements change and I also need to do I/O from within count_neighbors, I can easily accomplish this by adding async and await keywords to the existing functions and call sites instead of having to restructure everything as I would have to do if I were using Thread or Queue instances (see Item 76: "Know How to Port Threaded I/O to asyncio" for another example):

```
async def count_neighbors(y, x, get_cell):
    ...

async def step_cell(y, x, get_cell, set_cell):
    state = get_cell(y, x)
    neighbors = await count_neighbors(y, x, get_cell)
    next_state = await game_logic(state, neighbors)
    set_cell(y, x, next_state)

grid = Grid(5, 9)
grid.set(0, 3, ALIVE)
grid.set(1, 4, ALIVE)
grid.set(2, 2, ALIVE)
grid.set(2, 3, ALIVE)
grid.set(2, 4, ALIVE)

columns = ColumnPrinter()
for i in range(5):
```

```
    columns.append(str(grid))
    grid = asyncio.run(simulate(grid))

print(columns)

>>>
    0        |    1        |    2        |    3        |    4
---*-----   | ---------   | ---------   | ---------   | ---------
----*----   | --*-*----   | ----*----   | ---*-----   | ----*----
--*** ----  | ---**----   | --*-*----   | ----**---   | -----*---
---------   | ---*-----   | ---**----   | ---**----   | ---***---
---------   | ---------   | ---------   | ---------   | ---------
```

The beauty of coroutines is that they decouple your code's instructions for the external environment (i.e., I/O) from the implementation that carries out your wishes (i.e., the event loop). They let you focus on the logic of what you're actually trying to do instead of wasting time trying to figure out how you're going to accomplish your goals concurrently.

Things to Remember

✦ Functions that are defined using the async keyword are called coroutines. A caller can receive the result of a dependent coroutine by using the await keyword.

✦ Coroutines provide an efficient way to run tens of thousands of functions seemingly at the same time.

✦ Coroutines can use fan-out and fan-in in order to parallelize I/O, while also overcoming all the problems associated with doing I/O in threads.

Item 76: Know How to Port Threaded I/O to asyncio

Once you understand the advantage of coroutines (see Item 75: "Achieve Highly Concurrent I/O with Coroutines"), it may seem daunting to port an existing codebase to use them. Luckily, Python's support for asynchronous execution is well integrated into the language. This makes it straightforward to move code that does threaded, blocking I/O over to coroutines and asynchronous I/O.

For example, say that I have a TCP-based server for playing a "guess the number" game. The server takes lower and upper parameters that determine the range of numbers to consider. Then the server returns guesses for integer values in that range as they are requested by the client. Finally, the server collects reports from the client on whether each of those numbers was closer (warmer) or further away (colder) from the client's secret number.

The most common way to build this type of client/server system is by using blocking I/O and threads (see Item 68: "Use Threads for Blocking I/O; Avoid for Parallelism"). To do this, I need a helper class that can manage sending and receiving messages. For my purposes, each line sent or received represents a command to be processed:

```
class EOFError(Exception):
    pass

class Connection:
    def __init__(self, connection):
        self.connection = connection
        self.file = connection.makefile("rb")

    def send(self, command):
        line = command + "\n"
        data = line.encode()
        self.connection.send(data)

    def receive(self):
        line = self.file.readline()
        if not line:
            raise EOFError("Connection closed")
        return line[:-1].decode()
```

The server is implemented as a class that handles one connection at a time and maintains the game's session state:

```
import random

WARMER = "Warmer"
COLDER = "Colder"
SAME = "Same"
UNSURE = "Unsure"
CORRECT = "Correct"

class UnknownCommandError(Exception):
    pass

class ServerSession(Connection):
    def __init__(self, *args):
        super().__init__(*args)
        self.clear_state()
```

It has one primary method that handles incoming commands from the client and dispatches them to methods as needed. Here I use a `match` statement to parse the semi-structured data (see Item 9: "Consider `match` for Destructuring in Flow Control; Avoid When `if` Statements Are Sufficient" for details):

```
def loop(self):
    while command := self.receive():
        match command.split(" "):
            case "PARAMS", lower, upper:
                self.set_params(lower, upper)
            case ["NUMBER"]:
                self.send_number()
            case "REPORT", decision:
                self.receive_report(decision)
            case ["CLEAR"]:
                self.clear_state()
            case _:
                raise UnknownCommandError(command)
```

The first command sets the lower and upper bounds for the numbers that the server is trying to guess:

```
def set_params(self, lower, upper):
    self.clear_state()
    self.lower = int(lower)
    self.upper = int(upper)
```

The second command makes a new guess based on the previous state that's stored in the `ServerSession` instance. Specifically, this code ensures that the server will never try to guess the same number more than once per parameter assignment:

```
def next_guess(self):
    if self.secret is not None:
        return self.secret

    while True:
        guess = random.randint(self.lower, self.upper)
        if guess not in self.guesses:
            return guess

def send_number(self):
    guess = self.next_guess()
    self.guesses.append(guess)
    self.send(format(guess))
```

The third command receives the decision from the client about whether the guess was warmer, colder, the same, or correct, and it updates the ServerSession state accordingly:

```
def receive_report(self, decision):
    last = self.guesses[-1]
    if decision == CORRECT:
        self.secret = last

    print(f"Server: {last} is {decision}")
```

The last command clears the state to end a game whether it was successful or not:

```
def clear_state(self):
    self.lower = None
    self.upper = None
    self.secret = None
    self.guesses = []
```

A game is initiated by using a with statement to ensure that state is correctly managed on the server side (see Item 82: "Consider contextlib and with Statements for Reusable try/finally Behavior" for background and Item 78: "Maximize Responsiveness of asyncio Event Loops with async-Friendly Worker Threads" for another example). This new_game function sends the first and last commands to the server and provides a context object to use for the duration of the game:

```
import contextlib

@contextlib.contextmanager
def new_game(connection, lower, upper, secret):
    print(
        f"Guess a number between {lower} and {upper}!"
        f" Shhhhh, it's {secret}."
    )
    connection.send(f"PARAMS {lower} {upper}")
    try:
        yield ClientSession(
            connection.send,
            connection.receive,
            secret,
        )
    finally:
        connection.send("CLEAR")
```

I use a stateful class with helper methods for game actions and references to manage each game session (see Item 48: "Accept Functions Instead of Classes for Simple Interfaces" for why I pass in send and receive explicitly):

```
import math

class ClientSession:
    def __init__(self, send, receive, secret):
        self.send = send
        self.receive = receive
        self.secret = secret
        self.last_distance = None
```

New guesses are requested from the server using a method that implements the second command:

```
    def request_number(self):
        self.send("NUMBER")
        data = self.receive()
        return int(data)
```

Whether each guess from the server was warmer or colder than the last is reported using the third command:

```
    def report_outcome(self, number):
        new_distance = math.fabs(number - self.secret)

        if new_distance == 0:
            decision = CORRECT
        elif self.last_distance is None:
            decision = UNSURE
        elif new_distance < self.last_distance:
            decision = WARMER
        elif new_distance > self.last_distance:
            decision = COLDER
        else:
            decision = SAME

        self.last_distance = new_distance

        self.send(f"REPORT {decision}")
        return decision
```

The game session object can be iterated over (see Item 21: "Be Defensive when Iterating over Arguments" for background) to make new, unique guesses repeatedly until the correct answer is found:

```
def __iter__(self):
    while True:
        number = self.request_number()
        decision = self.report_outcome(number)
        yield number, decision
        if decision == CORRECT:
            return
```

I can run the server by having one thread listen on a socket and spawn additional threads to handle each new client connection:

```
import socket
from threading import Thread

def handle_connection(connection):
    with connection:
        session = ServerSession(connection)
        try:
            session.loop()
        except EOFError:
            pass

def run_server(address):
    with socket.socket() as listener:
        listener.bind(address)
        listener.listen()
        while True:
            connection, _ = listener.accept()
            thread = Thread(
                target=handle_connection,
                args=(connection,),
                daemon=True,
            )
            thread.start()
```

The client runs in the main thread and returns the results of the guessing game back to the caller. Perhaps a bit awkwardly, this code exercises a variety of Python language features (for loops, with statements, generators, comprehensions, the iterator protocol) so that below I can show what it takes to port each of these over to using coroutines:

```python
def run_client(address):
    with socket.create_connection(address) as server_sock:
        server = Connection(server_sock)

        with new_game(server, 1, 5, 3) as session:
            results = [outcome for outcome in session]

        with new_game(server, 10, 15, 12) as session:
            for outcome in session:
                results.append(outcome)

        with new_game(server, 1, 3, 2) as session:
            it = iter(session)
            while True:
                try:
                    outcome = next(it)
                except StopIteration:
                    break
                else:
                    results.append(outcome)

    return results
```

Finally, I can glue all this together and confirm that it works as expected:

```python
def main():
    address = ("127.0.0.1", 1234)
    server_thread = Thread(
        target=run_server, args=(address,), daemon=True
    )
    server_thread.start()

    results = run_client(address)
    for number, outcome in results:
        print(f"Client: {number} is {outcome}")

main()
```

```
>>>
Guess a number between 1 and 5! Shhhhh, it's 3.
Server: 4 is Unsure
```

```
Server: 1 is Colder
Server: 5 is Same
Server: 3 is Correct
Guess a number between 10 and 15! Shhhhh, it's 12.
Server: 11 is Unsure
Server: 10 is Colder
Server: 12 is Correct
Guess a number between 1 and 3! Shhhhh, it's 2.
Server: 3 is Unsure
Server: 2 is Correct
Client: 4 is Unsure
Client: 1 is Colder
Client: 5 is Same
Client: 3 is Correct
Client: 11 is Unsure
Client: 10 is Colder
Client: 12 is Correct
Client: 3 is Unsure
Client: 2 is Correct
```

How much effort is needed to convert this example to using async, await, and the asyncio built-in module?

First, I need to update my Connection class to provide coroutine methods for send and receive instead of blocking I/O methods. I've marked each line that's changed with a # Changed comment to make it clear what the delta is between this new example and the code above:

```python
class AsyncConnection:
    def __init__(self, reader, writer):        # Changed
        self.reader = reader                   # Changed
        self.writer = writer                   # Changed

    async def send(self, command):
        line = command + "\n"
        data = line.encode()
        self.writer.write(data)                # Changed
        await self.writer.drain()              # Changed

    async def receive(self):
        line = await self.reader.readline()    # Changed
        if not line:
            raise EOFError("Connection closed")
        return line[:-1].decode()
```

I can create another stateful class to represent the server session state for a single connection. The only changes here are the class's name and inheriting from AsyncConnection instead of Connection:

```
class AsyncServerSession(AsyncConnection):  # Changed
    def __init__(self, *args):
        ...
```

The primary entry point for the server's command-processing loop requires only minimal changes to become a coroutine:

```
async def loop(self):                          # Changed
    while command := await self.receive():  # Changed
        match command.split(" "):
            case "PARAMS", lower, upper:
                self.set_params(lower, upper)
            case ["NUMBER"]:
                await self.send_number()    # Changed
            case "REPORT", decision:
                self.receive_report(decision)
            case ["CLEAR"]:
                self.clear_state()
            case _:
                raise UnknownCommandError(command)
```

No changes are required for handling the first command:

```
def set_params(self, lower, upper):
    ...
```

The only change required for the second command is allowing asynchronous I/O to be used when guesses are transmitted to the client:

```
def next_guess(self):
    ...

async def send_number(self):                   # Changed
    guess = self.next_guess()
    self.guesses.append(guess)
    await self.send(format(guess))             # Changed
```

No changes are required in the third and fourth commands:

```
def receive_report(self, decision):
    ...

def clear_state(self):
    ...
```

Initiating a new game on the client requires a few async and await keywords to be added for sending the first and last commands. It also needs to use the asynccontextmanager helper function from the contextlib built-in module:

```
@contextlib.asynccontextmanager                       # Changed
async def new_async_game(
    connection, lower, upper, secret):                # Changed
    print(
        f"Guess a number between {lower} and {upper}!"
        f" Shhhhh, it's {secret}."
    )
    await connection.send(f"PARAMS {lower} {upper}")  # Changed
    try:
        yield AsyncClientSession(
            connection.send,
            connection.receive,
            secret,
        )
    finally:
        await connection.send("CLEAR")                # Changed
```

The asynchronous version of the ClientSession class for representing game state has the same constructor as before:

```
class AsyncClientSession:
    def __init__(self, send, receive, secret):
        ...
```

The second command only requires the addition of async and await anywhere asynchronous behavior is required:

```
    async def request_number(self):
        await self.send("NUMBER")      # Changed
        data = await self.receive()    # Changed
        return int(data)
```

The third command only requires adding one async and one await keyword:

```
    async def report_outcome(self, number):    # Changed
        new_distance = math.fabs(number - self.secret)

        if new_distance == 0:
            decision = CORRECT
```

```
        elif self.last_distance is None:
            decision = UNSURE
        elif new_distance < self.last_distance:
            decision = WARMER
        elif new_distance > self.last_distance:
            decision = COLDER
        else:
            decision = SAME

        self.last_distance = new_distance

        await self.send(f"REPORT {decision}")          # Changed
        return decision
```

To enable asynchronous iteration, I need to implement __aiter__ instead of __iter__, with corresponding additions of async and await:

```
    async def __aiter__(self):                         # Changed
        while True:
            number = await self.request_number()       # Changed
            decision = await self.report_outcome(
                number)                                 # Changed
            yield number, decision
            if decision == CORRECT:
                return
```

The code that runs the server needs to be completely reimplemented to use the asyncio built-in module and its start_server function:

```
import asyncio

async def handle_async_connection(reader, writer):
    session = AsyncServerSession(reader, writer)
    try:
        await session.loop()
    except EOFError:
        pass

async def run_async_server(address):
    server = await asyncio.start_server(
        handle_async_connection, *address
    )
    async with server:
        await server.serve_forever()
```

The run_client function that initiates the game requires changes on nearly every line. Any code that previously interacted with the blocking socket instances has to be replaced with asyncio versions of similar functionality (which are marked with # New below). All other lines in the function that require interaction with coroutines need to use async and await keywords; coroutine-specific functions like aiter and anext; or async-specific constants like StopAsyncIteration. If you forget to add one of these keywords in a necessary place, an exception will be raised at runtime.

```
async def run_async_client(address):
    streams = await asyncio.open_connection(*address)  # New
    client = AsyncConnection(*streams)                 # New

    async with new_async_game(client, 1, 5, 3) as session:
        results = [outcome async for outcome in session]

    async with new_async_game(client, 10, 15, 12) as session:
        async for outcome in session:
            results.append(outcome)

    async with new_async_game(client, 1, 3, 2) as session:
        it = aiter(session)
        while True:
            try:
                outcome = await anext(it)
            except StopAsyncIteration:
                break
            else:
                results.append(outcome)

    _, writer = streams                                # New
    writer.close()                                     # New
    await writer.wait_closed()                         # New

    return results
```

What's most interesting about run_async_client is that I didn't have to restructure any of the substantive parts of interacting with AsyncClient in order to port this function over to use coroutines. Each of the language features that I needed has a corresponding asynchronous version, which made the migration straightforward.

This transition won't always be easy. For example, in the standard library, there are currently no asynchronous versions of the utility functions from itertools (see Item 24: "Consider itertools for Working with Iterators and Generators"). There's also no asynchronous version of yield from (see Item 45: "Compose Multiple Generators with yield from"), which makes composing generators noisier. Many community libraries help fill these gaps (see Item 116: "Know Where to Find Community-Built Modules"), but it can still take extra work, depending on the complexity of your code.

Finally, the glue needs to be updated to run this new asynchronous example end-to-end. I use the asyncio.create_task function to enqueue the server for execution on the event loop so that it runs in parallel with the client when the await expression is reached. This is another approach to causing fan-out with different behavior than what occurs with the asyncio.gather function:

```
async def main_async():
    address = ("127.0.0.1", 4321)

    server = run_async_server(address)
    asyncio.create_task(server)

    results = await run_async_client(address)
    for number, outcome in results:
        print(f"Client: {number} is {outcome}")


asyncio.run(main_async())

>>>
Guess a number between 1 and 5! Shhhhh, it's 3.
Server: 5 is Unsure
Server: 4 is Warmer
Server: 2 is Same
Server: 1 is Colder
Server: 3 is Correct
Guess a number between 10 and 15! Shhhhh, it's 12.
Server: 14 is Unsure
Server: 10 is Same
Server: 15 is Colder
Server: 12 is Correct
Guess a number between 1 and 3! Shhhhh, it's 2.
Server: 2 is Correct
Client: 5 is Unsure
Client: 4 is Warmer
Client: 2 is Same
Client: 1 is Colder
Client: 3 is Correct
Client: 14 is Unsure
```

```
Client: 10 is Same
Client: 15 is Colder
Client: 12 is Correct
Client: 2 is Correct
```

This works as expected. The coroutine version is easier to follow because all the interactions with threads have been removed. The asyncio built-in module also provides many helper functions that reduce the amount of socket boilerplate code required to write a server like this.

Your use case may be more difficult to port for a variety of reasons. The asyncio module has a vast number of I/O, synchronization, and task management features that could make adopting coroutines easier for you (see Item 77: "Mix Threads and Coroutines to Ease the Transition to asyncio" and Item 78: "Maximize Responsiveness of asyncio Event Loops with async-Friendly Worker Threads"). Be sure to check out the online documentation for the library (https://docs.python.org/3/library/asyncio.html) to understand its full potential.

Things to Remember

✦ Python provides asynchronous versions of for loops, with statements, generators, comprehensions, iterators, and library helper functions that can be used as drop-in replacements in coroutines.

✦ The asyncio built-in module makes it straightforward to port existing code that uses threads and blocking I/O over to coroutines and asynchronous I/O.

Item 77: Mix Threads and Coroutines to Ease the Transition to asyncio

In the previous item (see Item 76: "Know How to Port Threaded I/O to asyncio"), I ported a TCP server that does blocking I/O with threads over to use asyncio with coroutines. It was a big-bang transition: I moved all of the code to the new style in one go. But it's rarely feasible to port a large program this way. Instead, you usually need to incrementally migrate your codebase while also updating your tests as needed and verifying that everything works at each step along the way.

In order to do that, your codebase needs to be able to use threads for blocking I/O (see Item 68: "Use Threads for Blocking I/O; Avoid for Parallelism") and coroutines for asynchronous I/O (see Item 75: "Achieve Highly Concurrent I/O with Coroutines") at the same time in a way that's mutually compatible. Practically, this means you need threads to be able to run coroutines, and you need coroutines to be able to start and wait on threads. Luckily, asyncio includes built-in facilities for making this type of interoperability straightforward.

For example, say that I'm writing a program that merges log files together into one output stream in order to aid with debugging. Given a file handle for an input log, I need a way to detect whether new data is available and return the next line of input. I can do this by using the tell method of the file handle to check whether the current read position matches the length of the file. When no new data is present, an exception should be raised (see Item 32: "Prefer Raising Exceptions to Returning None" for background):

```
class NoNewData(Exception):
    pass

def readline(handle):
    offset = handle.tell()
    handle.seek(0, 2)
    length = handle.tell()

    if length == offset:
        raise NoNewData

    handle.seek(offset, 0)
    return handle.readline()
```

By wrapping this function in a while loop, I can turn it into a worker thread. When a new line is available, I call a given callback function to write it to the output log (see Item 48: "Accept Functions Instead of Classes for Simple Interfaces" for why to use a function interface for this instead of a class). When no data is available, the thread sleeps to reduce the amount of busy waiting caused by polling for new data. When the input file handle is closed, the worker thread exits:

```
import time

def tail_file(handle, interval, write_func):
    while not handle.closed:
        try:
            line = readline(handle)
        except NoNewData:
            time.sleep(interval)
```

```
        else:
            write_func(line)
```

Now I can start one worker thread per input file and unify the output of these threads into a single output file. Below, the write closure function (see Item 33: "Know How Closures Interact with Variable Scope and nonlocal") needs to use a Lock instance (see Item 69: "Use Lock to Prevent Data Races in Threads") in order to serialize writes to the output stream and ensure that there are no intra-line conflicts:

```
from threading import Lock, Thread

def run_threads(handles, interval, output_path):
    with open(output_path, "wb") as output:
        lock = Lock()

        def write(data):
            with lock:
                output.write(data)

        threads = []
        for handle in handles:
            args = (handle, interval, write)
            thread = Thread(target=tail_file, args=args)
            thread.start()
            threads.append(thread)

        for thread in threads:
            thread.join()
```

As long as an input file handle is still alive, its corresponding worker thread will also stay alive. That means it's sufficient to wait for the join method from each thread to complete in order to know that the whole process is done.

Given a set of input paths and an output path, I can call run_threads and confirm that it works as expected. How the input file handles are created or separately closed isn't important in order to demonstrate this code's behavior, nor is the output verification function—defined in confirm_merge that follows—which is why I've left them out here:

```
def confirm_merge(input_paths, output_path):
    ...

input_paths = ...
handles = ...
```

```
output_path = ...
run_threads(handles, 0.1, output_path)

confirm_merge(input_paths, output_path)
```

With this threaded implementation as the starting point, how can I incrementally convert this code to use asyncio and coroutines instead? There are two approaches: top-down and bottom-up.

Top-Down Approach

Top-down means starting at the highest parts of a codebase, like in the main entry points, and working down to the individual functions and classes that are the leaves of the call hierarchy. This approach can be useful when you maintain a lot of common modules that you use across many different programs. By porting the entry points first, you can wait to port the common modules until you're already using coroutines everywhere else.

These are the concrete steps:

1. Change a top function to use async def instead of def.

2. Wrap all of its calls that do I/O—potentially blocking the event loop—to use asyncio.run_in_executor instead.

3. Ensure that the resources or callbacks used by run_in_executor invocations are properly synchronized (i.e., using Lock or the asyncio.run_coroutine_threadsafe function with a fan-in event loop instance).

4. Try to eliminate get_event_loop and run_in_executor calls by moving downward through the call hierarchy and converting intermediate functions and methods to coroutines (following the first three steps).

Here I apply steps 1–3 to the run_threads function:

```
import asyncio

async def run_tasks_mixed(handles, interval, output_path):
    loop = asyncio.get_event_loop()

    output = await loop.run_in_executor(
        None, open, output_path, "wb")
    try:
        async def write_async(data):
            await loop.run_in_executor(None, output.write, data)
```

```
def write(data):
    coro = write_async(data)
    future = asyncio.run_coroutine_threadsafe(coro, loop)
    future.result()

tasks = []
for handle in handles:
    task = loop.run_in_executor(
        None, tail_file, handle, interval, write
    )
    tasks.append(task)

await asyncio.gather(*tasks)

finally:
    await loop.run_in_executor(None, output.close)
```

The run_in_executor method instructs the event loop to run a given function—which may include blocking I/O—using a ThreadPoolExecutor, ensuring that it doesn't interfere with the event loop's thread (see Item 74: "Consider ThreadPoolExecutor When Threads Are Necessary for Concurrency" for background). By making multiple calls to run_in_executor without corresponding await expressions, the run_tasks_mixed coroutine fans out to have one concurrent line of execution for each input file. Then the asyncio.gather fans in the tail_file threads until they all complete (see Item 71: "Know How to Recognize When Concurrency Is Necessary" for more about fan-out and fan-in).

This code eliminates the need for the Lock instance in the write helper by using asyncio.run_coroutine_threadsafe. This function allows plain old threads to call a coroutine—write_async in this case—and have it execute in the event loop from the explicitly supplied main thread. This effectively synchronizes the worker threads together, ensuring that all writes to the output file happen one at a time. Once the asyncio.TaskGroup awaitable is resolved, I can assume that all writes to the output file have also completed, and thus I can close the output file handle without having to worry about race conditions.

I can verify that this code works as expected by using the asyncio.run function to start the coroutine and run the main event loop:

```
input_paths = ...
handles = ...
```

```
output_path = ...
asyncio.run(run_tasks_mixed(handles, 0.1, output_path))

confirm_merge(input_paths, output_path)
```

Now I can apply step 4 to the run_tasks_mixed function by moving down the call stack. I can redefine the tail_file dependent function to be an asynchronous coroutine instead of doing blocking I/O by following steps 1–3:

```
async def tail_async(handle, interval, write_func):
    loop = asyncio.get_event_loop()

    while not handle.closed:
        try:
            line = await loop.run_in_executor(
                None, readline, handle)
        except NoNewData:
            await asyncio.sleep(interval)
        else:
            await write_func(line)
```

The new tail_async function allows me to eliminate the run_tasks_mixed function's calls to run_coroutine_threadsafe and the write wrapper function. I can also use asyncio.TaskGroup (new in Python 3.11) to manage fan-out and fan-in for the tail_async coroutines, further shortening the code:

```
async def run_tasks(handles, interval, output_path):
    loop = asyncio.get_event_loop()

    output = await loop.run_in_executor(
        None, open, output_path, "wb")
    try:

        async def write_async(data):
            await loop.run_in_executor(None, output.write, data)

        async with asyncio.TaskGroup() as group:
            for handle in handles:
                group.create_task(
                    tail_async(handle, interval, write_async)
                )
    finally:
        await loop.run_in_executor(None, output.close)
```

I can verify that run_tasks works as expected, too:

```
input_paths = ...
handles = ...
output_path = ...
asyncio.run(run_tasks(handles, 0.1, output_path))

confirm_merge(input_paths, output_path)
```

It's possible to continue this refactoring approach and convert readline into an asynchronous coroutine as well. However, that function requires so many blocking file I/O operations that it doesn't seem worth porting, given how much that would reduce the clarity of the code. In some situations, it makes sense to move everything to asyncio, and in others it doesn't.

Bottom-Up Approach

The bottom-up approach to adopting coroutines has four steps that are similar to the steps of the top-down style, but the process traverses the call hierarchy in the opposite direction: from leaves to entry points.

These are the concrete steps:

1. Create a new asynchronous coroutine version of each leaf function that you're trying to port.

2. Change the existing synchronous functions so they call the coroutine versions and run the event loop instead of implementing any real asynchronous behavior.

3. Move up a level of the call hierarchy, make another layer of coroutines, and replace existing calls to synchronous functions with calls to the coroutines defined in step 1.

4. Delete synchronous wrappers around coroutines created in step 2 as you stop requiring them to glue the pieces together.

For the example above, I would start with the tail_file function since I decided that the readline function should keep using blocking I/O. I can rewrite tail_file so it merely wraps the tail_async coroutine that I defined above. The provided write_func, which uses blocking I/O, can be run by the write_async function using run_in_executor, making it compatible with what tail_async expects. To run each worker coroutine until it finishes, I can create an event loop for each tail_file thread and then call its run_until_complete method. This method will block the current thread and drive the event loop until the `tail_async` coroutine exits, achieving the same behavior as the threaded, blocking I/O version of `tail_file`:

```
def tail_file(handle, interval, write_func):
    loop = asyncio.new_event_loop()
    asyncio.set_event_loop(loop)

    async def write_async(data):
        await loop.run_in_executor(None, write_func, data)

    coro = tail_async(handle, interval, write_async)
    loop.run_until_complete(coro)
```

This new `tail_file` function is a drop-in replacement for the old one. I can verify that everything works as expected by calling run_threads again:

```
input_paths = ...
handles = ...
output_path = ...
run_threads(handles, 0.1, output_path)

confirm_merge(input_paths, output_path)
```

After wrapping `tail_async` with `tail_file`, the next step is to convert the run_threads function to a coroutine. This ends up being the same work as step 4 of the top-down approach above, so at this point, the styles converge.

This is all a great start for adopting asyncio, but there's even more that you could do to increase the responsiveness of your program (see Item 78: "Maximize Responsiveness of asyncio Event Loops with async-Friendly Worker Threads").

Things to Remember

✦ The awaitable `run_in_executor` method of the asyncio event loop enables coroutines to run synchronous functions in `ThreadPoolExecutor` worker threads. This facilitates top-down migration to asyncio.

✦ The `run_until_complete` method of the asyncio event loop enables synchronous code to run a coroutine until it finishes. The `asyncio.run_coroutine_threadsafe` function provides the same functionality across thread boundaries. Together these help with bottom-up migration to asyncio.

Item 78: Maximize Responsiveness of asyncio Event Loops with async-Friendly Worker Threads

In the previous item I showed how to migrate to asyncio incrementally (see Item 77: "Mix Threads and Coroutines to Ease the Transition to asyncio" for background and the implementation of various functions below). The resulting coroutine properly tails input files and merges them into a single output:

```
import asyncio

async def run_tasks(handles, interval, output_path):
    loop = asyncio.get_event_loop()

    output = await loop.run_in_executor(
        None, open, output_path, "wb")
    try:

        async def write_async(data):
            await loop.run_in_executor(None, output.write, data)

        async with asyncio.TaskGroup() as group:
            for handle in handles:
                group.create_task(
                    tail_async(handle, interval, write_async)
                )
    finally:
        await loop.run_in_executor(None, output.close)
```

This code is quite noisy and repetitive with all the run_in_executor boilerplate to handle the boundary between synchronous and asynchronous function calls. The function would be a lot shorter if I accepted the fact that calls to open, close, and write for the output file handle will block the event loop—and for the purpose of merging multiple file handles like this, it's functionally correct, too:

```
async def run_tasks_simpler(handles, interval, output_path):
    with open(output_path, "wb") as output:  # Changed

        async def write_async(data):
            output.write(data)                # Changed

        async with asyncio.TaskGroup() as group:
            for handle in handles:
                group.create_task(
                    tail_async(handle, interval, write_async)
                )
```

However, avoiding run_in_executor like this is bad because these operations all require making system calls to the program's host operating system, which may block the event loop for significant amounts of time and prevent other coroutines from making progress. This could hurt overall responsiveness and increase latency, especially for programs with event loops that are shared by many components, such as highly concurrent servers.

But how bad is it to block the event loop, really? And how often does it happen in practice? I can detect when this problem occurs in a real program by passing the debug=True parameter to the asyncio.run function. Here I show how the file and line of a bad coroutine, presumably blocked on a slow system call, can be identified:

```
import time

async def slow_coroutine():
    time.sleep(0.5)   # Simulating slow I/O

asyncio.run(slow_coroutine(), debug=True)

>>>
Executing <Task finished name='Task-1' coro=<slow_coroutine()
➥done, defined at example.py:61> result=None created at
➥.../asyncio/runners.py:100> took 0.506 seconds
...
```

If I want the most responsive program possible, then I need to minimize the potential system calls that are made from within the main event loop. Using run_in_executor is one way to do that, but it requires a lot of boilerplate, as shown above. One potentially better alternative is to create a new Thread subclass (see Item 68: "Use Threads for Blocking I/O; Avoid for Parallelism") that encapsulates everything required to write to the output file using its own independent event loop:

```
from threading import Thread

class WriteThread(Thread):
    def __init__(self, output_path):
        super().__init__()
        self.output_path = output_path
        self.output = None
        self.loop = asyncio.new_event_loop()
```

```
def run(self):
    asyncio.set_event_loop(self.loop)
    with open(self.output_path, "wb") as self.output:
        self.loop.run_forever()

    # Run one final round of callbacks so the await on
    # stop() in another event loop will be resolved.
    self.loop.run_until_complete(asyncio.sleep(0))
```

Coroutines in other threads can directly call and await on the write method of this class, since it's merely a thread-safe wrapper around the real_write method that actually does the I/O. This eliminates the need for Lock (see Item 69: "Use Lock to Prevent Data Races in Threads"):

```
async def real_write(self, data):
    self.output.write(data)

async def write(self, data):
    coro = self.real_write(data)
    future = asyncio.run_coroutine_threadsafe(
        coro, self.loop)
    await asyncio.wrap_future(future)
```

Other coroutines can tell the worker thread when to stop in a thread-safe manner, using similar boilerplate:

```
async def real_stop(self):
    self.loop.stop()

async def stop(self):
    coro = self.real_stop()
    future = asyncio.run_coroutine_threadsafe(
        coro, self.loop)
    await asyncio.wrap_future(future)
```

I can also define the __aenter__ and __aexit__ methods to allow this class to be used in with statements (see Item 82: "Consider contextlib and with Statements for Reusable try/finally Behavior" and Item 76: "Know How to Port Threaded I/O to asyncio" for background). This ensures that the worker thread starts and stops at the right times without slowing down the main event loop thread:

```
async def __aenter__(self):
    loop = asyncio.get_event_loop()
    await loop.run_in_executor(None, self.start)
    return self
```

```
async def __aexit__(self, *_):
    await self.stop()
```

With this new `WriteThread` class, I can refactor `run_tasks` into a fully asynchronous version that's easy to read, doesn't interfere with the main event loop's default executor, and completely avoids running slow system calls in the main event loop thread:

```
def readline(handle):
    ...


async def tail_async(handle, interval, write_func):
    ...


async def run_fully_async(handles, interval, output_path):
    async with (
        WriteThread(output_path) as output,
        asyncio.TaskGroup() as group,
    ):
        for handle in handles:
            group.create_task(
                tail_async(handle, interval, output.write)
            )
```

I can verify that this works as expected, given a set of input handles and an output file path:

```
def confirm_merge(input_paths, output_path):
    ...


input_paths = ...
handles = ...
output_path = ...
asyncio.run(run_fully_async(handles, 0.1, output_path))

confirm_merge(input_paths, output_path)
```

Things to Remember

✦ Making system calls in coroutines—including blocking I/O and starting threads—can reduce program responsiveness and increase the perception of latency.

✦ Pass the debug=True parameter to asyncio.run in order to detect when certain coroutines are preventing the event loop from reacting quickly.

✦ To improve the readability of code that must span the boundary between asynchronous and synchronous execution, consider defining helper thread classes that provide coroutine-friendly interfaces.

Item 79: Consider concurrent.futures for True Parallelism

At some point in writing Python programs, you might hit a performance wall. Even after optimizing your Python code (see Item 92: "Profile Before Optimizing"), your program's execution might still be too slow for your needs. On modern computers that have an increasing number of CPU cores, it's reasonable to assume that one solution could be parallelism. What if you could split your code's computation into independent pieces of work that run simultaneously across multiple CPU cores?

Unfortunately, Python's global interpreter lock (GIL) prevents true CPU parallelism in Python threads in most cases (see Item 68: "Use Threads for Blocking I/O; Avoid for Parallelism"). But the multiprocessing built-in module, which is easily accessed via the concurrent.futures built-in module, might be exactly what you need (see Item 74: "Consider ThreadPoolExecutor When Threads Are Necessary for Concurrency" for a related example). multiprocessing enables Python to utilize multiple CPU cores in parallel by running additional interpreters as child processes. These child processes are separate from the main interpreter, so their global interpreter locks are also separate. Each child can fully utilize one CPU core. Each child also has a link to the main process where it receives instructions to do computation and returns results.

For example, say that I want to do something computationally intensive with Python and utilize multiple CPU cores. I'll use an implementation of finding the greatest common divisor of two numbers as a proxy for a more computationally intense algorithm (like simulating fluid dynamics with the Navier–Stokes equation):

```
# my_module.py
def gcd(pair):
    a, b = pair
    low = min(a, b)
    for i in range(low, 0, -1):
        if a % i == 0 and b % i == 0:
            return i
    raise RuntimeError("Not reachable")
```

Running this function in serial takes a linearly increasing amount of time because there is no parallelism:

```
# run_serial.py
import my_module
import time

NUMBERS = [
    (19633090, 22659730),
    (20306770, 38141720),
    (15516450, 22296200),
    (20390450, 20208020),
    (18237120, 19249280),
    (22931290, 10204910),
    (12812380, 22737820),
    (38238120, 42372810),
    (38127410, 47291390),
    (12923910, 21238110),
]

def main():
    start = time.perf_counter()
    results = list(map(my_module.gcd, NUMBERS))
    end = time.perf_counter()
    delta = end - start
    print(f"Took {delta:.3f} seconds")

if __name__ == "__main__":
    main()

>>>
Took 5.643 seconds
```

Running this code on multiple Python threads will yield no speed improvement because the GIL prevents Python from using multiple CPU cores in parallel. Here I do the same computation as above but using the concurrent.futures module with its ThreadPoolExecutor class and eight worker threads (to match the number of CPU cores on my computer):

```
# run_threads.py
import my_module
from concurrent.futures import ThreadPoolExecutor
import time
```

```
NUMBERS = [
    ...
]

def main():
    start = time.perf_counter()
    pool = ThreadPoolExecutor(max_workers=8)
    results = list(pool.map(my_module.gcd, NUMBERS))
    end = time.perf_counter()
    delta = end - start
    print(f"Took {delta:.3f} seconds")

if __name__ == "__main__":
    main()

>>>
Took 5.810 seconds
```

It's even slower this time because of the overhead of starting and communicating with the pool of threads.

Now for the surprising part: Changing a single line of code causes
something magical to happen. If I replace ThreadPoolExecutor with
ProcessPoolExecutor from the concurrent.futures module, everything
speeds up:

```
# run_parallel.py
import my_module
from concurrent.futures import ProcessPoolExecutor
import time

NUMBERS = [
    ...
]

def main():
    start = time.perf_counter()
    pool = ProcessPoolExecutor(max_workers=8)   # The one change
    results = list(pool.map(my_module.gcd, NUMBERS))
    end = time.perf_counter()
    delta = end - start
    print(f"Took {delta:.3f} seconds")

if __name__ == "__main__":
    main()

>>>
Took 1.684 seconds
```

Running on my multi-core machine, this is significantly faster! How is this possible? Here's what the `ProcessPoolExecutor` class actually does (via the low-level constructs provided by the `multiprocessing` module):

1. It takes each item from the `numbers` input data to `map`.

2. It serializes the item into binary data by using the `pickle` module (see Item 107: "Make `pickle` Serialization Maintainable with `copyreg`").

3. It copies the serialized data from the main interpreter process to a child interpreter process over a local socket.

4. It deserializes the data back into Python objects, using `pickle` in the child process.

5. It imports the Python module containing the `gcd` function.

6. It runs the function on the input data in parallel with other child processes.

7. It serializes the result back into binary data.

8. It copies that binary data back through the socket.

9. It deserializes the binary data back into Python objects in the parent process.

10. It merges the results from multiple children into a single `list` to return.

Although using the `pool.map` method looks simple, the `multiprocessing` module and `ProcessPoolExecutor` class do a huge amount of work to make parallelism possible. In most other languages, the only touch point you need to coordinate two threads is a single lock or atomic operation (see Item 69: "Use `Lock` to Prevent Data Races in Threads" for an example). The overhead of using `multiprocessing` via `ProcessPoolExecutor` is high because of all the serialization and deserialization that must happen between the parent and child processes.

This scheme is well suited to certain types of isolated, high-leverage tasks. By *isolated*, I mean functions that don't need to share state with other parts of the program. By *high-leverage*, I mean situations in which only a small amount of data must be transferred between the parent and child processes to enable a large amount of computation. The greatest common divisor algorithm is one example of this, but many other mathematical algorithms work similarly.

If your computation doesn't have these characteristics, then the overhead of `ProcessPoolExecutor` may prevent it from speeding up your program through parallelization. When that happens, multiprocessing provides more advanced facilities for shared memory, cross-process locks, queues, and proxies. But all of these features are very complex. It's hard enough to reason about such tools in the memory space of a single process shared between Python threads. Extending that complexity to other processes and involving sockets makes this much more difficult to understand.

I suggest that you initially avoid all parts of the multiprocessing built-in module. You can start by using the ThreadPoolExecutor class to run isolated, high-leverage functions in threads. Later you can move to ProcessPoolExecutor to get a speedup. Finally, when you've completely exhausted the other options, you can consider using the multiprocessing module directly or using more advanced techniques (see Item 94: "Know When and How to Replace Python with Another Programming Language").

Things to Remember

+ The multiprocessing module provides powerful tools that can parallelize certain types of Python computation with minimal effort.

+ The power of multiprocessing is best accessed through the concurrent.futures built-in module and its simple ProcessPoolExecutor class.

+ Avoid the advanced (and complicated) parts of the multiprocessing module until you've exhausted all other options.

10

Robustness

A lot of useful Python code begins its life in a haphazardly developed script that solves a particular problem as a one-off. As these scripts are expanded, repurposed, and reused, they start to evolve from being short-term, throw-away code into substantial programs that are worth maintaining over the long term.

Once you've written a useful Python program like this, the critical next step is to *productionize* your code so it's bulletproof. Making programs dependable when they encounter unexpected circumstances is just as important as making programs with correct functionality. Python has built-in features and modules that aid in hardening your programs so they are robust in a wide variety of situations.

Item 80: Take Advantage of Each Block in try/except/ else/finally

There are four distinct times when you might want to take action during exception handling in Python: in try, except, else, and finally blocks. Each block serves a unique purpose in the compound statement, and the various combinations of these blocks are useful (see Item 121: "Define a Root Exception to Insulate Callers from APIs" for another example).

finally Blocks

Use try/finally when you want exceptions to propagate up and also want to run cleanup code, even when exceptions occur. One common usage of try/finally is for reliably closing file handles (see Item 82: "Consider contextlib and with Statements for Reusable try/finally Behavior" for another—likely better—approach):

```
def try_finally_example(filename):
    print("* Opening file")
```

```
    handle = open(filename, encoding="utf-8")   # May raise OSError
    try:
        print("* Reading data")
        return handle.read()                     # May raise UnicodeDecodeError
    finally:
        print("* Calling close()")
        handle.close()                           # Always runs after try block
```

Any exception raised by the read method will always propagate up to the calling code, but the close method of handle in the finally block will run first:

```
filename = "random_data.txt"


with open(filename, "wb") as f:
    f.write(b"\xf1\xf2\xf3\xf4\xf5")   # Invalid utf-8

data = try_finally_example(filename)
>>>
* Opening file
* Reading data
* Calling close()
Traceback ...
UnicodeDecodeError: 'utf-8' codec can't decode byte 0xf1 in
➡position 0: invalid continuation byte
```

You must call open before the try block because exceptions that occur when opening the file (like OSError if the file does not exist) should skip the finally block entirely:

```
try_finally_example("does_not_exist.txt")
>>>
* Opening file
Traceback ...
FileNotFoundError: [Errno 2] No such file or directory:
➡'does_not_exist.txt'
```

else Blocks

Use try/except/else to make it clear which exceptions will be handled by your code and which exceptions will propagate up. When the try block doesn't raise an exception, the else block runs. The else block helps you minimize the amount of code in the try block, which is good for isolating potential exception causes and improves readability (see Item 83: "Always Make try Blocks as Short as Possible"). For example, say that I want to load JSON dictionary data from a string and return the value of a key it contains:

```python
import json

def load_json_key(data, key):
    try:
        print("* Loading JSON data")
        result_dict = json.loads(data)  # May raise ValueError
    except ValueError:
        print("* Handling ValueError")
        raise KeyError(key)
    else:
        print("* Looking up key")
        return result_dict[key]          # May raise KeyError
```

In a successful case, the JSON data is decoded in the try block, and then the key lookup occurs in the else block:

```python
assert load_json_key('{"foo": "bar"}', "foo") == "bar"
>>>
* Loading JSON data
* Looking up key
```

If the input data isn't valid JSON, then decoding with json.loads raises a ValueError. The exception is caught by the except block and handled:

```python
load_json_key('{"foo": bad payload', "foo")
>>>
* Loading JSON data
* Handling ValueError
Traceback ...
JSONDecodeError: Expecting value: line 1 column 9 (char 8)

The above exception was the direct cause of the following
➡exception:

Traceback ...
KeyError: 'foo'
```

If the key lookup raises any exceptions, they will propagate up to the caller because they are outside the try block. The else clause ensures that what follows the try/except is visually distinguished from the except block. This makes the exception propagation behavior clear:

```
load_json_key('{"foo": "bar"}', "does not exist")

>>>
* Loading JSON data
* Looking up key
Traceback ...
KeyError: 'does not exist'
```

Everything Together

Use try/except/else/finally when you want to do everything in one compound statement. For example, say that I want to read a description of work to do from a file, process it, and then update the file in place. Here the try block is used to read the file and process it, the except block is used to handle exceptions from the try block that are expected, the else block is used to update the file in place and allow related exceptions to propagate up, and the finally block cleans up the file handle:

```
UNDEFINED = object()
def divide_json(path):
    print("* Opening file")
    handle = open(path, "r+")                        # May raise OSError
    try:
        print("* Reading data")
        data = handle.read()                         # May raise UnicodeDecodeError
        print("* Loading JSON data")
        op = json.loads(data)                        # May raise ValueError
        print("* Performing calculation")
        value = op["numerator"] / op["denominator"]  # May raise ZeroDivisionError
    except ZeroDivisionError:
        print("* Handling ZeroDivisionError")
        return UNDEFINED
    else:
        print("* Writing calculation")
        op["result"] = value
        result = json.dumps(op)
        handle.seek(0)                               # May raise OSError
        handle.write(result)                         # May raise OSError
        return value
    finally:
        print("* Calling close()")
        handle.close()                               # Always runs
```

In a successful case, the try, else, and finally blocks run:

```
temp_path = "random_data.json"

with open(temp_path, "w") as f:
    f.write('{"numerator": 1, "denominator": 10}')

assert divide_json(temp_path) == 0.1
>>>
* Opening file
* Reading data
* Loading JSON data
* Performing calculation
* Writing calculation
* Calling close()
```

If the calculation is invalid, the try, except, and finally blocks run, but the else block does not:

```
with open(temp_path, "w") as f:
    f.write('{"numerator": 1, "denominator": 0}')

assert divide_json(temp_path) is UNDEFINED
>>>
* Opening file
* Reading data
* Loading JSON data
* Performing calculation
* Handling ZeroDivisionError
* Calling close()
```

If the JSON data was invalid, the try block runs and raises an exception, the finally block runs, and then the exception is propagated up to the caller. The except and else blocks do not run:

```
with open(temp_path, "w") as f:
    f.write('{"numerator": 1 bad data')

divide_json(temp_path)
>>>
* Opening file
* Reading data
* Loading JSON data
* Calling close()
Traceback ...
JSONDecodeError: Expecting ',' delimiter: line 1 column 17
➥(char 16)
```

This layout is especially useful because all the blocks work together in intuitive ways. For example, here I simulate this by running the divide_json function at the same time that my hard drive runs out of disk space:

```
with open(temp_path, "w") as f:
    f.write('{"numerator": 1, "denominator": 10}')

divide_json(temp_path)

>>>
* Opening file
* Reading data
* Loading JSON data
* Performing calculation
* Writing calculation
* Calling close()
Traceback ...
OSError: [Errno 28] No space left on device
```

When the exception was raised in the else block while rewriting the result data, the finally block still ran and closed the file handle as expected.

Things to Remember

✦ The try/finally compound statement lets you run cleanup code regardless of whether exceptions were raised in the try block.

✦ The else block helps you minimize the amount of code in try blocks and visually distinguish a successful case from the try/except blocks.

✦ An else block can be used to perform additional actions after a successful try block but before common cleanup in a finally block.

Item 81: assert Internal Assumptions and raise Missed Expectations

Python includes the assert statement, which will raise an AssertionError exception at runtime if the given expression is a falsey value (see Item 7: "Consider Conditional Expressions for Simple Inline Logic" for background). For example, here I try to verify that two lists are not empty, and the second assertion fails because the expression is not a truthy value:

```
list_a = [1, 2, 3]
assert list_a, "a empty"
```

```
list_b = []
assert list_b, "b empty"  # Raises
>>>
Traceback ...
AssertionError: b empty
```

Python also provides the raise statement for reporting exceptional conditions to callers (see Item 32: "Prefer Raising Exceptions to Returning None" for when to use it). Here I use raise along with an if statement to report the same type of empty list problem:

```
class EmptyError(Exception):
    pass

list_c = []
if not list_c:
    raise EmptyError("c empty")
>>>
Traceback ...
EmptyError: c empty
```

The exceptions from raise statements can be caught with try/except statements (see Item 80: "Take Advantage of Each Block in try/except/else/finally"). This alternative type of control flow is the primary purpose of raise:

```
try:
    raise EmptyError("From raise statement")
except EmptyError as e:
    print(f"Caught: {e}")
>>>
Caught: From raise statement
```

But it's also possible to catch the exceptions from assert statements at runtime:

```
try:
    assert False, "From assert statement"
except AssertionError as e:
    print(f"Caught: {e}")
>>>
Caught: From assert statement
```

Why does Python provide two different ways (raise and assert) to report exceptional situations? The reason is that they serve separate roles.

Exceptions caused by raise statements are considered part of a function's interface, just like arguments and return values. These exceptions are meant to be caught by calling code and processed accordingly. The potential exceptions a function raises should be in the documentation (see Item 118: "Write Docstrings for Every Function, Class, and Module") so callers know that they might need to handle them. The behavior of these raise statements should also be verified in automated tests (see Item 109: "Prefer Integration Tests over Unit Tests").

Exceptions caused by assert statements are not meant to be caught by callers of a function. They're used to verify assumptions in an implementation that might not be obvious to new readers of the code. Assertions are self-documenting because they evaluate the second expression (after the comma) to create a debugging error message when the condition fails. These messages can be used by error reporting and logging facilities higher in the call stack to help developers find and fix bugs (see Item 87: "Use traceback for Enhanced Exception Reporting" for an example).

Code that implements identical functionality might use assert statements, raise statements, or both, depending on the context. For example, here I define a simple class that can be used to aggregate movie ratings. It provides a robust API that validates input and reports any problems to the caller using raise:

```
class RatingError(Exception):
    ...

class Rating:
    def __init__(self, max_rating):
        if not (max_rating > 0):
            raise RatingError("Invalid max_rating")
        self.max_rating = max_rating
        self.ratings = []

    def rate(self, rating):
        if not (0 < rating <= self.max_rating):
            raise RatingError("Invalid rating")
        self.ratings.append(rating)
```

The exceptions that this class raises are meant to be caught and, presumably, reported back to the end user or API caller who sent the invalid input:

```
movie = Rating(5)
movie.rate(5)
```

```
movie.rate(7)  # Raises
>>>
Traceback ...
RatingError: Invalid rating
```

Here's another implementation of the same functionality, but this version is not meant to report errors to the caller. Instead, this class assumes that other parts of the program have already done the necessary validation:

```
class RatingInternal:
    def __init__(self, max_rating):
        assert max_rating > 0, f"Invalid {max_rating=}"
        self.max_rating = max_rating
        self.ratings = []

    def rate(self, rating):
        assert 0 < rating <= self.max_rating, \
            f"Invalid {rating=}"
        self.ratings.append(rating)
```

When an assert statement in this class raises an exception, it's meant to report a bug in the code. The message should include information that a programmer can later use to find the cause and fix it:

```
movie = RatingInternal(5)
movie.rate(5)
movie.rate(7)  # Raises
>>>
Traceback ...
AssertionError: Invalid rating=7
```

For assertions like this to be useful, it's critical that calling code does not catch and silence AssertionError or Exception exceptions (see Item 85: "Beware of Catching the Exception Class").

Ultimately, it's on you to decide whether raise or assert will be the most appropriate choice. As the complexity of a Python program grows, the layers of interconnected functions, classes, and modules begin to take shape. Some of these systems are more externally facing APIs: library functions and interfaces meant to be leveraged by other components. In those cases, raise will be most useful (see Item 121: "Define a Root Exception to Insulate Callers from APIs"). Other code is internally facing and helps one part of the program implement larger requirements. In those cases, assert is the way to go; just make sure you don't disable assertions (see Item 90: "Never Set __debug__ to False").

Things to Remember

✦ The raise statement can be used to report expected error conditions back to the callers of a function.

✦ The exceptions that a function directly raises are part of its explicit interface and should be documented accordingly.

✦ The assert statement should be used to verify a programmer's assumptions in the code and convey them to other readers of the implementation.

✦ Failed assertions are not part of the explicit interface of a function and should not be caught by callers.

Item 82: Consider contextlib and with Statements for Reusable try/finally Behavior

The with statement in Python is used to indicate when code is running in a special context. For example, mutual-exclusion locks (see Item 69: "Use Lock to Prevent Data Races in Threads") can be used in with statements to indicate that the indented code block runs only while the lock is held:

```
from threading import Lock

lock = Lock()
with lock:
    # Do something while maintaining an invariant
    ...
```

The example above is equivalent to this try/finally construction (see Item 80: "Take Advantage of Each Block in try/except/else/finally") because the Lock class properly enables use in with statements:

```
lock.acquire()
try:
    # Do something while maintaining an invariant
    ...
finally:
    lock.release()
```

The with statement version of this is better because it eliminates the need to write the repetitive code of the try/finally compound statement, ensuring that you don't forget to have a corresponding release call for every acquire call.

It's easy to make your objects and functions work in with statements by using the contextlib built-in module. This module contains the contextmanager decorator (see Item 38: "Define Function Decorators with functools.wraps" for background), which lets a simple function be used in with statements. This is much easier than defining a new class with the special methods __enter__ and __exit__ (the standard object-oriented approach).

For example, say that I want a region of code to have more debug logging sometimes. Here I define a function that does logging at two severity levels:

```
import logging

def my_function():
    logging.debug("Some debug data")
    logging.error("Error log here")
    logging.debug("More debug data")
```

The default logging level for my program is WARNING, so only the logging.error message will print to screen when I run the function:

```
my_function()

>>>
Error log here
```

I can elevate the logging level of this function temporarily by defining a context manager. This helper function boosts the logging severity level before running the code in the with block and reduces the logging severity level afterward:

```
from contextlib import contextmanager

@contextmanager
def debug_logging(level):
    logger = logging.getLogger()
    old_level = logger.getEffectiveLevel()
    logger.setLevel(level)
    try:
        yield
    finally:
        logger.setLevel(old_level)
```

The yield expression is the point at which the with block's contents will execute (see Item 43: "Consider Generators Instead of Returning Lists" for background). Any exceptions that happen in the with block will be re-raised by the yield expression for you to catch in the helper function (see Item 47: "Manage Iterative State Transitions with a Class Instead of the Generator throw Method" for how that works).

Now I can call the same logging function again but in the debug_logging context. This time, all the debug messages are printed to the screen in the with block. The same function running outside the with block won't print debug messages:

```
with debug_logging(logging.DEBUG):
    print("* Inside:")
    my_function()

print("* After:")
my_function()
```

```
>>>
* Inside:
Some debug data
Error log here
More debug data
* After:
Error log here
```

Enabling as Targets

The context manager passed to a with statement may also return an object. This object is assigned to a local variable in the as part of the compound statement. This gives the code running in the with block the ability to directly interact with its context (see Item 76: "Know How to Port Threaded I/O to asyncio" for another example).

For example, say that I want to write a file and ensure that it's always closed correctly. I can do this by passing open to the with statement. open returns a file handle for the as target of with, and it closes the handle when the with block exits:

```
with open("my_output.txt", "w") as handle:
    handle.write("This is some data!")
```

The with approach is more Pythonic than manually opening and closing the file handle with a try/finally compound statement:

```
handle = open("my_output.txt", "w")
try:
    handle.write("This is some data!")
finally:
    handle.close()
```

Using the as target also gives you confidence that the file is eventually closed when execution leaves the with statement. By highlighting the critical section, it also encourages you to reduce the amount of code that executes while the file handle is open, which is good practice in general.

To enable your own functions to supply values for as targets, all you need to do is yield a value from your context manager. For example, here I define a context manager to fetch a Logger instance, set its level, and then yield it to become the as target:

```
@contextmanager
def log_level(level, name):
    logger = logging.getLogger(name)
    old_level = logger.getEffectiveLevel()
    logger.setLevel(level)
    try:
        yield logger
    finally:
        logger.setLevel(old_level)
```

Calling logging methods like debug on the as target produces output because the logging severity level is set low enough in the with block on that specific Logger instance. Using the logging module directly won't print anything because the default logging severity level for the default program logger is WARNING:

```
with log_level(logging.DEBUG, "my-log") as my_logger:
    my_logger.debug(f"This is a message for {my_logger.name}!")
    logging.debug("This will not print")

>>>
This is a message for my-log!
```

After the with statement exits, calling debug logging methods on the Logger named "my-log" will not print anything because the default logging severity level has been restored automatically. Error log messages will always print:

```
logger = logging.getLogger("my-log")
logger.debug("Debug will not print")
logger.error("Error will print")

>>>
Error will print
```

Later, I can change the name of the logger I want to use by simply updating the with statement. This will point the Logger object that's the as target in the with block to a different instance, but I won't have to update any of my other code to match:

```
with log_level(logging.DEBUG, "other-log") as my_logger:# Changed
    my_logger.debug(f"This is a message for {my_logger.name}!")
    logging.debug("This will not print")
```

```
>>>
This is a message for other-log!
```

This isolation of state and decoupling between creating a context and acting within that context is another benefit of the with statement.

Things to Remember

✦ The with statement allows you to reuse logic from try/finally blocks and reduce visual noise.

✦ The contextlib built-in module provides a contextmanager decorator that makes it easy to use your own functions in with statements.

✦ The value yielded by context managers is supplied to the as part of the with statement. It's useful for letting your code directly access the cause of the special context.

Item 83: Always Make try Blocks as Short as Possible

When handling an expected exception, there's quite a bit of overhead in getting all the various statement blocks set up properly (see Item 80: "Take Advantage of Each Block in try/except/else/finally"). For example, say that I want to make a remote procedure call (RPC) via a connection, which might encounter an error:

```
connection = ...
class RpcError(Exception):
    ...

def lookup_request(connection):
    ...

    raise RpcError("From lookup_request")
def close_connection(connection):
    ...
    print("Connection closed")

try:
    request = lookup_request(connection)
except RpcError:
    print("Encountered error!")
    close_connection(connection)
>>>
Error!
Connection closed
```

Later, imagine that I want to do more processing with the data gathered inside the try block or handle special cases. The simplest and most natural way to do this is to add code right where it's needed. Here I change the example above to have a fast path that checks for cached responses in order to avoid extra processing:

```
def lookup_request(connection):
    # No error raised
    ...

def is_cached(connection, request):
    ...
    raise RpcError("From is_cached")

try:
    request = lookup_request(connection)
    if is_cached(connection, request):
        request = None
except RpcError:
    print("Encountered error!")
    close_connection(connection)
>>>
Connection closed
```

The problem is that the is_cached function might also raise an RpcError exception. By calling lookup_request and is_cached in the same try/except statement, later on in the code I can't tell which of these functions actually raised the error and caused the connection to be closed:

```
if is_closed(connection):
    # Was the connection closed because of an error
    # in lookup_request or is_cached?
    ...
```

Instead, what you should do is put only one source of expected errors in each try block. Everything else should either be in an associated else block or a separate subsequent try statement:

```
try:
    request = lookup_request(connection)
except RpcError:
    close_connection(connection)
else:
    if is_cached(connection, request):  # Moved
        request = None
>>>
Traceback ...
RpcError: From is_cached
```

This approach ensures that exceptions you did *not* expect, such as those potentially raised by is_cached, will bubble up through your call stack and produce error messages that you can find, debug, and fix later.

Things to Remember

✦ Putting too much code inside a try block can cause your program to catch exceptions you didn't intend to handle.

✦ Instead of expanding a try block, put additional code into the else block following the associated except block or in a totally separate try statement.

Item 84: Beware of Exception Variables Disappearing

Unlike for loop variables (see Item 20: "Never Use for Loop Variables After the Loop Ends"), exception variables are not accessible on the line following an except block:

```
try:
    raise MyError(123)
except MyError as e:
    print(f"Inside {e=}")

print(f"Outside {e=}")  # Raises

>>>
Inside e=MyError(123)
Traceback ...
NameError: name 'e' is not defined
```

You might assume that the exception variable will still exist within scope of the finally block that is part of the exception handling machinery (see Item 80: "Take Advantage of Each Block in try/except/else/finally"). Unfortunately, it will not:

```
try:
    raise MyError(123)
except MyError as e:
    print(f"Inside {e=}")
finally:
    print(f"Finally {e=}")  # Raises

>>>
Inside e=MyError(123)
Traceback ...
NameError: name 'e' is not defined
```

Sometimes it's useful to save the result of each potential outcome of a try statement. For example, say that I want to log the result of each branch for debugging purposes. In order to accomplish this, I need to create a new variable and assign a value to it in each branch:

```
result = "Unexpected exception"
try:
    raise MyError(123)
except MyError as e:
    result = e
except OtherError as e:
    result = e
else:
    result = "Success"
finally:
    print(f"Log {result=}")
>>>
Log result=MyError(123)
```

It's important to note that the result variable is assigned in the example above even before the try block. This is necessary to address the situation where an exception is raised that is not covered by one of the except clauses. If you don't assign result up front, a runtime error will be raised instead of your original error:

```
try:
    raise OtherError(123)   # Not handled
except MyError as e:
    result = e
else:
    result = "Success"
finally:
    print(f"{result=}")     # Raises
>>>
Traceback ...
OtherError: 123

The above exception was the direct cause of the following
➥exception:

Traceback ...
NameError: name 'result' is not defined
```

This illustrates another way in which Python does not consistently scope variables to functions. The lifetime of a variable in an except block, generator expression, list comprehension, or for loop might be different than what you expect (see Item 42: "Reduce Repetition in Comprehensions with Assignment Expressions" for an example).

Things to Remember

✦ Exception variables assigned by except statements are only accessible within their associated except blocks.

✦ In order to access a caught Exception instance in the surrounding scope or subsequent finally block, you must assign it to another variable name.

Item 85: Beware of Catching the Exception Class

Errors in programs—both expected and unexpected—happen frequently. These issues are an aspect of building software that programmers must accept and attempt to mitigate. For example, say that I want to analyze the sales of a pizza restaurant and generate a daily summary report. Here I accomplish this with a simple pipeline of functions:

```
def load_data(path):
    ...

def analyze_data(data):
    ...

def run_report(path):
    data = load_data(path)
    summary = analyze(data)
    return summary
```

It would be useful to have an up-to-date summary always available, so I'll call the run_report function on a schedule every 5 minutes. However, sometimes transient errors might occur, such as at the beginning of the day before the restaurant opens, when no transactions have yet to be recorded in the daily file:

```
summary = run_report("pizza_data-2024-01-28.csv")
print(summary)

>>>
Traceback ...
FileNotFoundError: [Errno 2] No such file or directory:
➥'pizza_data-2024-01-28.csv'
```

Normally, I'd solve this problem by wrapping the run_report call with a try/except statement that logs a failure message to the console (see

Item 80: "Take Advantage of Each Block in try/except/else/finally" for details):

```
try:
    summary = run_report("pizza_data.csv")
except FileNotFoundError:
    print("Transient file error")
else:
    print(summary)

>>>
Transient file error
```

This will avoid one kind of problem, but the pipeline might raise many other types of transient exceptions that I haven't anticipated. I want to prevent any intermittent errors from crashing the rest of the restaurant's point-of-sale program in which the report is running. It's more important for transactions to keep being processed than for the periodic report to be refreshed.

One way to insulate the rest of the system from failures is to catch the broader Exception parent class instead of the more specific FileNotFoundError class:

```
try:
    summary = run_report("pizza_data.csv")
except Exception:  # Changed
    print("Transient report issue")
else:
    print(summary)

>>>
Transient report issue
```

When an exception is raised, each of the except clauses is considered in order. If the exception value's type is a subclass of the clause's specified class, then the corresponding error handling code will be executed. By providing the Exception class to match, I'll catch errors of any kind because they all inherit from this parent class.

Unfortunately, this approach has a big problem: The try/except statement might prevent me from noticing legitimate problems with my code. Once the pizza restaurant opens and the data file is definitely present, the run_report function surprisingly still fails. The cause is a typo in the original definition of run_report that called the analyze function—which does not exist—instead of the correct analyze_data function:

```
run_report("my_data.csv")

>>>
```

```
Traceback ...
NameError: name 'analyze' is not defined
```

Due to the highly dynamic nature of Python, the interpreter will only detect that the function is missing at execution time, not when the program first loads (see Item 3: "Never Expect Python to Detect Errors at Compile Time" for details). The interpreter will raise a NameError, which is a subclass of the Exception class. Thus, the corresponding except clause will catch the exception and report it as a transient error even though it's actually a critical problem.

One way to mitigate this issue is to always print or log the exception that's caught when matching the Exception class. At least that way the details about the error received will be visible; anyone looking at the console output might notice that there's a real bug in the program. For example, here I print both the exception value and its type to make it abundantly clear what went wrong:

```
try:
    summary = run_report("my_data.csv")
except Exception as e:
    print("Fail:", type(e), e)
else:
    print(summary)

>>>
Fail: <class 'NameError'> name 'analyze' is not defined
```

There are other ways that overly broad exception handling can cause problems that are worth knowing as well (see Item 86: "Understand the Difference Between Exception and BaseException" and Item 89: "Always Pass Resources into Generators and Have Callers Clean Them Up Outside"). In addition, there are more robust ways to report and handle errors for explicit APIs that help avoid these problems (see Item 121: "Define a Root Exception to Insulate Callers from APIs"). Catching exceptions to isolate errors can be useful, but you need to ensure that you're not accidentally hiding issues.

Things to Remember

✦ Using the Exception class in except clauses can help you insulate one part of your program from the others.

✦ Catching broad categories of exceptions might cause your code to handle errors you didn't intend, which can inadvertently hide problems.

✦ When using a broad exception handler, it's important to print or otherwise log any errors encountered to provide visibility into what's really happening.

Item 86: Understand the Difference Between Exception and BaseException

Python documentation will tell you that programmer-defined exception classes must inherit from the Exception class. But the root of the exception tree in Python is actually BaseException, which is the parent class of Exception. Branching off from BaseException are other exception classes that Python uses for its own internal purposes.

For example, when a user presses the Control-C key combination while a Python program runs, they expect to interrupt the running program and cause it to terminate. The precise way Python accomplishes this is platform dependent, but ultimately the interpreter runtime converts the interrupt signal into a KeyboardInterrupt exception and raises it in the program's main thread. KeyboardInterrupt does *not* inherit from Exception, which means that it should bypass exception handlers all the way up to the entry point of the program and cause it to exit with an error message. Here I show this behavior in action by exiting an infinite loop even though it catches the Exception class:

```
def do_processing():
    ...


def main(argv):
    while True:
        try:
            do_processing()  # Interrupted
        except Exception as e:
            print("Error:", type(e), e)

    return 0

if __name__ == "__main__":
    sys.exit(main(sys.argv))
>>>
Traceback ...
KeyboardInterrupt
```

Knowing this is possible, I might choose to catch the BaseException class so I can always do cleanup before program termination, such as flushing open files to disk to ensure that they're not corrupted. In other situations, catching a broad class of exceptions like this can be useful for insulating components against potential errors and providing resilient APIs (see Item 85: "Beware of Catching the Exception Class" and Item 121: "Define a Root Exception to Insulate Callers from APIs"). I can return 1 at the end of the exception handler to indicate that the program should exit with an error code:

```python
def do_processing(handle):
    ...


def main(argv):
    data_path = argv[1]
    handle = open(data_path, "w+")

    while True:
        try:
            do_processing(handle)
        except Exception as e:
            print("Error:", type(e), e)
        except BaseException:
            print("Cleaning up interrupt")
            handle.flush()
            handle.close()
            return 1

    return 0

if __name__ == "__main__":
    sys.exit(main(sys.argv))
```

```
>>>
Cleaning up interrupt
Traceback ...
SystemExit: 1
```

The problem is that there are other exception types that also inherit from BaseException, including SystemExit (caused by the sys.exit built-in function) and GeneratorExit (see Item 89: "Always Pass Resources into Generators and Have Callers Clean Them Up Outside"). Python might add more in the future as well. Python treats these exceptions as mechanisms for executing desired behavior instead of reporting error conditions, which is why they're in a separate part of the class hierarchy. The runtime relies on users generally not catching these exceptions in order to work properly; if you catch them, you might inadvertently cause harmful side effects in a program.

Thus, if you want to achieve this type of cleanup behavior, it's better to use constructs like try/finally statements (see Item 80: "Take

Advantage of Each Block in try/except/else/finally") and with statements (see Item 82: "Consider contextlib and with Statements for Reusable try/finally Behavior"). These constructs will ensure that the cleanup methods run regardless of whether the exception raised inherits from Exception or BaseException:

```
def main(argv):
    data_path = argv[1]
    handle = open(data_path, "w+")

    try:
        while True:
            try:
                do_processing(handle)
            except Exception as e:
                print("Error:", type(e), e)
    finally:
        print("Cleaning up finally")  # Always runs
        handle.flush()
        handle.close()

if __name__ == "__main__":
    sys.exit(main(sys.argv))
>>>
Cleaning up finally
Traceback ...
KeyboardInterrupt
```

If for some reason you really must catch and handle a direct child class of BaseException, it's important to propagate the error correctly so other code higher up in the call stack will still receive it. For example, I might catch KeyboardInterrupt exceptions and ask the user to confirm their intention to terminate the program. Here I use a bare raise at the end of the exception handler to ensure that the exception continues normally, without modifications to its traceback (see Item 87: "Use traceback for Enhanced Exception Reporting" for background):

```
def main(argv):
    while True:
        try:
            do_processing()
        except Exception as e:
            print("Error:", type(e), e)
        except KeyboardInterrupt:
            found = input("Terminate? [y/n]: ")
```

```
                if found == "y":
                    raise  # Propagate the error

if __name__ == "__main__":
    sys.exit(main(sys.argv))
>>>
Terminate? [y/n]: y
Traceback ...
KeyboardInterrupt
```

Another situation where you might decide to catch BaseException is for enhanced logging utilities (see Item 87: "Use traceback for Enhanced Exception Reporting" for a related use case). For example, I can define a function decorator that logs all inputs and outputs, including raised Exception subclass values (see Item 38: "Define Function Decorators with functools.wraps" for background):

```
import functools

def log(func):
    @functools.wraps(func)
    def wrapper(*args, **kwargs):
        try:
            result = func(*args, **kwargs)
        except Exception as e:
            result = e
            raise
        finally:
            print(
                f"Called {func.__name__}"
                f"(*{args!r}, **{kwargs!r}) "
                f"got {result!r}"
            )
    return wrapper
```

Calling a function decorated with log will print everything as expected:

```
@log
def my_func(x):
    x / 0

my_func(123)

>>>
Called my_func(*(123,), **{}) got ZeroDivisionError(
➥'division by zero')
```

```
Traceback ...
ZeroDivisionError: division by zero
```

However, if the exception that's raised inherits from BaseException instead of Exception, the decorator will break and cause unexpected errors:

```
@log
def other_func(x):
    if x > 0:
        sys.exit(1)


other_func(456)
>>>
Traceback ...
SystemExit: 1


The above exception was the direct cause of the following
➥exception:


Traceback ...
UnboundLocalError: cannot access local variable 'result'
➥where it is not associated with a value
```

It might seem counterintuitive, but the finally clause will run even in cases where there are no except clauses present or none of the provided except clauses actually match the exception value that was raised (see Item 84: "Beware of Exception Variables Disappearing" for another example). In the case above, that's exactly what happened: SystemExit is not a subclass of Exception, and so that handler never ran, and result was not assigned before the call to print in the finally clause. Simply catching BaseException instead of Exception solves the problem:

```
def fixed_log(func):
    @functools.wraps(func)
    def wrapper(*args, **kwargs):
        try:
            result = func(*args, **kwargs)
        except BaseException as e:  # Fixed
            result = e
            raise
        finally:
            print(
                f"Called {func.__name__}"
                f"(*{args!r}, **{kwargs!r}) "
```

```
                    f"got {result!r}"
            )
    return wrapper
```

Now the decorator works as expected for SystemExit:

```
@fixed_log
def other_func(x):
    if x > 0:
        sys.exit(1)


other_func(456)

>>>
Called other_func(*(456,), **{}) got SystemExit(1)
Traceback ...
SystemExit: 1
```

Handling BaseException and related classes can be useful, but it's also quite tricky, so it's important to pay close attention to the details and be careful.

Things to Remember

✦ For internal behaviors, Python sometimes raises BaseException child classes, which will skip except clauses that only handle the Exception base class.

✦ try/finally statements, with statements, and similar constructs properly handle raised BaseException child classes without extra effort.

✦ There are legitimate reasons to catch BaseException and related classes, but doing so can be error prone.

Item 87: Use traceback for Enhanced Exception Reporting

When a Python program encounters a problem, an exception is often raised. If the exception is not caught and handled (see Item 80: "Take Advantage of Each Block in try/except/else/finally"), it will propagate all the way up to the entry point of the program and cause it to exit with an error code. The Python interpreter will also print out a nicely formatted stack trace or *traceback* to aid developers in figuring out what went wrong. For example, here I use the assert statement to cause an exception and print out the corresponding traceback (see

Item 81: "assert Internal Assumptions, raise Missed Expectations" for background):

```
def inner_func(message):
    assert False, message

def outer_func(message):
    inner_func(message)

outer_func("Oops!")
>>>
Traceback (most recent call last):
  File "my_code.py", line 7, in <module>
    outer_func("Oops!")
    ~~~~~~~~~~~^^^^^^^^^^
  File "my_code.py", line 5, in outer_func
    inner_func(message)
    ~~~~~~~~~~^^^^^^^^^^
  File "my_code.py", line 2, in inner_func
    assert False, message
           ^^^^^
AssertionError: Oops!
```

This default printing behavior can be helpful for single-threaded code where all exceptions are happening in the main thread. But it won't work for programs or servers that are handling many requests concurrently (see Item 71: "Know How to Recognize When Concurrency Is Necessary"). If you allow exceptions from one request to propagate all the way up to the entry point, the program will crash and cause all other requests to fail as well.

One way to deal with this is to surround the root of a request handler with a blanket try statement (see Item 85: "Beware of Catching the Exception Class" and Item 86: "Understand the Difference Between Exception and BaseException"). For example, here I define a hypothetical Request class and handler function. When an exception is hit, I can print it out to the console log for the developer to see and then return an error code to the client. This ensures that all other handlers keep processing, even in the presence of bad requests:

```
class Request:
    def __init__(self, body):
        self.body = body
        self.response = None

def do_work(data):
```

```
    assert False, data
    ...


def handle(request):
    try:
        do_work(request.body)
    except BaseException as e:
        print(repr(e))
        request.response = 400  # Bad request error

request = Request("My message")
handle(request)

>>>
AssertionError('My message')
```

The problem with this code is that the string representation of the exception value doesn't provide enough information to debug the issue. I don't get a traceback as I would from an unhandled exception in the Python interpreter's main thread. Fortunately, Python can fill this gap with the `traceback` built-in module, which allows you to extract the traceback information from an exception at runtime. Here I use the `print_tb` function in the `traceback` built-in module to print a stack trace:

```
import traceback


def handle2(request):
    try:
        do_work(request.body)
    except BaseException as e:
        traceback.print_tb(e.__traceback__)   # Changed
        print(repr(e))
        request.response = 400


request = Request("My message 2")
handle2(request)

>>>
  File "my_code.py", line 70, in handle2
    do_work(request.body)
    ~~~~~~~~^^^^^^^^^^^^^^
  File "my_code.py", line 42, in do_work
    assert False, data
           ^^^^^
AssertionError('My message 2')
```

In addition to printing, you can process the traceback's detailed information—including filename, line number, source code line, and containing function name—however you like (e.g., to display in a GUI). Here I extract the function name for each frame in the traceback and print them to the console:

```python
def handle3(request):
    try:
        do_work(request.body)
    except BaseException as e:
        stack = traceback.extract_tb(e.__traceback__)
        for frame in stack:
            print(frame.name)
        print(repr(e))
        request.response = 400


request = Request("My message 3")
handle3(request)

>>>
handle3
do_work
AssertionError('My message 3')
```

Beyond printing to the console, I can also use the traceback module to provide more advanced error handling behaviors. For example, imagine that I wanted to save a log of exceptions encountered in a separate file, encoded as one JSON payload per line. Here I accomplish this with a wrapper function that processes the traceback frames:

```python
import json


def log_if_error(file_path, target, *args, **kwargs):
    try:
        target(*args, **kwargs)
    except BaseException as e:
        stack = traceback.extract_tb(e.__traceback__)
        stack_without_wrapper = stack[1:]
        trace_dict = dict(
            stack=[item.name
                   for item in stack_without_wrapper],
            error_type=type(e).__name__,
            error_message=str(e),
        )
        json_data = json.dumps(trace_dict)

        with open(file_path, "a") as f:
            f.write(json_data)
            f.write("\n")
```

Calling the wrapper with the erroring do_work function will properly encode errors and write them to disk:

```
log_if_error("my_log.jsonl", do_work, "First error")
log_if_error("my_log.jsonl", do_work, "Second error")
with open("my_log.jsonl") as f:
    for line in f:
        print(line, end="")
>>>
{"stack": ["do_work"], "error_type": "AssertionError",
➥"error_message": "First error"}
{"stack": ["do_work"], "error_type": "AssertionError",
➥"error_message": "Second error"}
```

The traceback built-in module also includes a variety of other functions that make it easy to format, print, and traverse exception stack traces in most of the ways you'll ever need (see https://docs.python.org/3/library/traceback.html). However, you'll still need to handle some of the edge cases yourself (see Item 88: "Consider Explicitly Chaining Exceptions to Clarify Tracebacks" for one such case).

Things to Remember

✦ When an unhandled exception propagates up to the entry point of a Python program, the interpreter will print a nicely formatted list of the stack frames that caused the error.

✦ In highly concurrent programs, exception tracebacks are often not printed in the same way, making errors more difficult to understand and debug.

✦ The traceback built-in module allows you to interact with the stack frames from an exception and process them in whatever way you see fit (i.e., to aid in debugging).

Item 88: Consider Explicitly Chaining Exceptions to Clarify Tracebacks

Python programs raise exceptions when they encounter errors or certain conditions in code (see Item 32: "Prefer Raising Exceptions to Returning None"). For example, here I try to access a nonexistent key in a dictionary, which results in an exception being raised:

```
my_dict = {}
my_dict["does_not_exist"]
>>>
Traceback ...
KeyError: 'does_not_exist'
```

I can catch this exception and handle it by using the try statement (see Item 80: "Take Advantage of Each Block in try/except/else/finally"):

```
my_dict = {}
try:
    my_dict["does_not_exist"]
except KeyError:
    print("Could not find key!")

>>>
Could not find key!
```

If another exception is raised while I'm already handling one, the output looks quite different. For example, here I raise a newly defined MissingError exception while handling the KeyError exception:

```
class MissingError(Exception):
    ...

try:
    my_dict["does_not_exist"]      # Raises first exception
except KeyError:
    raise MissingError("Oops!")   # Raises second exception

>>>
Traceback ...
KeyError: 'does_not_exist'

The above exception was the direct cause of the following
➡exception:

Traceback ...
MissingError: Oops!
```

The MissingError exception that's raised in the except KeyError block is the one propagated up to the caller. However, you can also see that the stack trace printed by Python included information about the exception that caused the initial problem: the KeyError raised by the my_dict["does_not_exist"] expression. This extra data is available because Python will automatically assign an exception's __context__ attribute to the exception instance being handled by the surrounding except block. Here is the same code as above, but now I catch the MissingError exception and print its __context__ attribute to show how the exceptions are *chained* together:

```
try:
    try:
```

```
        my_dict["does_not_exist"]
    except KeyError:
        raise MissingError("Oops!")
except MissingError as e:
    print("Second:", repr(e))
    print("First: ", repr(e.__context__))
>>>
Second: MissingError('Oops!')
First:  KeyError('does_not_exist')
```

In complex code with many layers of error handling, it can be useful to control these chains of exceptions to make the error messages more clear. To accomplish this, Python allows for explicitly chaining together exceptions by using the from clause in the raise statement.

For example, say that I want to define a helper function that implements the same dictionary lookup behavior as above:

```
def lookup(my_key):
    try:
        return my_dict[my_key]
    except KeyError:
        raise MissingError
```

When I look up a key that is present, I retrieve the value without a problem:

```
my_dict["my key 1"] = 123
print(lookup("my key 1"))
>>>
123
```

When the given key is missing, a MissingError exception is raised as expected:

```
print(lookup("my key 2"))
>>>
Traceback ...
KeyError: 'my key 2'

The above exception was the direct cause of the following
➥exception:

Traceback ...
MissingError
```

Now imagine that I want to augment the lookup function and be able to contact a remote database server and populate the my_dict dictionary in the event that a key is missing. Here I implement this behavior, assuming contact_server will do the database communication:

```python
def contact_server(my_key):
    print(f"Looking up {my_key!r} in server")
    ...


def lookup(my_key):
    try:
        return my_dict[my_key]
    except KeyError:
        result = contact_server(my_key)
        my_dict[my_key] = result  # Fill the local cache
        return result
```

Calling this function repeatedly, I can see that the server is only contacted on the first call, when the key is not yet present in the my_dict cache. The subsequent call avoids calling contact_server and returns the value that is already present in my_dict:

```python
print("Call 1")
print("Result:", lookup("my key 2"))
print("Call 2")
print("Result:", lookup("my key 2"))

>>>
Call 1
Looking up 'my key 2' in server
Result: my value 2
Call 2
Result: my value 2
```

Imagine that it's possible for the database server not to have a requested record. In this situation, perhaps the contact_server function raises a new type of exception to indicate the condition:

```python
class ServerMissingKeyError(Exception):
    ...


def contact_server(my_key):
    print(f"Looking up {my_key!r} in server")
    ...
    raise ServerMissingKeyError
    ...
```

Now when I try to look up a record that's missing, I see a traceback that includes the ServerMissingKeyError exception and the original KeyError for the my_dict cache miss:

```
print(lookup("my key 3"))
>>>
Looking up 'my key 3' in server
Traceback ...
KeyError: 'my key 3'

The above exception was the direct cause of the following
➥exception:

Traceback ...
ServerMissingKeyError
```

The problem is that the lookup function no longer adheres to the same interface as before when there was no call to contact_server. To abstract the details of the exception from the caller, I want a cache miss to always result in a MissingError, not a ServerMissingKeyError, which might be defined in a separate module that I don't control (see Item 121: "Define a Root Exception to Insulate Callers from APIs" for exception classes in APIs).

To fix this, I can wrap the call to contact_server in another try statement, catch the ServerMissingKeyError exception, and raise a MissingError instead (matching my desired API for lookup):

```
def lookup(my_key):
    try:
        return my_dict[my_key]
    except KeyError:
        try:
            result = contact_server(my_key)
        except ServerMissingKeyError:
            raise MissingError        # Convert the server error
        else:
            my_dict[my_key] = result  # Fill the local cache
            return result
```

Trying the new implementation of lookup, I can verify that the MissingError exception is what's propagated up to callers:

```
print(lookup("my key 4"))
>>>
Looking up 'my key 4' in server
Traceback ...
KeyError: 'my key 4'
```

```
The above exception was the direct cause of the following
➥exception:

Traceback ...
ServerMissingKeyError

The above exception was the direct cause of the following
➥exception:

Traceback ...
MissingError
```

This chain of exceptions shows three different errors because of how the except clauses are nested in the lookup function. First, the KeyError exception is raised. Then, while handling it, the contact_server function raises a ServerMissingKeyError, which is implicitly chained from the KeyError using the __context__ attribute. The ServerMissingKeyError is then caught, and the MissingError is raised with the __context__ attribute implicitly assigned to the ServerMissingKeyError currently being handled.

A lot of information was printed for this MissingError—so much that it seems like it could be confusing to programmers trying to debug a real problem. One way to reduce the output is to use the from clause in the raise statement to explicitly indicate the source of an exception. Here I hide the ServerMissingKeyError source error by having the exception handler explicitly chain the MissingError from the KeyError:

```
def lookup_explicit(my_key):
    try:
        return my_dict[my_key]
    except KeyError as e:              # Changed
        try:
            result = contact_server(my_key)
        except ServerMissingKeyError:
            raise MissingError from e   # Changed
        else:
            my_dict[my_key] = result
            return result
```

Calling the function again, I can confirm that the ServerMissingKeyError exception is no longer printed:

```
print(lookup_explicit("my key 5"))

>>>
Looking up 'my key 5' in server
```

```
Traceback ...
KeyError: 'my key 5'
```

The above exception was the direct cause of the following
➡exception:

```
Traceback ...
MissingError
```

Although in the exception output it appears that the
ServerMissingKeyError is no longer associated with the MissingError
exception, it is in fact still there, assigned to the __context__ attribute
as before. The reason it's not printed is that using the from e clause
in the raise statement assigns the raised exception's __cause__ attribute to the KeyError and the __suppress_context__ attribute to True.
Here I show the value of these attributes to clarify what Python uses
to control the printing of unhandled exceptions:

```
try:
    lookup_explicit("my key 6")
except Exception as e:
    print("Exception:", repr(e))
    print("Context:  ", repr(e.__context__))
    print("Cause:    ", repr(e.__cause__))
    print("Suppress: ", repr(e.__suppress_context__))
```

```
>>>
Looking up 'my key 6' in server
Exception: MissingError()
Context:   ServerMissingKeyError()
Cause:     KeyError('my key 6')
Suppress:  True
```

The exception chain traversal behavior that inspects __cause__ and
__suppress_context__ is only present for Python's built-in exception
printer. If you use the traceback module to process Exception stack
traces yourself (see Item 87: "Use traceback for Enhanced Exception
Reporting"), you might notice that chained exception data seems to be
missing:

```
import traceback
```

```
try:
    lookup("my key 7")
except Exception as e:
    stack = traceback.extract_tb(e.__traceback__)
```

```
        for frame in stack:
            print(frame.line)
>>>
Looking up 'my key 7' in server
lookup('my key 7')
raise MissingError        # Convert the server error
```

In order to extract the same chained exception information that Python prints for unhandled exceptions, you need to properly consider each exception's __cause__ and __context__ attributes:

```
def get_cause(exc):
    if exc.__cause__ is not None:
        return exc.__cause__
    elif not exc.__suppress_context__:
        return exc.__context__
    else:
        return None
```

The get_cause function can be applied in a loop or recursively to construct the full stack of chained exceptions:

```
try:
    lookup("my key 8")
except Exception as e:
    while e is not None:
        stack = traceback.extract_tb(e.__traceback__)
        for i, frame in enumerate(stack, 1):
            print(i, frame.line)
        e = get_cause(e)
        if e:
            print("Caused by")
>>>
Looking up 'my key 8' in server
1 lookup('my key 8')
2 raise MissingError        # Convert the server error
Caused by
1 result = contact_server(my_key)
2 raise ServerMissingKeyError
Caused by
1 return my_dict[my_key]
```

Another alternative way to shorten the MissingError exception chain is to suppress the KeyError source for the ServerMissingKeyError raised in `contact_server`. Here I do this by using the `from None` clause in the corresponding `raise` statement:

```
def contact_server(key):
    ...
    raise ServerMissingKeyError from None   # Suppress
    ...
```

Calling the `lookup` function again, I can confirm that the `KeyError` is no longer in Python's default exception handling output:

```
print(lookup("my key 9"))
>>>
Traceback ...

ServerMissingKeyError

The above exception was the direct cause of the following
➥exception:

Traceback ...
MissingError
```

Things to Remember

✦ When an exception is raised from inside an `except` clause, the original exception for that handler will always be saved to the newly raised `Exception` value's `__context__` attribute.

✦ The `from` clause in the `raise` statement lets you explicitly indicate—by setting the `__cause__` attribute—that a previously raised exception is the cause of a newly raised one.

✦ Explicitly chaining one exception from another will cause Python to only print the supplied cause (or lack thereof) instead of the automatically chained exception.

Item 89: Always Pass Resources into Generators and Have Callers Clean Them Up Outside

Python provides a variety of tools, such as exception handlers (see Item 80: "Take Advantage of Each Block in try/except/else/finally") and `with` statements (see Item 82: "Consider `contextlib` and `with` Statements for Reusable try/finally Behavior"), to help you ensure that resources like files, mutexes, and sockets are properly cleaned up at the right time. For example, in a normal function, a simple `finally` clause will be executed *before* the return value is actually received by the caller, making it an ideal location to reliably close file handles:

```
def my_func():
    try:
        return 123
    finally:
        print("Finally my_func")

print("Before")
print(my_func())
print("After")

>>>
Before
Finally my_func
123
After
```

In contrast, when using a generator function (see Item 43: "Consider Generators Instead of Returning Lists"), the finally clause won't execute until the StopIteration exception is raised to indicate that the sequence of values has been exhausted (see Item 21: "Be Defensive when Iterating over Arguments"). That means the finally clause is executed *after* the last item is received by the caller, unlike with a normal function:

```
def my_generator():
    try:
        yield 10
        yield 20
        yield 30
    finally:
        print("Finally my_generator")

print("Before")
for i in my_generator():
    print(i)

print("After")
>>>
Before
10
20
30
```

```
Finally my_generator
After
```

However, it's also possible for Python generators to not finish being iterated. In theory, this could prevent the StopIteration exception from ever being raised and thereby prevent the execution of the finally clause. Here I simulate this behavior by manually stepping forward the generator function's iterator; note how "Finally my_generator" doesn't print:

```
it = my_generator()
print("Before")
print(next(it))
print(next(it))
print("After")

>>>
Before
10
20
After
```

The finally clause hasn't executed yet. When will it? The answer is that it depends: It might never run. If the last reference to the iterator is dropped, garbage collection is enabled, and a collection cycle runs, which should cause the generator's finally clause to execute:

```
import gc

del it
gc.collect()

>>>
Finally my_generator
```

The mechanism that powers this is the GeneratorExit exception, which inherits from BaseException (see Item 86: "Understand the Difference Between Exception and BaseException"). Upon garbage collection, Python will send this special type of exception into the generator if it's not exhausted (see Item 46: "Pass Iterators into Generators as Arguments Instead of Calling the send Method" for background). Normally this causes the generator to return and clear its stack, but technically you can catch this type of exception and handle it:

```
def catching_generator():
    try:
        yield 40
```

```
        yield 50
        yield 60
    except BaseException as e:  # Catches GeneratorExit
        print("Catching handler", type(e), e)
        raise
```

At the end of the exception handler, I use a bare `raise` keyword with no arguments to ensure that the `GeneratorExit` exception propagates and none of Python's runtime machinery breaks. Here I step forward this new generator and then cause another garbage collecting cycle:

```
it = catching_generator()
print("Before")
print(next(it))
print(next(it))
print("After")
del it
gc.collect()

>>>
Before
40
50
After
Catching handler <class 'GeneratorExit'>
```

The exception handler is run separately by the `gc` module, not in the original call stack that created the generator and stepped it forward. What happens if a different exception is raised while handling the `GeneratorExit` exception? Here I define another generator to demonstrate this possibility:

```
def broken_generator():
    try:
        yield 70
        yield 80
    except BaseException as e:
        print("Broken handler", type(e), e)
        raise RuntimeError("Broken")

it = broken_generator()
print("Before")
print(next(it))
print("After")
del it
gc.collect()
```

```
print("Still going")
>>>
Before
70
After
Exception ignored in: <generator object broken_generator at
➥ 0x10099b2e0>
Traceback ...
RuntimeError: Broken
Broken handler <class 'GeneratorExit'>
Still going
```

This outcome is surprising: The gc module catches the RuntimeError raised by broken_generator and prints it out to sys.stderr. The exception is not raised back into the main thread where gc.collect was called. Instead, it's completely swallowed and hidden from the rest of the program, which continues running. This means that you can't rely on exception handlers or finally clauses in generators to always execute and report errors back to callers.

To work around this potential risk, you can allocate resources that need to be cleaned up outside a generator and pass them in as arguments. For example, imagine that I'm trying to build a simple utility that finds the maximum length of the first five lines of a file. Here I define a simple generator that yields line lengths given a file path:

```
def lengths_path(path):
    try:
        with open(path) as handle:
            for i, line in enumerate(handle):
                print(f"Line {i}")
                yield len(line.strip())
    finally:
        print("Finally lengths_path")
```

I can use the generator in a loop to calculate the maximum and then terminate the loop early, leaving the lengths_path generator in a partially executed state:

```
max_head = 0
it = lengths_path("my_file.txt")

for i, length in enumerate(it):
    if i == 5:
        break
    else:
```

```
        max_head = max(max_head, length)
```

```
print(max_head)
```

```
>>>
Line 0
Line 1
Line 2
Line 3
Line 4
Line 5
99
```

After the generator iterator goes out of scope sometime later, it will be garbage collected, and the `finally` clause will run as expected:

```
del it
gc.collect()
```

```
>>>
Finally lengths_path
```

This delayed behavior is what I'm trying to avoid. I need `finally` to run within the call stack of the original loop so that if any errors are encountered, they're properly raised back to the caller. This is especially important for resources like mutex locks that must avoid dead-locking. To accomplish the correct behavior, I can pass an open file handle into the generator function:

```
def lengths_handle(handle):
    try:
        for i, line in enumerate(handle):
            print(f"Line {i}")
            yield len(line.strip())
    finally:
        print("Finally lengths_handle")
```

I can use a `with` statement around the loop to make sure the file is opened and closed reliably and immediately so the generator doesn't have to manage the file handle itself:

```
max_head = 0
```

```
with open("my_file.txt") as handle:
    it = lengths_handle(handle)
    for i, length in enumerate(it):
        if i == 5:
            break
```

```
        else:
            max_head = max(max_head, length)

print(max_head)
print("Handle closed:", handle.closed)
>>>
Line 0
Line 1
Line 2
Line 3
Line 4
Line 5
99
Handle closed: True
```

Again, because the loop iteration ended before exhaustion, the generator function hasn't exited, and the finally clause hasn't executed. But this is okay with this different approach because I'm not relying on the generator to do any important cleanup.

The GeneratorExit exception represents a compromise between correctness and system health. If generators weren't forced to exit eventually, all prematurely stopped generators would leak memory and potentially cause the program to crash. Swallowing errors is the trade-off that Python makes because it's a reasonable thing to do most of the time. But it's up to you to make sure your generators expect this behavior and plan accordingly.

Things to Remember

✦ In normal functions, finally clauses are executed before values are returned, but in generator functions, finally clauses are only run after exhaustion, when the StopIteration exception is raised.

✦ In order to prevent memory leaks, the garbage collector injects GeneratorExit exceptions into unreferenced, partially iterated generators to cause them to exit and release resources.

✦ Due to this behavior, it's often better to pass resources (like files and mutexes) into generator functions instead of relying on them to allocate and clean up the resources properly.

Item 90: Never Set __debug__ to False

When you add an assert statement like this into a Python program:

```
n = 3
assert n % 2 == 0, f"{n=} not even"
```

it's essentially equivalent to the following code:

```
if __debug__:
    if not (n % 2 == 0):
        raise AssertionError(f"{n=} not even")
>>>
Traceback ...
AssertionError: n=3 not even
```

You can also use the __debug__ global built-in variable directly in order to gate the execution of more complex verification code:

```
def expensive_check(x):
    ...

items = [1, 2, 3]
if __debug__:
    for i in items:
        assert expensive_check(i), f"Failed {i=}"
>>>
Traceback ...
AssertionError: Failed i=2
```

The only way to set the __debug__ built-in global variable to False is by specifying the -O command-line argument at Python startup time. For example, here is a Python invocation that will start with __debug__ equal to True (the default):

```
$ python3 -c 'assert False, "FAIL"; print("OK")'
Traceback ...
AssertionError: FAIL
```

Adding the -O command-line option causes the assert statement to be skipped entirely, resulting in different output:

```
$ python3 -O -c 'assert False, "FAIL"; print("OK")'
OK
```

Although Python is an extremely dynamic language (see Item 3: "Never Expect Python to Detect Errors at Compile Time"), it won't allow you to modify the value of __debug__ at runtime:

```
__debug__ = False
>>>
Traceback ...
SyntaxError: cannot assign to __debug__
```

If the __debug__ constant is True, it will always stay that way during the life of a program.

The original intention of the __debug__ flag was to allow users to optimize the performance of their code by skipping seemingly unnecessary assertions at runtime. However, as time has gone on, more and more code, especially common frameworks and libraries, has become dependent on assertions being active in order to verify assumptions at program startup time and runtime. By disabling the assert statement and other debug code, you're undermining your program's validity for little practical gain.

If performance is what you're after, there are far better approaches to making programs faster (see Item 92: "Profile Before Optimizing" and Item 94: "Know When and How to Replace Python with Another Programming Language"). If you have very expensive verification code that you need to disable at runtime, then create your own enable_debug helper function and associated global variables to control these debugging operations in your own code instead of relying on __debug__.

There's still value in always keeping assertions active, especially in low-level code, even when you need to squeeze every ounce of performance out of your code, like when using MicroPython for microcontrollers (https://micropython.org). Somewhat counterintuitively, the presence of assert statements can help you debug even when these statements aren't failing. When you get a bug report, you can use successfully passing assertions to rule out possibilities and narrow the scope of what's gone wrong.

Ultimately, assertions are a powerful tool for ensuring correctness, and they should be used liberally throughout your code to help make assumptions explicit.

Things to Remember

✦ By default, the __debug__ global built-in variable is True, and Python programs will execute all assert statements.

✦ The -O command-line flag can be used to set __debug__ to False, which causes assert statements to be ignored.

✦ Having assert statements present can help narrow the cause of bugs even when the assertions themselves haven't failed.

Item 91: Avoid exec and eval Unless You're Building a Developer Tool

Python is a dynamic language that lets you do nearly anything at runtime (which can cause problems; see Item 3: "Never Expect Python to Detect Errors at Compile Time"). Many of its features enable these extremely flexible capabilities, such as setattr/getattr/hasattr (see Item 61: "Use __getattr__, __getattribute__, and __setattr__ for Lazy Attributes"), metaclasses (see Item 64: "Annotate Class Attributes with __set_name__") and descriptors (see Item 60: "Use Descriptors for Reusable @property Methods").

However, the most dynamic capability of all is executing arbitrary code from a string at runtime. This is possible in Python with the eval and exec built-in functions.

eval takes a single expression as a string and returns the result of its evaluation as a normal Python object:

```
x = eval("1 + 2")
print(x)
>>>
3
```

Passing a statement to eval will result in an error:

```
eval(
    """
if True:
    print('okay')
else:
    print('no')
"""
)
>>>
Traceback ...
SyntaxError: invalid syntax (<string>, line 2)
```

Instead, you can use exec to dynamically evaluate larger chunks of Python code. exec always returns None, and to get data out of it, you need to use the global and local scope dictionary arguments. Here, when I access the my_condition variable, it bubbles up to the global scope to be resolved, and my assignment of the x variable is made in the local scope (see Item 33: "Know How Closures Interact with Variable Scope and nonlocal" for background):

```
global_scope = {"my_condition": False}
local_scope = {}
```

```
exec(
    """
if my_condition:
    x = 'yes'
else:
    x = 'no'
""",
    global_scope,
    local_scope,
)

print(local_scope)
>>>
{'x': 'no'}
```

If you discover eval or exec in an otherwise normal application code-base, it's often a red flag indicating that something is seriously wrong. These features can cause severe security issues if they are inadvertently connected to an input channel that gives access to an attacker. Even for plug-in architectures, where these features might seem like a natural fit, Python has better ways to achieve similar outcomes (see Item 98: "Lazy-Load Modules with Dynamic Imports to Reduce Startup Time").

The only time it's actually appropriate to use eval and exec is in code that supports your application with an improved development experience, such as a debugger, notebook system, run-eval-print-loop (REPL), performance benchmarking tool, code generation utility, and so on. For any other purpose, avoid these insecure functions and use Python's other dynamic and metaprogramming features instead.

Things to Remember

✦ eval allows you to execute a string containing a Python expression and capture its return value.

✦ exec allows you to execute a block of Python code and affect variable scope and the surrounding environment.

✦ Due to potential security risks, these features should be used rarely or never, limited only to improving the development experience.

11

Performance

There are a wide range of metrics for judging the execution quality of a program, including CPU utilization, throughput, latency, response time, memory usage, and cache hit rate. These metrics can also be assessed in different ways with respect to their statistical distribution. For example, with latency, depending on your goals, you might need to consider average latency, median latency, 99th percentile latency, or worst-case latency. There are also application-specific metrics that build on these lower-level ones, such as transactions per second, time to first paint, maximum frame rate, and goodput.

Achieving good *performance* means that code you've written meets your expectations for one or more of the quantitative measurements that you care about most. Which metrics matter depends on the problem domain, production environment, and user profile; there's not a one-size-fits-all goal. *Performance engineering* is the discipline of analyzing program execution behavior, identifying areas for improvement, and implementing changes—large and small—to maximize or minimize the metrics that are most important.

Python is not considered to be a high-performance language, especially in comparison to lower-level languages built for the task. This reputation is understandable given the overhead and constraints of the Python runtime, especially when it comes to parallelism (see Item 68: "Use Threads for Blocking I/O; Avoid for Parallelism" for background). That said, Python includes a variety of capabilities that enable programs to achieve surprisingly impressive performance with relatively low amounts of effort. Using these features, it's possible to extract maximum performance from a host system while retaining the productivity gains afforded by Python's high-level nature.

Item 92: Profile Before Optimizing

The dynamic nature of Python causes surprising behaviors in its runtime performance. Operations you might assume would be slow are actually very fast (e.g., string manipulation, use of generators). Language features you might assume would be fast are actually very slow (e.g., attribute accesses, function calls). The true source of slowdowns in a Python program can be obscure.

The best approach is to ignore your intuition and directly measure the performance of a program before you try to optimize it. Python provides a built-in *profiler* for determining which parts of a program are responsible for its execution time. Profiling enables you to focus your optimization efforts on the biggest sources of trouble and ignore parts of the program that don't impact speed (i.e., follow Amdahl's law from academic literature).

For example, say that I want to determine why an algorithm in a program is slow. Here I define a function that sorts a list of data using an insertion sort:

```
def insertion_sort(data):
    result = []
    for value in data:
        insert_value(result, value)
    return result
```

The core mechanism of the insertion sort is the function that finds the insertion point for each piece of data. Here I define an extremely inefficient version of the insert_value function that does a linear scan over the input array:

```
def insert_value(array, value):
    for i, existing in enumerate(array):
        if existing > value:
            array.insert(i, value)
            return
    array.append(value)
```

To profile insertion_sort and insert_value, I create a data set of random numbers and define a test function to pass to the profiler (see Item 39: "Prefer functools.partial over lambda Expressions for Glue Functions" for background on lambda):

```
from random import randint

max_size = 12**4
data = [randint(0, max_size) for _ in range(max_size)]
test = lambda: insertion_sort(data)
```

Python provides two built-in profilers: one that is pure Python (profile) and another that is a C-extension module (cProfile). The cProfile built-in module is better because of its minimal impact on the performance of your program while it's being profiled. The pure-Python alternative imposes a high overhead that skews the results.

Note
When profiling a Python program, be sure that what you're measuring is the code itself and not any external systems. Beware of functions that access the network or resources on disk. These may appear to have a large impact on your program's execution time because of the slowness of the underlying systems. If your program uses a cache to mask the latency of slow resources like these, you should also ensure that it's properly warmed up before you start profiling.

Here I instantiate a Profile object from the cProfile module and run the test function through it by using the runcall method:

```
from cProfile import Profile

profiler = Profile()
profiler.runcall(test)
```

When the test function has finished running, I can extract statistics about its performance by using the pstats built-in module and its Stats class. Various methods on a Stats object adjust how to select and sort the profiling information to show only the things I care about:

```
from pstats import Stats

stats = Stats(profiler)
stats.strip_dirs()
stats.sort_stats("cumulative")
stats.print_stats()
```

The output is a table of information organized by function. The data sample is taken only from the time the profiler was active, during the runcall method above:

```
>>>
        41475 function calls in 2.198 seconds

  Ordered by: cumulative time

  ncalls tottime percall cumtime percall filename:lineno(function)
       1   0.000   0.000   2.198   2.198 main.py:35(<lambda>)
       1   0.003   0.003   2.198   2.198 main.py:10(insertion_sort)
```

```
20736    2.137    0.000    2.195    0.000 main.py:20(insert_value)
20729    0.058    0.000    0.058    0.000 {method 'insert' of 'list' objects}
    7    0.000    0.000    0.000    0.000 {method 'append' of 'list' objects}
```

Here's a quick guide to what the profiler statistics columns mean:

- **ncalls:** The number of calls to the function during the profiling period.

- **tottime:** The number of seconds spent executing the function, excluding time spent executing other functions it calls.

- **tottime percall:** The average number of seconds spent in the function each time it was called, excluding time spent executing other functions it calls. This is tottime divided by ncalls.

- **cumtime:** The cumulative number of seconds spent executing the function, including time spent in all other functions it calls.

- **cumtime percall:** The average number of seconds spent in the function each time it was called, including time spent in all other functions it calls. This is cumtime divided by ncalls.

Looking at the profiler statistics table above, I can see that the biggest use of CPU in my test is the cumulative time spent in the insert_value function. Here I redefine that function to use the more efficient bisect built-in module (see Item 102: "Consider Searching Sorted Sequences with bisect"):

```
from bisect import bisect_left

def insert_value(array, value):
    i = bisect_left(array, value)
    array.insert(i, value)
```

I can run the profiler again and generate a new table of profiler statistics. The new function is much faster, with a cumulative time spent that is nearly 40 times smaller than with the previous insert_value function:

```
>>>
        62211 function calls in 0.067 seconds

   Ordered by: cumulative time

   ncalls tottime percall cumtime percall filename:lineno(function)
        1   0.000   0.000   0.067   0.067 main.py:35(<lambda>)
        1   0.002   0.002   0.067   0.067 main.py:10(insertion_sort)
    20736   0.004   0.000   0.064   0.000 main.py:109(insert_value)
    20736   0.056   0.000   0.056   0.000 {method 'insert' of 'list' objects}
    20736   0.004   0.000   0.004   0.000 {built-in method _bisect.bisect_left}
```

Sometimes when you're profiling an entire program, you might find that a common utility function is responsible for the majority of execution time. The default output from the profiler makes such a situation difficult to understand because it doesn't show that the utility function is called by many different parts of your program.

For example, here the `my_utility` function is called repeatedly by two different functions in the program:

```python
def my_utility(a, b):
    c = 1
    for i in range(100):
        c += a * b

def first_func():
    for _ in range(1000):
        my_utility(4, 5)

def second_func():
    for _ in range(10):
        my_utility(1, 3)

def my_program():
    for _ in range(20):
        first_func()
        second_func()
```

Profiling this code and using the default `print_stats` output produces statistics that are confusing:

```
>>>
         20242 function calls in 0.040 seconds

   Ordered by: cumulative time

   ncalls  tottime  percall  cumtime  percall filename:lineno(function)
        1    0.000    0.000    0.040    0.040 main.py:172(my_program)
       20    0.002    0.000    0.040    0.002 main.py:164(first_func)
    20200    0.038    0.000    0.038    0.000 main.py:159(my_utility)
       20    0.000    0.000    0.000    0.000 main.py:168(second_func)
```

The `my_utility` function is clearly the source of most execution time, but it's not immediately obvious why that function is called so much. If you search through the program's code, you'll find multiple call sites for `my_utility` and will still be confused.

To deal with this, the Python profiler provides the `print_callers` method to show which callers contributed to the profiling information of each function:

```
stats.print_callers()
```

This profiler statistics table shows functions called on the left and which function was responsible for making the call on the right. Here it's clear that `my_utility` is most used by `first_func`:

```
>>>
    Ordered by: cumulative time

Function                    was called by...
                                ncalls  tottime  cumtime
main.py:172(my_program)     <-
main.py:164(first_func)     <-       20    0.002    0.040  main.py:172(my_program)
main.py:159(my_utility)     <-    20000    0.038    0.038  main.py:164(first_func)
                                    200    0.000    0.000  main.py:168(second_func)
main.py:168(second_func)    <-       20    0.000    0.000
```

Alternatively, you can call the `print_callees` method, which shows a top-down segmentation of how each function (on the left) spends time executing other dependent functions (on the right) deeper in the call stack:

```
stats.print_callees()
```

```
>>>
callees
    Ordered by: cumulative time

Function                    called...
                                ncalls  tottime  cumtime
main.py:172(my_program)     ->       20    0.002    0.041  Profiling.md:164(first_func)
                                     20    0.000    0.000  Profiling.md:168(second_func)
main.py:164(first_func)     ->    20000    0.038    0.038  Profiling.md:159(my_utility)
main.py:159(my_utility)     ->
main.py:168(second_func)    ->      200    0.000    0.000  Profiling.md:159(my_utility)
```

If you're not able to figure out why your program is slow using `cProfile`, fear not. Python includes other tools for assessing performance (see Item 93: "Optimize Performance-Critical Code Using `timeit` Micro-benchmarks," Item 98: "Lazy-Load Modules with Dynamic Imports to Reduce Startup Time," and Item 115: "Use `tracemalloc` to Understand Memory Usage and Leaks"). There are also community-built tools (see Item 116: "Know Where to Find Community-Built Modules") that have

additional capabilities for assessing performance, such as line profilers, sampling profilers, integration with Linux's `perf` tool, memory
usage profilers, and more.

Things to Remember

+ It's important to profile Python programs before optimizing because
the sources of slowdowns are often obscure.

+ Use the `cProfile` module instead of the `profile` module because it
provides more accurate profiling information.

+ The `Profile` object's `runcall` method provides everything you need
to profile a tree of function calls in isolation.

+ The `Stats` object lets you select and print the subset of profiling information you need to see to understand your program's performance.

Item 93: Optimize Performance-Critical Code Using `timeit` Microbenchmarks

When attempting to maximize the performance of a Python program, it's extremely important to use a profiler because the source
of slowness might not be obvious (see Item 92: "Profile Before Optimizing"). Once the real problem areas are identified, refactoring to
a better architecture or using more appropriate data structures can
often have a dramatic effect (see Item 104: "Know How to Use `heapq`
for Priority Queues"). However, some hotspots in the code might seem
inextinguishable even after many rounds of profiling and optimizing. Before attempting more complex solutions (see Item 94: "Know
When and How to Replace Python with Another Programming Language"), it's worth considering using the `timeit` built-in module to run
microbenchmarks.

The purpose of `timeit` is to precisely measure the performance of small
snippets of code. It lets you quantify and compare multiple solutions
to the same pinpointed problem. While profiling and whole-program
benchmarks do help with discovering room for optimization in larger
components, the number of potential improvements at such wide scope
might be limitless and costly to explore. Microbenchmarks, in contrast,
can be used to measure multiple implementations of the same nar-
rowly defined behavior, enabling you to take a scientific approach in
searching for the solution that performs best.

Using the `timeit` module is simple. Here I measure how long it takes to add two integers together:

```
import timeit

delay = timeit.timeit(stmt="1+2")
print(delay)

>>>
0.003767708025407046
```

The returned value is the number of seconds required to run 1 million iterations of the code snippet provided in the `stmt` argument. This default amount of repetition might be too much for slower microbenchmarks, so `timeit` lets you specify a more appropriate count by using the `number` argument:

```
delay = timeit.timeit(stmt="1+2", number=100)
print(delay)

>>>
7.500057108700275e-07
```

However, the 100 iterations specified above are so few that the measured microbenchmark time might start to disappear in the noise of the computer. There will always be some natural variation in performance due to other processes interfering with memory and cache status, the operating system running periodic background tasks, hardware interrupts being received, and so on. For a microbenchmark to be accurate, it needs to use a large number of iterations to compensate for this noise. The `timeit` module also disables garbage collection while it executes snippets to try to reduce variance.

I suggest providing the iteration count argument explicitly. I usually assign it to a variable that I use again later to calculate the average per-iteration time. This normalized value can then serve as a robust metric that can be compared to other implementations if desired or tracked over time (e.g., to detect regressions):

```
count = 1_000_000

delay = timeit.timeit(stmt="1+2", number=count)

print(f"{delay/count*1e9:.2f} nanoseconds")

>>>
4.36 nanoseconds
```

Running a single snippet of code over and over again isn't always sufficient to produce a useful microbenchmark. You often need to create some kind of scaffolding, harness, or data structure that can be used during iteration. `timeit`'s `setup` argument addresses this need by accepting a code snippet that runs a single time before all iterations and is excluded from the time measurement.

For example, imagine that I'm trying to determine if a number is present in a large randomized list of values. I don't want the microbenchmark to include the time spent creating a large list and randomizing it. Here I put these upfront tasks in the `setup` snippet; I also provide the `globals` argument so `stmt` and `setup` can refer to names defined elsewhere in the code, such as the imported `random` module (see Item 91: "Avoid `exec` and `eval` Unless You're Building a Developer Tool" for background):

```
import random

count = 100_000

delay = timeit.timeit(
    setup="""
numbers = list(range(10_000))
random.shuffle(numbers)
probe = 7_777
""",
    stmt="""
probe in numbers
""",
    globals=globals(),
    number=count,
)

print(f"{delay/count*1e9:.2f} nanoseconds")

>>>
13078.05 nanoseconds
```

With this baseline (13 milliseconds) established, I can try to produce the same behavior using a different approach to see how it affects the microbenchmark. Here I swap out the list created in the `setup` code snippet for a set data structure:

```
delay = timeit.timeit(
    setup="""
numbers = set(range(10_000))
probe = 7_777
```

```
""",
    stmt="""
probe in numbers
""",
    globals=globals(),
    number=count,
)

print(f"{delay/count*1e9:.2f} nanoseconds")

>>>
14.87 nanoseconds
```

This shows that checking for membership in a set is about 1,000 times faster than checking in a list. The reason is that the set data structure provides constant time access to its elements, similar to a dict, whereas a list requires time proportional to the number of elements it contains. Using timeit like this is a great way to find an ideal data structure or algorithm for your needs.

One problem that can arise in microbenchmarking like this is the need to measure the performance of tight loops, such as in mathematical kernel functions. For example, here I test the speed of summing a list of numbers:

```
def loop_sum(items):
    total = 0
    for i in items:
        total += i
    return total

count = 1000

delay = timeit.timeit(
    setup="numbers = list(range(10_000))",
    stmt="loop_sum(numbers)",
    globals=globals(),
    number=count,
)

print(f"{delay/count*1e9:.2f} nanoseconds")

>>>
142365.46 nanoseconds
```

This measurement is how long it takes for each call to loop_sum, which is meaningless on its own. What you need to make this microbenchmark robust is to normalize it by the number of itera-tions in the inner loop, which was hard-coded to 10_000 in the exam-ple above:

```
print(f"{delay/count/10_000*1e9:.2f} nanoseconds")
```

```
>>>
14.43 nanoseconds
```

Now I can see that this function will scale in proportion to the num-ber of items in the list by 14.43 nanoseconds per additional item.

The `timeit` module can also be executed as a command-line tool, which can help you rapidly investigate any curiosities you have about Python performance. For example, imagine that I want to determine the fastest way to look up a key that's already present in a dictionary (see Item 26: "Prefer `get` over `in` and `KeyError` to Handle Missing Dic-tionary Keys"). Here I use the `timeit` command-line interface to test using the `in` operator for this purpose:

```
$ python3 -m timeit \
--setup='my_dict = {"key": 123}' \
'if "key" in my_dict: my_dict["key"]'
20000000 loops, best of 5: 19.3 nsec per loop
```

The tool automatically determines how many iterations to run based on how much time a single iteration takes. It also runs five separate tests to compensate for system noise and presents the minimum as the best-case, lower-bound performance.

I can run the tool again using a different snippet that will show how the `dict.get` method compares to the `in` operator:

```
$ python3 -m timeit \
--setup='my_dict = {"key": 123}' \
'if (value := my_dict.get("key")) is not None: value'
20000000 loops, best of 5: 17.1 nsec per loop
```

Now I know that `get` is faster than `in`. What about the approach of catching a known exception type, which is a common style in Python programs (see Item 32: "Prefer Raising Exceptions to Returning None")?

```
$ python3 -m timeit \
--setup='my_dict = {"key": 123}' \
'try: my_dict["key"]
except KeyError: pass'
20000000 loops, best of 5: 10.6 nsec per loop
```

It turns out that the KeyError approach is actually fastest for keys that are expected to already exist in the dictionary. This might seem surprising, given all the extra machinery required to raise and catch exceptions in the missing key case. This non-obvious performance behavior illustrates why it's so important to test your assumptions and use profiling and microbenchmarks to measure before optimizing Python code.

Things to Remember

✦ The timeit built-in module can be used to run microbenchmarks that help you scientifically determine the best data structures and algorithms for performance-critical parts of programs.

✦ To make microbenchmarks robust, use the setup code snippet to exclude initialization time and be sure to normalize the returned measurements into comparable metrics.

✦ The python -m timeit command-line interface lets you quickly understand the performance of Python code snippets with little effort.

Item 94: Know When and How to Replace Python with Another Programming Language

At some point while using Python, you might feel that you're pushing the envelope of what it can do. This is understandable because in order to provide Python's enhanced developer productivity and ease of use, the language's execution model must be limiting in other ways. The CPython implementation's bytecode virtual machine and global interpreter lock (GIL), for example, negatively impact straight-line CPU performance, CPU parallelism, program startup time, and overall efficiency (see Item 68: "Use Threads for Blocking I/O; Avoid for Parallelism").

One potential solution is to rewrite all your code in another programming language and move away from Python. This might be the right choice in many circumstances, including:

- Your priority is critical path latency or 99th percentile latency, and you can't tolerate garbage collection pauses or non-deterministic data structure behaviors (such as dictionary resizes).

- You care a lot about program startup delay, and techniques like precompilation, zip imports, and late module loading fall short (see Item 97: "Rely on Precompiled Bytecode and File System Caching to Improve Startup Time" and Item 98: "Lazy-Load Modules with Dynamic Imports to Reduce Startup Time").

- You need to take advantage of libraries with APIs that are tightly coupled to an implementation language, such as platform-specific GUI frameworks, and it's impractical to bridge through C extensions (see details below).

- You need to target uncommon architectures like supercomputers or embedded systems, and the Python packages that support these environments (such as https://mpi4py.github.io and https://micropython.org) are insufficient.

- You need to distribute your program as an installable executable, and bundling tools (see Item 125: "Prefer Open Source Projects for Bundling Python Programs over zipimport and zipapp") don't meet your requirements.

- You've tried all the optimization techniques listed below, as well as alternative implementations of the Python language that can achieve better performance (such as PyPy: https://www.pypy.org), and you're still hitting a performance ceiling.

- You've tried to distribute computation across many Python processes on the same machine (see Item 79: "Consider concurrent.futures for True Parallelism") or spanning multiple computers using tools like Dask (https://www.dask.org) to no avail.

However, before you commit to a full rewrite of the software you've built, it's important to consider doing pinpointed optimizations using a variety of techniques, which each have unique trade-offs. What's possible largely depends on how much Python code you have, how complex it is, the constraints you're under, and the requirements you need to satisfy.

Many performance issues encountered in Python programs are from non-obvious causes. It's important to profile and benchmark your code (see Item 92: "Profile Before Optimizing" and Item 93: "Optimize Performance-Critical Code Using timeit Microbenchmarks") to find the true source of slowness or excess memory consumption (see Item 115: "Use tracemalloc to Understand Memory Usage and Leaks"). You should also seriously investigate replacing your program's core algorithms and data structures with better alternatives (see Item 104: "Know How to Use heapq for Priority Queues" and Item 102: "Consider Searching Sorted Sequences with bisect"), which can improve program performance by many orders of magnitude with surprisingly little effort.

Once you've fully exhausted these paths, migrating to another programming language or execution model can be achieved in many ways. For example, a common source of performance problems in Python is tight loops, which you often see in mathematical *kernel functions*. The following Python code, which computes the dot product of two vectors, will run orders of magnitude slower than would similar behavior implemented in C:

```
def dot_product(a, b):
    result = 0
    for i, j in zip(a, b):
        result += i * j
    return result
```

```
print(dot_product([1, 2], [3, 4]))
```

```
>>>
11
```

Luckily, a kernel function like this also defines a clear interface that can serve as a seam between the slow and fast parts of a program. If you can find a way to accelerate the interior implementation of the dot_product function, then all of its callers can benefit, without requiring you to make any other changes to the codebase. The same approach also works for much larger subcomponents if your program's structure is amenable. The standard version of Python (see Item 1: "Know Which Version of Python You're Using") provides two tools to help improve performance in this way:

- The ctypes built-in module makes it easy to describe the interfaces of native libraries on your system and call the functions they export (see Item 95: "Consider ctypes to Rapidly Integrate with Native Libraries" for details). These libraries can be implemented in any language that's compatible with the C calling convention (e.g., C, C++, Rust) and can leverage native threads, SIMD intrinsics, GPUs, and so on. No additional build system, compiler, or packaging is required.

- The Python C extension API allows you to create fully Pythonic APIs—taking advantage of all of Python's dynamic features—that are actually implemented in C to achieve better performance (see Item 96: "Consider Extension Modules to Maximize Performance and Ergonomics" for details). This approach often requires more work upfront, but it provides vastly improved ergonomics. However, you'll have to deal with additional build complexities, which can be difficult.

The larger Python ecosystem has also responded to the need for performance optimization by creating excellent libraries and tools. Here are a few highlights you should know about, though there are many others (see Item 116: "Know Where to Find Community-Built Modules"):

- The NumPy module (https://numpy.org) enables you to operate on arrays of values with ergonomic Python function calls that, under the covers, use the BLAS (Basic Linear Algebra Subprograms) to achieve high performance and CPU parallelism. You'll need to rewrite some of your data structures in order to use it, but the speedups can be enormous.

- The Numba module (https://numba.pydata.org) takes your existing Python functions and JIT (just-in-time) compiles them at runtime into highly optimized machine instructions. Some of your code might need to be slightly modified to use less dynamism and simpler data types. Like `ctypes`, Numba avoids additional build complexity, which is a huge benefit.

- The Cython tool (https://cython.org) provides a superset of the Python language with extra features that make it easy to create C extension modules without actually writing C code. It shares the build complexity of standard C extensions but can be much easier to use than the Python C API.

- Mypyc (https://github.com/mypyc/mypyc) is similar to Cython, but it uses standard annotations from the `typing` module (see Item 124: "Consider Static Analysis via `typing` to Obviate Bugs") instead of requiring nonstandard syntax. This can make it easier to adopt without code changes. It can also AOT (ahead-of-time) compile whole programs for faster startup time. Mypyc has similar build complexity to C extensions and doesn't include Cython's C integration features.

- The CFFI module (https://cffi.readthedocs.io) is similar to the `ctypes` built-in module except that it can read C header files directly in order to understand the interfaces of functions you want to call. This automatic mapping significantly reduces the developer toil of calling into native libraries that contain a lot of functions and data structures.

- SWIG (https://www.swig.org) is a tool that can automatically generate Python interfaces for C and C++ native libraries. It's similar to CFFI in this way, but the translation happens explicitly instead of at runtime, which can be more efficient. SWIG supports other target languages besides Python and a variety of customization options. It also requires build complexity like C extensions.

One important caveat to note is that these tools and libraries might require a non-trivial amount of developer time to learn and use effectively. It might be easier to rewrite components of a program from scratch in another language, especially given how great Python is at gluing together systems. You can use what you learned from building a Python implementation to inform the design of the rewrite.

That said, rewriting any of your Python code in C (or another language) also has a high cost. Code that is short and understandable in Python can become verbose and complicated in other languages. Porting also requires extensive testing to ensure that the functionality remains equivalent to the original Python code and that no bugs have been introduced.

Sometimes rewrites are worth it, which explains the large ecosystem of C extension modules in the Python community that speed up things like text parsing, image compositing, and matrix math. For your own code, you'll need to consider the risks vs. the potential rewards and decide on the best trade-off that's appropriate for your situation.

Things to Remember

- ✦ There are many valid reasons to rewrite Python code in another language, but you should investigate all the optimization techniques available before pursuing that option.

- ✦ Moving CPU bottlenecks to C extension modules and native libraries can be an effective way to improve performance while maximizing your investment in Python code. However, doing so has a high cost and may introduce bugs.

- ✦ There are a large number of tools and libraries available in the Python ecosystem that can accelerate the slow parts of a Python program with surprisingly few changes.

Item 95: Consider `ctypes` to Rapidly Integrate with Native Libraries

The `ctypes` built-in module enables Python to call functions that are defined in native libraries. Those libraries can be implemented in any other programming language that can export functions following the C calling convention (e.g., C, C++, Rust). The module provides two key benefits to Python developers:

- ▪ `ctypes` makes it easy to connect systems together using Python. If there's an existing native library with functionality you need, you will be able to use it without much effort.

- ctypes provides a straightforward path to optimizing slow parts of your program. If you find a hotspot you can't otherwise speed up, you can reimplement it in another language and then call the faster version by using ctypes.

For example, consider the dot_product function from the previous item (see Item 94: "Know When and How to Replace Python with Another Programming Language"):

```python
def dot_product(a, b):
    result = 0
    for i, j in zip(a, b):
        result += i * j
    return result
```

I can implement similar functionality using a simple C function that operates on arrays. Here I define the interface:

```c
/* my_library.h */
extern double dot_product(int length, double* a, double* b);
```

The implementation is simple and will be automatically vectorized by most C compilers to maximize performance using advanced processor features like SIMD (single instruction, multiple data) operations:

```c
/* my_library.c */
#include <stdio.h>
#include "my_library.h"

double dot_product(int length, double* a, double* b) {
    double result = 0;
    for (int i = 0; i < length; i++) {
        result += a[i] * b[i];
    }
    return result;
}
```

Now I need to compile this code into a library file. Doing so is beyond the scope of this book, but the command on my machine is:

```
$ cc -shared -o my_library.lib my_library.c
```

I can load this library file in Python simply by providing its path to the ctypes.cdll.LoadLibrary constructor:

```python
import ctypes

library_path = ...
my_library = ctypes.cdll.LoadLibrary(library_path)
```

The dot_product function that was implemented in C is now available as an attribute of my_library:

```
print(my_library.dot_product)
```

```
>>>
<_FuncPtr object at 0x10544cc50>
```

If you wrap the imported function pointer with a ctypes.CFUNCTYPE object, you might observe broken behavior due to implicit type conversions. Instead, it's best to directly assign the restype and argtypes attributes of an imported function to the ctypes types that match the signature of the function's native implementation:

```
my_library.dot_product.restype = ctypes.c_double

vector_ptr = ctypes.POINTER(ctypes.c_double)
my_library.dot_product.argtypes = (
    ctypes.c_int,
    vector_ptr,
    vector_ptr,
)
```

Calling the imported function is relatively easy. First, I define an array data type that contains three double values. Then I allocate two instances of that type to pass as arguments:

```
size = 3
vector3 = ctypes.c_double * size
a = vector3(1.0, 2.5, 3.5)
b = vector3(-7, 4, -12.1)
```

Finally, I call the dot_product imported function with these two arrays. I need to use the ctypes.cast helper function to ensure that the address of the first item in the array is supplied—matching C convention—instead of the address of the vector3 Python object. I don't need to do any casting of the return value because ctypes automatically converts it to a Python value:

```
result = my_library.dot_product(
    3,
    ctypes.cast(a, vector_ptr),
    ctypes.cast(b, vector_ptr),
)
print(result)
```

```
>>>
-39.35
```

It should be obvious by now that the ergonomics of the ctypes API are quite poor and not Pythonic. But it's impressive how quickly everything comes together and starts working. To make it feel more natural, here I wrap the imported native function with a Python function to do the data type mapping and verify assumptions (see Item 81: "assert Internal Assumptions and raise Missed Expectations" for background):

```python
def dot_product(a, b):
    size = len(a)
    assert len(b) == size
    a_vector = vector3(*a)
    b_vector = vector3(*b)
    result = my_library.dot_product(size, a_vector, b_vector)
    return result
```

```python
result = dot_product([1.0, 2.5, 3.5], [-7, 4, -12.1])
print(result)
```

```
>>>
-39.35
```

Alternatively, I can use Python's C extension API (see Item 96: "Consider Extension Modules to Maximize Performance and Ergonomics") to provide a more Pythonic interface with native performance. However, ctypes has some worthwhile advantages over C extensions:

- Pointer values that you hold with ctypes will be freed automatically when the Python object reference count goes to zero. C extensions must do manual memory management for C pointers and manual reference counting for Python objects.

- When you call a function with ctypes, it automatically releases the GIL while the call is executing, allowing other Python threads to progress in parallel (see Item 68: "Use Threads for Blocking I/O; Avoid for Parallelism"). With a C extension module, the GIL must be managed explicitly, and functionality is limited while not holding the lock.

- With ctypes, you simply provide a path to a shared object or dynamic library on disk, and it can be loaded. Compilation can be done separately with a build system that you already have in place. With Python C extensions, you need to leverage the Python build system to include the right paths, set linker flags, and so on; it's a lot of complexity and potentially duplicative.

But there are also important downsides to using the `ctypes` module instead of building a C extension:

- `ctypes` restricts you to the data types that C can describe. You lose most of the expressive power of Python, including extremely common functionality like iterators (see Item 21: "Be Defensive when Iterating over Arguments") and duck typing (see Item 25: "Be Cautious when Relying on Dictionary Insertion Ordering"). Even with wrappers, native functions imported using `ctypes` can feel strange to Python programmers and hamper productivity.

- Calling `ctypes` with the right data types often requires you to make copies or transformations of function inputs and outputs. The cost of this overhead might undermine the performance benefit of using a native library, rendering the whole optimization exercise worthless. C extensions allow you to bypass copies; the only speed limit is the inherent performance of the underlying data types.

- If you use `ctypes` slightly the wrong way, you might cause your program to corrupt its own memory and behave strangely. For example, if you accidentally provide `ctypes.c_double` where you should have specified `ctypes.c_int` for function arguments or return values, you might see unpredictable crashes with cryptic error messages. The `faulthandler` built-in module can help track down these problems, but they're still difficult to debug.

The best practice when using `ctypes` is to always write corresponding unit tests before putting it to work in more complex code (see Item 109: "Prefer Integration Tests over Unit Tests"). The goal of these tests is to exercise the basic surface area of a library that you're calling in order to confirm that it works as expected for simple usage. This can help you detect situations such as when a function in a shared library has its argument types modified but your `ctypes` usage hasn't been updated to match. Here I test the `my_library.dot_product` symbol from the imported library:

```
from unittest import TestCase

class MyLibraryTest(TestCase):

    def test_dot_product(self):
        vector3 = ctypes.c_double * size
        a = vector3(1.0, 2.5, 3.5)
        b = vector3(-7, 4, -12.1)
        vector_ptr = ctypes.POINTER(ctypes.c_double)
        result = my_library.dot_product(
```

```
            3,
            ctypes.cast(a, vector_ptr),
            ctypes.cast(b, vector_ptr),
        )
        self.assertAlmostEqual(-39.35, result)

...

>>>
.
----------------------------------------------------------------
--------
Ran 1 test in 0.000s

OK
```

The `ctypes` module includes additional functionality for mapping Python objects to C structs, copying memory, error checking, and a whole lot more (see the full manual at https://docs.python.org/3/library/ctypes.html for details). Ultimately, you'll need to decide if the ease and speed of development you get from using `ctypes` is worth its inferior ergonomics and overhead.

Things to Remember

✦ The `ctypes` built-in module makes it easy to integrate the functionality and performance of native libraries written in other languages into Python programs.

✦ In comparison to the Python C extension API, `ctypes` enables rapid development without additional build complexity.

✦ It's difficult to write Pythonic APIs using `ctypes` because the data types and protocols available are limited to what can be expressed in C.

Item 96: Consider Extension Modules to Maximize Performance and Ergonomics

The CPython implementation of the Python language (see Item 1: "Know Which Version of Python You're Using") supports *extension modules* that are written in C. These modules can directly use the Python API to take advantage of object-oriented features (see Chapter 7), duck typing protocols (see Item 25: "Be Cautious when Relying on Dictionary Insertion Ordering"), reference counting garbage collection, and nearly every other feature that makes Python great. The previous item (see

Item 95: "Consider ctypes to Rapidly Integrate with Native Libraries")
presented the upsides and downsides of the ctypes built-in module. If
you're looking to provide a Pythonic development experience without
compromising on performance or platform-specific capabilities, extension modules are the way to go.

Although creating an extension module is much more complicated
than using ctypes, the Python C API helps make it pretty straightforward. To demonstrate, I'll implement the same dot_product function
from before (see Item 94: "Know When and How to Replace Python
with Another Programming Language") but as an extension module.
First, I'll declare the C function that I want the extension to provide:

```
/* my_extension.h */
#define PY_SSIZE_T_CLEAN
#include <Python.h>


PyObject *dot_product(PyObject *self, PyObject *args);
```

Then I'll implement the function using C. The Python API I use to interface with inputs and outputs (e.g., PyList_Size, PyFloat_FromDouble)
is extensive, constantly evolving, and—luckily—well documented (see
https://docs.python.org/3/extending). This version of the function
expects to receive two equally sized lists of floating point numbers
and return a single floating point number:

```
/* dot_product.c */
#include "my_extension.h"

PyObject *dot_product(PyObject *self, PyObject *args)
{
    PyObject *left, *right;
    if (!PyArg_ParseTuple(args, "OO", &left, &right)) {
        return NULL;
    }
    if (!PyList_Check(left) || !PyList_Check(right)) {
        PyErr_SetString(PyExc_TypeError,
        "Both arguments must be lists");
        return NULL;
    }

    Py_ssize_t left_length = PyList_Size(left);
    Py_ssize_t right_length = PyList_Size(right);
    if (left_length == -1 || right_length == -1) {
        return NULL;
    }
```

```
    if (left_length != right_length) {
        PyErr_SetString(PyExc_ValueError,
        "Lists must be the same length");
        return NULL;
    }

    double result = 0;

    for (Py_ssize_t i = 0; i < left_length; i++) {
        PyObject *left_item = PyList_GET_ITEM(left, i);
        PyObject *right_item = PyList_GET_ITEM(right, i);

        double left_double = PyFloat_AsDouble(left_item);
        double right_double = PyFloat_AsDouble(right_item);
        if (PyErr_Occurred()) {
            return NULL;
        }

        result += left_double * right_double;
    }

    return PyFloat_FromDouble(result);
}
```

The function is about 40 lines of code, which is four times longer than a simple C implementation that can be called using the ctypes module. There's also some additional boilerplate code required to configure the extension module and initialize it:

```
/* init.c */
#include "my_extension.h"

static PyMethodDef my_extension_methods[] = {
    {
        "dot_product",
        dot_product,
        METH_VARARGS,
        "Compute dot product",
    },
    {
        NULL,
        NULL,
        0,
        NULL,
    },
};
```

```
static struct PyModuleDef my_extension = {
    PyModuleDef_HEAD_INIT,
    "my_extension",
    "My C-extension module",
    -1,
    my_extension_methods,
};

PyMODINIT_FUNC
PyInit_my_extension(void)
{
    return PyModule_Create(&my_extension);
}
```

Now I need to compile the C code into a native library that can be dynamically loaded by the CPython interpreter. The simplest way to do this is to define a minimal setup.py configuration file:

```
# setup.py
from setuptools import Extension, setup

setup(
    name="my_extension",
    ext_modules=[
        Extension(
            name="my_extension",
            sources=["init.c", "dot_product.c"],
        ),
    ],
)
```

I can use this configuration file, a virtual environment (see Item 117: "Use Virtual Environments for Isolated and Reproducible Dependencies"), and the setuptools package (see Item 116: "Know Where to Find Community-Built Modules") to properly drive my system's compiler with the right paths and flags; at the end, I'll get a native library file that can be imported by Python:

```
$ python3 -m venv .
$ source bin/activate
$ pip install setuptools
...
$ python3 setup.py develop
...
```

There are many ways to build Python extension modules and package them up for distribution. Unfortunately, the tools for this are constantly changing. In this example, I'm only focused on getting an extension module working in my local development environment. If you encounter problems or have other use cases, be sure to check the latest documentation from the official Python Packaging Authority (https://www.pypa.io).

After compilation, I can use tests written in Python (see Item 108: "Verify Related Behaviors in TestCase Subclasses") to verify that the extension module works as expected:

```python
# my_extension_test.py
import unittest
import my_extension

class MyExtensionTest(unittest.TestCase):

    def test_empty(self):
        result = my_extension.dot_product([], [])
        self.assertAlmostEqual(0, result)

    def test_positive_result(self):
        result = my_extension.dot_product(
            [3, 4, 5],
            [-1, 9, -2.5],
        )
        self.assertAlmostEqual(20.5, result)

    ...

if __name__ == "__main__":
    unittest.main()
```

This was a lot of effort compared to the basic C implementation. And the ergonomics of the interface are about the same as if I used the ctypes module: Both arguments to dot_product need to be lists that contain floats. If this is as far as you're going to go with the C extension API, then it's not worth it. You'd not be taking advantage of its most valuable features.

Now I'm going to create another version of this extension module that uses the iterator and number protocols that are provided by the Python API. This is 60 lines of code—50% more than the simpler dot_product function and six times more than the basic C version— but it enables the full set of features that make Python so powerful. By using the PyObject_GetIter and PyIter_Next APIs, the input types can be any kind of iterable container, such as tuples, lists, generators,

and so on (see Item 21: "Be Defensive when Iterating over Arguments").
By using the PyNumber_Multiply and PyNumber_Add APIs, the values
from the iterators can be any object that properly implements the
number special methods (see Item 57: "Inherit from collections.abc
Classes for Custom Container Types"):

```c
/* dot_product.c */
#include "my_extension2.h"

PyObject *dot_product(PyObject *self, PyObject *args)
{
    PyObject *left, *right;
    if (!PyArg_ParseTuple(args, "OO", &left, &right)) {
        return NULL;
    }
    PyObject *left_iter = PyObject_GetIter(left);
    if (left_iter == NULL) {
        return NULL;
    }
    PyObject *right_iter = PyObject_GetIter(right);
    if (right_iter == NULL) {
        Py_DECREF(left_iter);
        return NULL;
    }

    PyObject *left_item = NULL;
    PyObject *right_item = NULL;
    PyObject *multiplied = NULL;
    PyObject *result = PyLong_FromLong(0);

    while (1) {
        Py_CLEAR(left_item);
        Py_CLEAR(right_item);
        Py_CLEAR(multiplied);
        left_item = PyIter_Next(left_iter);
        right_item = PyIter_Next(right_iter);

        if (left_item == NULL && right_item == NULL) {
            break;
        } else if (left_item == NULL || right_item == NULL) {
            PyErr_SetString(PyExc_ValueError,
                "Arguments had unequal length");
            break;
        }
```

```
        multiplied = PyNumber_Multiply(left_item, right_item);
        if (multiplied == NULL) {
            break;
        }
        PyObject *added = PyNumber_Add(result, multiplied);
        if (added == NULL) {
            break;
        }
        Py_CLEAR(result);
        result = added;
    }

    Py_CLEAR(left_item);
    Py_CLEAR(right_item);
    Py_CLEAR(multiplied);
    Py_DECREF(left_iter);
    Py_DECREF(right_iter);

    if (PyErr_Occurred()) {
        Py_CLEAR(result);
        return NULL;
    }

    return result;
}
```

The implementation is further complicated by the need to properly manage object reference counts and the peculiarities of error propagation and reference borrowing. But the result is, perhaps, Python's holy grail: a module that is both fast and easy to use. Here I show that it works for multiple types of iterables and the Decimal numerical class (see Item 106: "Use decimal when Precision Is Paramount"):

```
# my_extension2_test.py
import unittest
import my_extension2

class MyExtension2Test(unittest.TestCase):

    def test_decimals(self):
        import decimal

        a = [decimal.Decimal(1), decimal.Decimal(2)]
        b = [decimal.Decimal(3), decimal.Decimal(4)]
```

```
        result = my_extension2.dot_product(a, b)
        self.assertEqual(11, result)

    def test_not_lists(self):
        result1 = my_extension2.dot_product(
            (1, 2),
            [3, 4],
        )
        result2 = my_extension2.dot_product(
            [1, 2],
            (3, 4),
        )
        result3 = my_extension2.dot_product(
            range(1, 3),
            range(3, 5),
        )
        self.assertAlmostEqual(11, result1)
        self.assertAlmostEqual(11, result2)
        self.assertAlmostEqual(11, result3)

    ...

if __name__ == "__main__":
    unittest.main()
```

This level of extensibility and flexibility in an API is what good ergonomics looks like. Achieving the same behaviors with basic C code
would require essentially reimplementing the core of the Python interpreter and API. Knowing that, the larger line count of these extension
modules seems reasonable, given how much functionality and performance you get in return.

Things to Remember

◆ Extension modules are written in C, executing at native speed, and
  can use the Python API to access nearly all of Python's powerful
  features.

◆ The peculiarities of the Python API, including memory management and error propagation, can be hard to learn and difficult to
  get right.

◆ The biggest value of a C extension comes from using the Python
  API's protocols and built-in data types, which are difficult to replicate in simple C code.

Item 97: Rely on Precompiled Bytecode and File System Caching to Improve Startup Time

Program startup time is an important performance metric to examine because it's directly observable by users. For command-line utilities, the startup time is how long it takes for a program to begin processing after you've pressed the Enter key. Users often execute the same command-line tools repeatedly in rapid succession, so the accumulation of startup delays can feel like a frustrating waste of time. For a web server, the startup time is how long it takes to begin processing the first incoming request after program launch. Web servers often use multiple threads or child processes to parallelize work, which can cause a *cold start* delay each time a new context is spun up. The end result is that some web requests can take a lot longer than others, annoying users with unpredictable delays.

Unfortunately, Python programs usually have a high startup time compared to programs written in languages that are compiled into machine code executables. There are two main contributors to this slowness in the CPython implementation of Python (see Item 1: "Know Which Version of Python You're Using"). First, on startup, CPython reads the source code for the program and compiles it into bytecode for its virtual machine interpreter, which requires both I/O and CPU processing (see Item 68: "Use Threads for Blocking I/O; Avoid for Parallelism" for details). Second, when the bytecode is ready, Python executes all of the modules imported by the main entry point. Loading modules requires running code to initialize global variables and constants, define classes, execute assertion statements, and so on—and it can be a lot of work.

To improve performance, modules are cached in memory after the first time they're loaded by a program, and they're reused for subsequent loads (see Item 122: "Know How to Break Circular Dependencies" for details). CPython also saves the bytecode it generates during compilation to a cache on disk so it can be reused for subsequent program starts. The cache is stored in a directory called __pycache__ next to the source code. Each bytecode file has a .pyc suffix and is usually smaller than the corresponding source file.

It's easy to see the effect of bytecode caching in action. For example, here I load all the modules from the Django web framework (https://www.djangoproject.com) and measure how long it takes (specifically, the "real" time). This is a source code–only snapshot of the open source project, and no bytecode cache files are present:

```
$ time python3 -c 'import django_all'
...
real    0m0.791s
user    0m0.495s
sys     0m0.145s
```

If I run the same program again with absolutely no modifications, it starts up in 70% less time than before—more than three times faster:

```
$ time python3 -c 'import django_all'
...
real    0m0.225s
user    0m0.182s
sys     0m0.038s
```

You might guess that this performance improvement is due to CPython using the bytecode cache the second time the program starts. However, if I remove the .pyc files, performance is surprisingly still better than the first time I executed Python and imported this module:

```
$ find django -name '*.pyc' -delete
$ time python3 -c 'import django_all'

real    0m0.613s
user    0m0.502s
sys     0m0.101s
```

This is a good example of how measuring performance is difficult and how the effects of optimizations can be confusing. What caused the subsequent Python invocation without .pyc files to be faster is the filesystem cache of my operating system. The Python source code files are already in memory because I recently accessed them. When I load them again, expensive I/O operations can be shortened, speeding up program start.

I can regenerate the bytecode files by using the compileall built-in module. This is usually done automatically when you install packages with pip (see Item 117: "Use Virtual Environments for Isolated and Reproducible Dependencies") to minimize startup time. But you can create new bytecode files manually for your own codebase when needed (e.g., before deploying to production):

```
$ python3 -m compileall django
Listing 'django'...
Compiling 'django/__init__.py'...
```

```
Compiling 'django/__main__.py'...
Listing 'django/apps'...
Compiling 'django/apps/__init__.py'...
Compiling 'django/apps/config.py'...
Compiling 'django/apps/registry.py'...
...
```

Most operating systems provide a way to purge the file system cache, which will cause subsequent I/O operations to go to the physical disk instead of memory. Here I force the cache to be empty (using the `purge` command) and then re-run the `django_all` import to see the performance impact of having bytecode files on disk and not in memory:

```
$ sudo purge
$ time python3 -c 'import django_all'
...
real    0m0.382s
user    0m0.169s
sys     0m0.085s
```

This startup time (382 milliseconds) is faster than having no bytecode and an empty filesystem cache (791 milliseconds) and faster that having no bytecode and the source code cached in memory (613 milliseconds), but it is slower than having both bytecode and source code in memory (225 milliseconds). Ultimately, you'll get the best startup performance by ensuring that your bytecode is precompiled and in the filesystem cache. For this reason, it can be valuable to put Python programs on a RAM disk so they are always in memory, regardless of access patterns. The effect of this will be even more pronounced when your computer has a spinning disk; I used an SSD (solid-state drive) in these tests. When caching in memory is not possible, other approaches to reduce startup time might be valuable (see Item 98: "Lazy-Load Modules with Dynamic Imports to Reduce Startup Time").

Finally, you might wonder if it's even faster to run a Python program without the source code files present at all, since it appears that the bytecode cache is all that CPython needs to execute a program. Indeed, this is possible. The trick is to use the -b flag when generating the bytecode, which causes the individual .pyc files to be placed next to source code instead of in __pycache__ directories. Here I modify the django package accordingly and then test the speed of importing the django_all module again:

```
$ find django -name '*.pyc' -delete
$ python3 -m compileall -b django
$ find django -name '*.py' -delete
```

```
$ time python3 -c 'import django_all'
...
real    0m0.226s
user    0m0.183s
sys     0m0.037s
```

The startup time in this case (226 milliseconds) is almost exactly the same as when the source code files were also present. Thus, there's no value in deleting the source code unless you have other constraints you need to satisfy, such as minimizing overall storage or system memory use (see Item 125: "Prefer Open Source Projects for Bundling Python Programs over zipimport and zipapp" for an example).

Things to Remember

✦ The CPython implementation of Python compiles a program's source files into bytecode that is then executed in a virtual machine.

✦ Bytecode is cached to disk, which enables subsequent runs of the same program, or loads of the same module, to avoid compiling bytecode again.

✦ With CPython, the best performance for program startup time is achieved when the program's bytecode files are generated in advance and they're already cached in operating system memory.

Item 98: Lazy-Load Modules with Dynamic Imports to Reduce Startup Time

The previous item investigated how Python program initialization can be slow and considered ways to improve performance (see Item 97: "Rely on Precompiled Bytecode and File System Caching to Improve Startup Time"). After following those best practices and further optimizing (see Item 92: "Profile Before Optimizing"), your Python programs might still feel like they take too long to start. Fortunately, there is one more technique to try: dynamic imports.

For example, imagine that I'm building an image processing tool with two features. The first module adjusts an image's brightness and contrast based on user-supplied settings:

```
# adjust.py
# Fast initialization
...

def do_adjust(path, brightness, contrast):
    ...
```

The second module intelligently enhances an image a given amount. To demonstrate a realistic situation, I'm going to assume that this requires loading a large native image processing library and thus initializes slowly:

```
# enhance.py
# Very slow initialization
...


def do_enhance(path, amount):
    ...
```

I can make these functions available as a command-line utility with the argparse built-in module. Here I use the add_subparsers feature to require a different set of flags, depending on the user-specified command. The adjust command accepts the --brightness and --contrast flags, and the enhance command only needs the --amount flag:

```
# parser.py
import argparse

PARSER = argparse.ArgumentParser()
PARSER.add_argument("file")

sub_parsers = PARSER.add_subparsers(dest="command")

enhance_parser = sub_parsers.add_parser("enhance")
enhance_parser.add_argument("--amount", type=float)

adjust_parser = sub_parsers.add_parser("adjust")
adjust_parser.add_argument("--brightness", type=float)
adjust_parser.add_argument("--contrast", type=float)
```

In the main function, I parse the arguments and then call into the enhance and adjust modules accordingly:

```
# mycli.py
import adjust
import enhance
import parser

def main():
    args = parser.PARSER.parse_args()

    if args.command == "enhance":
        enhance.do_enhance(args.file, args.amount)
```

```
    elif args.command == "adjust":
        adjust.do_adjust(
            args.file, args.brightness, args.contrast)
    else:
        raise RuntimeError("Not reachable")

if __name__ == "__main__":
    main()
```

Although the functionality here works well, the program is slow. For example, here I run the enhance command and observe that it takes over 1 second to complete:

```
$ time python3 ./mycli.py my_file.jpg enhance --amount 0.8
...
real    0m1.089s
user    0m0.035s
sys     0m0.022s
```

The cause of this long execution time is probably the dependency on the large native image processing library in the enhance module. I don't use that library for the adjust command, so I expect that it will go faster:

```
$ time python3 ./mycli.py my_file.jpg adjust --brightness
➡.3 --contrast -0.1
...
real    0m1.064s
user    0m0.040s
sys     0m0.016s
```

Unfortunately, it appears that the enhance and adjust commands are similarly slow. Upon closer inspection, I see that the problem is that I'm importing all of the modules that might ever be used by the command-line tool at the top of the main module, in keeping with PEP 8 style (see Item 2: "Follow the PEP 8 Style Guide"). On startup, my program pays the computational cost of preparing all functionality even when only part of it is actually used.

The CPython implementation of Python (see Item 1: "Know Which Version of Python You're Using") supports the -X importtime flag, which directly measures the performance of module loading. Here I use it to diagnose the slowness of my command-line tool:

```
$ python3 -X importtime mycli.py
import time: self [us] | cumulative | imported package
...
```

```
import time:           553 |           553 | adjust
import time:       1005348 |       1005348 | enhance
...
import time:          3347 |         14762 | parser
```

The `self` column shows how much time (in microseconds) each module took to execute all of its global statements, excluding imports. The cumulative column shows how much time it took to load each module, including all of its dependencies. Clearly, the enhance module is the culprit.

One solution is to delay importing dependencies until you actually need to use them. This is possible because Python supports importing modules at runtime—inside functions—in addition to using module-scoped `import` statements at program startup (see Item 122: "Know How to Break Circular Dependencies" for another use of this dynamism). Here I modify the command-line tool to only import the `adjust` module or the `enhance` module inside the `main` function after the command is dispatched:

```python
# mycli_faster.py
import parser

def main():
    args = parser.PARSER.parse_args()

    if args.command == "enhance":
        import enhance  # Changed

        enhance.do_enhance(args.file, args.amount)
    elif args.command == "adjust":
        import adjust  # Changed

        adjust.do_adjust(
            args.file, args.brightness, args.contrast)
    else:
        raise RuntimeError("Not reachable")

if __name__ == "__main__":
    main()
```

With this modification in place, the `adjust` command runs very quickly because the initialization of enhance can be skipped:

```
$ time python3 ./mycli_faster.py my_file.jpg adjust
➥--brightness .3 --contrast -0.1
...
```

```
real    0m0.049s
user    0m0.032s
sys     0m0.013s
```

The enhance command remains as slow as before:

```
$ time python3 ./mycli_faster.py my_file.jpg enhance
➥--amount 0.8
...
real    0m1.059s
user    0m0.036s
sys     0m0.014s
```

I can also use -X importtime to confirm that the adjust and enhance modules are not loaded when no command is specified:

```
$ time python3 -X importtime ./mycli_faster.py -h
import time: self [us] | cumulative | imported package
...
import time:      1118 |        6015 | parser
...
real    0m0.049s
user    0m0.032s
sys     0m0.013s
```

Lazy-loading modules works great for command-line tools like this that carry out a single task to completion and then terminate. But what if I need to reduce the latency of cold starts in a web application? Ideally, the cost of loading the enhance module wouldn't be incurred until the feature is actually requested by a user. Luckily, the same approach also works inside request handlers. Here I create a flask web application with one handler for each feature that dynamically imports the corresponding module:

```
# server.py
from flask import Flask, render_template, request

app = Flask(__name__)

@app.route("/adjust", methods=["GET", "POST"])
def do_adjust():
    if request.method == "POST":
        the_file = request.files["the_file"]
        brightness = request.form["brightness"]
        contrast = request.form["contrast"]
        import adjust    # Dynamic import
```

```
            return adjust.do_adjust(the_file, brightness, contrast)
        else:
            return render_template("adjust.html")

@app.route("/enhance", methods=["GET", "POST"])
def do_enhance():
    if request.method == "POST":
        the_file = request.files["the_file"]
        amount = request.form["amount"]
        import enhance  # Dynamic import

        return enhance.do_enhance(the_file, amount)
    else:
        return render_template("enhance.html")
```

When the do_enhance request handler is executed in the Python process for the first time, it imports the enhance module and pays a high initialization cost of 1 second. On subsequent calls to do_enhance, the import enhance statement will cause the Python process to merely verify that the module has already been loaded and then assign the enhance identifier in the local scope to the corresponding module object.

You might assume that the cost of a dynamic import statement is high, but it's actually not too bad. Here I use the timeit built-in module (see Item 93: "Optimize Performance-Critical Code Using timeit Microbenchmarks") to measure how much time it takes to dynamically import a previously imported module:

```
# import_perf.py
import timeit

trials = 10_000_000

result = timeit.timeit(
    setup="import enhance",
    stmt="import enhance",
    globals=globals(),
    number=trials,
)

print(f"{result/trials * 1e9:2.1f} nanos per call")

>>>
52.8 nanos per call
```

To put this overhead (52 nanoseconds) in perspective, here's another example that replaces the dynamic `import` statement with a lock-protected global variable (which is a common way to prevent multiple threads from dog-piling during program initialization):

```python
# global_lock_perf.py
import timeit
import threading

trials = 100_000_000

initialized = False
initialized_lock = threading.Lock()

result = timeit.timeit(
    stmt="""
global initialized
# Speculatively check without the lock
if not initialized:
    with initialized_lock:
        # Double check after holding the lock
        if not initialized:
            # Do expensive initialization
            ...
            initialized = True
""",
    globals=globals(),
    number=trials,
)

print(f"{result/trials * 1e9:2.1f} nanos per call")

>>>
5.5 nanos per call
```

The dynamic import version takes ten times longer than the approach using globals, so it's definitely much slower. Without any lock contention—which is the common case due to the speculative `if not initialized` statement—the global variable version runs just about as quickly as when you add together two integers in Python. But the dynamic import version is much simpler code that doesn't require any boilerplate. You wouldn't want a dynamic import to be present in CPU-bound code like a kernel function's inner loop (see Item 94: "Know When and How to Replace Python with Another Programming Language" for details), but it seems reasonable to do it once per web request.

Things to Remember

✦ The CPython -X importtime flag causes a Python program to print out how much time it takes to load imported modules and their dependencies, making it easy to diagnose the cause of startup time slowness.

✦ Modules can be imported dynamically inside a function, which makes it possible to delay the expensive initialization of dependencies until functionality actually needs to be used.

✦ The overhead of dynamically importing a module and checking that it was previously loaded is on the order of 20 addition operations, making it well worth the incremental cost if it can significantly improve the latency of cold starts.

Item 99: Consider memoryview and bytearray for Zero-Copy Interactions with bytes

Although Python isn't able to parallelize CPU-bound computation without extra effort (see Item 79: "Consider concurrent.futures for True Parallelism" and Item 94: "Know When and How to Replace Python with Another Programming Language"), it is able to support high-throughput, parallel I/O in a variety of ways (see Item 68: "Use Threads for Blocking I/O; Avoid for Parallelism" and Item 75: "Achieve Highly Concurrent I/O with Coroutines"). That said, it's surprisingly easy to use I/O tools the wrong way and reach the conclusion that the language is too slow for even I/O-bound workloads.

For example, say that I'm building a media server to stream television or movies over a network to users so they can watch without having to download the video data in advance. One of the key features of such a system is the ability for users to move forward or backward in the video playback so they can skip or repeat parts. In the client program, I can implement this by requesting a chunk of data from the server corresponding to the new time index selected by the user:

```
def timecode_to_index(video_id, timecode):
    ...
    # Returns the byte offset in the video data

def request_chunk(video_id, byte_offset, size):
    ...
    # Returns size bytes of video_id's data from the offset
```

```
video_id = ...
timecode = "01:09:14:28"
byte_offset = timecode_to_index(video_id, timecode)
size = 20 * 1024 * 1024
video_data = request_chunk(video_id, byte_offset, size)
```

How would you implement the server-side handler that receives the request_chunk request and returns the corresponding 20 MB chunk of video data? For the sake of this example, I assume that the command and control parts of the server have already been hooked up (see Item 76: "Know How to Port Threaded I/O to asyncio" for what that requires). I focus here on the last steps, where the requested chunk is extracted from gigabytes of video data that's cached in memory and is then sent over a socket back to the client. Here's what the implementation would look like:

```
socket = ...              # socket connection to client
video_data = ...          # bytes containing data for video_id
byte_offset = ...         # Requested starting position
size = 20 * 1024 * 1024   # Requested chunk size

chunk = video_data[byte_offset : byte_offset + size]
socket.send(chunk)
```

The latency and throughput of this code come down to two factors: how much time it takes to slice the 20 MB video chunk from video_data and how much time the socket takes to transmit that data to the client. If I assume that the socket is infinitely fast, I can run a microbenchmark by using the timeit built-in module to understand the performance characteristics of slicing bytes instances this way to create chunks (see Item 14: "Know How to Slice Sequences" for background):

```
import timeit

def run_test():
    chunk = video_data[byte_offset : byte_offset + size]
    # Call socket.send(chunk), but ignoring for benchmark

result = (
    timeit.timeit(
        stmt="run_test()",
        globals=globals(),
        number=100,
    )
```

```
    / 100
)
```

```
print(f"{result:0.9f} seconds")
```

```
>>>
0.004925669 seconds
```

Here it took roughly 5 milliseconds to extract the 20 MB slice of data
to transmit to the client. That means the overall throughput of my
server is limited to a theoretical maximum of 20 MB / 5 milliseconds
= 4 GB/second, since that's the fastest I can extract the video data
from memory. My server will also be limited to 1 CPU-second / 5 milliseconds = 200 clients requesting new chunks in parallel, which is
tiny compared to the tens of thousands of simultaneous connections
that tools like the asyncio built-in module can support. The problem
is that slicing a bytes instance causes the underlying data to be copied, which takes CPU time.

A better way to write this code is by using Python's built-in memoryview
type, which exposes CPython's high-performance *buffer protocol* to
programs. The buffer protocol is a low-level C API that allows the
Python runtime and C extensions (see Item 96: "Consider Extension
Modules to Maximize Performance and Ergonomics") to access the
underlying data buffers that are behind objects like bytes instances.
The best part about memoryview instances is that slicing them results
in another memoryview instance without copying the underlying data.
Here I create a memoryview instance that wraps a bytes instance and
inspect a slice of it:

```
data = b"shave and a haircut, two bits"
view = memoryview(data)
chunk = view[12:19]
print(chunk)
print("Size:            ", chunk.nbytes)
print("Data in view:    ", chunk.tobytes())
print("Underlying data:", chunk.obj)
```

```
>>>
<memory at 0x105407940>
Size:            7
Data in view:    b'haircut'
Underlying data: b'shave and a haircut, two bits'
```

By enabling *zero-copy* operations, memoryview can provide enormous
speedups for code that needs to quickly process large amounts of
memory, such as numerical C-extensions like NumPy and I/O-bound

programs like this one. Here I replace the simple bytes slicing above with `memoryview` slicing instead and repeat the same microbenchmark:

```
video_view = memoryview(video_data)

def run_test():
    chunk = video_view[byte_offset : byte_offset + size]
    # Call socket.send(chunk), but ignoring for benchmark

result = (
    timeit.timeit(
        stmt="run_test()",
        globals=globals(),
        number=100,
    )
    / 100
)

print(f"{result:0.9f} seconds")

>>>
0.000000250 seconds
```

The result is 250 nanoseconds. Now the theoretical maximum throughput of my server is 20 MB / 250 nanoseconds = 80 TB/second. For parallel clients, I can theoretically support up to 1 CPU-second / 250 nanoseconds = 4 million. That's more like it! This means that now my program is entirely bound by the underlying performance of the socket connection to the client and not by CPU constraints.

Now imagine that the data must flow in the other direction, where some clients are sending live video streams to the server in order to broadcast them to other users. In order to handle this, I need to store the latest video data from the user in a cache that other clients can read from. Here's what the implementation of reading 1 MB of new data from the incoming client would look like:

```
socket = ...          # socket connection to the client
video_cache = ...     # Cache of incoming video stream
byte_offset = ...     # Incoming buffer position
size = 1024 * 1024    # Incoming chunk size

chunk = socket.recv(size)
video_view = memoryview(video_cache)
before = video_view[:byte_offset]
after = video_view[byte_offset + size :]
new_cache = b"".join([before, chunk, after])
```

The socket.recv method returns a bytes instance. I can splice the new data with the existing cache at the current byte_offset by using simple slicing operations and the bytes.join method. To understand the performance of this, I can run another microbenchmark. I'm using a dummy socket implementation, so the performance test is only for the memory operations, not the I/O interaction:

```
def run_test():
    chunk = socket.recv(size)
    before = video_view[:byte_offset]
    after = video_view[byte_offset + size :]
    new_cache = b"".join([before, chunk, after])

result = (
    timeit.timeit(
        stmt="run_test()",
        globals=globals(),
        number=100,
    )
    / 100
)

print(f"{result:0.9f} seconds")

>>>
0.033520550 seconds
```

It takes 33 milliseconds to receive 1 MB and update the video cache. This means my maximum receive throughput is 1 MB / 33 milliseconds = 31 MB/second, and I'm limited to 31 MB / 1 MB = 31 simultaneous clients streaming in video data this way. This doesn't scale.

A better way to write this code is to use Python's built-in bytearray type in conjunction with memoryview. One limitation with bytes instances is that they are read-only and don't allow for individual indexes to be updated:

```
my_bytes = b"hello"
my_bytes[0] = 0x79

>>>
Traceback ...
TypeError: 'bytes' object does not support item assignment
```

The bytearray type is like a mutable version of bytes that allows for arbitrary positions to be overwritten. bytearray uses integers for its values instead of bytes:

```
my_array = bytearray(b"hello")
my_array[0] = 0x79
print(my_array)

>>>
bytearray(b'yello')
```

A memoryview object can also be used to wrap a bytearray instance. When you slice a memoryview, the resulting object can be used to assign data to a particular portion of the underlying buffer. This eliminates the copying costs from above that were required to splice the bytes instances back together after data was received from the client:

```
my_array = bytearray(b"row, row, row your boat")
my_view = memoryview(my_array)
write_view = my_view[3:13]
write_view[:] = b"-10 bytes-"
print(my_array)

>>>
bytearray(b'row-10 bytes- your boat')
```

Many library methods in Python, such as socket.recv_into and RawIOBase.readinto, use the buffer protocol to receive or read data quickly. The benefit of these methods is that they avoid allocating memory and creating another copy of the data; what's received goes straight into an existing buffer. Here I use socket.recv_into along with a memoryview slice to receive data into an underlying bytearray without the need for any splicing:

```
video_array = bytearray(video_cache)
write_view = memoryview(video_array)
chunk = write_view[byte_offset : byte_offset + size]
socket.recv_into(chunk)
```

I can run another microbenchmark to compare the performance of this approach to the earlier example that used socket.recv:

```
def run_test():
    chunk = write_view[byte_offset : byte_offset + size]
    socket.recv_into(chunk)
```

```
result = (
    timeit.timeit(
        stmt="run_test()",
        globals=globals(),
        number=100,
    )
    / 100
)

print(f"{result:0.9f} seconds")

>>>
0.000033925 seconds
```

It took 33 microseconds to receive a 1 MB video transmission. This means my server can support 1 MB / 33 microseconds = 31 GB/second of max throughput, and 31 GB / 1 MB = 31,000 parallel streaming clients. That's the type of scalability I'm looking for!

Things to Remember

✦ The memoryview built-in type provides a zero-copy interface for reading and writing slices of objects that support Python's high-performance buffer protocol.

✦ The bytearray built-in type provides a mutable bytes-like type that can be used for zero-copy data reads with functions like socket.recv_from.

✦ A memoryview can wrap a bytearray, allowing for received data to be spliced into an arbitrary buffer location without copying costs.

12

Data Structures and Algorithms

When you're implementing Python programs that handle a non-trivial amount of data, you'll often encounter slowdowns caused by the algorithmic complexity of your code. For example, programs you expected to scale linearly in the size of input data might actually grow quadratically, causing problems in production. Luckily, Python includes optimized implementations of many standard data structures and algorithms that can help you achieve high performance with minimal effort.

Similarly, Python provides built-in data types and helper functions for handling common tasks that frequently come up in programs: manipulating dates, times, and time zones; working with money values while preserving precision and controlling rounding behavior; and saving and restoring program state for users even as your software evolves over time. Writing code to handle these situations is fiddly and hard to get right. Having battle-tested implementations built into the language to handle them is a blessing.

Item 100: Sort by Complex Criteria Using the key Parameter

The list built-in type provides a sort method for ordering the items in a list instance based on a variety of criteria. (Don't confuse the sort method with sorted; see Item 101: "Know the Difference Between sort and sorted.") By default, sort orders a list's contents by the natural ascending order of the items. For example, here I sort a list of integers from smallest to largest:

```
numbers = [93, 86, 11, 68, 70]
numbers.sort()
print(numbers)

>>>
[11, 68, 70, 86, 93]
```

The `sort` method works for nearly all built-in types (strings, floats, etc.) that have a natural ordering. What does `sort` do with objects? As an example, here I define a class—including a `__repr__` method so instances are printable (see Item 12: "Understand the Difference Between `repr` and `str` when Printing Objects")—to represent various tools you might need to use on a construction site:

```
class Tool:
    def __init__(self, name, weight):
        self.name = name
        self.weight = weight

    def __repr__(self):
        return f"Tool({self.name!r}, {self.weight})"

tools = [
    Tool("level", 3.5),
    Tool("hammer", 1.25),
    Tool("screwdriver", 0.5),
    Tool("chisel", 0.25),
]
```

Sorting objects of this type doesn't work because the `sort` method tries to call comparison special methods that aren't defined by the class:

```
tools.sort()

>>>
Traceback ...
TypeError: '<' not supported between instances of 'Tool' and
➥'Tool'
```

If your class should have a natural ordering as integers do, then you can define the necessary special methods (see Item 104: "Know How to Use heapq for Priority Queues" for an example and Item 57: "Inherit from collections.abc Classes for Custom Container Types" for background) to make `sort` work without any extra parameters. But the more common case is that your objects might need to support multiple orderings, in which case defining a single natural ordering really doesn't make sense.

Often there's an attribute on the object that you'd like to use for sorting. To support this use case, the `sort` method accepts a key parameter that's expected to be a function (see Item 48: "Accept Functions Instead of Classes for Simple Interfaces" for background). The key function is passed a single argument, which is an item from the list that is being sorted. The return value of the key function should be a comparable value (i.e., with a natural ordering) to use in place of an item for sorting purposes.

Here I use the lambda keyword (see Item 39: "Prefer functools.partial over lambda Expressions for Glue Functions" for background) to define a function for the key parameter that enables me to sort the list of Tool objects alphabetically by the name attribute:

```
print("Unsorted:", repr(tools))
tools.sort(key=lambda x: x.name)
print("\nSorted: ", tools)
```

```
>>>
Unsorted: [Tool('level', 3.5), Tool('hammer', 1.25),
➡Tool('screwdriver', 0.5), Tool('chisel', 0.25)]

Sorted:   [Tool('chisel', 0.25), Tool('hammer', 1.25),
➡Tool('level', 3.5), Tool('screwdriver', 0.5)]
```

I can just as easily define another lambda function to sort by the weight attribute and pass it as the key parameter to the sort method:

```
tools.sort(key=lambda x: x.weight)
print("By weight:", tools)
```

```
>>>
By weight: [Tool('chisel', 0.25), Tool('screwdriver', 0.5),
➡Tool('hammer', 1.25), Tool('level', 3.5)]
```

Within the lambda function that's passed as the key parameter, you can access attributes of items as I've done here, index into items (for sequences, tuples, and dictionaries), or use any other valid expression.

For basic types like strings, you might even want to use the key function to do transformations on the values before sorting. For example, here I apply the lower method to each item in a list of place names to ensure that they're in alphabetical order, ignoring any capitalization (since in the natural lexical ordering of strings, uppercase letters appear before lowercase letters):

```
places = ["home", "work", "New York", "Paris"]
places.sort()
print("Case sensitive:  ", places)
places.sort(key=lambda x: x.lower())
print("Case insensitive:", places)
```

```
>>>
Case sensitive:   ['New York', 'Paris', 'home', 'work']
Case insensitive: ['home', 'New York', 'Paris', 'work']
```

Sometimes you might need to use multiple criteria for sorting. For example, say that I have a list of power tools, and I want to sort them first by the `weight` attribute and then by `name`. How can I accomplish this?

```
power_tools = [
    Tool("drill", 4),
    Tool("circular saw", 5),
    Tool("jackhammer", 40),
    Tool("sander", 4),
]
```

The simplest solution in Python is to use the `tuple` type (see Item 56: "Prefer dataclasses for Creating Immutable Objects" for another approach). A tuple is an immutable sequence of arbitrary Python values. Tuples are comparable by default and have a natural ordering, meaning that they implement all the special methods, such as `__lt__`, that are required by the `sort` method. The `tuple` type implements special comparator methods by iterating over each position in the tuple and comparing the corresponding values, one index at a time. Here I show how this works when one tool is heavier than another:

```
saw = (5, "circular saw")
jackhammer = (40, "jackhammer")
assert not (jackhammer < saw)  # Matches expectations
```

If the first position in the tuples being compared are equal—weight in this case—the tuple comparison will move to the second position and so on:

```
drill = (4, "drill")
sander = (4, "sander")
assert drill[0] == sander[0]   # Same weight
assert drill[1] < sander[1]    # Alphabetically less
assert drill < sander          # Thus, drill comes first
```

You can take advantage of this tuple comparison behavior in order to sort the list of power tools first by weight and then by name. Here I define a key function that returns a tuple containing the two attributes that I want to sort on, in order of priority:

```
power_tools.sort(key=lambda x: (x.weight, x.name))
print(power_tools)
```

```
>>>
[Tool('drill', 4), Tool('sander', 4), Tool('circular saw', 5),
➥Tool('jackhammer', 40)]
```

One limitation of having the key function return a tuple is that the direction of sorting for all criteria must be the same (either all in ascending order or all in descending order). If I provide the reverse parameter to the sort method, it will affect both criteria in the tuple the same way (note how sander now comes before drill instead of after):

```
power_tools.sort(
    key=lambda x: (x.weight, x.name),
    reverse=True,   # Makes all criteria descending
)
print(power_tools)
```

```
>>>
[Tool('jackhammer', 40), Tool('circular saw', 5),
➥Tool('sander', 4), Tool('drill', 4)]
```

For numerical values, it's possible to mix sorting directions by using the unary minus operator in the key function. This negates one of the values in the returned tuple, effectively reversing its sort order while leaving the others intact. Here I use this approach to sort by weight descending and then by name ascending (note how sander now comes after drill instead of before):

```
power_tools.sort(key=lambda x: (-x.weight, x.name))
print(power_tools)
```

```
>>>
[Tool('jackhammer', 40), Tool('circular saw', 5), Tool
➥('drill', 4), Tool('sander', 4)]
```

Unfortunately, unary negation isn't possible for all types. Here I try to achieve the same outcome by using the reverse argument to sort by weight descending and then negating the name attribute to put it in ascending order:

```
power_tools.sort(key=lambda x: (x.weight, -x.name),
reverse=True)
```

```
>>>
Traceback ...
TypeError: bad operand type for unary -: 'str'
```

For situations like this, Python provides a *stable* sorting algorithm. The sort method of the list type preserves the order of the input list when the key function returns values that are equal to each other. This means I can call sort multiple times on the same list to combine different criteria together. Here I produce the same sort ordering of weight descending and name ascending as I did above, but now I do it by using two separate calls to sort:

```
power_tools.sort(
    key=lambda x: x.name,    # Name ascending
)
power_tools.sort(
    key=lambda x: x.weight,  # Weight descending
    reverse=True,
)
print(power_tools)

>>>
[Tool('jackhammer', 40), Tool('circular saw', 5),
Tool('drill', 4), Tool('sander', 4)]
```

To understand why this works, note how the first call to sort puts the names in alphabetical order:

```
power_tools.sort(key=lambda x: x.name)
print(power_tools)

>>>
[Tool('circular saw', 5), Tool('drill', 4),
➥Tool('jackhammer', 40), Tool('sander', 4)]
```

When the second sort call by weight descending is made, the code sees that both sander and drill have a weight of 4. This causes the sort method to put both items into the final result list in the same order in which they appeared in the original list, thus preserving their relative ordering by name ascending:

```
power_tools.sort(
    key=lambda x: x.weight,
    reverse=True,
)
print(power_tools)

>>>
[Tool('jackhammer', 40), Tool('circular saw', 5),
➥Tool('drill', 4), Tool('sander', 4)]
```

This same approach can be used to combine as many different types of sorting criteria as you'd like in any direction. You just need to make sure that you execute the sorts in the opposite sequence of what you want the final list to contain. In this example, I wanted the sort order to be by weight descending and then by name ascending, so I had to do the name sort first, followed by the weight sort.

That said, the approach of having the key function return a tuple and using unary negation to mix sort orders is simpler to read and requires less code. I recommend using multiple calls to sort only if absolutely necessary.

Things to Remember

✦ The sort method of the list type can be used to rearrange a list's contents by the natural ordering of built-in types like strings, integers, tuples, and so on.

✦ The sort method doesn't work for objects unless they define a natural ordering using special methods, which is uncommon.

✦ The key parameter of the sort method can be used to supply a helper function that returns the value to use in place of each item from the list while sorting.

✦ Returning a tuple from the key function allows you to combine multiple sorting criteria together. The unary minus operator can be used to reverse individual sort orders for types that allow it.

✦ For types that can't be negated, you can combine many sorting criteria together by calling the sort method multiple times using different key functions and reverse values, in the order of lowest-rank sort call to highest-rank sort call.

Item 101: Know the Difference Between sort and sorted

The most familiar way to sort data in Python is by using the list type's built-in sort method (see Item 100: "Sort by Complex Criteria Using the key Parameter"). This method causes the data to be sorted in place, meaning the original list is modified, and the unsorted arrangement is no longer available. For example, here I alphabetize a list of butterfly names:

```
butterflies = ["Swallowtail", "Monarch", "Red Admiral"]
print(f"Before {butterflies}")
butterflies.sort()
print(f"After {butterflies}")

>>>
Before ['Swallowtail', 'Monarch', 'Red Admiral']
After ['Monarch', 'Red Admiral', 'Swallowtail']
```

Another way to sort data in Python is by using the `sorted` built-in function. This function sorts the contents of the given object and returns the results as a list while leaving the original intact:

```
original = ["Swallowtail", "Monarch", "Red Admiral"]
alphabetical = sorted(original)
print(f"Original {original}")
print(f"Sorted   {alphabetical}")

>>>
Original ['Swallowtail', 'Monarch', 'Red Admiral']
Sorted   ['Monarch', 'Red Admiral', 'Swallowtail']
```

The `sorted` built-in function can be used with any iterable object (see Item 21: "Be Defensive when Iterating over Arguments"), including tuples, dictionaries, and sets:

```
patterns = {"solid", "spotted", "cells"}
print(sorted(patterns))

>>>
['cells', 'solid', 'spotted']
```

It also supports the `reverse` and `key` parameters, just like the `sort` built-in function (see Item 100: "Sort by Complex Criteria Using the key Parameter"):

```
legs = {"insects": 6, "spiders": 8, "lizards": 4}
sorted_legs = sorted(
    legs,
    key=lambda x: legs[x],
    reverse=True,
)
print(sorted_legs)

>>>
['spiders', 'insects', 'lizards']
```

There are two benefits of using `sort` over `sorted`. First, `sort` modifies the list in place, which means the memory consumed by your program will stay the same during and after the sort. On the other hand, `sorted` needs to make a copy of the iterable's contents in order to produce a sorted list, which might double your program's memory requirements. Second, `sort` can be a lot faster because it's doing less work overall. The result list is already known and doesn't need to be allocated or resized. Iteration only needs to occur over a list instead of over arbitrary iterable objects. If the data is already partially ordered, index reassignments can be avoided altogether.

However, there are two primary benefits of using `sorted` instead of `sort`. First, the original object is left alone, ensuring that you don't inadvertently modify arguments supplied to your functions and cause perplexing bugs (see Item 30: "Know That Function Arguments Can Be Mutated" and Item 56: "Prefer dataclasses for Creating Immutable Objects" for background). Second, sorted works for any type of iterator, not just lists, which means your functions can rely on *duck typing* and be more flexible in the types they accept (see Item 25: "Be Cautious when Relying on Dictionary Insertion Ordering" for an example).

Arguably, sorted is more Pythonic than sort because it enables additional flexibility and is more explicit in how it produces results. The choice of which to use depends on the circumstances and what you're trying to accomplish.

Things to Remember

◆ sort achieves maximum performance with minimal memory overhead but requires the target list to be modified in place.

◆ sorted can process all types of iterators and collections as input, and won't inadvertently mutate data.

Item 102: Consider Searching Sorted Sequences with bisect

It's common to find yourself with a large amount of data in memory as a sorted list that you then want to search. For example, you may have loaded an English language dictionary to use for spell checking, or perhaps you have a list of dated financial transactions to audit for correctness.

Regardless of the data your specific program needs to process, searching for a specific value in a list takes linear time proportional to the list's length when you call the index method:

```
data = list(range(10**5))
index = data.index(91234)
assert index == 91234
```

If you're not sure whether the exact value you're searching for is in the list, you might want to search for the closest index that is equal to or exceeds your goal value. The simplest way to do this is to linearly scan the list and compare each item to your goal value:

```
def find_closest(sequence, goal):
    for index, value in enumerate(sequence):
        if goal < value:
            return index
    raise ValueError(f"{goal} is out of bounds")
```

```
index = find_closest(data, 91234.56)
assert index == 91235
```

Python's built-in bisect module provides better ways to accomplish these types of searches through ordered lists. You can use the bisect_left function to do an efficient binary search through any sequence of sorted items. The index it returns will either be where the item is already present in the list or where you'd want to insert the item in the list to keep it in sorted order:

```
from bisect import bisect_left

index = bisect_left(data, 91234)       # Exact match
assert index == 91234

index = bisect_left(data, 91234.56)  # Closest match
assert index == 91235
```

The complexity of the binary search algorithm used by the bisect module is logarithmic. This means searching in a list of length 1 million takes roughly the same amount of time with bisect as linearly searching a list of length 20 using the list.index method (math.log2(10**6) == 19.93...). So bisect is way faster!

I can verify this speed improvement for the example from above by using the timeit built-in module to run a microbenchmark (see Item 93: "Optimize Performance-Critical Code Using timeit Microbenchmarks" for details):

```
import random
import timeit

size = 10**5
iterations = 1000

data = list(range(size))
to_lookup = [random.randint(0, size)
             for _ in range(iterations)]

def run_linear(data, to_lookup):
    for index in to_lookup:
        data.index(index)

def run_bisect(data, to_lookup):
    for index in to_lookup:
        bisect_left(data, index)
```

```
baseline = (
    timeit.timeit(
        stmt="run_linear(data, to_lookup)",
        globals=globals(),
        number=10,
    )
    / 10
)
print(f"Linear search takes {baseline:.6f}s")

comparison = (
    timeit.timeit(
        stmt="run_bisect(data, to_lookup)",
        globals=globals(),
        number=10,
    )
    / 10
)
print(f"Bisect search takes {comparison:.6f}s")

slowdown = 1 + ((baseline - comparison) / comparison)
print(f"{slowdown:.1f}x slower")

>>>
Linear search takes 0.317685s
Bisect search takes 0.000197s
1610.1x time
```

The best part about bisect is that it's not limited to the list type; you can use it with any Python object that acts like a sequence (see Item 57: "Inherit from collections.abc Classes for Custom Container Types" for how to do that) containing values that have a natural ordering (see Item 104: "Know How to Use heapq for Priority Queues" for background). The module also provides additional features for more advanced situations (see https://docs.python.org/3/library/bisect.html).

Things to Remember

✦ Searching sorted data contained in a list takes linear time using the index method or a for loop with simple comparisons.

✦ The bisect built-in module's bisect_left function takes logarithmic time to search for values in sorted lists, which can be orders of magnitude faster than other approaches.

Item 103: Prefer deque for Producer–Consumer Queues

A common need in writing programs is a first-in, first-out (FIFO) queue, also known as a *producer–consumer queue*. A FIFO queue is used when one function gathers values to process and another function handles them in the order in which they were received. Often, programmers turn to Python's built-in list type to act as a FIFO queue.

For example, say that I'm writing a program that processes incoming emails for long-term archival, and it's using a list for a producer–consumer queue. Here I define a class to represent the messages:

```
class Email:
    def __init__(self, sender, receiver, message):
        self.sender = sender
        self.receiver = receiver
        self.message = message

    ...
```

I also define a placeholder function for receiving a single email, presumably from a socket, the file system, or some other type of I/O system. The implementation of this function doesn't matter; what's important is its interface: It will either return an Email instance or raise a NoEmailError exception (see Item 32: "Prefer Raising Exceptions to Returning None" for more about this convention):

```
class NoEmailError(Exception):
    pass


def try_receive_email():
    # Returns an Email instance or raises NoEmailError
    ...
```

The producing function receives emails and enqueues them to be consumed at a later time. This function uses the append method on the list to add new messages to the end of the queue so they are processed after all messages that were previously received:

```
def produce_emails(queue):
    while True:
        try:
            email = try_receive_email()
        except NoEmailError:
            return
        else:
            queue.append(email)  # Producer
```

The consuming function is what does something useful with the emails. This function calls pop(0) on the queue, which removes the very first item from the list and returns it to the caller. By always processing items from the beginning of the queue, the consumer ensures that the items are processed in the order in which they were received:

```
def consume_one_email(queue):
    if not queue:
        return
    email = queue.pop(0)   # Consumer
    # Index the message for long-term archival
    ...
```

Finally, I need a looping function that connects the pieces together. This function alternates between producing and consuming until the keep_running function returns False (see Item 75: "Achieve Highly Concurrent I/O with Coroutines" on how to do this concurrently):

```
def loop(queue, keep_running):
    while keep_running():
        produce_emails(queue)
        consume_one_email(queue)


def my_end_func():
    ...


loop([], my_end_func)
```

Why not process each Email object in produce_emails as it's returned by try_receive_email? It comes down to the trade-off between latency and throughput. When using producer–consumer queues, you often want to minimize the latency of accepting new items so they can be collected as fast as possible. The consumer can then process through the backlog of items at a consistent pace—one item per loop in this case—which provides a stable performance profile and consistent throughput at the cost of end-to-end latency (see Item 70: "Use Queue to Coordinate Work Between Threads" for related best practices).

Using a list for a producer–consumer queue like this works fine up to a point, but as the *cardinality*—the number of items in the list—increases, the list type's performance can degrade superlinearly. To analyze the performance of using list as a FIFO queue, I can run some microbenchmarks using the timeit built-in module (see Item 93: "Optimize Performance-Critical Code Using timeit Microbenchmarks" for details). Here I define a benchmark for the performance of adding new items to the queue using the append method of list (matching the producer function's usage):

```python
import timeit

def list_append_benchmark(count):
    def run(queue):
        for i in range(count):
            queue.append(i)

    return timeit.timeit(
        setup="queue = []",
        stmt="run(queue)",
        globals=locals(),
        number=1,
    )
```

Running this benchmark function with different levels of cardinality lets me compare its performance in relationship to data size:

```python
for i in range(1, 6):
    count = i * 1_000_000
    delay = list_append_benchmark(count)
    print(f"Count {count:>5,} takes: {delay*1e3:>6.2f}ms")

>>>
Count 1,000,000 takes:  13.23ms
Count 2,000,000 takes:  26.50ms
Count 3,000,000 takes:  39.06ms
Count 4,000,000 takes:  51.98ms
Count 5,000,000 takes:  65.19ms
```

This shows that the append method takes roughly constant time for the list type, and the total time for enqueueing scales linearly as the data size increases. There is overhead for the list type to increase its capacity under the covers as new items are added, but it's reasonably low and is amortized across repeated calls to append.

Here I define a similar benchmark for the pop(0) call that removes items from the beginning of the queue (matching the consumer function's usage):

```python
def list_pop_benchmark(count):
    def prepare():
        return list(range(count))

    def run(queue):
        while queue:
            queue.pop(0)
```

```
    return timeit.timeit(
        setup="queue = prepare()",
        stmt="run(queue)",
        globals=locals(),
        number=1,
    )
```

I can similarly run this benchmark for queues of different sizes to see how performance is affected by cardinality:

```
for i in range(1, 6):
    count = i * 10_000
    delay = list_pop_benchmark(count)
    print(f"Count {count:>5,} takes: {delay*1e3:>6.2f}ms")
```

```
>>>
Count 10,000 takes:    4.98ms
Count 20,000 takes:   22.21ms
Count 30,000 takes:   60.04ms
Count 40,000 takes:  109.96ms
Count 50,000 takes:  176.92ms
```

Surprisingly, this shows that the total time for dequeuing items from a list with pop(0) scales quadratically as the length of the queue increases. This happens because pop(0) needs to move every item in the list back an index, effectively reassigning the entire list's contents. I need to call pop(0) for every item in the list, and so I end up doing roughly len(queue) * len(queue) operations to consume the queue. This doesn't scale.

Python provides the deque class from the collections built-in module to solve this problem. deque is a *double-ended queue* implementation. It provides constant time operations for inserting or removing items from its beginning or end. This makes it ideal for FIFO queues.

To use the deque class, the call to append in produce_emails can stay the same as it was when using a list for the queue. The list.pop method call in consume_one_email must change to call the deque.popleft method with no arguments instead. And the loop method must be called with a deque instance instead of a list. Everything else stays the same. Here I redefine the one function affected to use the new method and run loop again:

```
import collections

def consume_one_email(queue):
    if not queue:
        return
```

```
    email = queue.popleft()   # Consumer
    # Process the email message
    ...

def my_end_func():
    ...

loop(collections.deque(), my_end_func)
```

I can run another version of the benchmark to verify that the performance of append (matching the producer function's usage) has stayed
roughly the same (modulo a constant factor):

```
def deque_append_benchmark(count):
    def prepare():
        return collections.deque()

    def run(queue):
        for i in range(count):
            queue.append(i)

    return timeit.timeit(
        setup="queue = prepare()",
        stmt="run(queue)",
        globals=locals(),
        number=1,
    )

for i in range(1, 6):
    count = i * 100_000
    delay = deque_append_benchmark(count)
    print(f"Count {count:>5,} takes: {delay*1e3:>6.2f}ms")

>>>
Count 100,000 takes:    1.68ms
Count 200,000 takes:    3.16ms
Count 300,000 takes:    5.05ms
Count 400,000 takes:    6.81ms
Count 500,000 takes:    8.43ms
```

And I can also benchmark the performance of calling popleft to
mimic the consumer function's usage of deque:

```
def dequeue_popleft_benchmark(count):
    def prepare():
        return collections.deque(range(count))
```

```
    def run(queue):
        while queue:
            queue.popleft()

    return timeit.timeit(
        setup="queue = prepare()",
        stmt="run(queue)",
        globals=locals(),
        number=1,
    )

for i in range(1, 6):
    count = i * 100_000
    delay = dequeue_popleft_benchmark(count)
    print(f"Count {count:>5,} takes: {delay*1e3:>6.2f}ms")

>>>
Count 100,000 takes:    1.67ms
Count 200,000 takes:    3.59ms
Count 300,000 takes:    5.65ms
Count 400,000 takes:    7.50ms
Count 500,000 takes:    9.58ms
```

The popleft usage scales linearly, in contrast to the superlinear behavior of pop(0) that I measured before—hooray! If you know that the performance of your program critically depends on the speed of your producer–consumer queues, then deque is a great choice. If you're not sure, then you should instrument your program to find out (see Item 92: "Profile Before Optimizing").

Things to Remember

✦ The list type can be used as a FIFO queue by having the producer call append to add items and the consumer call pop(0) to receive items. However, this may cause problems because the performance of pop(0) degrades superlinearly as the queue length increases.

✦ The deque class from the collections built-in module takes constant time—regardless of length—for append and popleft, making it ideal for FIFO queues.

Item 104: Know How to Use heapq for Priority Queues

One of the limitations of Python's other queue implementations (see Item 103: "Prefer deque for Producer-Consumer Queues" and Item 70: "Use Queue to Coordinate Work Between Threads") is that they are first-in, first-out (FIFO) queues: Their contents are sorted by the order in which they were received. Often, you need a program to process items in order of relative importance instead. To accomplish this, a *priority queue* is the right tool for the job.

For example, say that I'm writing a program to manage books borrowed from a library. There are people constantly borrowing new books. There are people returning their borrowed books on time. And there are people who need to be reminded to return their overdue books. Here I define a class to represent a book that's been borrowed:

```
class Book:
    def __init__(self, title, due_date):
        self.title = title
        self.due_date = due_date
```

I need a system that will send a reminder message when each book passes its due date. Unfortunately, I can't use a FIFO queue for this because the amount of time each book is allowed to be borrowed varies based on its recency, popularity, and other factors. For example, a book that is borrowed today may be due back later than a book that's borrowed tomorrow. Here I achieve this behavior by using a standard list and sorting it by the due_date attribute each time a new Book object is added:

```
def add_book(queue, book):
    queue.append(book)
    queue.sort(key=lambda x: x.due_date, reverse=True)

queue = []
add_book(queue, Book("Don Quixote", "2019-06-07"))
add_book(queue, Book("Frankenstein", "2019-06-05"))
add_book(queue, Book("Les Misérables", "2019-06-08"))
add_book(queue, Book("War and Peace", "2019-06-03"))
```

If I can assume that the queue of borrowed books is always in sorted order, then all I need to do to check for overdue books is to inspect the final element in the list. Here I define a function to return the next overdue book, if any, and remove it from the queue:

```
class NoOverdueBooks(Exception):
    pass

def next_overdue_book(queue, now):
    if queue:
        book = queue[-1]
        if book.due_date < now:
```

```
        queue.pop()
        return book

    raise NoOverdueBooks
```

I can call this function repeatedly to get overdue books to remind people about in order from most overdue to least overdue:

```
now = "2019-06-10"

found = next_overdue_book(queue, now)
print(found.due_date, found.title)

found = next_overdue_book(queue, now)
print(found.due_date, found.title)

>>>
2019-06-03 War and Peace
2019-06-05 Frankenstein
```

If a book is returned before the due date, I can remove the scheduled reminder message by removing the book from the list:

```
def return_book(queue, book):
    queue.remove(book)

queue = []
book = Book("Treasure Island", "2019-06-04")

add_book(queue, book)
print("Before return:", [x.title for x in queue])

return_book(queue, book)
print("After return: ", [x.title for x in queue])

>>>
Before return: ['Treasure Island']
After return:  []
```

And I can confirm that when all books are returned, the return_book function will raise the right exception (see Item 32: "Prefer Raising Exceptions to Returning None" for this convention):

```
try:
    next_overdue_book(queue, now)
except NoOverdueBooks:
    pass           # Expected
else:
    assert False   # Doesn't happen
```

However, the computational complexity of this solution isn't ideal. Although checking for and removing an overdue book has a constant cost, every time I add a book, I pay the cost of sorting the whole list again. If I have `len(queue)` books to add, and the cost of sorting them is roughly `len(queue)` * `math.log(len(queue))`, the time it takes to add books will grow superlinearly (`len(queue)` * `len(queue)` * `math.log(len(queue))`).

Here I define a microbenchmark to measure this performance behavior experimentally by using the `timeit` built-in module (see Item 93: "Optimize Performance-Critical Code Using `timeit` Microbenchmarks" for details):

```
import random
import timeit

def list_overdue_benchmark(count):
    def prepare():
        to_add = list(range(count))
        random.shuffle(to_add)
        return [], to_add

    def run(queue, to_add):
        for i in to_add:
            queue.append(i)
            queue.sort(reverse=True)

        while queue:
            queue.pop()

    return timeit.timeit(
        setup="queue, to_add = prepare()",
        stmt="run(queue, to_add)",
        globals=locals(),
        number=1,
    )
```

I can verify that the runtime of adding and removing books from the queue scales superlinearly as the number of books being borrowed increases:

```
for i in range(1, 6):
    count = i * 1_000
    delay = list_overdue_benchmark(count)
    print(f"Count {count:>5,} takes: {delay*1e3:>6.2f}ms")
```

```
>>>
Count 1,000 takes:    1.74ms
Count 2,000 takes:    5.87ms
Count 3,000 takes:   11.12ms
Count 4,000 takes:   19.80ms
Count 5,000 takes:   31.02ms
```

When a book is returned before the due date, I need to do a linear scan in order to find the book in the queue and remove it. Removing a book causes all subsequent items in the list to be shifted back an index, which has a high cost that also scales superlinearly. Here I define another microbenchmark to test the performance of returning a book using this function:

```
def list_return_benchmark(count):
    def prepare():
        queue = list(range(count))
        random.shuffle(queue)

        to_return = list(range(count))
        random.shuffle(to_return)

        return queue, to_return

    def run(queue, to_return):
        for i in to_return:
            queue.remove(i)

    return timeit.timeit(
        setup="queue, to_return = prepare()",
        stmt="run(queue, to_return)",
        globals=locals(),
        number=1,
    )
```

And again, I can verify that indeed the performance degrades super-linearly as the number of books increases:

```
for i in range(1, 6):
    count = i * 1_000
    delay = list_return_benchmark(count)
    print(f"Count {count:>5,} takes: {delay*1e3:>6.2f}ms")
```

```
>>>
Count 1,000 takes:    1.97ms
Count 2,000 takes:    6.99ms
Count 3,000 takes:   14.59ms
```

```
Count 4,000 takes:   26.12ms
Count 5,000 takes:   40.38ms
```

Using the methods of list may work for a tiny library, but it certainly won't scale to the size of the Great Library of Alexandria, as I want it to!

Fortunately, Python has the built-in heapq module that solves this problem by implementing priority queues efficiently. A *heap* is a data structure that allows for a list of items to be maintained where the computational complexity of adding a new item or removing the smallest item has logarithmic computational complexity (i.e., even better than linear scaling). In the book-borrowing example, smallest means the book with the earliest due date. The best part about heapq is that you don't have to understand how heaps are implemented in order to use the module's functions correctly.

Here I reimplement the add_book function using the heapq module. The queue is still a plain list. The heappush function replaces the list.append call from before. And I no longer have to call list.sort on the queue:

```
from heapq import heappush

def add_book(queue, book):
    heappush(queue, book)
```

If I try to use this with the Book class as previously defined, I get this somewhat cryptic error:

```
queue = []
add_book(queue, Book("Little Women", "2019-06-05"))
add_book(queue, Book("The Time Machine", "2019-05-30"))

>>>
Traceback ...
TypeError: '<' not supported between instances of 'Book' and
➥'Book'
```

This happens because the heapq module requires items in the priority queue to be comparable and have a natural sort order (see Item 100: "Sort by Complex Criteria Using the key Parameter" for details). You can quickly give the Book class this behavior by using the total_ordering class decorator from the functools built-in module (see Item 66: "Prefer Class Decorators over Metaclasses for Composable Class Extensions" for background) and implementing the __lt__ special method (see Item 57: "Inherit from collections.abc Classes for Custom Container Types" for background).

Here I redefine the class with a less-than method (__lt__) that simply compares the due_date fields between two Book instances:

```
import functools

@functools.total_ordering
class Book:
    def __init__(self, title, due_date):
        self.title = title
        self.due_date = due_date

    def __lt__(self, other):
        return self.due_date < other.due_date
```

Now I can add books to the priority queue without any issues by using the heapq.heappush function:

```
queue = []
add_book(queue, Book("Pride and Prejudice", "2019-06-01"))
add_book(queue, Book("The Time Machine", "2019-05-30"))
add_book(queue, Book("Crime and Punishment", "2019-06-06"))
add_book(queue, Book("Wuthering Heights", "2019-06-12"))
```

Alternatively, I can create a list with all the books in any order and then use the sort method of list to produce the heap:

```
queue = [
    Book("Pride and Prejudice", "2019-06-01"),
    Book("The Time Machine", "2019-05-30"),
    Book("Crime and Punishment", "2019-06-06"),
    Book("Wuthering Heights", "2019-06-12"),
]
queue.sort()
```

Or I can use the heapq.heapify function to create a heap in linear time (as opposed to the sort method's len(queue) * log(len(queue)) complexity):

```
from heapq import heapify

queue = [
    Book("Pride and Prejudice", "2019-06-01"),
    Book("The Time Machine", "2019-05-30"),
    Book("Crime and Punishment", "2019-06-06"),
    Book("Wuthering Heights", "2019-06-12"),
]
heapify(queue)
```

To check for overdue books, I inspect the first element in the list instead of the last, and then I use the heapq.heappop function instead of the list.pop function to remove the book from the heap:

```
from heapq import heappop

def next_overdue_book(queue, now):
    if queue:
        book = queue[0]       # Most overdue first
        if book.due_date < now:
            heappop(queue)  # Remove the overdue book
            return book

    raise NoOverdueBooks
```

Now I can find and remove overdue books in order until there are none left for the current time:

```
now = "2019-06-02"

book = next_overdue_book(queue, now)
print(book.due_date, book.title)

book = next_overdue_book(queue, now)
print(book.due_date, book.title)

try:
    next_overdue_book(queue, now)
except NoOverdueBooks:
    pass            # Expected
else:
    assert False  # Doesn't happen

>>>
2019-05-30 The Time Machine
2019-06-01 Pride and Prejudice
```

I can write another microbenchmark to test the performance of this implementation that uses the heapq module:

```
def heap_overdue_benchmark(count):
    def prepare():
        to_add = list(range(count))
        random.shuffle(to_add)
        return [], to_add
```

```
def run(queue, to_add):
    for i in to_add:
        heappush(queue, i)
    while queue:
        heappop(queue)

return timeit.timeit(
    setup="queue, to_add = prepare()",
    stmt="run(queue, to_add)",
    globals=locals(),
    number=1,
)
```

This benchmark experimentally verifies that the heap-based priority queue implementation scales much better (roughly `len(queue) * math.log(len(queue))`) without superlinearly degrading performance:

```
for i in range(1, 6):
    count = i * 10_000
    delay = heap_overdue_benchmark(count)
    print(f"Count {count:>5,} takes: {delay*1e3:>6.2f}ms")

>>>
Count 10,000 takes:    1.73ms
Count 20,000 takes:    3.83ms
Count 30,000 takes:    6.50ms
Count 40,000 takes:    8.85ms
Count 50,000 takes:   11.43ms
```

With the heapq implementation, one question remains: How should I handle returns that are on time? The solution is to never remove a book from the priority queue until its due date. At that time, it will be the first item in the list, and I can simply ignore the book if it's already been returned. Here I implement this behavior by adding a new field to track the book's return status:

```
@functools.total_ordering
class Book:
    def __init__(self, title, due_date):
        self.title = title
        self.due_date = due_date
        self.returned = False  # New field

    ...
```

Then I change the `next_overdue_book` function to repeatedly ignore any book that's already been returned:

```
def next_overdue_book(queue, now):
    while queue:
        book = queue[0]
        if book.returned:
            heappop(queue)
            continue

        if book.due_date < now:
            heappop(queue)
            return book

        break

    raise NoOverdueBooks
```

This approach makes the `return_book` function extremely fast because it makes no modifications to the priority queue:

```
def return_book(queue, book):
    book.returned = True
```

The downside of this solution for returns is that the priority queue may grow to the maximum size needed if all books from the library were checked out and went overdue. Although the queue operations will be fast thanks to `heapq`, this storage overhead might require significant memory (see Item 115: "Use `tracemalloc` to Understand Memory Usage and Leaks" for how to debug such usage).

If you're trying to build a robust system, you will need to plan for the worst-case scenario; thus, you should expect that it's possible for every library book to go overdue for some reason (e.g., a natural disaster closes the road to the library). This memory cost is a design consideration that you should have already planned for and mitigated through additional constraints (e.g., imposing a maximum number of simultaneously lent books).

Beyond the priority queue primitives that I've used in this example, the `heapq` module also provides additional functionality for advanced use cases (see https://docs.python.org/3/library/heapq.html). The module is a great choice when its functionality matches the problem you're facing (see the `queue.PriorityQueue` class for another thread-safe option).

Things to Remember

✦ A priority queue allows you to process items in order of importance instead of in first-in, first-out order.

✦ If you try to use list operations to implement a priority queue, your program's performance will degrade superlinearly as the queue grows.

✦ The heapq built-in module provides all the functions you need to implement a priority queue that scales efficiently.

✦ To use heapq, the items being prioritized must have a natural sort order, which requires special methods like __lt__ to be defined for classes.

Item 105: Use datetime **Instead of** time **for Local Clocks**

Coordinated Universal Time (UTC) is the standard, time zone–independent representation of time. UTC works great for computers that represent time as seconds since the UNIX epoch. But UTC isn't ideal for humans. Humans reference time relative to where they're currently located. People say "noon" or "8 a.m." instead of "UTC 15:00 minus 7 hours." If your program handles time, you'll probably find yourself converting time between UTC and local clocks for the sake of human understanding.

Python provides two ways of accomplishing time zone conversions. The old way, using the time built-in module, is terribly error prone. The new way, using datetime, works great with some help from the built-in zoneinfo module.

You should be acquainted with both time and datetime to thoroughly understand why datetime is the best choice and time should be avoided.

The time Module

The localtime function from the time built-in module lets you convert a UNIX timestamp (seconds since the UNIX epoch in UTC) to a local time that matches the host computer's time zone (Pacific Daylight Time in my case). This local time can be printed in human-readable format using the strftime function:

```
import time

now = 1710047865.0
local_tuple = time.localtime(now)
```

```
time_format = "%Y-%m-%d %H:%M:%S"
time_str = time.strftime(time_format, local_tuple)
print(time_str)
```

```
>>>
2024-03-09 21:17:45
```

You'll often need to go the other way as well, starting with user input in human-readable local time and converting it to UTC time. You can do this by using the `strptime` function to parse the time string and then calling `mktime` to convert local time to a UNIX timestamp:

```
time_tuple = time.strptime(time_str, time_format)
utc_now = time.mktime(time_tuple)
print(utc_now)
```

```
>>>
1710047865.0
```

How do you convert local time in one time zone to local time in another time zone? For example, say that I'm taking a flight between San Francisco and New York, and I want to know what time it will be in San Francisco when I've arrived in New York.

I might initially assume that I can directly manipulate the return values from the `time`, `localtime`, and `strptime` functions to do time zone conversions. But this is a very bad idea. Time zones change all the time due to local laws. It's too complicated to manage yourself, especially if you want to handle every global city for flight departures and arrivals.

Many operating systems have configuration files that automatically keep up with the time zone changes. Python lets you use these time zones through the `time` module if your platform supports it. On other platforms, such as Windows, some time zone functionality isn't available from `time` at all. For example, here I parse a departure time from the San Francisco time zone, Pacific Standard Time (PST):

```
parse_format = "%Y-%m-%d %H:%M:%S %Z"
depart_sfo = "2024-03-09 21:17:45 PST"
time_tuple = time.strptime(depart_sfo, parse_format)
time_str = time.strftime(time_format, time_tuple)
print(time_str)
```

```
>>>
2024-03-09 21:17:45
```

After seeing that "PST" works with the `strptime` function, I might also assume that other time zones known to my computer will work.

Unfortunately, this isn't the case. strptime raises an exception when it sees Eastern Daylight Time (EDT), which is the time zone for New York (when the flight arrives after the time change):

```
arrival_nyc = "2024-03-10 03:31:18 EDT"
time_tuple = time.strptime(arrival_nyc, parse_format)
```

```
>>>
Traceback ...
ValueError: time data '2024-03-10 03:31:18 EDT' does not match
➥format '%Y-%m-%d %H:%M:%S %Z'
```

The problem here is the platform-dependent nature of the time module. Its actual behavior is determined by how the underlying C functions work with the host operating system. This makes the functionality of the time module unreliable in Python. The time module fails to consistently work properly for multiple local times. Thus, you should avoid using the time module for this purpose. If you must use time, use it only to convert between UTC and the host computer's local time. For all other types of conversions, use the datetime module.

The datetime Module

The second option for representing times in Python is the datetime class from the datetime built-in module. Like the time module, datetime can be used to convert from the current time in UTC to local time.

Here I convert the present time in UTC to my computer's local time, PDT:

```
from datetime import datetime, timezone

now = datetime(2024, 3, 10, 5, 17, 45)
now_utc = now.replace(tzinfo=timezone.utc)
now_local = now_utc.astimezone()
print(now_local)
```

```
>>>
2024-03-09 21:17:45-08:00
```

The datetime module can also easily convert a local time back to a UNIX timestamp in UTC (matching the value above):

```
time_str = "2024-03-09 21:17:45"
now = datetime.strptime(time_str, time_format)
time_tuple = now.timetuple()
utc_now = time.mktime(time_tuple)
print(utc_now)
```

```
>>>
1710047865.0
```

Unlike the `time` module, the `datetime` module has facilities for reliably converting from one local time to another local time. However, `datetime` only provides the machinery for time zone operations with its `tzinfo` class and related methods.

Fortunately, since Python version 3.9, on many systems the `zoneinfo` built-in module contains a full database of every time zone definition you might need. On other systems, such as Windows, the officially endorsed `tzdata` community package might need to be installed to provide the time zone database that the `zoneinfo` module needs to function properly (see Item 116: "Know Where to Find Community-Built Modules" for details).

To use `zoneinfo` effectively, you should always convert local times to UTC first. Next, perform any `datetime` operations you need on the UTC values (such as offsetting). Finally, convert to local times.

For example, here I convert a New York City flight arrival time to a UTC datetime:

```
from zoneinfo import ZoneInfo

arrival_nyc = "2024-03-10 03:31:18"
nyc_dt_naive = datetime.strptime(arrival_nyc, time_format)
eastern = ZoneInfo("US/Eastern")
nyc_dt = nyc_dt_naive.replace(tzinfo=eastern)
utc_dt = nyc_dt.astimezone(timezone.utc)
print("EDT:", nyc_dt)
print("UTC:", utc_dt)

>>>
EDT: 2024-03-10 03:31:18-04:00
UTC: 2024-03-10 07:31:18+00:00
```

Once I have a UTC datetime, I can convert it to San Francisco local time:

```
pacific = ZoneInfo("US/Pacific")
sf_dt = utc_dt.astimezone(pacific)
print("PST:", sf_dt)

>>>
PST: 2024-03-09 23:31:18-08:00
```

Just as easily, I can convert it to the local time in Nepal:

```
nepal = ZoneInfo("Asia/Katmandu")
nepal_dt = utc_dt.astimezone(nepal)
print("NPT", nepal_dt)

>>>
NPT 2024-03-10 13:16:18+05:45
```

With datetime and zoneinfo, these conversions are consistent across all environments, regardless of what operating system the host computer is running.

Things to Remember

✦ Avoid using the time module for translating between different time zones.

✦ Use the datetime and zoneinfo built-in modules to reliably convert between times and dates in different time zones.

✦ Always represent time in UTC and do conversions to local time as the very final step before presentation.

Item 106: Use decimal when Precision Is Paramount

Python is an excellent language for writing code that interacts with numerical data. Python's integer type can represent values of any practical size. Its double-precision floating point type complies with the IEEE 754 standard. The language also provides a standard complex number type for imaginary values. However, these aren't enough for every situation.

For example, say that I want to compute the amount to charge a customer for an international phone call via a portable satellite phone. I know the time in minutes and seconds that the customer was on the phone (say, 3 minutes 42 seconds). I also have a set rate for the cost of calling Antarctica from the United States (say, $1.45/minute). What should the charge be?

With floating point math, the computed charge seems reasonable:

```
rate = 1.45
seconds = 3 * 60 + 42
cost = rate * seconds / 60
print(cost)
```

```
>>>
5.364999999999999
```

The result is 0.0001 short of the correct value (5.365) due to how IEEE 754 floating point numbers are represented. I might want to round up this value to 5.37 to properly cover all costs incurred by the customer. However, due to floating point error, rounding to the nearest whole cent actually reduces the final charge (from 5.364 to 5.36) instead of increasing it (from 5.365 to 5.37):

```
print(round(cost, 2))
```

```
>>>
```

5.36

The solution is to use the Decimal class from the decimal built-in module. The Decimal class provides fixed point math of 28 decimal places by default—and it can go even higher, if required. This works around the precision issues in IEEE 754 floating point numbers. The class also gives you more control over rounding behaviors.

For example, redoing the Antarctica calculation with Decimal results in the exact expected charge instead of an approximation:

```
from decimal import Decimal

rate = Decimal("1.45")
seconds = Decimal(3 * 60 + 42)
cost = rate * seconds / Decimal(60)
print(cost)

>>>
5.365
```

Decimal instances can be given starting values in two different ways. The first way is by passing a str containing the number to the Decimal constructor. This ensures that there is no loss of precision due to the inherent nature of Python floating point values and number constants. The second way is by directly passing a float or an int instance to the constructor. Here you can see that the two construction methods result in different behavior:

```
print(Decimal("1.45"))
print(Decimal(1.45))

>>>
1.45
1.4499999999999999555910790149937383830547332763671875
```

This problem doesn't occur if I supply integers to the Decimal constructor:

```
print("456")
print(456)

>>>
456
456
```

If you care about exact answers, err on the side of caution and always use the str constructor for the Decimal type.

Getting back to the phone call example, say that I also want to support very short phone calls between places (like Toledo and Detroit) that are much cheaper to connect via an auxiliary cellular connection. Here I compute the charge for a phone call that was 5 seconds long with a rate of $0.05/minute:

```
rate = Decimal("0.05")
seconds = Decimal("5")
small_cost = rate * seconds / Decimal(60)
print(small_cost)
```

```
>>>
0.004166666666666666666666666667
```

The result is so low that it is decreased to zero when I tried to round it to the nearest whole cent. This won't do!

```
print(round(small_cost, 2))
```

```
>>>
0.00
```

Luckily, the Decimal class has a built-in function for rounding to exactly the decimal place needed with the desired rounding behavior. This works for the higher-cost case from earlier:

```
from decimal import ROUND_UP

rounded = cost.quantize(Decimal("0.01"), rounding=ROUND_UP)
print(f"Rounded {cost} to {rounded}")
```

```
>>>
Rounded 5.365 to 5.37
```

Using the quantize method this way also properly handles the small usage case for short, cheap phone calls:

```
rounded = small_cost.quantize(Decimal("0.01"),
rounding=ROUND_UP)
print(f"Rounded {small_cost} to {rounded}")
```

```
>>>
Rounded 0.004166666666666666666666666667 to 0.01
```

While Decimal works great for fixed point numbers, it still has limitations in its precision (e.g., 1/3 will be an approximation). For representing rational numbers with no limit to precision, consider using the Fraction class from the fractions built-in module.

Things to Remember

✦ Python has built-in types and classes in modules that can represent practically every type of numerical value.

- ✦ The `Decimal` class is ideal for situations that require high precision and control over rounding behavior, such as computations of monetary values.

- ✦ Pass `str` instances to the `Decimal` constructor instead of `float` instances if it's important to compute exact answers and not floating point approximations.

Item 107: Make `pickle` Serialization Maintainable with `copyreg`

The `pickle` built-in module can serialize Python objects into a stream of bytes and deserialize bytes back into objects (see Item 10: "Know the Differences Between `bytes` and `str`" for background). Pickled byte streams shouldn't be used to communicate between untrusted parties. The purpose of `pickle` is to let you pass Python objects between programs that you control over binary channels.

Note

The `pickle` module's serialization format is unsafe by design. The serialized data contains what is essentially a program that describes how to reconstruct the original Python objects. This means a malicious `pickle` payload could be used to compromise any part of the Python program that attempts to deserialize it.

In contrast, the `json` module is safe by design. Serialized JSON data contains a simple description of an object hierarchy. Deserializing JSON data does not expose a Python program to any additional risk beyond out-of-memory errors. Formats like JSON should be used for communication between programs or people that don't trust each other.

For example, say that I want to use a Python object to represent the state of a player's progress in a game. The game state includes the level the player is on and the number of lives they have remaining:

```
class GameState:
    def __init__(self):
        self.level = 0
        self.lives = 4
```

The program modifies this object as the game runs:

```
state = GameState()
state.level += 1  # Player beat a level
state.lives -= 1  # Player had to try again

print(state.__dict__)
```

```
>>>
{'level': 1, 'lives': 3}
```

When the user quits playing, the program can save the state of the game to a file so it can be resumed at a later time. The pickle module makes it easy to do this. Here I dump the GameState object directly to a file:

```
import pickle
```

```
state_path = "game_state.bin"
with open(state_path, "wb") as f:
    pickle.dump(state, f)
```

Later, I can load the file and get back the GameState object as if it had never been serialized:

```
with open(state_path, "rb") as f:
    state_after = pickle.load(f)
```

```
print(state_after.__dict__)
```

```
>>>
{'level': 1, 'lives': 3}
```

The problem with this approach is what happens as the game's features expand over time. Imagine that I want the player to earn points toward a high score. To track the player's points, I can add a new field to the GameState class:

```
class GameState:
    def __init__(self):
        self.level = 0
        self.lives = 4
        self.points = 0  # New field
```

Serializing the new version of the GameState class using pickle will work exactly as before. Here I simulate the round trip through a file by serializing to a string with dumps and back to a GameState object with loads:

```
state = GameState()
serialized = pickle.dumps(state)
state_after = pickle.loads(serialized)
```

```
print(state_after.__dict__)
```

```
>>>
{'level': 0, 'lives': 4, 'points': 0}
```

But what happens to older saved GameState objects that the user may want to resume? Here I unpickle an old game file using a program with the new definition of the GameState class:

```
with open(state_path, "rb") as f:
    state_after = pickle.load(f)

print(state_after.__dict__)

>>>
{'level': 1, 'lives': 3}
```

The points attribute is missing! This is especially confusing because the returned object is an instance of the new GameState class:

```
assert isinstance(state_after, GameState)
```

This behavior is a by-product of the way the pickle module works. Its primary use case is making it easy to serialize objects. As soon as your use of pickle expands beyond trivial usage, the module's functionality starts to break down in surprising ways.

Fixing these problems is straightforward using the copyreg built-in module. The copyreg module lets you register the functions responsible for serializing and deserializing Python objects, allowing you to control the behavior of pickle and make it more reliable and adaptable.

Default Attribute Values

In the simplest case, you can use a constructor with default arguments (see Item 35: "Provide Optional Behavior with Keyword Arguments" for background) to ensure that GameState objects will always have all attributes after unpickling. Here I redefine the constructor this way:

```
class GameState:
    def __init__(self, level=0, lives=4, points=0):
        self.level = level
        self.lives = lives
        self.points = points
```

To use this constructor for pickling, I define a helper function that takes a GameState object and turns it into a tuple of parameters for the copyreg module. The returned tuple contains the function to use for unpickling and the parameters to pass to the unpickling function:

```
def pickle_game_state(game_state):
    kwargs = game_state.__dict__
    return unpickle_game_state, (kwargs,)
```

Now I need to define the unpickle_game_state helper. This function takes serialized data and parameters from pickle_game_state and returns the corresponding GameState object. It's a tiny wrapper around the constructor:

```
def unpickle_game_state(kwargs):
    return GameState(**kwargs)
```

Now I register these functions with the copyreg built-in module:

```
import copyreg

copyreg.pickle(GameState, pickle_game_state)
```

After registration, serializing and deserializing works as before:

```
state = GameState()
state.points += 1000
serialized = pickle.dumps(state)
state_after = pickle.loads(serialized)
print(state_after.__dict__)

>>>
{'level': 0, 'lives': 4, 'points': 1000}
```

With this registration done, now I'll change the definition of GameState again to give the player a count of magic spells to use. This change is similar to when I added the points field to GameState:

```
class GameState:
    def __init__(self, level=0, lives=4, points=0, magic=5):
        self.level = level
        self.lives = lives
        self.points = points
        self.magic = magic  # New field
```

But unlike before, deserializing an old GameState object will result in valid game data instead of missing attributes. This works because unpickle_game_state calls the GameState constructor directly instead of using the pickle module's default behavior of saving and restoring only the attributes that belong to an object. The GameState constructor's keyword arguments have default values that will be used for any parameters that are missing. This causes old game state files to receive the default value for the new magic field when they are deserialized:

```
print("Before:", state.__dict__)
state_after = pickle.loads(serialized)
print("After: ", state_after.__dict__)
```

```
>>>
Before: {'level': 0, 'lives': 4, 'points': 1000}
After:  {'level': 0, 'lives': 4, 'points': 1000, 'magic': 5}
```

Versioning Classes

Sometimes you need to make backward-incompatible changes to your Python objects by removing fields. Doing so prevents the default argument approach to migrating serializations from working.

For example, say I realize that a limited number of lives is a bad idea, and I want to remove the concept of lives from the game. Here I redefine the GameState class to no longer have a lives field:

```
class GameState:
    def __init__(self, level=0, points=0, magic=5):
        self.level = level
        self.points = points
        self.magic = magic
```

The problem is that this breaks deserialization of old game data. All fields from the old data—even ones removed from the class—will be passed to the GameState constructor by the unpickle_game_state function:

```
pickle.loads(serialized)
```

```
>>>
Traceback ...
TypeError: GameState.__init__() got an unexpected keyword
➥argument 'lives'. Did you mean 'level'?
```

I can fix this by adding a version parameter to the functions supplied to copyreg. New serialized data will have a version of 2 specified when pickling a new GameState object:

```
def pickle_game_state(game_state):
    kwargs = game_state.__dict__
    kwargs["version"] = 2
    return unpickle_game_state, (kwargs,)
```

Old versions of the data will not have a version argument present, which means I can manipulate the arguments passed to the GameState constructor accordingly:

```
def unpickle_game_state(kwargs):
    version = kwargs.pop("version", 1)
    if version == 1:
        del kwargs["lives"]
    return GameState(**kwargs)
```

Now deserializing an old object works properly:

```
copyreg.pickle(GameState, pickle_game_state)
print("Before:", state.__dict__)
state_after = pickle.loads(serialized)
print("After: ", state_after.__dict__)

>>>
Before: {'level': 0, 'lives': 4, 'points': 1000}
After:  {'level': 0, 'points': 1000, 'magic': 5}
```

I can continue using this approach to handle changes between future versions of the same class. Any logic I need to adapt an old version of the class to a new version of the class can go in the unpickle_game_state function.

Stable Import Paths

One other issue you may encounter with pickle is breakage from renaming a class. Often over the life cycle of a program, you'll refactor your code by renaming classes and moving them to other modules. Unfortunately, doing so breaks the pickle module unless you're careful.

Here I rename the GameState class to BetterGameState and remove the old class from the program entirely:

```
class BetterGameState:
    def __init__(self, level=0, points=0, magic=5):
        self.level = level
        self.points = points
        self.magic = magic
```

Attempting to deserialize an old GameState object now fails because the class can't be found:

```
pickle.loads(serialized)

>>>
Traceback ...
AttributeError: Can't get attribute 'GameState'
➥on <module '__main__' from 'my_code.py'>
```

This exception occurs because the import path of the serialized object's class is encoded in the pickled data:

```
print(serialized)

>>>
b'\x80\x04\x95A\x00\x00\x00\x00\x00\x00\x00\x8c\x08__main__\
x94\x8c\tGameState\x94\x93\x94)\x81\x94}\x94(\x8c\x05level\
x94K\x00\x8c\x06points\x94K\x00\x8c\x05magic\x94K\x05ub.'
```

The solution is to use copyreg again. I can specify a stable identifier for the function to use for unpickling an object. This allows me to transition pickled data to different classes with different names when it's deserialized. It gives me a level of indirection:

```
copyreg.pickle(BetterGameState, pickle_game_state)
```

After I use copyreg, it's evident that the import path to unpickle_game_state is encoded in the serialized data instead of BetterGameState:

```
state = BetterGameState()
serialized = pickle.dumps(state)
print(serialized)
```

```
>>>
b'\x80\x04\x95W\x00\x00\x00\x00\x00\x00\x00\x8c\x08__main__\
➥x94\x8c\x13unpickle_game_state\x94\x93\x94}\x94(\x8c\
➥x05level\x94K\x00\x8c\x06points\x94K\x00\x8c\x05magic\x94K\
➥x05\x8c\x07version\x94K\x02u\x85\x94R\x94.'
```

The only gotcha is that I can't change the path of the module in which the unpickle_game_state function is present. Once I serialize data with a function, it must remain available on that import path for deserialization in the future.

Things to Remember

✦ The pickle built-in module is useful only for serializing and deserializing objects between trusted programs.

✦ Deserializing previously pickled objects may break if the classes involved have changed over time (e.g., attributes have been added or removed).

✦ Use the copyreg built-in module with pickle to ensure backward compatibility for serialized objects.

13

Testing and Debugging

The dynamic behavior of Python and its lack of static type checking by default is both a blessing and a curse (see Item 3: "Never Expect Python to Detect Errors at Compile Time" for details). However, large numbers of Python programmers out there say it's worth using because of the productivity gained from the resulting brevity and simplicity. But most people using Python have at least one horror story about a program encountering a boneheaded error at runtime. One of the worst examples I've heard of involved a SyntaxError exception being raised in production as a side effect of a dynamic import (see Item 98: "Lazy-Load Modules with Dynamic Imports to Reduce Startup Time" for an example), resulting in a crashed server process. The programmer I know who was hit by this surprising occurrence has since ruled out using Python ever again.

But I have to wonder: Why wasn't the code more well tested before the program was deployed to production? Compile-time static type safety isn't everything. You should always test your code, regardless of what language it's written in. However, I'll admit that in Python it may be more important to write tests to verify correctness than in other languages. Luckily, the same dynamic features that create these risks also make it extremely easy to write tests for your code and to debug malfunctioning programs. You can use Python's dynamic nature and easily overridable behaviors to implement tests and ensure that your programs work as expected.

Item 108: Verify Related Behaviors in TestCase Subclasses

The canonical way to write tests in Python is to use the unittest built-in module. For example, say I have the following utility function defined that I would like to verify works correctly across a variety of inputs:

```
# utils.py
def to_str(data):
    if isinstance(data, str):
        return data
    elif isinstance(data, bytes):
        return data.decode("utf-8")
    else:
        raise TypeError(
            f"Must supply str or bytes, found: {data}")
```

To define tests, I create a second file named test_utils.py or utils_test.py—the naming scheme is a style choice—that contains tests for each behavior I expect:

```
# utils_test.py
from unittest import TestCase, main
from utils import to_str

class UtilsTestCase(TestCase):
    def test_to_str_bytes(self):
        self.assertEqual("hello", to_str(b"hello"))

    def test_to_str_str(self):
        self.assertEqual("hello", to_str("hello"))

    def test_failing(self):
        self.assertEqual("incorrect", to_str("hello"))

if __name__ == "__main__":
    main()
```

Then I run the test file using the Python command line. In this case, two of the test methods pass and one fails, printing out a helpful error message about what went wrong:

```
$ python3 utils_test.py
F..
================================================================
FAIL: test_failing (__main__.UtilsTestCase)
----------------------------------------------------------------
Traceback (most recent call last):
  File "utils_test.py", line 15, in test_failing
    self.assertEqual('incorrect', to_str('hello'))
AssertionError: 'incorrect' != 'hello'
```

```
- incorrect
+ hello
```

```
----------------------------------------------------------------
Ran 3 tests in 0.002s
```

```
FAILED (failures=1)
```

Tests are organized into TestCase subclasses. Each test case is a method that begins with the word test. If a test method runs without raising any kind of exception (including AssertionError from assert statements; see Item 81: "assert Internal Assumptions and raise Missed Expectations"), the test is considered to have passed successfully. If one test fails, the TestCase subclass continues running the other test methods so you can get a full picture of how all your tests are doing instead of stopping at the first sign of trouble.

If you want to iterate quickly to fix or improve a specific test, you can run only that test method by specifying its path within the test module on the command line:

```
$ python3 utils_test.py UtilsTestCase.test_to_str_bytes
.
----------------------------------------------------------------
Ran 1 test in 0.000s
```

```
OK
```

You can also invoke the debugger from directly within test methods at specific breakpoints in order to dig more deeply into the cause of failures (see Item 114: "Consider Interactive Debugging with pdb" for how to do that).

The TestCase class provides helper methods for making assertions in your tests, such as assertEqual for verifying equality, assertTrue for verifying Boolean expressions, assertAlmostEqual for when precision is a concern (see Item 113: "Use assertAlmostEqual to Control Precision in Floating Point Tests"), and many more (see https://docs.python.org/3/library/unittest.html for the full list). These are better than the built-in assert statement because they print out all the inputs and outputs to help you understand the exact reason the test is failing. For example, here I have the same test case written with and without a helper assertion method:

```
# assert_test.py
from unittest import TestCase, main
```

```
from utils import to_str

class AssertTestCase(TestCase):
    def test_assert_helper(self):
        expected = 12
        found = 2 * 5
        self.assertEqual(expected, found)

    def test_assert_statement(self):
        expected = 12
        found = 2 * 5
        assert expected == found

if __name__ == "__main__":
    main()
```

Which of these failure messages seems more helpful to you? Note how the second message doesn't show the values of expected or found:

```
$ python3 assert_test.py
FF
======================================================================
FAIL: test_assert_helper (__main__.AssertTestCase)
----------------------------------------------------------------------
Traceback (most recent call last):
  File "assert_test.py", line 16, in test_assert_helper
    self.assertEqual(expected, found)
AssertionError: 12 != 10


======================================================================
FAIL: test_assert_statement (__main__.AssertTestCase)
----------------------------------------------------------------------
Traceback (most recent call last):
  File "assert_test.py", line 11, in test_assert_statement
    assert expected == found
AssertionError


----------------------------------------------------------------------
Ran 2 tests in 0.001s

FAILED (failures=2)
```

There's also an assertRaises helper method for verifying exceptions, which can be used as a context manager in with statements (see Item 82: "Consider contextlib and with Statements for Reusable try/finally Behavior" for how that works). This appears similar to a try/except statement and makes it abundantly clear where the exception is expected to be raised:

```
# utils_error_test.py
from unittest import TestCase, main
from utils import to_str

class UtilsErrorTestCase(TestCase):
    def test_to_str_bad(self):
        with self.assertRaises(TypeError):
            to_str(object())

    def test_to_str_bad_encoding(self):
        with self.assertRaises(UnicodeDecodeError):
            to_str(b"\xfa\xfa")

if __name__ == "__main__":
    main()
```

You can also define your own helper methods with complex logic in TestCase subclasses to make your tests more readable. Just ensure that your method names don't begin with the word test, or they'll be run as if they're test cases. In addition to calling TestCase assertion methods, these custom test helpers often use the fail method to clarify which assumption or invariant wasn't met. For example, here I define a custom test helper method for verifying the behavior of a generator:

```
# helper_test.py
from unittest import TestCase, main

def sum_squares(values):
    cumulative = 0
    for value in values:
        cumulative += value**2
        yield cumulative

class HelperTestCase(TestCase):
    def verify_complex_case(self, values, expected):
        expect_it = iter(expected)
        found_it = iter(sum_squares(values))
        test_it = zip(expect_it, found_it, strict=True)
```

```
        for i, (expect, found) in enumerate(test_it):
            if found != expect:
                self.fail(f"Index {i} is wrong: "
                          f"{found} != {expect}")

    def test_too_short(self):
        values = [1.1, 2.2]
        expected = [1.1**2]
        self.verify_complex_case(values, expected)

    def test_too_long(self):
        values = [1.1, 2.2]
        expected = [
            1.1**2,
            1.1**2 + 2.2**2,
            0,  # Value doesn't matter
        ]
        self.verify_complex_case(values, expected)

    def test_wrong_results(self):
        values = [1.1, 2.2, 3.3]
        expected = [
            1.1**2,
            1.1**2 + 2.2**2,
            1.1**2 + 2.2**2 + 3.3**2 + 4.4**2,
        ]
        self.verify_complex_case(values, expected)

if __name__ == "__main__":
    main()
```

The helper method makes the test cases short and readable, and the outputted error messages are easy to understand:

```
$ python3 helper_test.py
EEF
================================================================
ERROR: test_too_long (__main__.HelperTestCase.test_too_long)
----------------------------------------------------------------
Traceback (most recent call last):
  File "helper_test.py", line 36, in test_too_long
    self.verify_complex_case(values, expected)
    ~~~~~~~~~~~~~~~~~~~~~~~~~^^^^^^^^^^^^^^^^^^^
```

```
    File "helper_test.py", line 20, in verify_complex_case
        for i, (expect, found) in enumerate(test_it):
                                 ~~~~~~~~~~^^^^^^^^^^
ValueError: zip() argument 2 is shorter than argument 1


======================================================================
ERROR: test_too_short (__main__.HelperTestCase.test_too_short)
----------------------------------------------------------------------
Traceback (most recent call last):
    File "helper_test.py", line 27, in test_too_short
        self.verify_complex_case(values, expected)
        ~~~~~~~~~~~~~~~~~~~~~~~~~^^^^^^^^^^^^^^^^^^^
    File "helper_test.py", line 20, in verify_complex_case
        for i, (expect, found) in enumerate(test_it):
                                 ~~~~~~~~~~^^^^^^^^^^
ValueError: zip() argument 2 is longer than argument 1


======================================================================
FAIL: test_wrong_results
➥(__main__.HelperTestCase.test_wrong_results)
----------------------------------------------------------------------
Traceback (most recent call last):
    File "helper_test.py", line 45, in test_wrong_results
        self.verify_complex_case(values, expected)
        ~~~~~~~~~~~~~~~~~~~~~~~~~^^^^^^^^^^^^^^^^^^^
    File "helper_test.py", line 22, in verify_complex_case
        self.fail(f"Index {i} is wrong: {found} != {expect}")
        ~~~~~~~~~^^^^^^^^^^^^^^^^^^^^^^^^^^^^^^^^^^^^^^^^^^^^^^
AssertionError: Index 2 is wrong: 16.939999999999998 != 36.3


----------------------------------------------------------------------
Ran 3 tests in 0.001s

FAILED (failures=1, errors=2)
```

I usually define one TestCase subclass for each set of related tests. Sometimes, I have one TestCase subclass for each function that has many edge cases. Other times, a TestCase subclass spans all functions in a single module. I often create one TestCase subclass for testing each basic class and all of its methods (see Item 109: "Prefer Integration Tests over Unit Tests" for more guidance).

The TestCase class also provides a subTest helper method that enables you to avoid boilerplate by defining multiple tests within a single test method. This is especially helpful for writing data-driven tests, and it allows the test method to continue testing other cases even after one of them fails (similar to the behavior of TestCase with its contained test methods; see Item 110: "Isolate Tests from Each Other with setUp, tearDown, setUpModule, and tearDownModule" for another approach). To show this, here I define an example data-driven test:

```python
# data_driven_test.py
from unittest import TestCase, main
from utils import to_str

class DataDrivenTestCase(TestCase):
    def test_good(self):
        good_cases = [
            (b"my bytes", "my bytes"),
            ("no error", b"no error"),   # This one will fail
            ("other str", "other str"),
            ...
        ]
        for value, expected in good_cases:
            with self.subTest(value):
                self.assertEqual(expected, to_str(value))

    def test_bad(self):
        bad_cases = [
            (object(), TypeError),
            (b"\xfa\xfa", UnicodeDecodeError),
            ...
        ]
        for value, exception in bad_cases:
            with self.subTest(value):
                with self.assertRaises(exception):
                    to_str(value)

if __name__ == "__main__":
    main()
```

The "no error" test case fails, printing a helpful error message, but all of the other cases are still tested and confirmed to pass:

```
$ python3 data_driven_test.py
.
```

```
=================================================================
FAIL: test_good (__main__.DataDrivenTestCase) [no error]
-----------------------------------------------------------------
Traceback (most recent call last):
  File "testing/data_driven_test.py", line 18, in test_good
    self.assertEqual(expected, to_str(value))
AssertionError: b'no error' != 'no error'


-----------------------------------------------------------------
Ran 2 tests in 0.001s

FAILED (failures=1)
```

At some point, depending on your project's complexity and testing requirements, you might outgrow unittest and its capabilities. If and when that happens, the pytest (https://pytest.org) open source package and its large number of community plug-ins can be especially useful as an alternative test runner.

Things to Remember

✦ You can create tests by subclassing the TestCase class from the unittest built-in module and defining one method per behavior you'd like to test. A test method on a TestCase class must start with the word test.

✦ Use the various helper methods defined by the TestCase class, such as assertEqual, to confirm expected behaviors in your tests instead of using the built-in assert statement.

✦ Consider writing data-driven tests using the subTest helper method in order to reduce boilerplate.

Item 109: Prefer Integration Tests over Unit Tests

There are many approaches to software testing that are far broader than Python, including test-driven development, property-based testing, mutation testing, and code and branch coverage reporting. You will find great tools for writing every type and style of automated test imaginable in Python's built-in and community packages (see Item 116: "Know Where to Find Community-Built Modules"). So the question in Python isn't whether you can and should write tests, but instead: How much testing is enough, and what exactly should your tests verify?

It's best to think of tests in Python as an insurance policy on your code. Good tests give you confidence that your code is correct. If you refactor or expand your code, tests that verify behavior—*not* implementation—make it easy to identify what's changed. It sounds counterintuitive, but having well-built tests actually makes it easier to modify Python code, not harder.

As in other languages, testing can exercise many different levels of a codebase. *Unit tests* verify focused pieces of a much larger system. They are useful when you have a lot of edge cases and you need to ensure that everything is handled properly. They are fast to run because they use only a small part of the program. Often they're built using mocks (see Item 111: "Use Mocks to Test Code with Complex Dependencies").

Integration tests verify that multiple components work together. They're often slower to run and harder to write (see Item 110: "Isolate Tests from Each Other with setUp, tearDown, setUpModule, and tearDownModule" for an example). However, integration tests are especially important in Python because you have no guarantee that your subsystems will actually interoperate unless you prove it (see Item 3: "Never Expect Python to Detect Errors at Compile Time"). Statically typed languages can use type information to approximate rough fitting of components, but similarly leveraging types can be much more difficult in dynamic languages (see Item 124: "Consider Static Analysis via typing to Obviate Bugs") or practically infeasible.

Generally in Python it's best to write integration tests. But if you notice that some parts of your code also have a lot of boundary conditions to explore, then it might be worth writing unit tests for those behaviors as well. What you don't want to do is only write unit tests. For example, imagine that I'm building embedded software to control a toaster. Here I define a toaster class that lets me set the "doneness" level, push down the bread, or pop up the toast:

```
class Toaster:
    def __init__(self, timer):
        self.timer = timer
        self.doneness = 3
        self.hot = False

    def _get_duration(self):
        return max(0.1, min(120, self.doneness * 10))

    def push_down(self):
        if self.hot:
            return
```

```
        self.hot = True
        self.timer.countdown(self._get_duration(), self.pop_up)

    def pop_up(self):
        print("Pop!")  # Release the spring
        self.hot = False
        self.timer.end()
```

The Toaster class relies on a timer that ejects the toast when it's done. It should be possible to reset the timer any number of times. Here I use the Timer class from the threading built-in module to implement this:

```
import threading

class ReusableTimer:
    def __init__(self):
        self.timer = None

    def countdown(self, duration, callback):
        self.end()
        self.timer = threading.Timer(duration, callback)
        self.timer.start()

    def end(self):
        if self.timer:
            self.timer.cancel()
```

With these two classes defined, I can easily exercise the toaster's functionality to show that it can apply heat to bread and pop it up before burning it:

```
toaster = Toaster(ReusableTimer())
print("Initially hot:  ", toaster.hot)
toaster.doneness = 5
toaster.push_down()
print("After push down:", toaster.hot)

# Time passes
...
print("After time:     ", toaster.hot)

>>>
Initially hot:   False
After push down: True
```

```
Pop!
After time:      False
```

If I wanted to write a unit test for the Toaster class, I might do something like this with the built-in unittest module (see Item 108: "Verify Related Behaviors in TestCase Subclasses"), where I mock out the
ReusableTimer class entirely:

```
from unittest import TestCase
from unittest.mock import Mock

class ToasterUnitTest(TestCase):

    def test_start(self):
        timer = Mock(spec=ReusableTimer)
        toaster = Toaster(timer)
        toaster.push_down()
        self.assertTrue(toaster.hot)
        timer.countdown.assert_called_once_with(
            30, toaster.pop_up)

    def test_end(self):
        timer = Mock(spec=ReusableTimer)
        toaster = Toaster(timer)
        toaster.hot = True
        toaster.pop_up()
        self.assertFalse(toaster.hot)
        timer.end.assert_called_once()

...

>>>
Pop!
..
----------------------------------------------------------------
Ran 2 tests in 0.000s

OK
```

Writing a unit test for the ReusableTimer class could similarly mock its
dependencies:

```
from unittest import mock

class ReusableTimerUnitTest(TestCase):

    def test_countdown(self):
```

```
        my_func = lambda: None
        with mock.patch("threading.Timer"):
            timer = ReusableTimer()
            timer.countdown(0.1, my_func)
            threading.Timer.assert_called_once_with(0.1, my_func)
            timer.timer.start.assert_called_once()

    def test_end(self):
        my_func = lambda: None
        with mock.patch("threading.Timer"):
            timer = ReusableTimer()
            timer.countdown(0.1, my_func)
            timer.end()
            timer.timer.cancel.assert_called_once()

...

>>>
..
----------------------------------------------------------------
Ran 2 tests in 0.001s

OK
```

These unit tests work, but they require quite a lot of set up and fiddling with mocks. Instead, consider this single integration test that verifies the Toaster and ReusableTimer classes together, without using any mocks:

```
class ToasterIntegrationTest(TestCase):

    def setUp(self):
        self.timer = ReusableTimer()
        self.toaster = Toaster(self.timer)
        self.toaster.doneness = 0

    def test_wait_finish(self):
        self.assertFalse(self.toaster.hot)
        self.toaster.push_down()
        self.assertTrue(self.toaster.hot)
        self.timer.timer.join()
        self.assertFalse(self.toaster.hot)
```

```
def test_cancel_early(self):
    self.assertFalse(self.toaster.hot)
    self.toaster.push_down()
    self.assertTrue(self.toaster.hot)
    self.toaster.pop_up()
    self.assertFalse(self.toaster.hot)
```

```
...

>>>
Pop!
.Pop!

.
----------------------------------------------------------------
Ran 2 tests in 0.108s

OK
```

This test is clear, concise, and focused on the end-to-end behavior instead of implementation details. Perhaps the only gripe I have with it is that it accesses the internals of the ReusableTimer class in order to properly wait for the threading.Timer instance to finish (using the join method). But this is Python, and having that kind of access for testing is one of the language's primary benefits.

The earlier unit tests for the Toaster and ReusableTimer classes, respectively, appear redundant and unnecessarily complex in comparison to this single integration test. However, there is one potential benefit that a unit test could bring to this code: testing the boundaries of the doneness setting to make sure it's never too long or too short:

```
class DonenessUnitTest(TestCase):
    def setUp(self):
        self.toaster = Toaster(ReusableTimer())

    def test_min(self):
        self.toaster.doneness = 0
        self.assertEqual(0.1, self.toaster._get_duration())

    def test_max(self):
        self.toaster.doneness = 1000
        self.assertEqual(120, self.toaster._get_duration())

...
```

```
>>>
..
----------------------------------------------------------------
Ran 2 tests in 0.000s

OK
```

This is the right balance for the tests you should write in Python: Definitely have integration tests for end-to-end behaviors and maybe have unit tests for intricate edge cases. It's easy to avoid mocks most of the time and use them only when there's a compelling reason (see Item 112: "Encapsulate Dependencies to Facilitate Mocking and Testing"). Otherwise, don't forget that you'll still need even larger system tests to verify how your Python programs interact with corresponding web clients, API endpoints, mobile applications, databases, and so on.

Things to Remember

✦ An integration test verifies the behavior of multiple components together, whereas a unit test verifies only an individual component on its own.

✦ Due to the highly dynamic nature of Python, integration tests are the best way—sometimes the only way—to gain confidence about the correctness of a program.

✦ Unit tests can be used in addition to integration tests for verifying parts of a codebase that have a lot of edge cases or boundary conditions.

Item 110: Isolate Tests from Each Other with `setUp`, `tearDown`, `setUpModule`, and `tearDownModule`

`TestCase` subclasses (see Item 108: "Verify Related Behaviors in TestCase Subclasses") often need to have the test environment set up before test methods can be run; this is sometimes called the *test harness*. To do this setup, you can override the `setUp` and `tearDown` methods of the `TestCase` parent class. These methods are called before and after each test method, respectively, allowing you to ensure that each test runs in isolation, which is an important best practice of proper testing.

For example, here I define a `TestCase` subclass that creates a temporary directory before each test and deletes its contents after each test finishes:

```
# environment_test.py
from pathlib import Path
```

```
from tempfile import TemporaryDirectory
from unittest import TestCase, main

class EnvironmentTest(TestCase):
    def setUp(self):
        self.test_dir = TemporaryDirectory()
        self.test_path = Path(self.test_dir.name)

    def tearDown(self):
        self.test_dir.cleanup()

    def test_modify_file(self):
        with open(self.test_path / "data.bin", "w") as f:
            ...

if __name__ == "__main__":
    main()
```

When programs get complicated, you can use additional tests to verify the end-to-end interactions between your modules instead of only testing code in isolation (see Item 109: "Prefer Integration Tests over Unit Tests"). One common problem is that setting up your test environment for integration tests can be computationally expensive and may require a lot of wall-clock time. For example, you might need to start a database process and wait for it to finish loading indexes before you can run your integration tests. This type of latency makes it impractical to do test preparation and cleanup for every test in the TestCase subclass's setUp and tearDown methods.

To handle this situation, the unittest module also supports module-level test harness initialization. You can configure expensive resources a single time, and then have all TestCase classes and their test methods run without repeating that initialization. Later, when all tests in the module are finished, the test harness can be torn down a single time. Here I take advantage of this behavior by defining setUpModule and tearDownModule functions within the module that contains the TestCase subclasses:

```
# integration_test.py
from unittest import TestCase, main

def setUpModule():
    print("* Module setup")

def tearDownModule():
    print("* Module clean-up")
```

```
class IntegrationTest(TestCase):
    def setUp(self):
        print("* Test setup")

    def tearDown(self):
        print("* Test clean-up")

    def test_end_to_end1(self):
        print("* Test 1")

    def test_end_to_end2(self):
        print("* Test 2")

if __name__ == "__main__":
    main()
$ python3 integration_test.py
* Module setup
* Test setup
* Test 1
* Test clean-up
.* Test setup
* Test 2
* Test clean-up
.* Module clean-up


----------------------------------------------------------------
Ran 2 tests in 0.000s

OK
```

The `setUpModule` function is run by `unittest` only once, and it happens before any `setUp` methods are called. Similarly, `tearDownModule` happens after the `tearDown` method is called.

Things to Remember

✦ Use the `setUp` and `tearDown` methods of `TestCase` to make sure your tests are isolated from each other and ensure a clean test environment.

✦ For integration tests, use the `setUpModule` and `tearDownModule` module-level functions to manage any test harnesses you need for the entire lifetime of a test module and all the `TestCase` subclasses that it contains.

Item 111: Use Mocks to Test Code with Complex Dependencies

Another common need when writing tests (see Item 108: "Verify Related Behaviors in TestCase Subclasses") is to use mocked functions and classes to simulate behaviors when it's too difficult or slow to use the real thing. For example, say that I need a program to maintain the feeding schedule for animals at the zoo. Here I define a function to query a database for all the animals of a certain species and then return when they most recently ate:

```
class DatabaseConnection:
    ...

def get_animals(database, species):
    # Query the Database
    ...
    # Return a list of (name, last_mealtime) tuples
```

How do I get a DatabaseConnection instance to use for testing this function? Here I try to create one and pass it into the function being tested:

```
database = DatabaseConnection("localhost", "4444")

get_animals(database, "Meerkat")

>>>
Traceback ...
DatabaseConnectionError: Not connected
```

There's no database running, so of course this fails. One solution is to actually stand up a database server and connect to it in the test. However, it's a lot of work to fully automate starting up a database, configuring its schema, populating it with data, and so on in order to just run a simple unit test. Further, it will probably take a lot of wall-clock time to set up a database server, which would slow down these unit tests and make them harder to maintain (see Item 110: "Isolate Tests from Each Other with setUp, tearDown, setUpModule, and tearDownModule" for one potential solution).

An alternative approach is to mock out the database. A *mock* lets you provide expected responses for dependent functions, given a set of expected calls. It's important not to confuse mocks with fakes. A *fake* would provide most of the behavior of the DatabaseConnection class but with a simpler implementation, such as a basic in-memory, single-threaded database with no persistence.

Python has the `unittest.mock` built-in module for creating mocks and using them in tests. Here I define a `Mock` instance that simulates the `get_animals` function without actually connecting to the database:

```
from datetime import datetime
from unittest.mock import Mock

mock = Mock(spec=get_animals)
expected = [
    ("Spot", datetime(2024, 6, 5, 11, 15)),
    ("Fluffy", datetime(2024, 6, 5, 12, 30)),
    ("Jojo", datetime(2024, 6, 5, 12, 45)),
]
mock.return_value = expected
```

The `Mock` class creates a mock function. The `return_value` attribute of the mock is the value to return when it is called. The `spec` argument indicates that the mock should act like the given object, which is a function in this case, and error if it's used the wrong way. For example, here I try to treat the mock function as if it were a mock object with attributes:

```
mock.does_not_exist
```

```
>>>
Traceback ...
AttributeError: Mock object has no attribute 'does_not_exist'
```

Once it's created, I can call the mock, get its return value, and verify that what it returns matches expectations. I use a unique `object()` value as the database argument because it won't actually be used by the mock to do anything; all I care about is that the database parameter was correctly plumbed through to any dependent functions that needed a `DatabaseConnection` instance in order to work:

```
database = object()
result = mock(database, "Meerkat")
assert result == expected
```

This verifies that the mock responded correctly, but how do I know if the code that called the mock provided the correct arguments? For this, the `Mock` class provides the `assert_called_once_with` method, which verifies that a single call with exactly the given parameters was made:

```
mock.assert_called_once_with(database, "Meerkat")
```

If I supply the wrong parameters, an exception is raised, and any TestCase that the assertion is used in fails:

```
mock.assert_called_once_with(database, "Giraffe")
```

```
>>>
Traceback ...
AssertionError: expected call not found.
Expected: mock(<object object at 0x104728900>, 'Giraffe')
  Actual: mock(<object object at 0x104728900>, 'Meerkat')
```

If I actually don't care about some of the individual parameters, such as exactly which database object was used, then I can indicate that any value is okay for an argument by using the unittest.mock.ANY constant. I can also use the assert_called_with method of Mock to verify that the most recent call to the mock—and there may have been multiple calls in this case—matches my expectations:

```
from unittest.mock import ANY

mock = Mock(spec=get_animals)
mock("database 1", "Rabbit")
mock("database 2", "Bison")
mock("database 3", "Meerkat")

mock.assert_called_with(ANY, "Meerkat")
```

ANY is useful in tests when a parameter is not core to the behavior that's being tested. It's often worth erring on the side of underspecifying tests by using ANY more liberally instead of overspecifying tests and having to plumb through various test parameter expectations.

The Mock class also makes it easy to mock exceptions being raised:

```
class MyError(Exception):
    pass

mock = Mock(spec=get_animals)
mock.side_effect = MyError("Whoops! Big problem")
result = mock(database, "Meerkat")
```

```
>>>
Traceback ...
MyError: Whoops! Big problem
```

There are many more features available, so be sure to see the module documentation for the full range of options (https://docs.python.org/3/library/unittest.mock.html).

Now that I've shown the mechanics of how a Mock object works, I can apply it to an actual testing situation to show how to use it effectively in writing tests. Here I define a function to do the rounds of feeding animals at the zoo, given a set of database-interacting functions:

```python
def get_food_period(database, species):
    # Query the Database
    ...
    # Return a time delta

def feed_animal(database, name, when):
    # Write to the Database
    ...

def do_rounds(database, species):
    now = datetime.now()
    feeding_timedelta = get_food_period(database, species)
    animals = get_animals(database, species)
    fed = 0

    for name, last_mealtime in animals:
        if (now - last_mealtime) > feeding_timedelta:
            feed_animal(database, name, now)
            fed += 1

    return fed
```

The goal of my test is to verify that when do_rounds is run, the right animals got fed, that the latest feeding time was recorded to the database, and that the total number of animals fed returned by the function matches the correct total. In order to do all this, I need to mock out datetime.now so my tests can expect a stable time that isn't affected by when the program is executed. I need to mock out get_food_period and get_animals to return values that would have come from the database. And I need to mock out feed_animal to accept data that would have been written back to the database.

The question is: Even if I know how to create these mock functions and set expectations, how do I get the do_rounds function that's being tested to use the mock dependent functions instead of the real versions? One approach is to inject everything as keyword-only arguments (see Item 37: "Enforce Clarity with Keyword-Only and Positional-Only Arguments" for background):

```python
def do_rounds(
    database,
```

```
    species,
    *,
    now_func=datetime.now,
    food_func=get_food_period,
    animals_func=get_animals,
    feed_func=feed_animal
):
    now = now_func()
    feeding_timedelta = food_func(database, species)
    animals = animals_func(database, species)
    fed = 0

    for name, last_mealtime in animals:
        if (now - last_mealtime) > feeding_timedelta:
            feed_func(database, name, now)
            fed += 1

    return fed
```

To test this function, I need to create all the Mock instances upfront and set their expectations:

```
from datetime import timedelta

now_func = Mock(spec=datetime.now)
now_func.return_value = datetime(2024, 6, 5, 15, 45)

food_func = Mock(spec=get_food_period)
food_func.return_value = timedelta(hours=3)

animals_func = Mock(spec=get_animals)
animals_func.return_value = [
    ("Spot", datetime(2024, 6, 5, 11, 15)),
    ("Fluffy", datetime(2024, 6, 5, 12, 30)),
    ("Jojo", datetime(2024, 6, 5, 12, 45)),
]

feed_func = Mock(spec=feed_animal)
```

Then I can run the test by passing the mocks into the do_rounds function to override the defaults:

```
result = do_rounds(
    database,
    "Meerkat",
```

```
        now_func=now_func,
        food_func=food_func,
        animals_func=animals_func,
        feed_func=feed_func,
)
```

```
assert result == 2
```

Finally, I can verify that all the calls to dependent functions matched my expectations:

```
from unittest.mock import call
```

```
food_func.assert_called_once_with(database, "Meerkat")
```

```
animals_func.assert_called_once_with(database, "Meerkat")
```

```
feed_func.assert_has_calls(
    [
        call(database, "Spot", now_func.return_value),
        call(database, "Fluffy", now_func.return_value),
    ],
    any_order=True,
)
```

I don't verify the parameters to the `datetime.now` mock or how many times it was called because that's indirectly verified by the return value of the function. For `get_food_period` and `get_animals`, I verify a single call with the specified parameters by using `assert_called_once_with`. For the `feed_animal` function, I verify that two calls were made— and their order didn't matter—to write to the database using the `unittest.mock.call` helper and the `assert_has_calls` method.

This approach of using keyword-only arguments for injecting mocks works, but it's quite verbose and requires changing every function you want to test. The `unittest.mock.patch` family of functions makes injecting mocks easier. It temporarily reassigns an attribute of a module or class, such as the database-accessing functions that I defined above. For example, here I override `get_animals` to be a mock using patch:

```
from unittest.mock import patch
```

```
print("Outside patch:", get_animals)
```

```
with patch("__main__.get_animals"):
    print("Inside patch: ", get_animals)

print("Outside again:", get_animals)

>>>
Outside patch: <function get_animals at 0x104eda160>
Inside patch:  <MagicMock name='get_animals' id='4397863264'>
Outside again: <function get_animals at 0x104eda160>
```

patch works for many modules, classes, and attributes. It can be used in with statements (see Item 82: "Consider contextlib and with Statements for Reusable try/finally Behavior"), as a function decorator (see Item 38: "Define Function Decorators with functools.wraps"), or in the setUp and tearDown methods of TestCase classes (see Item 110: "Isolate Tests from Each Other with setUp, tearDown, setUpModule, and tearDownModule").

However, patch doesn't work in all cases. For example, to test do_rounds, I need to mock out the current time returned by the datetime.now class method. Python won't let me do that because the datetime class is defined in a C-extension module, which can't be modified in this way:

```
fake_now = datetime(2024, 6, 5, 15, 45)

with patch("datetime.datetime.now"):
    datetime.now.return_value = fake_now

>>>
Traceback ...
TypeError: cannot set 'now' attribute of immutable type
➡'datetime.datetime'

The above exception was the direct cause of the following
➡exception:

Traceback ...
TypeError: cannot set 'now' attribute of immutable type
➡'datetime.datetime'
```

To work around this, I can create another helper function to fetch time that can be patched:

```
def get_do_rounds_time():
    return datetime.now()
```

```
def do_rounds(database, species):
    now = get_do_rounds_time()
    ...


with patch("__main__.get_do_rounds_time"):
    ...
```

Alternatively, I can use a keyword-only argument for the datetime.now mock and use patch for all of the other mocks:

```
def do_rounds(database, species, *, now_func=datetime.now):
    now = now_func()
    feeding_timedelta = get_food_period(database, species)
    animals = get_animals(database, species)
    fed = 0

    for name, last_mealtime in animals:
        if (now - last_mealtime) > feeding_timedelta:
            feed_animal(database, name, now)
            fed += 1

    return fed
```

I'm going to go with the latter approach. Now I can use the patch.multiple function to create many mocks and then set their expectations:

```
from unittest.mock import DEFAULT


with patch.multiple(
    "__main__",
    autospec=True,
    get_food_period=DEFAULT,
    get_animals=DEFAULT,
    feed_animal=DEFAULT,
):
    now_func = Mock(spec=datetime.now)
    now_func.return_value = datetime(2024, 6, 5, 15, 45)
    get_food_period.return_value = timedelta(hours=3)
    get_animals.return_value = [
        ("Spot", datetime(2024, 6, 5, 11, 15)),
        ("Fluffy", datetime(2024, 6, 5, 12, 30)),
        ("Jojo", datetime(2024, 6, 5, 12, 45)),
    ]
```

The keyword arguments to patch.multiple correspond to names in the __main__ module that I want to override during the test. The DEFAULT value indicates that I want a standard Mock instance to be created for each name. All the generated mocks will adhere to the specification of the objects they are meant to simulate, thanks to the autospec=True parameter.

With the setup ready, I can run the test and verify that the calls were correct inside the with statement that used patch.multiple:

```
result = do_rounds(database, "Meerkat", now_func=now_func)
assert result == 2

get_food_period.assert_called_once_with(database, "Meerkat")
get_animals.assert_called_once_with(database, "Meerkat")
feed_animal.assert_has_calls(
    [
        call(database, "Spot", now_func.return_value),
        call(database, "Fluffy", now_func.return_value),
    ],
    any_order=True,
)
```

These mocks work as expected, but it's important to realize that it's possible to further improve the readability of these tests and reduce boilerplate by refactoring your code to be more testable by design (see Item 112: "Encapsulate Dependencies to Facilitate Mocking and Testing").

Things to Remember

✦ The unittest.mock module provides a way to simulate the behavior of interfaces using the Mock class. Mocks are useful in tests when it's difficult to set up the dependencies that are required by the code that's being tested.

✦ When using mocks, it's important to verify both the behavior of the code being tested and how dependent functions were called by that code, using the Mock.assert_called_once_with family of methods.

✦ Keyword-only arguments and the unittest.mock.patch family of functions can be used to inject mocks into the code being tested.

Item 112: Encapsulate Dependencies to Facilitate Mocking and Testing

In the previous item (see Item 111: "Use Mocks to Test Code with Complex Dependencies"), I showed how to use the facilities of the unittest.mock built-in module—including the Mock class and patch family of functions—to write tests that have complex dependencies, such as a database. However, the resulting test code requires a lot of boilerplate, which could make it more difficult for new readers of the code to understand what the tests are trying to verify.

One way to improve these tests is to use a wrapper object to encapsulate the database's interface instead of passing a DatabaseConnection object to functions as an argument. It's often worth refactoring your code (see Item 123: "Consider warnings to Refactor and Migrate Usage" for one approach) to use better abstractions because it facilitates creating mocks and writing tests. Here I redefine the various database helper functions from the previous item as methods on a class instead of as independent functions:

```python
class ZooDatabase:
    ...

    def get_animals(self, species):
        ...

    def get_food_period(self, species):
        ...

    def feed_animal(self, name, when):
        ...
```

Now I can redefine the do_rounds function to call methods on a ZooDatabase object:

```python
from datetime import datetime

def do_rounds(database, species, *, now_func=datetime.now):
    now = now_func()
    feeding_timedelta = database.get_food_period(species)
    animals = database.get_animals(species)
    fed = 0

    for name, last_mealtime in animals:
        if (now - last_mealtime) >= feeding_timedelta:
```

```
        database.feed_animal(name, now)
        fed += 1

    return fed
```

Writing a test for do_rounds is now a lot easier because I no longer need to use unittest.mock.patch to inject the mock into the code being tested. Instead, I can create a Mock instance to represent a ZooDatabase and pass that in as the database parameter. The Mock class returns a mock object for any attribute name that is accessed. Those attributes can be called like methods, which I can then use to set expectations and verify calls. This makes it easy to mock out all the methods of a class:

```
from unittest.mock import Mock

database = Mock(spec=ZooDatabase)
print(database.feed_animal)
database.feed_animal()
database.feed_animal.assert_any_call()

>>>
<Mock name='mock.feed_animal' id='4386901024'>
```

I can rewrite the Mock setup code using the ZooDatabase encapsulation:

```
from datetime import timedelta
from unittest.mock import call

now_func = Mock(spec=datetime.now)
now_func.return_value = datetime(2019, 6, 5, 15, 45)

database = Mock(spec=ZooDatabase)
database.get_food_period.return_value = timedelta(hours=3)
database.get_animals.return_value = [
    ("Spot", datetime(2019, 6, 5, 11, 15)),
    ("Fluffy", datetime(2019, 6, 5, 12, 30)),
    ("Jojo", datetime(2019, 6, 5, 12, 55)),
]
```

Then I can run the function being tested and verify that all dependent methods were called as expected:

```
result = do_rounds(database, "Meerkat", now_func=now_func)
assert result == 2

database.get_food_period.assert_called_once_with("Meerkat")
database.get_animals.assert_called_once_with("Meerkat")
```

```
database.feed_animal.assert_has_calls(
    [
        call("Spot", now_func.return_value),
        call("Fluffy", now_func.return_value),
    ],
    any_order=True,
)
```

Using the spec parameter to Mock is especially useful when mocking classes because it ensures that the code under test doesn't call a misspelled method name by accident. This allows you to avoid a common pitfall where the same bug is present in both the code and the unit test, masking a real error that will later reveal itself in production:

```
database.bad_method_name()
```

```
>>>
Traceback ...
AttributeError: Mock object has no attribute 'bad_method_name'
```

If I want to test this program end-to-end with a midlevel integration test (see Item 109: "Prefer Integration Tests over Unit Tests"), I still need a way to inject a mock ZooDatabase into the program. I can do this by creating a helper function that acts as a seam for *dependency injection*. Here I define such a helper function that caches a ZooDatabase object in module scope by using a global statement (see Item 120: "Consider Module-Scoped Code to Configure Deployment Environments" for background):

```
DATABASE = None

def get_database():
    global DATABASE
    if DATABASE is None:
        DATABASE = ZooDatabase()
    return DATABASE

def main(argv):
    database = get_database()
    species = argv[1]
    count = do_rounds(database, species)
    print(f"Fed {count} {species}(s)")
    return 0
```

Now I can inject the mock ZooDatabase using patch, run the test, and verify the program's output. I'm not using a mock datetime.now here; instead, I'm relying on the database records returned by the mock to be relative to the current time in order to produce similar behavior to the unit test. This approach is more flaky than mocking everything, but it also tests more surface area:

```
import contextlib
import io
from unittest.mock import patch

with patch("__main__.DATABASE", spec=ZooDatabase):
    now = datetime.now()

    DATABASE.get_food_period.return_value = timedelta(hours=3)
    DATABASE.get_animals.return_value = [
        ("Spot", now - timedelta(minutes=4.5)),
        ("Fluffy", now - timedelta(hours=3.25)),
        ("Jojo", now - timedelta(hours=3)),
    ]

    fake_stdout = io.StringIO()
    with contextlib.redirect_stdout(fake_stdout):
        main(["program name", "Meerkat"])

    found = fake_stdout.getvalue()
    expected = "Fed 2 Meerkat(s)\n"

    assert found == expected
```

The results match my expectations. Creating this integration test was straightforward because I designed the implementation to make it easier to test.

Things to Remember

✦ When unit tests require a lot of repeated boilerplate to set up mocks, one solution may be to encapsulate the functionality of dependencies into classes that are more easily mocked.

✦ The Mock class of the unittest.mock built-in module simulates classes by returning a new mock, which can act as a mock method, for each attribute that is accessed.

✦ For end-to-end tests, it's valuable to refactor your code to have more helper functions that can act as explicit seams to use for injecting mock dependencies in tests.

Item 113: Use assertAlmostEqual to Control Precision in Floating Point Tests

Python's float type is a double-precision floating point number (following the IEEE 754 standard). This scheme has limitations (see Item 106: "Use decimal when Precision Is Paramount"), but floating point numbers are useful for many purposes and are well supported in Python.

Often, it's important to test mathematical code for boundary conditions and other potential sources of error (see Item 109: "Prefer Integration Tests over Unit Tests" for details). Unfortunately, writing automated tests involving floating point numbers can be tricky. For example, here I use the unittest built-in module to define a test that tries (and fails) to verify the result of the expression 5 / 3:

```
import unittest

class MyTestCase(unittest.TestCase):
    def test_equal(self):
        n = 5
        d = 3
        self.assertEqual(1.667, n / d)   # Raises

...

>>>
Traceback ...
AssertionError: 1.667 != 1.6666666666666667
```

The issue is that in Python the expression 5 / 3 results in a number that can't be represented exactly as a float value (which is evidenced by the repeating 6 after the decimal point). The expected value passed to assertEqual, 1.667, isn't sufficiently precise to exactly match the calculated result. (They're different by 0.000333....) Thus, the assertEqual method call fails. I could solve this problem by making the expected result more precise, such as the literal 1.6666666666666667. But in practice, using this level of precision makes numerical tests hard to maintain. The order of operations can produce different results due to rounding behavior. It's also possible for architectural differences (such as x86 vs. AArch64) to affect the results.

Here I show this rounding problem by reordering a calculation in a way that doesn't look like it should affect the results but it does (note the last digit):

```
print(5 / 3 * 0.1)
print(0.1 * 5 / 3)
```

```
>>>
0.16666666666666669
0.16666666666666666
```

To deal with this in automated tests, the assertAlmostEqual helper method in the TestCase class can be used to do approximate comparisons between floating point numbers. It properly deals with infinity and NaN conditions, and minimizes the introduction of error due to rounding. Here I use this method to verify that the numbers are equal when rounded to two decimal places after the decimal point:

```
class MyTestCase2(unittest.TestCase):
    def test_equal(self):
        ...
        # Changed
        self.assertAlmostEqual(1.667, n / d, places=2)
```

```
...

>>>
.
-----------------------------------------------------------------
Ran 1 test in 0.000s

OK
```

The places parameter for assertAlmostEqual works well in verifying numbers with a fractional portion between zero and one. But floating point behavior and repeating decimals might affect larger numbers as well. For example, consider the large difference, in absolute terms, between these two calculations, even though the only change is the addition of 0.001 to one coefficient:

```
print(1e24 / 1.1e16)
print(1e24 / 1.101e16)
```

```
>>>
90909090.9090909
90826521.34423251
```

The difference between these values is approximately 82,569. Depending on the use case, that margin might matter, or it might not. To enable you to express your tolerance for imprecision, you can provide a delta argument to the assertAlmostEqual helper method. This parameter causes the method to consider the absolute difference between the numbers and raise an AssertionError exception only if it's larger than the delta provided.

Here I use this option to specify a tolerance of 100,000, which is more than the 82,569 difference, allowing both assertions to pass:

```
class MyTestCase3(unittest.TestCase):
    def test_equal(self):
        a = 1e24 / 1.1e16
        b = 1e24 / 1.101e16
        self.assertAlmostEqual(90.9e6, a, delta=0.1e6)
        self.assertAlmostEqual(90.9e6, b, delta=0.1e6)
```

In some situations, you might need to assert the opposite: that two numbers are not close to each other given a tolerance or number of decimal places. The TestCase class also provides the assertNotAlmostEqual method to make this easy. To handle more complex use cases when comparing numbers in test code or outside tests, the math built-in module provides the isclose function, which has similar functionality, and more.

Things to Remember

✦ Due to rounding behavior, floating point numbers, especially their fractional parts, might change as a result of the order of operations applied.

✦ Testing floating point values with assertEqual can lead to flaky tests because this method considers the full precision of the numbers being compared.

✦ The assertAlmostEqual and assertNotAlmostEqual methods allow you to specify places or delta parameters to indicate your tolerance for differences when comparing floating point numbers.

Item 114: Consider Interactive Debugging with pdb

Everyone encounters bugs in their code while developing programs. Using the print function can help you track down the sources of many issues (see Item 12: "Understand the Difference Between repr and str when Printing Objects"). Writing tests for specific cases that cause trouble is another great way to identify problems (see Item 109: "Prefer Integration Tests over Unit Tests").

But these tools aren't enough to find every root cause. When you need something more powerful, it's time to try Python's built-in *interactive debugger*. The debugger lets you inspect the state of a running program, print local variables, and step through execution one statement at a time.

In most other programming languages, you use a debugger by specifying what line of a source file you'd like to stop on and then execute the program. In contrast, with Python, the easiest way to use the debugger is by modifying your program to directly initiate the debugger just before you think you'll have an issue worth investigating. This means there is no difference between starting a Python program in order to run the debugger and starting it normally.

To initiate the debugger, all you have to do is call the breakpoint built-in function. This is equivalent to importing the pdb built-in module and running its set_trace function:

```python
# always_breakpoint.py
import math

def compute_rmse(observed, ideal):
    total_err_2 = 0
    count = 0
    for got, wanted in zip(observed, ideal):
        err_2 = (got - wanted) ** 2
        breakpoint()  # Start the debugger here
        total_err_2 += err_2
        count += 1

    mean_err = total_err_2 / count
    rmse = math.sqrt(mean_err)
    return rmse

result = compute_rmse(
    [1.8, 1.7, 3.2, 6],
    [2, 1.5, 3, 5],
)
print(result)
```

As soon as the breakpoint function runs, the program pauses its execution before the line of code immediately following the breakpoint call. The terminal that started the program will turn into a Python debugging shell:

```
$ python3 always_breakpoint.py
> always_breakpoint.py(12)compute_rmse()
-> total_err_2 += err_2
(Pdb)
```

At the (Pdb) prompt, you can type in the names of local variables to see their values printed out (or use p <name>). You can see a list of all local variables by calling the locals built-in function. You can import modules, inspect global state, construct new objects, and even modify parts of the running program. Some Python statements and language features aren't supported in this debugging prompt, but you can access a standard Python REPL with access to program state by using the interact command.

In addition, the debugger has a variety of special commands to control and understand program execution; type help to see the full list. Three very useful commands make inspecting the running program easier:

- **where:** Print the current execution call stack. This lets you figure out where you are in your program and how you arrived at the breakpoint trigger.

- **up:** Move your scope up the execution call stack to the caller of the current function. This allows you to inspect the local variables in higher levels of the program that led to the breakpoint.

- **down:** Move your scope back down the execution call stack one level.

When you're done inspecting the current state, you can use these five debugger commands to control the program's execution in different ways:

- **step:** Run the program until the next line of execution in the program and then return control to the debugger prompt. If the next line of execution includes calling a function, the debugger stops within the function that was called.

- **next:** Run the program until the next line of execution in the current function and then return control to the debugger prompt. If the next line of execution includes calling a function, the debugger will not stop until the called function has returned.

- **return:** Run the program until the current function returns and then return control to the debugger prompt.

- **continue:** Continue running the program until the next breakpoint is hit (either through an explicit breakpoint call or when encountering a breakpoint added by a prior debugger command).

- **quit:** Exit the debugger and end the program. Run this command if you've found the problem, gone too far, or need to make program modifications and try again.

The breakpoint function can be called anywhere in a program. If you know that the problem you're trying to debug happens only under special circumstances, then you can just write plain old Python code to call breakpoint after a specific condition is met. For example, here I start the debugger only if the squared error for a datapoint is more than 1:

```
# conditional_breakpoint.py
def compute_rmse(observed, ideal):
    ...
    for got, wanted in zip(observed, ideal):
        err_2 = (got - wanted) ** 2
        if err_2 >= 1:   # Start the debugger if True
            breakpoint()
        total_err_2 += err_2
        count += 1
    ...

result = compute_rmse(
    [1.8, 1.7, 3.2, 7],
    [2, 1.5, 3, 5],
)
print(result)
```

When I run the program and it enters the debugger, I can confirm that the condition was true by inspecting local variables:

```
$ python3 conditional_breakpoint.py
> conditional_breakpoint.py(14)compute_rmse()
-> total_err_2 += err_2
(Pdb) wanted
5
(Pdb) got
7
(Pdb) err_2
4
```

Another useful way to reach the debugger prompt is by using *postmortem debugging*. This enables you to debug a program *after* it's already raised an exception and crashed. This is especially helpful when you're not quite sure where to put the breakpoint function call. Here I have a script that will crash due to the 7j complex number being present in one of the function's arguments:

```
# postmortem_breakpoint.py
import math
```

```
def compute_rmse(observed, ideal):
    ...


result = compute_rmse(
    [1.8, 1.7, 3.2, 7j],  # Bad input
    [2, 1.5, 3, 5],
)
print(result)
```

I use the command line `python3 -m pdb -c continue <program path>` to run the program under control of the pdb module. The `continue` command tells pdb to get the program started immediately. Once it's running, the program hits a problem and automatically enters the interactive debugger, at which point I can inspect the program state:

```
$ python3 -m pdb -c continue postmortem_breakpoint.py
Traceback (most recent call last):
  File "pdb.py", line 1944, in main
    pdb._run(target)
  File "pdb.py", line 1738, in _run
    self.run(target.code)
  File "bdb.py", line 606, in run
    exec(cmd, globals, locals)
  File "<string>", line 1, in <module>
  File "postmortem_breakpoint.py", line 22, in <module>
    result = compute_rmse(
        [1.8, 1.7, 3.2, 7j],  # Bad input
        [2, 1.5, 3, 5],
    )
  File "postmortem_breakpoint.py", line 17, in compute_rmse
    rmse = math.sqrt(mean_err)
TypeError: must be real number, not complex
Uncaught exception. Entering post mortem debugging
Running 'cont' or 'step' will restart the program
> postmortem_breakpoint.py(17)compute_rmse()
-> rmse = math.sqrt(mean_err)
(Pdb) mean_err
(-5.97-17.5j)
```

You can also use postmortem debugging after hitting an uncaught exception in the interactive Python interpreter by calling the `pm` function of the pdb module (which is often done in a single line as `import pdb; pdb.pm()`):

```
$ python3
>>> import my_module
```

```
>>> my_module.compute_stddev([5])
Traceback (most recent call last):
  File "<stdin>", line 1, in <module>
  File "my_module.py", line 20, in compute_stddev
    variance = compute_variance(data)
               ^^^^^^^^^^^^^^^^^^^^^^
  File "my_module.py", line 15, in compute_variance
    variance = err_2_sum / (len(data) - 1)
               ~~~~~~~~~~~^~~~~~~~~~~~~~~~~
ZeroDivisionError: float division by zero
>>> import pdb; pdb.pm()
> my_module.py(15)compute_variance()
-> variance = err_2_sum / (len(data) - 1)
(Pdb) err_2_sum
0.0
(Pdb) len(data)
1
```

Things to Remember

✦ You can initiate the Python interactive debugger at a point of interest directly in your program by calling the breakpoint built-in
function.

✦ pdb shell commands let you precisely control program execution
and allow you to alternate between inspecting program state and
progressing program execution.

✦ The pdb module can be used to debug exceptions after they happen in independent Python programs (using python   -m   pdb   -c
continue   <program   path>) or the interactive Python interpreter
(using import pdb; pdb.pm()).

Item 115: Use tracemalloc to Understand Memory Usage and Leaks

Memory management in the default implementation of Python, CPython, uses reference counting. This ensures that as soon as all references to an object have expired, the referenced object is also cleared
from memory, freeing up that space for other data. CPython also has
a built-in cycle detector to ensure that self-referencing objects are
eventually garbage collected.

In theory, this means that most Python developers don't have to
worry about allocating or deallocating memory in their programs. It's

taken care of automatically by the language and the CPython runtime. However, in practice, programs eventually do run out of memory when references that are no longer useful are still being held. Figuring out where a Python program is using or leaking memory can be challenging.

One way to debug memory usage is to ask the `gc` built-in module to list every object currently known by the garbage collector. Although it's quite a blunt tool, this approach lets you quickly get a sense of where your program's memory is being used. Here I define a module that fills up memory by keeping references:

```python
# waste_memory.py
import os

class MyObject:
    def __init__(self):
        self.data = os.urandom(100)

def get_data():
    values = []
    for _ in range(100):
        obj = MyObject()
        values.append(obj)
    return values

def run():
    deep_values = []
    for _ in range(100):
        deep_values.append(get_data())
    return deep_values
```

Then I run a program that uses the `gc` built-in module to print out how many objects were created during execution, along with a small sample of allocated objects:

```python
# using_gc.py
import gc

found_objects = gc.get_objects()
print("Before:", len(found_objects))

import waste_memory

hold_reference = waste_memory.run()
```

```
found_objects = gc.get_objects()
print("After: ", len(found_objects))
for obj in found_objects[:3]:
    print(repr(obj)[:100])

>>>
Before: 6207
After:  16801
<waste_memory.MyObject object at 0x10390aeb8>
<waste_memory.MyObject object at 0x10390aef0>
<waste_memory.MyObject object at 0x10390af28>
...
```

The problem with gc.get_objects is that it doesn't tell you anything about *how* the objects were allocated. In complicated programs, objects of a specific class could be allocated many different ways. Knowing the overall number of objects isn't nearly as important as identifying the code responsible for allocating the objects that are leaking memory.

Python 3.4 introduced a new tracemalloc built-in module for solving this problem. tracemalloc makes it possible to connect an object back to where it was allocated. You use it by taking before and after snapshots of memory usage and comparing them to see what's changed. Here I use this approach to print out the top three memory usage offenders in a program:

```
# top_n.py
import tracemalloc

tracemalloc.start(10)                        # Set stack depth
time1 = tracemalloc.take_snapshot()          # Before snapshot

import waste_memory

x = waste_memory.run()                       # Usage to debug
time2 = tracemalloc.take_snapshot()          # After snapshot

stats = time2.compare_to(time1, "lineno")    # Compare snapshots
for stat in stats[:3]:
    print(stat)

>>>
waste_memory.py:5: size=2392 KiB (+2392 KiB), count=29994
➡(+29994), average=82 B
waste_memory.py:10: size=547 KiB (+547 KiB), count=10001
➡(+10001), average=56 B
```

```
waste_memory.py:11: size=82.8 KiB (+82.8 KiB), count=100
➥(+100), average=848 B
```

The size and count labels in the output make it immediately clear which objects are dominating my program's memory usage and where in the source code they were allocated.

The `tracemalloc` module can also print out the full stack trace of each allocation (up to the number of frames passed to the `tracemalloc.start` function). Here I print out the stack trace of the biggest source of memory usage in the program:

```python
# with_trace.py
import tracemalloc

tracemalloc.start(10)
time1 = tracemalloc.take_snapshot()

import waste_memory

x = waste_memory.run()
time2 = tracemalloc.take_snapshot()

stats = time2.compare_to(time1, "traceback")
top = stats[0]
print("Biggest offender is:")
print("\n".join(top.traceback.format()))
```

```
>>>
Biggest offender is:
  File "with_trace.py", line 11
    x = waste_memory.run()
  File "waste_memory.py", line 20
    deep_values.append(get_data())
  File "waste_memory.py", line 12
    obj = MyObject()
  File "waste_memory.py", line 6
    self.data = os.urandom(100)
```

A stack trace like this is most valuable for figuring out which particular usage of a common function or class is responsible for memory consumption in a program.

For more advanced memory profiling needs there are also community packages (see Item 116: "Know Where to Find Community-Built Modules") to consider, such as Memray (https://github.com/bloomberg/memray).

Things to Remember

✦ It can be difficult to understand how Python programs use and leak memory.

✦ The gc module can help you understand which objects exist, but it has no information about how they were allocated.

✦ The tracemalloc built-in module provides powerful tools for understanding the sources of memory usage.

14

Collaboration

Python has language features that help you construct well-defined APIs with clear interface boundaries. The Python community has established best practices to maximize the maintainability of code over time. In addition, some standard tools that ship with Python enable large teams to work together across disparate environments.

Collaborating with others on Python programs requires being deliberate in how you write your code. Even if you're working on your own, chances are you'll be using code written by someone else via the standard library or open source packages. It's important to understand the mechanisms that make it easy to collaborate with other Python programmers.

Item 116: Know Where to Find Community-Built Modules

Python has a central repository of modules (https://pypi.org) that you can install and use in your programs. These modules are built and maintained by people like you: the Python community. When you find yourself facing an unfamiliar challenge, the Python Package Index (PyPI) is a great place to look for code that will get you closer to your goal.

To use the Package Index, you need to use the command-line tool named pip (a recursive acronym for "pip installs packages"). You can run python3 -m pip to ensure that packages are installed for the correct version of Python on your system (see Item 1: "Know Which Version of Python You're Using"). Using pip to install a new module is simple. For example, here I install the numpy module (see Item 94: "Know When and How to Replace Python with Another Programming Language" for related info):

```
$ python3 -m pip install numpy
Collecting numpy
```

```
 Downloading ...
Installing collected packages: numpy
Successfully installed numpy-2.0.0
```

pip is best used together with the built-in module venv to consistently track sets of packages to install for your projects (see Item 117: "Use Virtual Environments for Isolated and Reproducible Dependencies"). You can also create your own PyPI packages to share with the Python community or host your own private package repositories for use with pip.

Each module in PyPI has its own software license. For most of the packages, especially the popular ones, the licenses are free or open source (see https://opensource.org for details). Such a license typically allows you to include a copy of the module with your program (including for end-user distribution; see Item 125: "Prefer Open Source Projects for Bundling Python Programs over zipimport and zipapp"); when in doubt, talk to a lawyer.

Things to Remember

◆ The Python Package Index (PyPI) contains a wealth of common packages that are built and maintained by the Python community.

◆ pip is the command-line tool you can use to install packages from PyPI.

◆ The majority of PyPI modules are free and open source software.

Item 117: Use Virtual Environments for Isolated and Reproducible Dependencies

Building larger and more complex programs often leads you to rely on various packages from the Python community (see Item 116: "Know Where to Find Community-Built Modules"). You'll find yourself running the python3 -m pip command-line tool to install packages like numpy, pandas, and many others.

The problem is that, by default, pip installs new packages in a global location. That causes all Python programs on your system to be affected by these installed modules. In theory, this shouldn't be an issue. If you install a package and never import it, how could it affect your programs?

The trouble comes from transitive dependencies: the packages that the packages you install depend on. For example, after installing the Sphinx package, you can see what it depends on by asking pip:

```
$ python3 -m pip show Sphinx
Name: Sphinx
Version: 7.4.6
Summary: Python documentation generator
Location: /usr/local/lib/python3.13/site-packages
Requires: alabaster, babel, docutils, imagesize, Jinja2,
➥ packaging, Pygments, requests, snowballstemmer,
➥ sphinxcontrib-applehelp, sphinxcontrib-devhelp,
➥ sphinxcontrib-htmlhelp, sphinxcontrib-jsmath,
➥ sphinxcontrib-qthelp, sphinxcontrib-serializinghtml
```

If you install another package like flask, you can see that it, too, depends on the Jinja2 package:

```
$ python3 -m pip show flask
Name: Flask
Version: 3.0.3
Summary: A simple framework for building complex web applications.
Location: /usr/local/lib/python3.13/site-packages
Requires: blinker, click, itsdangerous, Jinja2, Werkzeug
```

A dependency conflict can arise as Sphinx and flask diverge over time. Perhaps right now they both require the same version of Jinja2, and everything is fine. But six months or a year from now, Jinja2 may release a new version that makes breaking changes to users of the library. If you update your global version of Jinja2 with python3 -m pip install --upgrade Jinja2, you may find that Sphinx breaks, while flask keeps working.

The cause of such breakage is that Python can have only a single global version of a module installed at a time. If one of your installed packages must use the new version and another package must use the old version, your system isn't going to work properly; this situation is often called *dependency hell*.

Such breakage can even happen when package maintainers try their best to preserve API compatibility between releases (see Item 119: "Use Packages to Organize Modules and Provide Stable APIs"). New versions of a library can subtly change behaviors that API-consuming code relies on. Users on a system may upgrade one package to a new version but not others, which could break dependencies. If you're not careful, there's a constant risk of the ground moving beneath your feet.

These difficulties are magnified when you collaborate with other developers who do their work on separate computers. It's best to assume the worst: that the versions of Python and global packages that they have installed on their machines will be slightly different than yours. These differences can cause frustrating situations such as a codebase working perfectly on one programmer's machine and being completely broken on another's.

The solution to all of these problems is to use a tool called venv, which provides *virtual environments*. Since Python 3.4, pip and the venv module have been available by default along with the Python installation (accessible with python -m venv).

venv allows you to create isolated versions of the Python environment. Using venv, you can have many different versions of the same package installed on the same system at the same time without conflicts. This means you can work on many different projects and use many different tools on the same computer.

venv does this by installing explicit versions of packages and their dependencies into completely separate directory structures. This makes it possible to reproduce a Python environment that you know will work with your code. It's a reliable way to avoid surprising breakages.

Using venv on the Command Line

Here's a quick tutorial on how to use venv effectively. Before using the tool, it's important to note the meaning of the python3 command line on your system. On my computer, python3 is located in the /usr/local/bin directory and evaluates to version 3.13 (see Item 1: "Know Which Version of Python You're Using"):

```
$ which python3
/usr/local/bin/python3
$ python3 --version
Python 3.13.0
```

To demonstrate the setup of my environment, I can test that running a command to import the numpy module doesn't cause an error. This works because I already have the numpy package installed as a global module:

```
$ python3 -c 'import numpy'
$
```

Now I use venv to create a new virtual environment called myproject. Each virtual environment must live in its own unique directory. The result of the command is a tree of directories and files that are used to manage the virtual environment:

```
$ python3 -m venv myproject
$ cd myproject
$ ls
bin      include     lib     pyvenv.cfg
```

To start using the virtual environment, I use the source command from my shell on the bin/activate script. activate modifies all my environment variables to match the virtual environment. It also updates my command-line prompt to include the virtual environment name (myproject) to make it extremely clear what I'm working on:

```
$ source bin/activate
(myproject)$
```

On Windows the same script is available as:

```
C:\> myproject\Scripts\activate.bat
(myproject) C:>
```

And with PowerShell it is available as:

```
PS C:\> myproject\Scripts\activate.ps1
(myproject) PS C:>
```

After activation, you can see that the path to the python3 command-line tool has moved to within the virtual environment directory:

```
(myproject)$ which python3
/tmp/myproject/bin/python3
(myproject)$ ls -l /tmp/myproject/bin/python3
... -> /usr/local/bin/python3
```

This ensures that changes to the outside system will not affect the virtual environment. Even if the outer system upgrades its default python3 to version 3.14, my virtual environment will still explicitly point to version 3.13.

The virtual environment I created with venv starts with no packages installed except for pip and setuptools. Trying to use the numpy package that was installed as a global module in the outside system will fail because it's unknown to the virtual environment:

```
(myproject)$ python3 -c 'import numpy'
Traceback (most recent call last):
  File "<string>", line 1, in <module>
```

```
    import numpy
ModuleNotFoundError: No module named 'numpy'
```

I can use the `pip` command-line tool to install the `numpy` module into my virtual environment:

```
(myproject)$ python3 -m pip install numpy
Collecting numpy
  Downloading ...
Installing collected packages: numpy
Successfully installed numpy-2.0.0
```

Once it's installed, I can verify that it's working by using the same test import command:

```
(myproject)$ python3 -c 'import numpy'
(myproject)$
```

When I'm done with a virtual environment and want to go back to my default system, I use the `deactivate` command. This restores my environment to the system defaults, including the location of the `python3` command-line tool:

```
(myproject)$ which python3
/tmp/myproject/bin/python3
(myproject)$ deactivate
$ which python3
/usr/local/bin/python3
```

If I ever want to work in the `myproject` environment again, I can just run `source bin/activate` (or the similar command on Windows) in the directory, as before.

Reproducing Dependencies

Once you are in a virtual environment, you can continue installing packages in it with `pip` as you need them. Eventually, you might want to copy your environment somewhere else. For example, say that I want to reproduce the development environment from my workstation on a server in a datacenter. Or maybe I want to clone someone else's environment on my own machine so I can help debug their code. `venv` makes such tasks easy.

I can use the `python3 -m pip freeze` command to save all my explicit package dependencies into a file (which, by convention, is named `requirements.txt`):

```
(myproject)$ python3 -m pip freeze > requirements.txt
(myproject)$ cat requirements.txt
```

```
certifi==2024.7.4
charset-normalizer==3.3.2
idna==3.7
numpy==2.0.0
requests==2.32.3
urllib3==2.2.2
```

Now imagine that I'd like to have another virtual environment that matches the `myproject` environment. I can create a new directory as before by using venv and activating it:

```
$ python3 -m venv otherproject
$ cd otherproject
$ source bin/activate
(otherproject)$
```

The new environment will have no extra packages installed:

```
(otherproject)$ python3 -m pip list
Package Version
------- -------
pip     24.1.1
```

I can install all of the packages from the first environment by running `python3 -m pip install` on the `requirements.txt` file that I generated with the `python3 -m pip freeze` command:

```
(otherproject)$ python3 -m pip install -r
➥/tmp/myproject/ requirements.txt
```

This command cranks along for a little while as it retrieves and installs all the packages required to reproduce the first environment. When it's done, I can list the set of installed packages in the second virtual environment and should see the same list of dependencies found in the first virtual environment:

```
(otherproject)$ python3 -m pip list
Package               Version
------------------    --------
certifi               2024.7.4
charset-normalizer    3.3.2
idna                  3.7
pip                   24.1.1
urllib3               2.2.2
```

Using a `requirements.txt` file is ideal for collaborating with others through a revision control system. You can commit changes to your code at the same time you update your list of package dependencies, ensuring that they move in lockstep. However, it's important to note

that the specific version of Python you're using is *not* included in the
`requirements.txt` file, so that must be managed separately.

The gotcha with virtual environments is that moving them breaks
everything because all the paths, including the `python3` command-line
tool, are hard-coded to the environment's install directory. But ultimately this limitation doesn't matter. The whole purpose of virtual
environments is to make it easy to reproduce a setup. Instead of moving a virtual environment directory, just use `python3 -m pip freeze`
on the old one, create a new virtual environment somewhere else, and
reinstall everything from the `requirements.txt` file.

Things to Remember

✦ Virtual environments allow you to use `pip` to install many different versions of the same package on the same machine without
conflicts.

✦ Virtual environments are created with `python -m venv`, enabled with
`source bin/activate`, and disabled with `deactivate`.

✦ You can dump all the requirements of an environment with
`python3 -m pip freeze`. You can reproduce an environment by running `python3 -m pip install -r requirements.txt`.

Item 118: Write Docstrings for Every Function, Class, and Module

Documentation in Python is extremely important because of the
dynamic nature of the language. Python provides built-in support
for attaching documentation to blocks of code. Unlike with many
other languages, the documentation from a program's source code is
directly accessible as the program runs.

For example, you can add documentation by providing a *docstring*
immediately after the `def` statement of a function:

```
def palindrome(word):
    """Return True if the given word is a palindrome."""
    return word == word[::-1]

assert palindrome("tacocat")
assert not palindrome("banana")
```

You can retrieve the docstring from within the Python program itself
by accessing the function's `__doc__` special attribute:

```
print(palindrome.__doc__)
```

```
>>>
Return True if the given word is a palindrome.
```

You can also use the built-in pydoc module from the command line to run a local web server on your computer that hosts all of the Python documentation that's accessible to your interpreter, including modules that you've written:

```
$ python3 -m pydoc -p 1234
Server ready at http://localhost:1234/
Server commands: [b]rowser, [q]uit
server> b
```

Docstrings can be attached to functions, classes, and modules. Making such a connection is part of the process of compiling and running a Python program. Support for docstrings and the __doc__ attribute has three consequences:

- The accessibility of documentation makes interactive development easier. You can inspect functions, classes, and modules to see their documentation by using the help built-in function. This makes the Python interactive interpreter and tools like Jupyter (https://jupyter.org) a joy to use while you're developing algorithms, testing APIs, and writing code snippets.

- Using a standard way of defining documentation makes it easy to build tools that convert the text into more appealing formats (like HTML). This has led to excellent documentation-generating tools for the Python community, such as Sphinx (https://www.sphinx-doc.org). It has also enabled services like Read the Docs (https://readthedocs.org) that provide free hosting of beautiful-looking documentation for open source Python projects.

- Python's first-class, accessible, and good-looking documentation encourages people to write more documentation. The members of the Python community have a strong belief in the importance of documentation. There's an assumption that "good code" also means well-documented code, and so you can expect most open source Python libraries to have decent documentation.

To participate in this excellent culture of documentation, you need to follow a few guidelines when you write docstrings. The full details are discussed online in PEP 257 (https://www.python.org/dev/peps/pep-0257/). Here are some of the best practices you should be sure to follow.

Documenting Modules

Each module should have a top-level docstring—a string literal that is the first statement in a source file. It should use three double quotes ("""). The goal of this docstring is to introduce the module and its contents.

The first line of the docstring should be a single sentence describing the module's purpose. The paragraphs that follow should contain the details that all users of the module should know about its operation. The module docstring is also a jumping-off point where you can highlight important classes and functions found in the module.

Here's an example of a module docstring:

```
# words.py
#!/usr/bin/env python3
"""Library for finding linguistic patterns in words.

Testing how words relate to each other can be tricky sometimes!
This module provides easy ways to determine when words you've
found have special properties.

Available functions:
- palindrome: Determine if a word is a palindrome.
- check_anagram: Determine if two words are anagrams.
...
"""


...
```

If the module is a command-line utility, the module docstring is also a great place to put usage information for running the tool.

Documenting Classes

Each class should have a class-level docstring that largely follows the same pattern as the module-level docstring. The first line is the single-sentence purpose of the class. Paragraphs that follow discuss important details of the class's operation.

Important public attributes and methods of the class should be highlighted in the class-level docstring. It should also provide guidance to subclasses on how to properly interact with protected attributes (see Item 55: "Prefer Public Attributes over Private Ones") and the superclass's methods (see Item 53: "Initialize Parent Classes with super").

Here's an example of a class docstring:

```
class Player:
    """Represents a player of the game.

    Subclasses may override the 'tick' method to provide
    custom animations for the player's movement depending
    on their power level, etc.

    Public attributes:
    - power: Unused power-ups (float between 0 and 1).
    - coins: Coins found during the level (integer).
    """

    ...
```

Documenting Functions

Each public function and method should have a docstring that follows the same pattern as the docstrings for modules and classes. The first line is a single-sentence description of what the function does. The paragraphs that follow describe any specific behaviors and the arguments for the function. Any return values should be mentioned, and any exceptions that callers must handle as part of the function's interface should be explained (see Item 32: "Prefer Raising Exceptions to Returning None" for an example).

Here's an example of a function docstring:

```
def find_anagrams(word, dictionary):
    """Find all anagrams for a word.

    This function only runs as fast as the test for
    membership in the 'dictionary' container.

    Args:
        word: String of the target word.
        dictionary: collections.abc.Container with all
            strings that are known to be actual words.

    Returns:
        List of anagrams that were found. Empty if
        none were found.
    """

    ...
```

There are also some special cases in writing docstrings for functions that are important to know:

- If a function has no arguments and a simple return value, a single-sentence description is probably good enough.

- If a function doesn't return anything, it's better to leave out any mention of the return value than to say "returns `None`."

- If a function's interface includes raising exceptions, then your docstring should describe each exception that's raised and when it's raised.

- If you don't expect a function to raise an exception during normal operation, don't mention that fact.

- If a function accepts a variable number of arguments (see Item 34: "Reduce Visual Noise with Variable Positional Arguments") or keyword arguments (see Item 35: "Provide Optional Behavior with Keyword Arguments"), use `*args` and `**kwargs` in the documented list of arguments to describe their purpose.

- If a function has arguments with default values, those defaults should be mentioned (see Item 36: "Use `None` and Docstrings to Specify Dynamic Default Arguments").

- If a function is a generator (see Item 43: "Consider Generators Instead of Returning Lists"), its docstring should describe what the generator yields when it's iterated.

- If a function is an asynchronous coroutine (see Item 75: "Achieve Highly Concurrent I/O with Coroutines"), its docstring should explain when it will stop execution.

Using Docstrings and Type Annotations

Python now supports type annotations for a variety of purposes (see Item 124: "Consider Static Analysis via `typing` to Obviate Bugs" for how to use them). The information they contain may be redundant with typical docstrings. For example, here is the function signature for `find_anagrams` with type annotations applied:

```
from collections.abc import Container

def find_anagrams(word: str,
                  dictionary: Container[str]) -> list[str]:
    ...
```

There is no longer a need to specify in the docstring that the word argument is a string, since the type annotation has that information. The same goes for the dictionary argument being a collections.abc.Container. There's no reason to mention that the return type will be a list, since this fact is clearly annotated as such. And when no anagrams are found, the return value still must be a list, so it's implied that it will be empty; that doesn't need to be noted in the docstring. Here I write the same function signature from above along with the docstring that has been shortened accordingly:

```
def find_anagrams(word: str,
                  dictionary: Container[str]) -> list[str]:
    """Find all anagrams for a word.

    This function only runs as fast as the test for
    membership in the 'dictionary' container.

    Args:
        word: Target word.
        dictionary: All known actual words.

    Returns:
        Anagrams that were found.
    """
    ...
```

The redundancy between type annotations and docstrings should be similarly avoided for instance fields, class attributes, and methods. It's best to have type information in only one place so there's less risk that it will skew from the actual implementation.

Things to Remember

✦ Write documentation for every module, class, method, and function using docstrings. Keep them up-to-date as your code changes.

✦ For a module, introduce the contents of the module and any important classes or functions that all users should know about.

✦ For a class, document behavior, important attributes, and subclass behavior in the docstring following the class statement.

✦ For a function or method, document every argument, returned value, raised exception, and other behaviors in the docstring following the def statement.

✦ If you're using type annotations, omit that information from docstrings since it would be redundant to have it in both places.

Item 119: Use Packages to Organize Modules and Provide Stable APIs

As the size of a program's codebase grows, it's natural for you to reorganize its structure. You'll split larger functions into smaller functions. You'll refactor data structures into helper classes (see Item 29: "Compose Classes Instead of Deeply Nesting Dictionaries, Lists, and Tuples" for an example). You'll separate functionality into various modules that depend on each other.

At some point, you'll find yourself with so many modules that you need another layer in your program to make it understandable. For this purpose, Python provides *packages*. Packages are modules that contain other modules.

In most cases, packages are defined by putting an empty file named __init__.py into a directory. Once __init__.py is present, any other Python files in that directory will be available for import, using a path relative to the directory. For example, imagine that I have the following directory structure in a program:

```
main.py
mypackage/__init__.py
mypackage/models.py
mypackage/utils.py
```

To import the `utils` module, I can use the absolute module name that includes the package directory's name:

```
# main.py
import mypackage.utils
```

I can also import a child module name relative to its containing package using the `from` clause:

```
# main2.py
from mypackage import utils
```

This dotted path pattern for the `import` statement continues when I have package directories nested within other packages (like `import mypackage.foo.bar` and `from mypackage.foo import bar`).

The functionality provided by packages has two primary purposes in Python programs.

Namespaces

The first use of packages is to help divide your modules into separate namespaces. They enable you to have many modules with the same filename but different absolute paths that are unique. For example, here's a program that imports attributes from two modules with the same filename, utils.py:

```
# main.py
from analysis.utils import log_base2_bucket
from frontend.utils import stringify

bucket = stringify(log_base2_bucket(33))
```

This approach breaks when the functions, classes, or submodules defined in packages have the same names. For example, say that I want to use the inspect function from both the analysis.utils and the frontend.utils modules. Importing the attributes directly won't work because the second import statement will overwrite the value of inspect in the current scope.

```
# main2.py
from analysis.utils import inspect
from frontend.utils import inspect  # Overwrites!
```

The solution is to use the as clause of the import statement to rename whatever I've imported for the current scope:

```
# main3.py
from analysis.utils import inspect as analysis_inspect
from frontend.utils import inspect as frontend_inspect

value = 33
if analysis_inspect(value) == frontend_inspect(value):
    print("Inspection equal!")
```

The as clause can be used to rename anything retrieved with the import statement, including entire modules. This facilitates accessing namespaced code and makes its identity clear when you use it.

Another approach for avoiding imported name conflicts is to always access names by their highest unique module name. For the example above, this means I'd use basic import statements instead of the from clause:

```
# main4.py
import analysis.utils
import frontend.utils

value = 33
if (analysis.utils.inspect(value) ==
        frontend.utils.inspect(value)):
    print("Inspection equal!")
```

This approach allows you to avoid the as clause altogether. It also makes it abundantly clear to new readers of the code where each of the similarly named functions is defined.

Stable APIs

The second use of packages in Python is to provide strict, stable APIs for external consumers.

When you're writing an API for wider consumption, such as an open source package (see Item 116: "Know Where to Find Community-Built Modules" for examples), you'll want to provide stable functionality that doesn't change between releases. To ensure that happens, it's important to hide your internal code organization from external users. This way, you can refactor and improve your package's internal modules without breaking existing users.

Python can limit the surface area exposed to API consumers by using the __all__ special attribute of a module or package. The value of __all__ is a list of every name to export from the module as part of its public API. When consuming code executes from foo import *—details on this below—only the attributes in foo.__all__ will be imported from foo. If __all__ isn't present in foo, then only public attributes—those without a leading underscore—are imported (see Item 55: "Prefer Public Attributes over Private Ones" for details about that convention).

For example, say that I want to provide a package for calculating collisions between moving projectiles. Here I define the models module of mypackage to contain the representation of projectiles:

```
# models.py
__all__ = ["Projectile"]

class Projectile:
    def __init__(self, mass, velocity):
        self.mass = mass
        self.velocity = velocity
```

I also define a utils module in mypackage to perform operations on the Projectile instances, such as simulating collisions between them:

```
# utils.py
from .models import Projectile


__all__ = ["simulate_collision"]
```

```
def _dot_product(a, b):
    ...

def simulate_collision(a, b):
    ...
```

Now I'd like to provide all of the public parts of this API as a set of attributes that are available on the mypackage module. This will allow downstream consumers to always import directly from mypackage instead of importing from mypackage.models or mypackage.utils. This ensures that the API consumer's code will continue to work even if the internal organization of mypackage changes (e.g., if models.py is deleted).

To do this with Python packages, you need to modify the __init__.py file in the mypackage directory. This file is what actually becomes the contents of the mypackage module when it's imported. Thus, you can specify an explicit API for mypackage by limiting what you import into __init__.py. Since all of my internal modules already specify __all__, I can expose the public interface of mypackage by simply import-ing everything from the internal modules and updating __all__ accordingly:

```
# __init__.py
__all__ = []
from .models import *

__all__ += models.__all__
from .utils import *

__all__ += utils.__all__
```

Here's a consumer of the API that directly imports from mypackage instead of accessing the inner modules:

```
# api_consumer.py
from mypackage import *

a = Projectile(1.5, 3)
b = Projectile(4, 1.7)
after_a, after_b = simulate_collision(a, b)
```

Notably, internal-only functions like mypackage.utils._dot_product will not be available to the API consumer on mypackage because they weren't present in __all__. Being omitted from __all__ also means that they weren't imported by the from mypackage import * state-ment. The internal-only names are effectively hidden.

This whole approach works great when it's important to provide an explicit, stable API. However, if you're building an API for use between your own modules, the functionality of __all__ is probably unnecessary and should be avoided. The namespacing provided by packages is usually enough for a team of programmers to collaborate on large amounts of code they control while maintaining reasonable interface boundaries.

Beware of import *

Import statements like from x import y are clear because the source of y is explicitly the x package or module. Wildcard imports like from foo import * can also be useful, especially in interactive Python sessions. However, wildcards make code more difficult to understand:

- from foo import * hides the sources of names from new readers of the code. If a module has multiple import * statements, the reader needs to check all of the referenced modules to figure out where a name was defined.

- Names from import * statements will overwrite any conflicting names within the containing module. This can lead to strange bugs caused by accidental interactions between your code and names reassigned by successive import * statements.

The safest approach is to avoid import * in your code and explicitly import names with the from x import y style.

Things to Remember

✦ Packages in Python are modules that contain other modules. Packages allow you to organize your code into separate, non-conflicting namespaces with unique absolute module names.

✦ Simple packages are defined by adding an __init__.py file to a directory that contains other source files. These files become the child modules of the directory's package. Package directories may also contain other packages.

✦ You can provide an explicit API for a module by listing its publicly visible names in its __all__ special attribute.

✦ You can hide a package's internal implementation by only importing public names in the package's __init__.py file or by naming internal-only members with a leading underscore.

✦ When collaborating within a single team or on a single codebase, using __all__ for explicit APIs is probably unnecessary.

Item 120: Consider Module-Scoped Code to Configure Deployment Environments

A deployment environment is a configuration in which a program runs. Every program has at least one deployment environment: the *production environment*. The goal of writing a program in the first place is to put it to work in the production environment and achieve some kind of outcome.

Writing or modifying a program requires being able to run it on the computer you use for developing. The configuration of your *development environment* might be very different from that of your production environment. For example, you might be using a tiny single-board computer to develop a program that's meant to run on enormous supercomputers.

Tools like venv (see Item 117: "Use Virtual Environments for Isolated and Reproducible Dependencies") make it easy to ensure that all environments have the same Python packages installed. The trouble is that production environments often require many external assumptions that are hard to reproduce in development environments.

For example, say that I want to run a program in a web server container and give it access to a database. Every time I want to modify my program's code, I need to run a server container, the database schema must be set up properly, and my program needs the password for access. This is a very high cost if all I'm trying to do is verify that a one-line change to my program works correctly.

The best way to work around such issues is to override parts of a program at startup time to provide different functionality depending on the deployment environment. For example, I can have two different __main__ files—one for production and one for development:

```
# dev_main.py
TESTING = True

import db_connection

db = db_connection.Database()
```

```
# prod_main.py
TESTING = False

import db_connection

db = db_connection.Database()
```

The only difference between the two files is the value of the TESTING constant. Other modules in my program can then import the __main__ module and use the value of TESTING to decide how they define their own attributes:

```
# db_connection.py
import __main__

class TestingDatabase:
    ...

class RealDatabase:
    ...

if __main__.TESTING:
    Database = TestingDatabase
else:
    Database = RealDatabase
```

The key behavior to notice here is that code running in module scope—not inside a function or method—is just normal Python code (see Item 98: "Lazy-Load Modules with Dynamic Imports to Reduce Startup Time" for details). You can use an if statement at the module level to decide how the module will define names. This makes it easy to tailor modules to your various deployment environments. You can avoid having to reproduce costly assumptions like database configurations when they aren't needed. You can inject local or fake implementations that ease interactive development, or you can use mocks for writing tests (see Item 111: "Use Mocks to Test Code with Complex Dependencies").

Note

When your deployment environment configuration gets really complicated, you should consider moving it out of Python constants (like TESTING) and into dedicated configuration files. Tools like the configparser built-in module let you maintain production configurations separately from code, a distinction that's crucial for collaborating with an operations team.

Module-scoped code can be used for more than dealing with external configurations. For example, if I know that my program must work differently depending on its host platform, I can inspect the sys module before defining top-level constructs in a module:

```
# db_connection.py
import sys
```

```
class Win32Database:
    ...

class PosixDatabase:
    ...

if sys.platform.startswith("win32"):
    Database = Win32Database
else:
    Database = PosixDatabase
```

Similarly, I could use environment variables from os.environ to guide my module definitions to match other constraints and requirements of the system.

Things to Remember

◆ Programs often need to run in multiple deployment environments that each have unique assumptions and configurations.

◆ You can tailor a module's contents to different deployment environments by using normal Python statements in module scope.

◆ Module contents can be the product of any external condition, including host introspection through the sys and os modules.

Item 121: Define a Root Exception to Insulate Callers from APIs

When you're defining a module's API, the exceptions you raise are just as much a part of your interface as the functions and classes you define (see Item 32: "Prefer Raising Exceptions to Returning None" for an example of why).

Python has a built-in hierarchy of exceptions for the language and standard library (see Item 86: "Understand the Difference Between Exception and BaseException" for background). There's a draw to using the built-in exception types for reporting errors instead of defining your own new types. For example, I could raise a ValueError exception whenever an invalid parameter is passed to a function in one of my modules:

```
# my_module.py
def determine_weight(volume, density):
    if density <= 0:
        raise ValueError("Density must be positive")
    ...
```

In some cases, using ValueError makes sense, but for APIs, it's much more powerful to define a new hierarchy of exceptions. I can do this by providing a root Exception class in my module and having all other exceptions raised by that module inherit from the root exception:

```
# my_module.py
class Error(Exception):
    """Base-class for all exceptions raised by this module."""

class InvalidDensityError(Error):
    """There was a problem with a provided density value."""

class InvalidVolumeError(Error):
    """There was a problem with the provided weight value."""

def determine_weight(volume, density):
    if density < 0:
        raise InvalidDensityError("Density must be positive")
    if volume < 0:
        raise InvalidVolumeError("Volume must be positive")
    if volume == 0:
        density / volume
```

Having a root exception in a module makes it easy for consumers of an API to catch all the exceptions that were raised deliberately. For example, here a consumer of my API makes a function call with a try/except statement that catches my root exception:

```
try:
    weight = my_module.determine_weight(1, -1)
except my_module.Error:
    logging.exception("Unexpected error")

>>>
Unexpected error
Traceback (most recent call last):
  File ".../example.py", line 3, in <module>
    weight = my_module.determine_weight(1, -1)
  File ".../my_module.py", line 10, in determine_weight
    raise InvalidDensityError("Density must be positive")
InvalidDensityError: Density must be positive
```

The logging.exception function prints the full stack trace of the caught exception so it's easier to debug in this situation. The try/except also prevents my API's exceptions from propagating too far upward and breaking the calling program. It insulates the calling code from my API. This insulation has three helpful effects.

First, root exceptions let callers understand when there's a problem with their usage of an API. If callers are using my API properly, they should catch the various exceptions that I deliberately raise. If they don't handle such an exception, it will propagate all the way up to the insulating except block that catches my module's root exception. That block can bring the exception to the attention of the API consumer, providing an opportunity for them to add proper handling of the missed exception type:

```
try:
    weight = my_module.determine_weight(-1, 1)
except my_module.InvalidDensityError:
    weight = 0
except my_module.Error:
    logging.exception("Bug in the calling code")

>>>
Bug in the calling code
Traceback (most recent call last):
  File ".../example.py", line 3, in <module>
    weight = my_module.determine_weight(-1, 1)
  File ".../my_module.py", line 12, in determine_weight
    raise InvalidVolumeError("Volume must be positive")
InvalidVolumeError: Volume must be positive
```

The second advantage of using root exceptions is that they can help find bugs in an API module's code. If my code only deliberately raises exceptions that I define within my module's hierarchy, then all other types of exceptions raised by my module must be the ones that I didn't intend to raise. These are bugs in my API's code.

Using the try/except statement above will not insulate API consumers from bugs in my API module's code. To do that, the caller needs to add another except block that catches Python's Exception base class (see Item 85: "Beware of Catching the Exception Class" for details). This allows the API consumer to detect when there's a bug in the API module's implementation that needs to be fixed.

The output for this example includes both the logging.exception message and the default interpreter output for the exception since it was re-raised:

```
try:
    weight = my_module.determine_weight(0, 1)
except my_module.InvalidDensityError:
    weight = 0
except my_module.Error:
```

```
    logging.exception("Bug in the calling code")
except Exception:
    logging.exception("Bug in the API code!")
    raise  # Re-raise exception to the caller

>>>
Bug in the API code!
Traceback (most recent call last):
  File ".../example.py", line 3, in <module>
    weight = my_module.determine_weight(0, 1)
  File ".../my_module.py", line 14, in determine_weight
    density / volume
    ~~~~~~~~^~~~~~~~
ZeroDivisionError: division by zero
Traceback ...
ZeroDivisionError: division by zero
```

The third impact of using root exceptions is future-proofing an API.
Over time, I might want to expand my API to provide more specific exceptions in certain situations. For example, I could add an
Exception subclass that indicates the error condition of supplying
negative densities:

```
# my_module.py
...


class NegativeDensityError(InvalidDensityError):
    """A provided density value was negative."""


...


def determine_weight(volume, density):
    if density < 0:
        raise NegativeDensityError("Density must be positive")
    ...
```

The calling code would continue to work exactly as before because it
already catches InvalidDensityError exceptions (the parent class of
NegativeDensityError). In the future, the caller could decide to spe-
cial-case the new type of exception and change the handling behavior
accordingly:

```
try:
    weight = my_module.determine_weight(1, -1)
except my_module.NegativeDensityError:
    raise ValueError("Must supply non-negative density")
```

```
except my_module.InvalidDensityError:
    weight = 0
except my_module.Error:
    logging.exception("Bug in the calling code")
except Exception:
    logging.exception("Bug in the API code!")
    raise

>>>
Traceback ...
NegativeDensityError: Density must be positive

The above exception was the direct cause of the following
➥ exception:

Traceback ...
ValueError: Must supply non-negative density
```

I can take API future-proofing further by providing a broader set of exceptions directly below the root exception. For example, imagine that that I have one set of errors related to calculating weights, another related to calculating volume, and a third related to calculating density:

```
# my_module.py
class Error(Exception):
    """Base-class for all exceptions raised by this module."""

class WeightError(Error):
    """Base-class for weight calculation errors."""

class VolumeError(Error):
    """Base-class for volume calculation errors."""

class DensityError(Error):
    """Base-class for density calculation errors."""

...
```

Specific exceptions would inherit from these general exceptions. Each intermediate exception acts as its own kind of root exception. This makes it easier to insulate layers of calling code from API code based on broad functionality. This is much better than having all callers catch a long list of very specific Exception subclasses.

Things to Remember

✦ When a module defines a root exception and only raises its child classes, API consumers have a simple way to isolate themselves from unexpected situations encountered by the module.

✦ Catching root exceptions can help you find bugs in code that consumes an API.

✦ Catching the Python Exception base class can help you find bugs in API implementations.

✦ Intermediate root exceptions let you raise more specific types of exceptions in the future without breaking API consumers.

Item 122: Know How to Break Circular Dependencies

Inevitably, while you're collaborating with others, you'll find a mutual interdependence between modules. This can even happen when you work by yourself on the various parts of a single program.

For example, say that I want my GUI application to show a dialog box for choosing where to save a document. The data displayed by the dialog could be specified through arguments to my event handlers. But the dialog also needs to read global state, such as user preferences, to know how to render properly.

Here I define a dialog that retrieves the default document save location from global preferences:

```
# dialog.py
import app

class Dialog:
    def __init__(self, save_dir):
        self.save_dir = save_dir

    ...

save_dialog = Dialog(app.prefs.get("save_dir"))

def show():
    ...
```

The problem is that the app module that contains the prefs object also imports the dialog class in order to show the same dialog on program start:

```
# app.py
import dialog
```

```
class Prefs:
    ...
    def get(self, name):
        ...

prefs = Prefs()
dialog.show()
```

It's a circular dependency. If I try to import the app module from my main program like this:

```
# main.py
import app
```

I get an exception:

```
$ python3 main.py
Traceback (most recent call last):
  File ".../main.py", line 4, in <module>
    import app
  File ".../app.py", line 4, in <module>
    import dialog
  File ".../dialog.py", line 15, in <module>
    save_dialog = Dialog(app.prefs.get("save_dir"))
                         ^^^^^^^^^
AttributeError: partially initialized module 'app' has no
➥ attribute 'prefs' (most likely due to a circular import)
```

To understand what's happening here, you need to know how Python's import machinery works in general. When a module is imported, here's what Python actually does, in depth-first order (see https://docs.python.org/3/library/importlib.html for the full details):

1. Searches for the module in locations from `sys.path`

2. Loads the code from the module and ensures that it compiles

3. Creates a corresponding empty module object

4. Inserts the module into `sys.modules`

5. Runs the code in the module object to define its contents

The problem with a circular dependency is that the attributes of a module aren't defined until the code for those attributes has executed (after step 5). But the module can be loaded with the `import` statement immediately after it's inserted into `sys.modules` (after step 4).

In the example above, the app module imports `dialog` before defining anything. Then the `dialog` module imports app. Since app still hasn't finished running—it's currently importing dialog—the app module is empty (from step 4). The AttributeError exception is raised (during step 5 for dialog) because the code that defines prefs hasn't run yet (i.e., step 5 for app isn't complete).

The best solution to this problem is to refactor the code so that the prefs data structure is at the bottom of the dependency tree. Then both app and dialog can import the same utility module and avoid any circular dependencies. But such a clear division isn't always possible or could require too much refactoring to be worth the effort.

There are three other ways to break circular dependencies.

Reordering Imports

The first approach to the circular imports problem is to change the order of imports. For example, if I import the dialog module toward the bottom of the app module, after the app module's other contents have run, the AttributeError exception goes away:

```
# app.py
class Prefs:
    ...

prefs = Prefs()

import dialog  # Moved

dialog.show()
```

This works because, when the dialog module is loaded late, its recursive import of app finds that app.prefs has already been defined (i.e., step 5 is mostly done for app).

Although this solution avoids the AttributeError exception, it goes against the PEP 8 style guide (see Item 2: "Follow the PEP 8 Style Guide"). The style guide suggests that you always put imports at the top of your Python files. This makes your module's dependencies clear to new readers of the code. It also ensures that any module you depend on is in scope and available to all the code in your module.

Having imports later in a file can be brittle and can cause small changes in the ordering of your code to break the module entirely. I suggest not using import reordering to solve your circular dependency issues.

Import, Configure, Run

A second solution to the circular imports problem is to have modules minimize side effects at import time. For example, I can have my modules only define functions, classes, and constants. I specifically avoid running any functions at import time. Then I have each module provide a configure function that I can call when all other modules have finished importing. The purpose of configure is to prepare each module's state by accessing the attributes of other modules. I run configure after all modules have been imported (i.e., when step 5 is complete), so all attributes must be defined.

Here I redefine the dialog module to only access the prefs object when configure is called:

```
# dialog.py
import app

class Dialog:
    ...

save_dialog = Dialog()

def show():
    ...

def configure():
    save_dialog.save_dir = app.prefs.get("save_dir")
```

I also redefine the app module to not run any activities on import:

```
# app.py
import dialog

class Prefs:
    ...

prefs = Prefs()

def configure():
    ...
```

Finally, the main module has three distinct phases of execution—import everything, configure everything, and run the first activity:

```
# main.py
import app
```

```
import dialog

app.configure()
dialog.configure()

dialog.show()
```

This works well in many situations and enables patterns like *dependency injection* (see Item 112: "Encapsulate Dependencies to Facilitate Mocking and Testing" for a similar example). But sometimes it can be difficult to structure your code so that an explicit configure step is possible. Having two distinct phases within a module can also make your code harder to read because it separates the definition of objects from their configuration.

Dynamic Import

The third—and often simplest—solution to the circular imports problem is to use an import statement within a function or method. This is called a *dynamic import* because the module import happens while the program is running, not while the program is first starting up and initializing its modules.

Here I redefine the dialog module to use a dynamic import. The dialog.show function imports the app module at runtime instead of the dialog module importing app at initialization time:

```
# dialog.py
class Dialog:
    ...

save_dialog = Dialog()

def show():
    import app  # Dynamic import

    save_dialog.save_dir = app.prefs.get("save_dir")
    ...
```

The app module can now be the same as it was in the original example. It imports dialog at the top and calls dialog.show at the bottom:

```
# app.py
import dialog

class Prefs:
    ...
```

```
prefs = Prefs()
dialog.show()
```

This approach has a similar effect to the import, configure, and run steps from before. The difference is that it requires no structural changes to the way the modules are defined and imported. I'm simply delaying the circular import until the moment I must access the other module. At that point, I can be pretty sure that all other modules have already been initialized (as step 5 is complete for everything).

In general, it's good to avoid dynamic imports like this. The cost of the import statement is not negligible and can be especially bad in tight loops (see Item 98: "Lazy-Load Modules with Dynamic Imports to Reduce Startup Time" for an example). By delaying execution, dynamic imports also set you up for surprising failures at runtime, such as SyntaxError exceptions long after your program has started running (see Item 108: "Verify Related Behaviors in TestCase Subclasses" for how to avoid that). However, these downsides are often better than the alternative of restructuring your entire program.

Things to Remember

+ Circular dependencies happen when two modules must call into each other at import time. They can cause your program to crash at startup.

+ The best way to break a circular dependency is to refactor mutual dependencies into a separate module at the bottom of the dependency tree.

+ Dynamic imports are the simplest solution for breaking a circular dependency between modules while minimizing refactoring and complexity.

Item 123: Consider warnings to Refactor and Migrate Usage

It's natural for APIs to change in order to satisfy new requirements that meet formerly unanticipated needs. When an API is small and has few upstream or downstream dependencies, making such changes is straightforward. One programmer can often update a small API and all of its callers in a single commit to the source code repository.

However, as a codebase grows, the number of callers of an API can become so large or fragmented across repositories that it's infeasible or impractical to make API changes in lockstep with updating callers to match. Instead, you need a way to notify and encourage the people you collaborate with to refactor their code and migrate their API usage to the latest forms.

For example, say that I want to provide a module for calculating how far a car will travel at a given average speed and duration. Here I define such a function and assume that speed is in miles per hour and duration is in hours:

```
def print_distance(speed, duration):
    distance = speed * duration
    print(f"{distance} miles")

print_distance(5, 2.5)

>>>
12.5 miles
```

Imagine that this works so well that I quickly gather a large number of dependencies on this function. Other programmers that I collaborate with need to calculate and print distances like this all across our shared codebase.

Despite its success, this implementation is error prone because the units for the arguments are implicit. For example, if I wanted to see how far a bullet travels in 3 seconds at 1000 meters per second, I would get the wrong result:

```
print_distance(1000, 3)

>>>
3000 miles
```

I can address this problem by expanding the API of print_distance to include optional keyword arguments (see Item 37: "Enforce Clarity with Keyword-Only and Positional-Only Arguments") for the units of speed, duration, and the computed distance to print out:

```
CONVERSIONS = {
    "mph": 1.60934 / 3600 * 1000,    # m/s
    "hours": 3600,                   # seconds
    "miles": 1.60934 * 1000,         # m
    "meters": 1,                     # m
    "m/s": 1,                        # m/s
    "seconds": 1,                    # s
}

def convert(value, units):
```

```
    rate = CONVERSIONS[units]
    return rate * value

def localize(value, units):
    rate = CONVERSIONS[units]
    return value / rate

def print_distance(
    speed,
    duration,
    *,
    speed_units="mph",
    time_units="hours",
    distance_units="miles",
):
    norm_speed = convert(speed, speed_units)
    norm_duration = convert(duration, time_units)
    norm_distance = norm_speed * norm_duration
    distance = localize(norm_distance, distance_units)
    print(f"{distance} {distance_units}")
```

Now I can modify the speeding bullet call and produce an accurate result with a unit conversion to miles:

```
print_distance(
    1000,
    3,
    speed_units="meters",
    time_units="seconds",
)
```

```
>>>
1.8641182099494205 miles
```

It seems like requiring units to be specified for this function is a much better way to go. Making them explicit reduces the likelihood of errors and is easier for new readers of the code to understand. But how can I migrate all callers of the API over to always specifying units? How do I minimize breakage of any code that's dependent on print_distance while also encouraging callers to adopt the new units arguments as soon as possible?

For this purpose, Python provides the built-in warnings module. Using warnings is a programmatic way to inform other programmers that their code needs to be modified due to a change to an underlying library that they depend on. While exceptions are primarily for automated error handling by machines (see Item 81: "assert Internal Assumptions and raise Missed Expectations"), warnings are all about communication between humans about what to expect in their collaboration with each other.

I can modify print_distance to issue warnings when the optional keyword arguments for specifying units are not supplied. This way, the arguments can continue being optional temporarily, while providing an explicit notice to people running dependent programs that they should expect breakage in the future if they fail to take action:

```
import warnings

def print_distance(
    speed,
    duration,
    *,
    speed_units=None,
    time_units=None,
    distance_units=None,
):
    if speed_units is None:
        warnings.warn(
            "speed_units required",
            DeprecationWarning,
        )
        speed_units = "mph"

    if time_units is None:
        warnings.warn(
            "time_units required",
            DeprecationWarning,
        )
        time_units = "hours"

    if distance_units is None:
        warnings.warn(
            "distance_units required",
            DeprecationWarning,
        )
        distance_units = "miles"

    norm_speed = convert(speed, speed_units)
    norm_duration = convert(duration, time_units)
    norm_distance = norm_speed * norm_duration
```

```
distance = localize(norm_distance, distance_units)
print(f"{distance} {distance_units}")
```

I can verify that this code issues a warning by calling the function with the same arguments as before and capturing the sys.stderr output from the warnings module:

```
import contextlib
import io

fake_stderr = io.StringIO()
with contextlib.redirect_stderr(fake_stderr):
    print_distance(
        1000,
        3,
        speed_units="meters",
        time_units="seconds",
    )

print(fake_stderr.getvalue())

>>>
1.8641182099494205 miles
.../example.py:121: DeprecationWarning: distance_units required
  warnings.warn(
```

Adding warnings to this function required quite a lot of repetitive boilerplate that's hard to read and maintain. Also, the warning message indicates the line where warning.warn was called, but what I really want to point out is where the call to print_distance was made *without* soon-to-be-required keyword arguments.

Luckily, the warnings.warn function supports the stacklevel parameter, which makes it possible to report the correct place in the stack as the cause of the warning. stacklevel also makes it easy to write functions that can issue warnings on behalf of other code, reducing boilerplate. Here I define a helper function that warns if an optional argument wasn't supplied and then provides a default value for it:

```
def require(name, value, default):
    if value is not None:
        return value
    warnings.warn(
        f"{name} will be required soon, update your code",
        DeprecationWarning,
        stacklevel=3,
    )
```

```
        return default

def print_distance(
    speed,
    duration,
    *,
    speed_units=None,
    time_units=None,
    distance_units=None,
):
    speed_units = require(
        "speed_units",
        speed_units,
        "mph",
    )
    time_units = require(
        "time_units",
        time_units,
        "hours",
    )
    distance_units = require(
        "distance_units",
        distance_units,
        "miles",
    )

    norm_speed = convert(speed, speed_units)
    norm_duration = convert(duration, time_units)
    norm_distance = norm_speed * norm_duration
    distance = localize(norm_distance, distance_units)
    print(f"{distance} {distance_units}")
```

I can verify that this propagates the proper offending line by inspecting the captured output:

```
import contextlib
import io

fake_stderr = io.StringIO()
with contextlib.redirect_stderr(fake_stderr):
    print_distance(
        1000,
        3,
        speed_units="meters",
        time_units="seconds",
```

```
    )

print(fake_stderr.getvalue())

>>>
1.8641182099494205 miles
.../example.py:208: DeprecationWarning: distance_units will be
➥required soon, update your code
  print_distance(
```

The warnings module also lets you configure what should happen when a warning is encountered. One option is to make all warnings become errors, which raises the warning as an exception instead of printing it out to sys.stderr:

```
warnings.simplefilter("error")
try:
    warnings.warn(
        "This usage is deprecated",
        DeprecationWarning,
    )
except DeprecationWarning:
    pass  # Expected
```

This exception-raising behavior is especially useful for automated tests in order to detect changes in upstream dependencies and fail tests accordingly. Using such test failures is a great way to make it clear to the people you collaborate with that they will need to update their code. You can use the -W error command-line argument to the Python interpreter or the PYTHONWARNINGS environment variable to apply this policy:

```
$ python3 -W error example_test.py
Traceback (most recent call last):
  File ".../example_test.py", line 6, in <module>
    warnings.warn("This might raise an exception!")
UserWarning: This might raise an exception!
```

Once the people responsible for code that depends on a deprecated API are aware that they'll need to do a migration, they can tell the warnings module to ignore the error by using the simplefilter and filterwarnings functions (see https://docs.python.org/3/library/warnings for details):

```
warnings.simplefilter("ignore")
warnings.warn("This will not be printed to stderr")
```

After a program is deployed into production, it doesn't make sense for warnings to cause errors because they might crash the program at a critical time. Instead, a better approach is to replicate warnings into the `logging` built-in module. Here I accomplish this by calling the `logging.captureWarnings` function and configuring the corresponding `"py.warnings"` logger:

```
import logging

fake_stderr = io.StringIO()
handler = logging.StreamHandler(fake_stderr)
formatter = logging.Formatter(
    "%(asctime)-15s WARNING] %(message)s")
handler.setFormatter(formatter)

logging.captureWarnings(True)
logger = logging.getLogger("py.warnings")
logger.addHandler(handler)
logger.setLevel(logging.DEBUG)

warnings.resetwarnings()
warnings.simplefilter("default")
warnings.warn("This will go to the logs output")

print(fake_stderr.getvalue())

>>>
2019-06-11 19:48:19,132 WARNING] .../example.py:227:
➥UserWarning: This will go to the logs output
  warnings.warn("This will go to the logs output")
```

Using logging to capture warnings ensures that any error-reporting systems that my program already has in place will also receive notice of important warnings in production. This can be especially useful if my tests don't cover every edge case that I might see when the program is undergoing real usage.

API library maintainers should also write unit tests to verify that warnings are generated under the correct circumstances with clear and actionable messages (see Item 108: "Verify Related Behaviors in TestCase Subclasses"). Here I use the `warnings.catch_warnings` function as a context manager (see Item 82: "Consider `contextlib` and `with` Statements for Reusable `try`/`finally` Behavior" for background) to wrap a call to the `require` function that I defined above:

```
with warnings.catch_warnings(record=True) as found_warnings:
    found = require("my_arg", None, "fake units")
```

```
    expected = "fake units"
    assert found == expected
```

Once I've collected the warning messages, I can verify that their number, detail messages, and categories match my expectations:

```
assert len(found_warnings) == 1
single_warning = found_warnings[0]
assert str(single_warning.message) == (
    "my_arg will be required soon, update your code"
)
assert single_warning.category == DeprecationWarning
```

Things to Remember

✦ The warnings module can be used to notify callers of your API about deprecated usage. Warning messages encourage such callers to fix their code before later changes break their programs.

✦ Raise warnings as errors by using the -W error command-line argument to the Python interpreter. This is especially useful in automated tests to catch potential regressions of dependencies.

✦ In production, you can replicate warnings into the logging module to ensure that your existing error-reporting systems will capture warnings at runtime.

✦ It's useful to write tests for the warnings that your code generates to make sure they'll be triggered at the right time in any of your downstream dependencies.

Item 124: Consider Static Analysis via typing to Obviate Bugs

Providing documentation is a great way to help users of an API understand how to use it properly (see Item 118: "Write Docstrings for Every Function, Class, and Module"), but often it's not enough, and incorrect usage still causes bugs. Ideally, there would be a programmatic mechanism to verify that callers are using your APIs the right way and that you are using your downstream dependencies correctly as well. Many programming languages address part of this need with compile-time type checking, which can identify and eliminate some categories of bugs.

Historically Python has focused on dynamic features and has not provided compile-time type safety of any kind (see Item 3: "Never Expect Python to Detect Errors at Compile Time"). However, more recently

Python has introduced special syntax and the built-in typing module, which allow you to annotate variables, class fields, functions, and methods with type information. These *type hints* allow for *gradual typing*, which means a codebase can be progressively updated to specify types as desired.

The benefit of adding type information to a Python program is that you can run *static analysis* tools to ingest a program's source code and identify where bugs are most likely to occur. The typing built-in module doesn't actually implement any of the type checking functionality itself. It merely provides a common library for defining types that can be applied to Python code and consumed by separate tools.

Much as there are multiple distinct implementations of the Python interpreter (e.g., CPython, PyPy; see Item 1: "Know Which Version of Python You're Using"), there are multiple implementations of static analysis tools for Python that use typing. As of this writing, the most popular tools are mypy (https://github.com/python/mypy), pyright (https://github.com/microsoft/pyright), pyre (https://pyre-check.org), and pytype (https://github.com/google/pytype). For the typing examples in this book, I've used mypy with the --strict flag, which enables all the various warnings supported by the tool. Here's an example of what running the command line looks like:

```
$ python3 -m mypy --strict example.py
```

These tools can be used to detect a large number of common errors before a program is ever run, which can provide an added layer of safety in addition to having good tests (see Item 109: "Prefer Integration Tests over Unit Tests"). For example, can you find the bug that causes this simple function to compile fine but throw an exception at runtime?

```
def subtract(a, b):
    return a - b


subtract(10, "5")

>>>
Traceback ...
TypeError: unsupported operand type(s) for -: 'int' and 'str'
```

Parameter and variable type annotations are delineated with a colon (such as name: type). Return value types are specified with -> type following the argument list. Using such type annotations and mypy, I can easily spot the bug:

```
def subtract(a: int, b: int) -> int:  # Function annotation
    return a - b
```

```
subtract(10, "5")  # Oops: passed string value

$ python3 -m mypy --strict example.py
.../example.py:4: error: Argument 2 to "subtract" has
➥ incompatible type "str"; expected "int"  [arg-type]
Found 1 error in 1 file (checked 1 source file)
```

Type annotations can also be applied to classes. For example, this class has two bugs in it that will raise exceptions when the program is run:

```
class Counter:
    def __init__(self):
        self.value = 0

    def add(self, offset):
        value += offset

    def get(self) -> int:
        self.value
```

The first one happens when I call the add method:

```
counter = Counter()
counter.add(5)

>>>
Traceback ...
UnboundLocalError: cannot access local variable 'value' where
➥it is not associated with a value
```

The second bug happens when I call get:

```
counter = Counter()
found = counter.get()
assert found == 0, found

>>>
Traceback ...
AssertionError: None
```

Both of these problems are easily found in advance by mypy:

```
class Counter:
    def __init__(self) -> None:
        self.value: int = 0  # Field / variable annotation

    def add(self, offset: int) -> None:
        value += offset       # Oops: forgot "self."
```

```
    def get(self) -> int:
        self.value              # Oops: forgot "return"

counter = Counter()
counter.add(5)
counter.add(3)
assert counter.get() == 8
```

```
$ python3 -m mypy --strict example.py
.../example.py:9: error: Name "value" is not defined
➥[name-defined]
.../example.py:11: error: Missing return statement   [return]
Found 2 errors in 1 file (checked 1 source file)
```

One of the strengths of Python's dynamism is the ability to write generic functionality that operates on duck types (see Item 25: "Be Cautious when Relying on Dictionary Insertion Ordering" and Item 57: "Inherit from collections.abc Classes for Custom Container Types"). This allows one implementation to accept a wide range of types, saving a lot of duplicative effort and simplifying testing. Here I've defined such a generic function for combining values from a list together, but the assert statement on the last line fails for a non-obvious reason:

```
def combine(func, values):
    assert len(values) > 0

    result = values[0]
    for next_value in values[1:]:
        result = func(result, next_value)

    return result

def add(x, y):
    return x + y

inputs = [1, 2, 3, 4j]
result = combine(add, inputs)
assert result == 10, result   # Fails

>>>
Traceback ...
AssertionError: (6+4j)
```

I can use the typing module's support for generics to annotate this function and detect the problem statically:

```
from collections.abc import Callable
from typing import TypeVar
```

```
Value = TypeVar("Value")
Func = Callable[[Value, Value], Value]

def combine(func: Func[Value], values: list[Value]) -> Value:
    assert len(values) > 0

    result = values[0]
    for next_value in values[1:]:
        result = func(result, next_value)

    return result

Real = TypeVar("Real", int, float)

def add(x: Real, y: Real) -> Real:
    return x + y

inputs = [1, 2, 3, 4j]  # Oops: included a complex number
result = combine(add, inputs)
assert result == 10
```

```
$ python3 -m mypy --strict example.py
.../example.py:22: error: Argument 1 to "combine" has
➡incompatible type "Callable[[Real, Real], Real]"; expected
➡"Callable[[complex, complex], complex]"  [arg-type]
Found 1 error in 1 file (checked 1 source file)
```

Another extremely common error is a None value appearing where you thought you'd have a valid object (see Item 32: "Prefer Raising Exceptions to Returning None"). This problem can affect seemingly simple code, like the following snippet where the last assert statement fails:

```
def get_or_default(value, default):
    if value is not None:
        return value
    return value

found = get_or_default(3, 5)
assert found == 3

found = get_or_default(None, 5)
assert found == 5, found  # Fails

>>>
Traceback ...
AssertionError: None
```

The typing module supports *option types*—indicated with type | None—which ensure that programs only interact with values after proper null checks have been performed. This allows mypy to infer that there's a bug in this code. The type used in the return statement must be None, and that doesn't match the int type required by the function signature:

```
def get_or_default(value: int | None, default: int) -> int:
    if value is not None:
        return value
    return value  # Oops: should have returned "default"
```

```
$ python3 -m mypy --strict example.py
.../example.py:4: error: Incompatible return value type
➥ (got "None", expected "int")  [return-value]
Found 1 error in 1 file (checked 1 source file)
```

A wide variety of other options are available in the typing module. (See https://docs.python.org/3/library/typing.html for all the details.) Notably, exceptions are not included. Unlike Java, which has checked exceptions that are enforced at the API boundary of every method, Python's type annotations are more similar to those of C#: Exceptions are not considered part of an interface's definition. Thus, if you want to verify that you're raising and catching exceptions properly, you need to write tests.

One common gotcha in using the typing module occurs when you need to deal with forward references (see Item 122: "Know How to Break Circular Dependencies" for a similar problem). For example, imagine that I have two classes where one holds a reference to the other. Usually the definition order of these classes doesn't matter because they will both be defined before their instances are created later in the program:

```
class FirstClass:
    def __init__(self, value):
        self.value = value

class SecondClass:
    def __init__(self, value):
        self.value = value

second = SecondClass(5)
first = FirstClass(second)
```

If you apply type hints to this program and run mypy, it will say that there are no issues:

```
class FirstClass:
    def __init__(self, value: SecondClass) -> None:
        self.value = value


class SecondClass:
    def __init__(self, value: int) -> None:
        self.value = value


second = SecondClass(5)
first = FirstClass(second)
```

```
$ python3 -m mypy --strict example.py
Success: no issues found in 1 source file
```

However, if you actually try to run this code, it fails because SecondClass is referenced by the type annotation in the FirstClass.__init__ method's parameters before it's actually defined:

```
class FirstClass:
    def __init__(self, value: SecondClass) -> None:  # Breaks
        self.value = value


class SecondClass:
    def __init__(self, value: int) -> None:
        self.value = value


second = SecondClass(5)
first = FirstClass(second)
```

```
>>>
Traceback ...
NameError: name 'SecondClass' is not defined
```

The recommended workaround that's supported by these static analysis tools is to use a string as the type annotation that contains the forward reference. The string value is later parsed and evaluated to extract the type information to check:

```
class FirstClass:
    def __init__(self, value: "SecondClass") -> None:  # OK
        self.value = value


class SecondClass:
    def __init__(self, value: int) -> None:
```

```
        self.value = value

second = SecondClass(5)
first = FirstClass(second)
```

Now that you've seen how to use type hints and their potential benefits, it's important to be thoughtful about when to use them. Here are some of the best practices to keep in mind:

- It's going to slow you down if you try to use type annotations from the start when writing a new piece of code. A general strategy is to write a first version without annotations, then write tests, and then add type information where it's most valuable.

- Type hints are most important at the boundaries of a codebase, such as an API you provide that many callers (and thus other people) depend on. Type hints complement tests (see Item 108: "Verify Related Behaviors in TestCase Subclasses") and warnings (see Item 123: "Consider warnings to Refactor and Migrate Usage") to ensure that your API callers aren't surprised or broken by your changes.

- It can be useful to apply type hints to the most complex and error-prone parts of your codebase that aren't part of an API. However, it may not be worth striving for 100% coverage in your type annotations because you'll quickly encounter diminishing returns.

- If possible, you should include static analysis as part of your automated build and test system to ensure that every commit to your codebase is vetted for errors. In addition, the configuration used for type checking should be maintained in the repository to ensure that all the people you collaborate with are using the same rules.

- It's important to run the type checker as you add type information to your code. If you don't, you may nearly finish sprinkling type hints everywhere and then be hit by a huge wall of errors from the type checking tool, which can be disheartening and make you want to abandon type hints altogether.

Finally, it's important to acknowledge that in many situations, you might not need or want to use type annotations at all. For small to medium-sized programs, ad hoc code, legacy codebases, and prototypes, type hints may require far more effort than they're worth.

Things to Remember

✦ Python has special syntax and the `typing` built-in module for annotating variables, fields, functions, and methods with type information.

✦ Static type checkers can leverage this type information to help you avoid many common bugs that would otherwise happen at runtime.

✦ There are a variety of best practices for adopting types in your programs, using them in APIs, and making sure they don't get in the way of your productivity.

Item 125: Prefer Open Source Projects for Bundling Python Programs over `zipimport` and `zipapp`

Imagine that you've finished building a web application in Python using the `flask` open source project, and it's time to ship it to production for real users (see Item 120: "Consider Module-Scoped Code to Configure Deployment Environments" for background). There are a variety of options for doing this with package managers (see Item 116: "Know Where to Find Community-Built Modules"). However, an often easier way is to simply copy the source code and dependencies to a server (or into a container image).

To that end, I've pulled together my application and all of its related modules into a directory—similar to the `site-packages` directory created by tools like `pip` (see Item 117: "Use Virtual Environments for Isolated and Reproducible Dependencies"):

```
$ ls flask_deps
Jinja2-3.1.3.dist-info
MarkupSafe-2.1.5.dist-info
blinker
blinker-1.7.0.dist-info
click
click-8.1.7.dist-info
flask
flask-3.0.2.dist-info
itsdangerous
itsdangerous-2.1.2.dist-info
jinja2
markupsafe
myapp.py
werkzeug
werkzeug-3.0.1.dist-info
```

These dependencies include more than 330 files and 56,000 lines of source code, with an uncompressed size of 5.1 MB. Copying this many relatively small files to another server can be annoyingly slow. Such transfers can also unexpectedly change important details like file permissions. In the past, a common way to work around these pitfalls was to archive a codebase into a zip file before deployment.

To make archives like this easier to work with, Python has the zipimport built-in module. It enables programs to be decompressed and loaded on the fly from zip files that appear in the PYTHONPATH environment variable or sys.path list. Here I create a zip archive of the flask_deps directory and then verify that it's working correctly when executed directly from a zip file:

```
$ cd flask_deps
$ zip -r ../flask_deps.zip *
$ cd ..
$ PYTHONPATH=flask_deps.zip python3 -m flask --app=myapp routes
Endpoint     Methods  Rule
-----------  -------  ----------------------
hello_world  GET      /
static       GET      /static/<path:filename>
```

You might expect that there's a performance penalty in loading Python modules from a zip file due to the CPU overhead of decompression. Here I measure the startup time loading from a zip archive:

```
$ time PYTHONPATH=flask_deps.zip python3 -m flask --app=myapp
➥routes
...
real    0m0.123s
user    0m0.097s
sys     0m0.022s
```

And here I measure startup time loading from plain files on disk:

```
$ time PYTHONPATH=flask_deps python3 -m flask --app=myapp
➥routes
Endpoint     Methods  Rule
-----------  -------  ----------------------
hello_world  GET      /
static       GET      /static/<path:filename>

real    0m0.126s
user    0m0.098s
sys     0m0.023s
```

The performance is nearly identical. There are two main reasons for this. First, modern computers have a huge amount of processing power compared to their I/O capacity and memory bandwidth, so the slowdown from additional decompression is often negligible. Second, large file system caches and SSD (solid-state drive) performance can practically hide I/O delays for relatively small amounts of data (see Item 97: "Rely on Precompiled Bytecode and File System Caching to Improve Startup Time" for details). Although the flask_deps.zip file is 1.6 MB compared to the uncompressed directory size of 5.1 MB, the performance difference is effectively zero.

One conclusion might be that you should always compress your Python programs into zip files as it seems like there would be no downsides. Python even provides the zipapp built-in module for rapidly archiving whole applications because of this benefit. Here I use this tool to create a compressed, single-file executable (with the .pyz suffix) for my web application that's easy to copy around and interact with:

```
$ python -m zipapp flask_deps -m "flask.__main__:main" -p
➥'/usr/bin/env python3' -c
$ ./flask_deps.pyz --app myapp routes
Endpoint      Methods   Rule
-----------   -------   ----------------------
hello_world   GET       /
static        GET       /static/<path:filename>
```

Unfortunately, executing Python code from zip files causes real programs to break in two ways: data file accesses and extension modules.

As an example of the first issue, here I create a zip archive of the Django web framework and try to run a web application that depends on it:

```
$ python3 -m compileall django
$ zip -r django.zip Django-5.0.3.dist-info django
$ rm -R Django-5.0.3.dist-info django
$ PYTHONPATH=django.zip python3 django_project/manage.py check
Traceback (most recent call last):
...
OSError: No translation files found for default language en-us.
```

This didn't work because Django is looking for the translations data file next to the source files. In the Django code excerpt below, the value of the localedir variable is ".../django.zip/django/conf/locale", which is not a directory on the filesystem. When that path is passed to the gettext module to load translations, the files can't be found by the Django library code, causing the OSError exception shown above:

```
# trans_real.py
# Copyright (c) Django Software Foundation and
# individual contributors. All rights reserved.
class DjangoTranslation(gettext_module.GNUTranslations):
    ...

    def _init_translation_catalog(self):
        settingsfile = \
            sys.modules[settings.__module__].__file__
        localedir = os.path.join(
            os.path.dirname(settingsfile),
            "locale",
        )
        translation = self._new_gnu_trans(localedir)
        self.merge(translation)

...
```

Python provides the pkgutil built-in module to work around this problem. It intelligently inspects modules to determine how to properly access their data resources even if they're in zip archives or require a custom module loader. Here I use pkgutil to load the translations file that Django couldn't find due to the zip archive:

```
# django_pkgutil.py
import pkgutil

data = pkgutil.get_data(
    "django.conf.locale",
    "en/LC_MESSAGES/django.po",
)
print(data.decode("utf-8"))

>>>
# This file is distributed under the same license as the Django
➥ package.
#
msgid ""
msgstr ""
"Project-Id-Version: Django\n"
"Report-Msgid-Bugs-To: \n"
...
```

Few projects actually use pkgutil; even an extremely popular project like Django doesn't use it. Python programs are most commonly executed as files on disk with their original directory structure. In contrast, other languages compile programs into an executable that is placed into a separate build artifacts directory, far from the code. This causes programmers to assume that they can't access the source tree and need to handle data dependencies more explicitly. With Python code, however, the assumption is that the code is nearby, and thus the data files in the source tree must also be nearby. Don't expect common packages to work when imported from zip archives.

The second issue is that you can't import native extension modules (see Item 96: "Consider Extension Modules to Maximize Performance and Ergonomics") from zip archives due to operating system constraints. Here I show how this breaks for the NumPy package:

```
$ zip -r ./numpy.zip numpy numpy-1.26.4.dist-info
$ rm -R numpy numpy-1.26.4.dist-info
$ PYTHONPATH=numpy.zip python -c 'import numpy'
Traceback (most recent call last):
...
ModuleNotFoundError: No module named
➥'numpy.core._multiarray_umath'

During handling of the above exception, another exception
➥ occurred:

Traceback (most recent call last):
...
ImportError:

IMPORTANT: PLEASE READ THIS FOR ADVICE ON HOW TO SOLVE THIS
➥ ISSUE!

Importing the numpy C-extensions failed. This error can happen for
many reasons, often due to issues with your setup or how NumPy was
installed.
...
```

Extension modules are extremely valuable and popular because they help Python go faster for CPU-intensive tasks (see Item 96: "Consider Extension Modules to Maximize Performance and Ergonomics"). This is ultimately the biggest deal-breaker for both zipimport and zipapps.

Fortunately, the Python community has built a variety of open source solutions that are better at deploying Python applications. The Pex tool (https://github.com/pex-tool/pex) and a derivative project, Shiv (https://github.com/linkedin/shiv), provide similar functionality to zipapp, but these tools automatically work around the problems with data files and native modules. For example, here I use Pex to create a single executable file for the same Django web application from earlier—and this one actually works:

```
$ pip install -e django_project
$ pex django_project -o myapp.pex
$ ./django_project.pex -m manage check
System check identified no issues (0 silenced).
```

Another alternative is PyInstaller (https://pyinstaller.org), which goes even further by bundling the Python executable itself so the user doesn't need anything else installed on their system in order to run an application. Whatever route you decide to take, be sure to read the documentation carefully and experimentally verify that it's compatible with the modules you need to use and the assumptions they make about their execution environment.

Things to Remember

✦ Python has the ability to load modules directly from zip archives, which makes it easier to deploy whole applications as a single file.

✦ Many common open source Python packages break when imported from a zip archive due to reliance on data files and extension modules.

✦ The community has built alternatives to Python's built-in zipapp module, such as Pex, which provide the deployment benefits of zip archives without the downsides.

Index